Improper Pursuits

Improper Pursuits

The Scandalous Life of an
Earlier Lady Diana Spencer

CAROLA HICKS

ST. MARTIN'S PRESS ❧ NEW YORK

To Elsie Duncan-Jones

www.stmartins.com

ISBN 0-312-29157-4

First published in Great Britain under the title *Improper Pursuits:
The Scandalous Life of Lady Di Beauclerk* by Macmillan
An imprint of Macmillan Publishers Ltd

First U.S. Edition: June 2002

10 9 8 7 6 5 4 3 2 1

Contents

List of Illustrations

List of Illustrations

Lydiard House (Lydiard House/John Gibbons)
Stained-glass window, Lydiard House
George St John (Lydiard House/John Gibbons)
Mary and Elizabeth Beauclerk (Lewis Walpole Library, Yale University)
Gimcrack with John Pratt by George Stubbs (Fitzwilliam Museum, Cambridge)
The Out of Town Party, or A Conversation, 1759 by Joshua Reynolds (Bristol
    City Musuem and Art Gallery, UK/Bridgeman Art Library)
Turk's Head Tavern by Samuel Percy (Museum of London)
The Duke of York and Companions by Richard Brompton (The Royal Collection
    copyright © 2001, Her Majesty Queen Elizabeth II)
Johnson and Mrs Thrale
Horace Walpole by Joshua Reynolds (National Portrait Gallery, London)
James Boswell by Joshua Reynolds (National Portrait Gallery, London)

SECTION THREE

Triumph of Bacchantes by Diana Beauclerk (Fitzwilliam Museum, Cambridge)
The Drunken Silenus by Diana Beauclerk (Fitzwilliam Museum, Cambridge)
Bacchanalian tablet by Wedgwood (City of Nottingham Museums and Galleries)
The Mysterious Mother, Act Two, Scene 3 by Diana Beauclerk (Lewis Walpole
    Library, Yale University)
The Mysterious Mother, Act Five, Scene 6 by Diana Beauclerk (Lewis Walpole
    Library, Yale University)
Faerie Queen, Book One, Canto 6 by Diana Beauclerk (Lewis Walpole Library,
    Yale University)
Faerie Queen, Book Three, Canto 12 by Diana Beauclerk (Lewis Walpole
    Library, Yale University)
Theodore and Honoria by Diana Beauclerk (Lewis Walpole Library, Yale
    University)
The Beauclerk Cabinet (Lewis Walpole Library, Yale University)

Endpapers
Basket of Flowers by Diana Beauclerk (Lydiard House/John Gibbons)
Chapter openers
Cupid with a Mirror and *Cupid with a Bow* by Diana Beauclerk (The British
    Museum)

Every effort has been made to trace all copyright holders but if any has been
inadvertently overlooked, the author and publishers will be pleased to make the
necessary arrangement at the first opportunity.

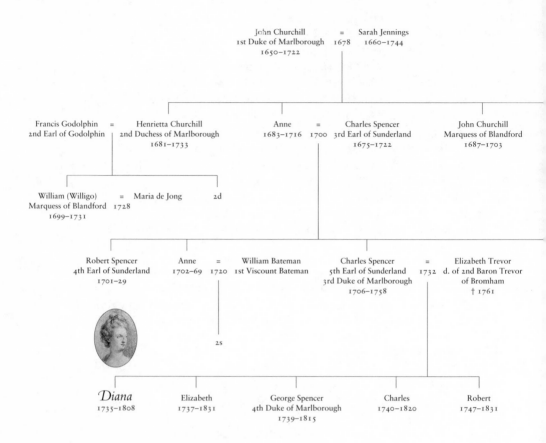

John Churchill = Sarah Jennings
1st Duke of Marlborough 1678 1660–1744
1650–1722

Francis Godolphin = Henrietta Churchill   Anne = Charles Spencer   John Churchill
2nd Earl of Godolphin | 2nd Duchess of Marlborough   1683–1716 1700 3rd Earl of Sunderland   Marquess of Blandford
1681–1733   1675–1722   1687–1703

William (Willigo) = Maria de Jong   2d
Marquess of Blandford 1728
1699–1731

Robert Spencer   Anne = William Bateman   Charles Spencer = Elizabeth Trevor
4th Earl of Sunderland   1702–69 1720 1st Viscount Bateman   5th Earl of Sunderland   1732 d. of 2nd Baron Trevor
1701–29   3rd Duke of Marlborough   of Bromham
                                                 1706–1758   † 1761

                                  2s

Diana   Elizabeth   George Spencer   Charles   Robert
1735–1808   1737–1831   4th Duke of Marlborough 1740–1820   1747–1831
                                  1739–1815

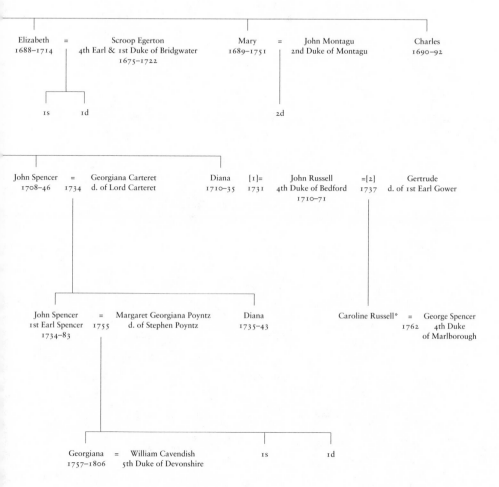

Elizabeth	=	Scroop Egerton		Mary	=	John Montagu		Charles
1688–1714		4th Earl & 1st Duke of Bridgwater		1689–1751		2nd Duke of Montagu		1690–92
		1675–1722						

1s   1d   2d

John Spencer	=	Georgiana Carteret		Diana	[1]=	John Russell	=[2]	Gertrude
1708–46	1734	d. of Lord Carteret		1710–35	1731	4th Duke of Bedford	1737	d. of 1st Earl Gower
						1710–71		

John Spencer	=	Margaret Georgiana Poyntz		Diana		Caroline Russell*	=	George Spencer
1st Earl Spencer	1755	d. of Stephen Poyntz		1735–43			1762	4th Duke
1734–83								of Marlborough

| Georgiana | = | William Cavendish | | 1s | | 1d |
| 1757–1806 | | 5th Duke of Devonshire | | | | |

* duplication in the family tree

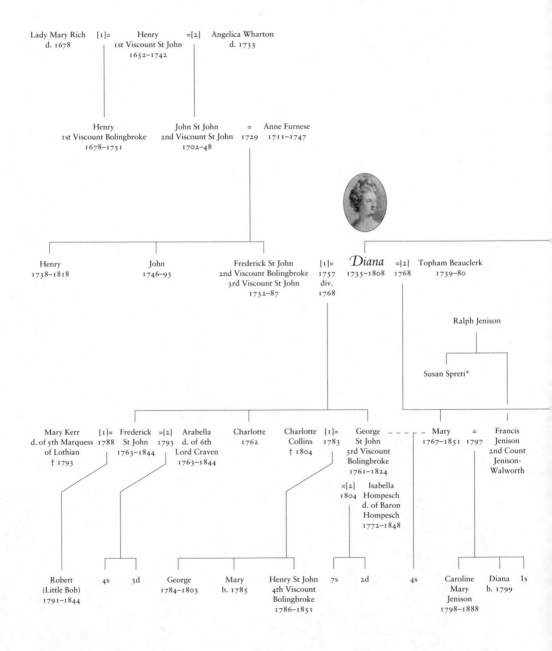

Lady Mary Rich   [1]=   Henry   =[2]   Angelica Wharton
d. 1678   1st Viscount St John   d. 1735
                                  1652–1742

Henry   John St John   =   Anne Furnese
1st Viscount Bolingbroke   2nd Viscount St John   1729   1711–1747
1678–1751   1702–48

Henry   John   Frederick St John   [1]=   *Diana*   =[2]   Topham Beauclerk
1738–1818   1746–93   2nd Viscount Bolingbroke 1757   1735–1808   1768   1739–80
                                     3rd Viscount St John   div.
                                     1732–87   1768

                                                                                    Ralph Jenison

                                                                                    Susan Spreti*

Mary Kerr   [1]= Frederick =[2] Arabella   Charlotte   Charlotte [1]=   George   - - - - ┌─ Mary   =   Francis
d. of 5th Marquess 1788   St John   1793 d. of 6th   1762   Collins   1783   St John   1767–1851 1797   Jenison
of Lothian   1763–1844   Lord Craven   † 1804   3rd Viscount   2nd Count
† 1793   1763–1844   Bolingbroke   Jenison-
                                                                                        1761–1824   Walworth

                                                                                        =[2]   Isabella
                                                                                        1804   Hompesch
                                                                                                d. of Baron
                                                                                                Hompesch
                                                                                                1772–1848

Robert   4s   3d   George   Mary   Henry St John   7s   2d   4s   Caroline   Diana   1s
(Little Bob)   1784–1803   b. 1785   4th Viscount   Mary   b. 1799
1791–1844   Bolingbroke   Jenison
                                                      1786–1851   1798–1888

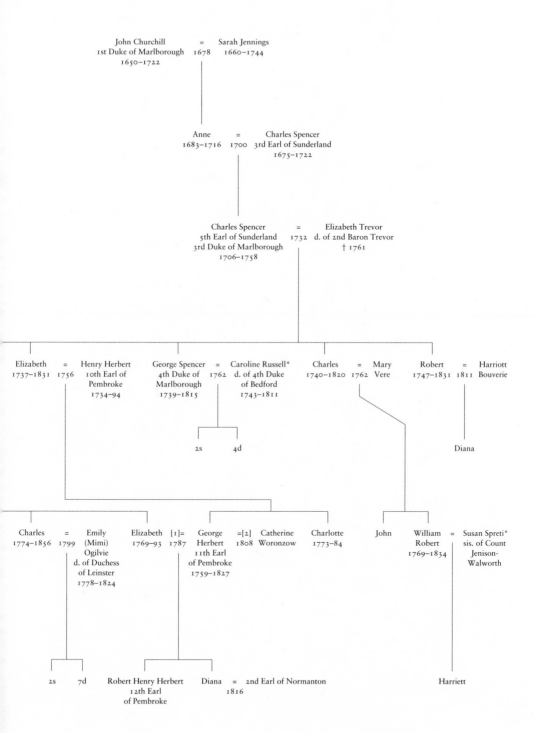

John Churchill = Sarah Jennings
1st Duke of Marlborough 1678 1660–1744
1650–1722

Anne = Charles Spencer
1683–1716 1700 3rd Earl of Sunderland
1675–1722

Charles Spencer = Elizabeth Trevor
5th Earl of Sunderland 1732 d. of 2nd Baron Trevor
3rd Duke of Marlborough † 1761
1706–1758

Elizabeth = Henry Herbert   George Spencer = Caroline Russell*   Charles = Mary   Robert = Harriott
1737–1831 1756 10th Earl of   4th Duke of 1762 d. of 4th Duke   1740–1820 1762 Vere   1747–1831 1811 Bouverie
Pembroke   Marlborough   of Bedford
1734–94   1739–1815   1743–1811

2s   4d   Diana

Charles = Emily   Elizabeth [1]= George =[2] Catherine   Charlotte   John   William = Susan Spreti*
1774–1856 1799 (Mimi)   1769–93 1787 Herbert 1808 Woronzow   1773–84   Robert sis. of Count
Ogilvie   11th Earl   1769–1834 Jenison-
d. of Duchess   of Pembroke   Walworth
of Leinster   1759–1827
1778–1824

2s   7d   Robert Henry Herbert   Diana = 2nd Earl of Normanton   Harriett
12th Earl   1816
of Pembroke

* duplication in the family tree

Introduction

The artist's studio, a spacious octagonal room, has just one source of light, a large window high up in one of the walls, through which London's cold grey sky casts an even wash over the painter and the sitter. A fire burns in the grate, which is surmounted by an elegant mantelshelf, and the smell of smoke mingles with the more pungent odours of linseed oil and turpentine. There are several easels, supporting various works in progress, and a four-foot-high fire screen whose surface is a looking glass which can either reflect light onto the sitter's face, or, if placed at the correct angle to the easel in use, enable the subject to inspect the artist's progress. On a low plinth stands an upholstered chair whose feet have been modified by the addition of castors so that its occupant can be swivelled by the portrait painter to the most precise and flattering angle. Background colour and texture, and more light control, are provided by a tall two-leaved screen, over which different fabrics from the painter's rich stock can be draped to emulate tapestries or high-hanging curtains.

Joshua Reynolds, the most fashionable portrait-painter of the day, is at work. His sitter appears to be another artist, also at work – a woman, who has momentarily lowered the drawing implement in her right hand but holds in her left hand a large portfolio. She presents herself as a serious artist. Dressed simply in a loosely draped gown of some soft material, sash knotted under her breasts in the classical manner, but the sleeve tied up in workmanlike style, she turns away from her drawing pad to contemplate the studio. Her expression is grave, belying a reputation for wit and gaiety, and her features composed – lustrous dark eyes, firm brows, a determined chin. She looks like someone who is in control of her life.

But the artist's work is the creation of images. Self-presentation can be as deceptive as the most flattering of portraits. As the young Viscountess Bolingbroke posed as a maker of art, it was her perform-ance that imperceptibly moderated Reynolds' oil and canvas interpre-tation of her. To be depicted as an artist meant that her commitment to a noble activity which concerned eternal values and ideals, and which enabled the practitioner to soar above the petty and mundane, was recorded both for the contemporary spectator and for posterity. The practice of art, for this woman, already represented an escape from daily tensions and underlying deeper worries. Her poise masked personal problems – of health, of money, of the heart.

Being fitted into Reynolds' busy schedule in the spring of 1763 required dukes and duchesses, politicians, actors, respectable and dis-reputable women alike to attend his recently extended premises in Leicester Fields, with its impressive purpose-built studio and adjoining gallery. Recently completed portraits were exhibited for the admiration of friends and family, who were welcome to visit the sitter (Reynolds booked in several subjects each day); one such work, displayed while the Viscountess was sitting, depicted one of her husband's mistresses, a coincidence which had attracted the attention of the gossips.

But it was not only her husband's infidelity which was causing concern. There was his uncontrollable extravagance – the debts, which had been temporarily alleviated by her own marriage portion (admit-tedly rather modest considering that she was born Lady Diana Spencer, the eldest daughter of the Duke of Marlborough), had again piled up, and the hard-earned salary from the mind-numbing service which she endured at the dowdy court might be thrown away by him in one afternoon at the races. He was even now exploring ways of eating into his own inheritance, and therefore that of their two-year-old son, by selling off lands and properties that had belonged to his family for generations. Enshrined in the very background of the portrait being painted was a large and rare French vase, the sort of item whose compulsive purchase had contributed to their financial plight. Boling-broke's reckless collection of such treasured status symbols undermined her self-projection as industrious, independent artist: a wife, like a vase, is owned by a husband.

A more ominous shadow was being cast by his emotional instability. A wild young man had not been settled by marriage, extremes of mood were further fuelled by drink. She was pregnant again, the third time in three years – the sash of her robe is tied discreetly high over a gently swelling belly. Her firstborn, George, was healthy, but the second baby, a girl, had died when just a few months old, less than a year before. There was obviously fear for the future, further aggravated by the sickening awareness that her husband was sporadically infecting her with a sexually transmitted disease. The projected image of a serene, noble artist veiled a restless, anxious woman.

Although this was the role she had managed to create for Reynolds, posterity knows her better from a later part, in which she has been irrevocably cast by Reynolds' friend Dr Samuel Johnson. As recorded by his devoted biographer James Boswell, Johnson said of Lady Di: 'My dear Sir, never accustom your mind to mingle virtue and vice. The woman's a whore and there's an end on't'. We do not know his tone of voice, whether he was smiling, or speaking with tongue in cheek. But he was talking about someone who had now become the wife of one of his dearest friends, in whose house he was welcomed and at whose table he regularly dined. Her crime, in Johnson's eyes, was to have broken the sacred bonds of matrimony through her well-publicized adultery with Topham Beauclerk, which had resulted in a notorious divorce from Bolingbroke, followed by marriage to her lover. Johnson's view was an extreme one, at the end of a whole spectrum of disapproving responses which served to give her name an aura of glamour and sin.

And it was the resulting ambiguity of Lady Di's personal reputation that she managed to turn to advantage in the pursuit of her career as an artist, so that she was able eventually to earn money from her skills, a factor that singles her out from so many other women practising art at the time. The term 'amateur' was barely formulated in the second half of the eighteenth century, and it did not have the derogatory meaning it has today. People of rank were well trained to practise art, as well as to collect and to appreciate it, all morally improving activities whose status had to be defended at a time when patronage was extending from the aristocracy to the professional and merchant classes. There was almost a fear that the encouragement and acquisition of art was being seen as a form of financial investment rather than as the reinforcement of social standards; there were debates about the influence and role of the fine arts, in an attempt to offset the undeniably commercial function of art in an age of leisure. It was certainly a time of widening access, through the first public exhibitions, the vigorous print market, and the new genre of art criticism in the expanding popular press. Polite society decreed that it was necessary to develop genuine taste in order to promote morality through art. So the study of painting and the liberal arts remained an important element of education and of daily life. Art was respectable, and women participated fully as patrons, viewers and practitioners.

But Lady Di Beauclerk's name became better known than those of many other women artists because of the public perception of her as an adulterous aristocrat; it was this which helped to ensure that her works were acquired, commissioned and sold, whether the true motivation of her patrons and public was prurience or the genuine admiration of her work. The later poverty, which was directly caused by the reckless choices that she had made in life, meant that she needed to work for money, and was able and willing to sell her drawings and designs. This was not the intention of the making of art; genteel female practitioners should not expect to get paid. And unlike those who did manage to earn a living, she had no family tradition of supportive artist father or husband, and was restricted by the limitations of her training in subject matter, media, and opportunities for display. These were common enough problems for most women artists, who also had to face the sort of disapproval expressed by Dr Johnson: 'the public practice of any art, and staring in men's faces is very indelicate in a female', perhaps an additional factor inspiring to his particular hostility to Lady Di. Yet, for a variety of reasons, she was able to overcome the handicaps of her background and of the perceived constraints on women's activities.

By looking at one life, we learn more about women's lives in general. For the privileged and literate, the second half of the eighteenth century was a time of self-expression, confidence, openness, debate and discussion, in which women were major players; the salons, correspondences, and relationships with husbands, children and friends reveal a sex not so much discriminated against as regarded differently. At the same time the rigid and stultifying conventions of court and polite society provided a structure in which people knew their place and were meant to be defined by it. Someone who transgressed the boundaries, by divorce (which undermined the whole pattern of family relationships and inheritance) and by receiving recognition for marketable skills (despite being a woman of a class not expected to work), was hardly a victim of society. Lady Di is yet another representative of the many splendid and vigorous, determined or outrageous women of the time, whose lives are gradually being recovered.

ONE

The Dowager and the Duke

(1700–34)

'That B.B.B.B. Old B. the Duchess of Marlborough'

SIR JOHN VANBRUGH

In August 1744, in a grand house in Piccadilly, a very old woman was purposefully completing the final codicil of the twenty-sixth version of her will. Aged eighty-four, so crippled with arthritic pain that she had to be carried everywhere in a chair, in constant discomfort from the skin irritation from which she had suffered for many years, her mind was as acute and manipulative as it had ever been. The document covered four massive skins of parchment (the printed version would run to ninety pages). Almost at the end, there was a bequest of £5,000 to her great-granddaughter Lady Diana Spencer, then aged nine, a moderately generous sum yet characteristically hedged around with conditions – the bequest should not be paid until the girl's younger brother, Charles, had reached the age of twenty-one, and it would be cancelled if her father or her eldest brother breached the terms of another will, that of the old woman's late husband. There was also a sarcastic reference to the marriage settlement of Diana's parents, which had been the source of an earlier lawsuit. Although frail now, this woman had outlived all her contemporaries, all but one of her children and even some of her grandchildren, necessitating the constant rewriting of this document which was intended to ensure that the descendants of Sarah Churchill, first Duchess of Marlborough, should continue to obey her beyond the grave.

Yet Sarah's greatest legacy was one which she could not withhold or divide. If we are dominated by nature, not nurture, the charisma and powerful presence of this woman, reinforced by looks, intelligence and stamina, were passed on to more of her female than male descendants, an appropriate inversion of the contemporary laws of inheritance. Her beauty was striking, both in youth and maturity; even in her sixties (at a time when most women even reaching this point were worn-out wrecks) 'she had still at a great age, considerable remains of beauty, most expressive eyes and the finest fair hair imaginable, the colour of which she said she had preserved unchanged by the constant use of honey-water'. Her surviving charms (and huge personal fortune) continued to attract admirers and suitors whom she rejected both as a devoted widow and one determined to retain her independence. Her energy was phenomenal throughout her life, her good health and exceptional longevity attributable in some degree to a regime which included a firm belief in long walks and fresh air as well as the medical skills which she had mastered and believed to be superior to those of most doctors. No family member could fall ill without Sarah becoming involved, writing instructions, and turning up with potions, which in many cases were just as effective as professional remedies.[1]

But like many clever, confident, energetic people, Sarah Churchill thought she had a right and a duty to organize other people's lives, and took terrible offence when this was resisted. Sarah's most successful relationship, her mutually loving and happy marriage with John Churchill, first Duke of Marlborough, was entirely offset by disastrous ones with most of their children and grandchildren. This resulted directly from her unceasing attempts to run their lives, a course of behaviour to which she always felt that she was fully entitled. According to Horace Walpole (youngest son of a man whom she especially hated, the Prime Minister Sir Robert Walpole), because she was 'incapable of due respect to superiors, it was no wonder she treated her children and inferiors with supercilious contempt'.[2]

Her career in public life had also exemplified the principle of always seeking your own way through the noblest of motives: these however were viewed differently by commentators such as Jonathan Swift – 'three Furies reigned in her breast, the most mortal enemies of all softer passions, which were sordid Avarice, disdainful Pride and ungovernable Rage'. Or the smooth courtier Lord Hervey, who referred

6

to her as Mount Aetna, or the Beldame of Bedlam. For Horace Walpole, she was 'ever proud and ever malignant', for her former friend Lady Mary Wortley Montagu, she was 'eternally disappointed and eternally fretting'.[3]

Swift's accusation of avarice was an extreme interpretation of her great skill with money, the ability to make shrewd investments, amassing properties and capital, and the cool head to make a profit of £100,000 by selling out before the South Sea Bubble burst. But her massive personal fortune was used as a weapon in family management, since it was quite separate from the inheritance of the Marlborough title, over which she had no control. Sarah's long-standing quarrel with Diana's father, Charles, was fairly typical of her relationships with most of her immediate family – those who did not immediately obey her were regarded as enemies contravening the intentions of her late husband's will, which she had helped devise and of which she was the chief trustee. Sarah and John Churchill's only son, John, had died suddenly in 1703, aged just sixteen, barely two months after they had been created Duke and Duchess of Marlborough by a grateful Queen Anne. The eldest of their four daughters, Henrietta, became heiress to the title and a duchess in her own right as a result of the private Act of Parliament passed in 1706 ensuring that the Marlborough title could pass to the female line in the absence of a male heir. (However, this privilege only extended to the first female in line, with the title then passing to the nearest male heir.) Henrietta had been married off to the son of the Churchills' friend and ally the first Earl of Godolphin and had already produced a son, who thus became the heir presumptive.

John and Sarah's second daughter, Anne (the most beautiful of the four, according to Horace Walpole), also had a fine marriage arranged by her parents to another political ally, the third Earl of Sunderland, whose family seat was Althorp in Northamptonshire. More subtle than Sarah in her desire and ability to influence people, Anne was alleged by Walpole, who described her as 'a great politician', to have manipulated people through the mermaid-like enchantment of letting them watch her comb her 'beautiful head of hair' while at her toilette. Anne was Sarah's favourite daughter, and the grandchildren produced by this marriage were initially adored. By the unpredictable and fatal illnesses that so frequently upset the expected succession, it was Charles, the younger son of this younger daughter, who would eventually become the next Duke of Marlborough. But by this time Sarah had turned against him, one reason for her hostility perhaps being the fact that his inheritance of the sacred title had never been part of her plans for the future. She had also failed to control his selection of a wife and his irresponsible expenditure.

His mother, Anne Sunderland, had inherited Sarah's charm and guile but not the robust health: she died in 1716, aged only thirty-two, leaving five children aged from fifteen to five. Sarah, devastated, made herself responsible for the youngest, a girl named Diana (a family name of the Spencers of Althorp), who came to live with her, and after whom Charles would name his firstborn as a gesture of appeasement and an attempt to regain Sarah's favour at a time when their problematic but inextricable relationship was at its lowest ebb. Sunderland remarried in 1717. Following such perceived disloyalty to his late wife, Sarah quarrelled with him and even came to blame him for Anne's death. When he too suddenly and unexpectedly died in 1722, Sarah stepped in and took charge of the two other younger children, Charles and Johnny, then aged fifteen and thirteen. This was in accordance with their mother's request, which she had made in a testamentary letter written some time before her death.

Sarah also turned her attention to their older brother Robert, aged twenty, who had become the fourth Earl of Sunderland. He was now summoned back from Rome, where he was finishing his education doing the Grand Tour in company with his first cousin William, Henrietta Godolphin's son. Sarah wrote winningly: 'I hope I shall find in you all the comforts I have lost in your dear mother . . . as I believe from what you write that you will act like a son, I shall have all the pleasure in the world in making you mine'. And to reinforce his dependency on her, when he was invited to become a Lord of the Bedchamber to King George I, a salaried court position as well as a standard honour for one of his rank, she offered him £1,000 a year, together with support for his younger brothers and the promise of inheriting her personal fortune, on condition that he refuse the post. He accepted her terms and her money. This determination that her kin should be independent of court or political favour or salary remained an obsession over the next twenty years – a manifestation not just of her hostility to the Hanoverians but also her personal antagonism to the Prime Minister, Sir Robert Walpole. It was not a paradox that they should be dependent on her instead.[4]

Caring for the Spencer grandchildren provided some comfort to Sarah after the death of her beloved husband on 16 June 1722, just two months after that of her son-in-law Sunderland. Marlborough's deathbed was public and theatrical, attended by the various members of his family as well as his agonized wife. At first reclining on a couch in a reception room at the Lodge in Windsor Great Park (her own house, which she had acquired in 1702 when made Ranger of the Park by Queen Anne, and not his beloved Blenheim), he was moved, as the long day wore on, to his own bedroom, where he lay in the company of 'doctors, surgeons, apothecaries and servants' as well as his daughters and grandchildren. Young Charles Spencer was present with his older and younger brothers and sisters. When dusk fell and candles were lit, Sarah in her grief made them all leave; the most reluctant to go were her daughters, Henrietta, Countess of Godolphin, and Mary, Duchess of Montagu, to neither of whom was she was any longer speaking. Even on this terrible day, they communicated with each other only through intermediaries.

On John Churchill's death, Henrietta now became the second Duchess of Marlborough and her son William (Willigo) became the Marquess of Blandford. Sarah was now technically the Dowager Duchess of Marlborough, a title she hated, and which people seldom dared to use, referring to her generally as 'the old Duchess'. Under the first Duke's will, which appointed her chief of the seven trustees, she retained during her lifetime the use of Blenheim (still unfinished and subject to litigation with architects, builders and workmen) and Marlborough House in London, which she had commissioned from Sir Christopher Wren as a deliberate and restrained contrast to the grand ostentation of Vanbrugh's Blenheim, her husband's monument.

Sarah's overwhelming attentions, increased by loneliness and depression, affected her grandchildren in different ways: they found themselves having to make a deliberate choice whether to resist or submit to her. The elder girl, Anne, was for the moment out of the picture, for she had been married since 1720 – at Sarah's arrangement, and in opposition to her own father's wishes – to William (later Viscount) Bateman, a man of fairly undistinguished background but whose father, like Sarah, had made a fortune out of the South Sea Bubble. The young Lord Sunderland had already submitted, although Sarah confessed her underlying feelings about him: 'he is as easy with me as I can desire and I believe we shall always live so with one another, but I can't say that the love I have for him is like what I had for my own children'. Relationships remained cordial however, despite his heavy gambling, subsidized of course by her handouts, and reluctance to marry. Therefore when Sarah, shaken by a bout of illnesses, decided to update her will in 1729, she made him her main heir. The loyalties of his younger brothers Charles and Johnny Spencer were less clear cut. Inevitably confused and disturbed by the loss of a mother, acquisition of a stepmother, death of a father, then dependence on the whims and dominance of a grandmother who used her wealth as a weapon, one gave in to her while the other did not.

Sarah believed that she had taken care of all her daughter's children 'with the same tenderness as if they had been my own'. This care had earlier included nursing Charles, when thirteen, through an attack of potentially fatal smallpox (the killer of her own son). Taken ill at school, he had been carried by relays of chairmen to Marlborough House where 'he lay beside my bedside' and was nursed 'with as true an affection as if he had been my only son'. Yet even at this time, she was critical, commenting on his poor understanding and constant resemblance to his father ('violent and ill-natured'). And she later recalled a typical confrontation with Charles:

When he was a very great boy, he had burnt the hair of his head almost down to his forehead. I was frightened at it and asked him how it came in that condition, and who had cut it to hide its having been burnt, but he stiffly denied that it was either burnt or cut, saying for half an hour together till I was tired and let it drop, that he knew nothing of it. It is a very bad sign of the nature of a boy when he will so obstinately deny the truth, and in this there was a great addition of folly, as well as the falsehood of it.

This is an incident which in fact reveals great stamina in the young Charles to have the courage to challenge and wear out his normally inexhaustible grandmother.[5]

Charles and Johnny had been sent to Eton by their father, the normal practice for boys of rank, but Sarah's first act of control was to remove them from the school and have them privately educated by a tutor, James Stephens, at her favourite country property, Windsor Lodge. Her growing disenchantment with Charles is suggested by her justification for this action: 'A great deal of time he passed at school and in learning, though it can scarce be called either writing or reading well. How much better would it have been if that time had been spent in teaching him principles and what returns are due to a good parent and friend'.[6]

Increasingly preferring Johnny to his brother, she sent Charles abroad in 1725 to finish his disrupted education at M. Gallatin's private academy in Geneva, which she claimed, unconvincingly, 'to have been in the nature of Oxford'. Here he was later joined by Johnny (spotted in Paris en route for Geneva on his voyage of escape from his grandmother 'as happy and brisk as a bird out of a cage'), to improve his French and 'to keep them out of harm's way while they are so young that they can't keep the best company in England, and to make them see that nothing is so agreeable as England, take it altogether'. What Geneva did have in common with Oxford was the way it taught young noblemen to spend large sums of money. The Spencer boys were very good at that, assisted by the equally extravagant Gallatin. His carefully kept accounts of their lavish budgets (luxurious clothes, not only for them but for their servants too, fifty bottles of burgundy consumed at one party) so appalled the careful Sarah that in 1727 she removed them from Gallatin's control and put them under the charge of Humphrey Fish, a former page and protégé of hers. His remit included preventing the boys from gambling on pain of total disinheritance, and he accompanied them to Lorraine, Germany and Paris. She wanted the boys to study the subjects which she regarded as most useful – French, history and accounting – and not to dabble in those topics which most young aristocrats studied on the Grand Tour, such as music, art and architecture. For they were after all only younger sons and needed to earn a living. 'As to architecture, I think it will be of no use to Charles nor John, no more than music; which are all things proper for people that have time on their hands and like passing it in idleness rather than in what will be profitable'.[7]

Charles continued to disappoint. He had always been an unconfident and mumbling speaker of his own language (Sarah complaining of his 'ill habit of speaking through his teeth, one can't tell whether he is saying Yes or No; it is disagreeable not to speak distinctly'; years later Horace Walpole mentioned 'the greatest bashfulness and indistinction in his articulation'), and Fish now reported that despite three years abroad he still had a very poor French accent and that 'he has never had a familiar acquaintance that has not told him about it and at times rallied and laughed at him about it'. Nor was he happy in Paris: 'he thinks of nothing but England and pines after it: the more he sees of foreign countries the more that desire increases. Paris does not answer his hopes, he is not easy nor happy. If he employs the morning in study, that is as much as one can expect at one-and-twenty . . . the world offers nothing agreeable to his imagination but England'.[8]

These restrictions and interferences were too much for Charles: Sarah was still treating him like a child at an age when his grandfather was a serving soldier and had already had the Duchess of Cleveland as mistress. As soon as he reached the age of majority, in November 1727, he announced his intention of returning to England; having gone through the merely polite motion of seeking Sarah's permission, he came back in February 1728. Wishing him to take the political role that she could not directly perform herself – that of being in opposition to Walpole's government – she tried to fix him up with the parliamentary seat of Woodstock, which was in the Marlborough gift. This had already been given by her to Henrietta's son, the Marquess of Blandford ('It would be shameful that one of the Duke of Marlborough's family should not be chosen in that town'). However, Blandford's father, Godolphin, refused to agree to this handover, although the incumbent, and current heir to the Marlborough title, was proving a sad disappointment, living happily in Paris away from Sarah's influence, with no desire to return to England or work towards the great political career to which he should have been aspiring. Yet it was Sarah herself who had already sapped the ambition of her once favourite grandson by persuading the first Duke to add a codicil to his will which made Blandford financially independent of his parents. He already received an income of £8,000 a year, which would rise to £20,000 after Sarah's death. But she had failed to foresee that this would also make him independent of her.

Even had the seat been available, it is unlikely that Charles would have taken it, for fear of remaining under obligation to Sarah any longer; on his return, she commented: 'they say he has sense but he has nothing at least before me that is entertaining, though you know my manner does not constrain anybody', adding disapprovingly but perceptively to Fish, his former tutor, that he was 'much too expensive for a younger brother'. When she would not give him any more money, Charles happily ceased contact with her, and went to live with his brother Sunderland.

It was their younger brother Johnny who now became the favourite grandson ('I love him more than any body that is now in the world' she wrote in May 1728). He returned from his Continental education that November, having mercifully survived the fever which carried off Humphrey Fish in Dijon. Sarah expressed her relief: 'no words can express how dear you are to me, and I shall be in torture till I see you, therefore pray let it be as soon as you can come with safety'. Johnny was more amenable, or duplicitous, than his elder brother, and moved into a self-contained apartment in Marlborough House.

His status as favourite was enhanced by Blandford's unfortunate marriage, in August 1728, to a Dutch girl of humble birth whom he had met in Paris. He had the courtesy to come to England and inform Sarah and his father (true to family tradition he was not now on speaking terms with his mother). He did not need to ask their permission, in order to obtain a good financial settlement, because, as he reminded Sarah, although his bride's 'fortune be not so very large, surely it is a point not worth thinking of one minute in my case, whom your Grace has been so kind as to make easy that way.' Sarah begged him not to break her heart 'which it will certainly do to see the Duke of Marlborough's heir marryd to a burger master's daughter', an appeal which had no effect. Blandford married his bourgeoise love and went to live near her family in Utrecht.

A far greater blow was the sudden death in September 1729 of the eldest Spencer grandson, Robert, Earl of Sunderland, at the age of twenty-seven. This was in Paris, which he could afford to visit whenever he pleased, as a result of Sarah's generosity to him. Taken ill with a fever, he succumbed to blood-poisoning following treatment by the all-purpose remedy of blood-letting. His brother Charles, the least favourite grandson, the over-expensive younger son, became the fifth Earl of Sunderland, master of Althorp and heir, for the moment, to the bulk of Sarah's fortune (which was willed to the Sunderland grandson rather than Blandford, who would inherit Marlborough's money). However, as she threatened, this depended on his behaviour: 'if the present Lord Sunderland or others greatly concerned in this will should behave ill or marry without my approbation, I will certainly alter it'.

Charles now had to master new responsibilities; his dying brother had left him instructions for the care of his servants and the settlement of current debts, most caused by the gambling that Sarah so dreaded, incurred with the money-lender Matthew Lamb, who would soon be providing his services to Charles.

The formerly portionless young man was now a marriageable prize, and his choice of bride became the source of a contest between two strong women. Sarah's determination to control the family had been inherited by her own granddaughter, Charles' elder sister Anne, Lady Bateman. Unhappy in her childless marriage, her husband rumoured to be homosexual, Anne had the time and energy to bear Sarah a great grudge for having arranged this match, and remained more involved with her own family than the one into which she had married. She was now preparing to take revenge on her grandmother by obtaining dominance over her tractable and newly significant younger brother. According to Horace Walpole, Anne Bateman had 'the intriguing spirit of her father and grandfather, the Earls of Sunderland', to which should of course be added the equally intriguing spirit of her grand-mother the Duchess of Marlborough.

Sarah tried to pre-empt the situation by considering the possibility of a marriage between Charles and his first cousin – whose mother, the Duchess of Montagu, was the second daughter with whom Sarah was not on speaking terms. Mary Montagu had already been trying to effect a reconciliation with her mother, so the proposed match between the cousins would have confirmed the situation, as well as providing an extremely advantageous future for her own daughter. But, according to Sarah, it was Lady Bateman (whom she also accused of pro-curing mistresses for Charles) who managed to discourage him from this match.

It was also through the Batemans that Charles began to move into social and political circles of which Sarah strongly disapproved, those who supported the court and Walpole's government. There was the jovial, ambitious Henry Fox, slightly older than Charles, but with whom he had been at Eton, whose extravagant tastes and amusements in town and country he shared; as a result of Fox's friendship and beliefs, Charles started to develop views which would take him far from Sarah. Another member of this circle was John, Lord Hervey, a younger son of the Earl of Bristol, Member of Parliament, Vice-Chamberlain at the court of George II and loyal friend to Queen Caroline. Sexually ambiguous, delicately featured and of fragile health, Hervey had fathered eight children within his own marriage, made apparently for love, to the widely admired Molly Lepell, former maid of honour to Caroline when Princess of Wales; he had shared a mistress with Caroline's son Frederick, Prince of Wales but had also been in love for some years with Henry Fox's older brother Stephen, whom Hervey had taken on an extended fifteen-month 'honeymoon' on the Continent. (On his return, however, he seemed to have gone straight back into his wife's bed, for she had another baby exactly nine months later.) It was about Hervey, in the persona of Sporus, that Alexander Pope had written the vicious lines: 'Yet let me flap this bug with gilded wings, this painted child of dirt that stinks and stings . . .' in his *Epistle to Dr Arbuthnot* (1735), and it was the whole family whom Pope's sharp friend Lady Mary Wortley Montagu was describing when she defined the world as being divided into Men, Women and Herveys. Sarah was an old acquaintance of Hervey's mother, and was godmother to one of his children; but she came to dislike him extremely, not just for his political allegiance to Walpole and dedicated service at the Hanoverian court but also for his personal conduct. She referred to him as Lady Fanny, and described him as 'the most wretched profligate man that ever was born, besides ridiculous; a painted face and not a tooth in his head'. But there was also jealousy and resentment that Charles could be happy with very different sorts of people than those of whom she approved: Hervey's intellectual skills and balance of satirical wit with supreme tact provided a very different role model for Charles, as did his other new friends the Fox brothers. Stephen Fox became an MP in 1726, but preferred life in the country – his hunting box at Maddington was a favourite spot for relaxation, frequented by Charles and by Henry Fox, who would join his brother in the House of Commons in 1735.[9]

Hervey's letters to Stephen and Henry Fox describe the goings-on of their friend Charles – taking his place in society as Lord Sunderland, visiting the Batemans, dining with Hervey, joining the Freemasons, hunting in the country. There are also glimpses of Sarah, who was having more success with the youngest Spencer, Charles' sister Diana, whom Sarah had adopted and still adored as a daughter, whose charm, tact and compliance compensated for those real daughters whom Sarah had alienated or lost to death. A mother's main function was to arrange a good match. Sarah's first attempt for Diana aimed at the highest in the land, Frederick, Prince of Wales, a young man loathed by his parents George II and Caroline (who described her son as 'the greatest ass and the greatest liar in the whole world') and kept embarrassingly short of money. As recounted later by Horace Walpole, who was at the time a schoolboy at Eton, Sarah offered to the Prince of Wales 'her favourite granddaughter Lady Diana Spencer, with a fortune of £100,000. He accepted the proposal and the day was fixed for a secret wedding at the Duchess's Lodge in the Great Park at Windsor. Sir Robert Walpole got intelligence of the project, prevented it, and the Secret was buried in Silence'. As the son of Sir Robert, Horace presumably obtained this information at first hand. It also seems to be confirmed by Hervey; writing from Windsor, where he was in attendance on George II during the autumn of 1730, he mentions the Batemans being intimate with the Prince of Wales, and how 'Old Marlborough is come to the Lodge, and lets Lady Di sometimes be of the party. Thereby hangs a tale'. So perhaps Sarah was trying to marry Diana to the Prince of Wales to undermine the Batemans' influence on him just as much as to annoy the King and Queen. The match foiled, Hervey described how 'Old Marlborough is come to town, cross as the devil and flaming like Mount Vesuvius'.[10]

Although she had lost this greatest of prizes, Sarah kept on with her search for a worthy suitor and finally settled on Lord John Russell, younger brother and heir to the childless and gravely ill Duke of Bedford. The Duke was married to another of Sarah's granddaughters, Anne (daughter of Sarah's third daughter Elizabeth, who married the fourth Earl of Bridgwater); Anne's match had been made without Sarah's approval since she already had him in her sights for Diana. However, Bedford's galloping consumption meant that Lord John would become the Duke and Diana his Duchess barely a year after their marriage. It is a mark of Sarah's paranoia at this time that the match was kept secret from the grandchildren whom she currently disliked most. As described by Hervey, 'Lady Di is to be married in a few days to Lord John Russell. Negotiation has been carried on with so much affected secrecy by old Aetna that it has never been communicated to Lord Sunderland and Lady Bateman till last week, tho it has been in every mouth and Gazette within a hundred miles of London this week . . . she wrote a letter to excuse her not acquainting Lord Sunderland with his sister Di's match sooner, and said the reason was for fear he should have told Lady Bateman.' Hervey also noted Sarah's carefulness with money: 'the old Beldame of Bedlam, after offering £50,000 with Lady Di to Lord John gives but £30,000; which is in reality giving but £14,000 for £16,000 Lady Di has of her own.' However, Charles was permitted to attend his sister's wedding, as were her other siblings Johnny and Lady Bateman. The architect of the match stayed away.[11]

It was in the summer of 1731 that Charles became the direct heir to the Dukedom of Marlborough itself, as a result of the sudden death of that other privileged young man, the Marquess of Blandford. The Blandfords had left Utrecht to live in England the year before, and Sarah, still fond of Willigo despite his heavy drinking and complete lack of ambition, had made a genuine effort at reconciliation. She agreed to receive his wife – of whom however she wrote 'if anybody saw her by chance, they would be ready to ask her to shew them what Lace she had to sell' – and visited them socially. But he quite literally drank himself to death in an epic session in Oxford which caused fatal alcoholic poisoning. Sarah rushed there with her box of medicines but could not save him. According to Hervey, his uncaring mother Henrietta, Duchess of Marlborough, pronounced a dreadful epitaph on her son: 'Anybody who had any regard to Papa's memory must be glad that the Duke of Marlborough was not now in danger of being represented in the next generation by one who must have brought any name he bore into contempt'.

As Blandford and his wife were childless, the succession passed to the Spencer line, in the person of Charles. Hervey commented to Stephen Fox: 'It is a fine accident for our lucky friend Lord Sunderland. He will be no longer obliged to manage that unloving, capricious, extravagant Fury of a grandmother.' And he wrote to Henry Fox, then in Spain, avoiding his English creditors, of 'your friend Lord Sunderland's good fortune by the death of Lord Blandford. He gets nothing immediately but an independency on Mount Aetna, who never gave him anything in present, and who, if she was as partial to him as she is prejudiced against him, would now certainly never think of leaving him a shilling at her death.' Two weeks later, he went into more details about Charles' finances: 'notwithstanding he is only the heir presumptive of the young Duchess of Marlborough, the words of the will (the oddest that was ever made in this particular) put him exactly in the place of a Lord Blandford, the title only excepted: that is, £8,000 a year rent-charge comes to him immediately, and £12,000 a year at the death of his grandmother.' The 'young' Duchess of Marlborough, Henrietta Godolphin, was then aged fifty, but had given birth to a daughter just six years earlier, more than twenty years after her last confinement; this baby was the product of her affair with the playwright William Congreve.[12]

Sarah now had to arrange more marriages urgently. If Charles and Johnny produced no heirs, there was the alarming possibility that the title might pass to Henrietta's love child, who was officially legitimate since her father Godolphin was still very much alive although living well apart from his wife. The succession of little 'Moll Congreve', as the child was commonly known, would be infinitely worse, in Sarah's eyes, than the succession of Charles' children. Therefore his marriage became even more essential. And given the unpredictable nature of the succession, Johnny should also be made to produce a family as added security. But Charles was still enjoying his liberty, with the aid of the generous income which he had inherited on Blandford's death. Hervey reported him gloating that he was 'no longer obliged to that unloving, capricious, extravagant old Fury of a Grandmother . . . he intended to kick her A--- and bid her kiss his own'. He spent money on his current passions, hunting, a mistress and the refurbishment and rebuilding of Althorp – the latter particularly maddened Sarah since, under the terms of Marlborough's will, if and when Charles did become Duke of Marlborough, Althorp would revert to Johnny.

Hervey described Charles' new lifestyle:

I saw Lord Sunderland Sunday, Monday and Tuesday, which is every day he has been in town since his sister was married. He is grown so confirmed a fox-hunter, that he has two packs of hounds, in order not to lose one day of the week besides the Sabbath. Lord John and Lady Russell, Lord and Lady Bateman . . . have been with him at Althrop [as Althorp was pronounced] where I hear their recreations all day were galloping and hallooing, and their pleasures all night stale beer and tobacco . . . how essential riches must needs be to happiness, when people with twenty thousand a year take the same pleasures with those who carry chairs and burdens for two or three shillings a day.[13]

To get him away from these trivial pursuits and dangerous company, as well as protecting the succession from Congreve's bastard, Sarah strove to encourage Charles to contemplate marriage. A good moment occurred in the spring of 1732, when Sarah learned that he had broken with his current mistress. She summoned him to Marlborough House, according to Hervey, and pointed out that she was 'glad to hear he had not so great an Aversion to Marriage as he formerly had; for our Family wanted posterity very much'. But Charles only replied, 'with a stiff air and disagreeable voice, "I won't marry without telling you."' And he kept his word, in a way, for he came to tell her, just two days later, that he would be marrying Elizabeth Trevor the very next day. As Sarah was ill in bed on this occasion and had refused to see him in person, this terrible news was simply communicated by a message.

This was a threefold blow – the marriage had been arranged without her knowledge or approval, it had been organized through the hated Lady Bateman, and it was into a family totally unacceptable to Sarah, both politically and socially. The bride was the granddaughter of an old enemy of the Marlboroughs, Thomas Trevor, who had been appointed first Baron Trevor by Queen Anne, as one of the twelve Tory peers created to ensure the safe passage through the House of Lords of the measure establishing the Treaty of Utrecht, which eventually ended the War of the Spanish Succession; this making of peace with the French and their allies had been strongly opposed by Marlborough. As a final insult, Elizabeth was the daughter of a first cousin of Lord Bateman, at whose house the details of the marriage settlement were finalized. Sarah did not find out all the particulars until early in the following year, although she was convinced from the beginning that the Trevors had actually paid Lady Bateman to fix up the match; when the details emerged, she was shocked to learn that not only would Charles receive nothing of his wife's miserly £15,000 dowry until after Lord Trevor's death – despite being 'something between a madman and a fool' he was still only forty – but that as an additional shame, in order to provide the new Lady Sunderland with an income of £2,000 a year immediately (increasing to £4,000 a year when she became Duchess) Lady Bateman and the Trevors were attempting to overturn some of the provisions of the complex Marlborough will. 'This is being very ungrateful and dishonourable to his grandfather', she stormed.[14]

The wedding took place on 23 May 1732. Sarah was beside herself with rage, venting her temper by deeds as well as words. Assuming that Lady Bateman had deliberately chosen an insignificant and low-bred bride for her brother who would not therefore provide a threat to her 'so that she might continue in the Post of her Brother's Premier Minister and govern all his Affairs', Sarah wrote a vicious letter to Charles attacking both his sister and new wife, and she used the familiar weapon of altering her will in order to deprive him of as much as she could. To which he replied:

> I receiv'd Your Grace's extraordinary letter last night . . . I shan't endeavour to convince Your Grace that it is a match of my own seeking and not of my overbearing sister (as you are pleased to call her) because in the Passion Your Grace must be in, when you wrote such a Letter, all Arguments would be of very little use. As for your putting me out of your Will, it is some time since I neither expected or desir'd to be in it. I have nothing more to add but to assure Your Grace that this is the last time I shall ever Trouble you by Letter or Conversation.[15]

Charles must have showed a copy of this letter to Hervey, who quoted it almost verbatim to his own mother, in a long letter which provides a favourable account of the new Lady Sunderland:

> the first reflection your Ladyship will naturally make on this piece of news (when I tell you the young lady is pretty and sensible and has £30,000) to be sure, will be that bellowing Aetna, after the frequent desire she has expressed to see Lord Sunderland married, must be overjoyed; and that those streams of sulphur, fire and smoke that used to flow in such outrageous torrents from the foul mouth at the summit of this tremendous mountain, are all converted into the soft murmurs of the Land of Canaan that flows with milk and honey. But . . . she proceeded to calling the young lady's father a madman, her mother a fool, her grandfather a rogue and her grandmother a w----.[16]

Sarah then summoned Johnny Spencer to show him the changes in her will, having transferred such lands and properties as she could from his brother to him, and reminded him that he could inherit around £300,000 from her on condition that he would always behave as if he were her son – this meant total obedience. Johnny promised that he would not marry without her consent, but did have the courage to defend his brother's action, to the reckless extent of admitting that he had attended the wedding, which had taken place at one of Lord Bateman's properties. The furious Sarah immediately disinherited him and burnt the latest will. Then she wrote him a bitter letter, continuing her attacks on Lady Bateman, and the Trevors – 'beggars and odd people . . . for the sake of a woman . . . who don't know how to behave on any occasion, has a very indifferent person and very bad teeth'. This letter was subsequently annotated by Charles, who wrote 'All Lies' over the last sentence, signed 'M'.

She felt even angrier, if possible, with Lady Bateman, when she heard that the latter had invited her sister Diana, now the only favourite left, to the wedding; but the demure and loyal Lady Russell, at that time the only person capable of mollifying Sarah, had had the tact not to attend. Sarah declared Lady Bateman's motivation was to make Diana 'appear to the world as black as herself. Who is certainly the worst Woman that I ever knew in my Life'. Sarah then literally blackened the face of Lady Bateman's portrait, which hung in a public room at Marlborough House, and wrote underneath it 'Now her outside is as black as her inside'.[17]

She flatly refused to meet Charles' bride but claimed to describe her to Diana in a letter written from Scarborough, one of the fashionable spa resorts, where she had taken herself in July 1732 to drink the waters in hopes of improving her 'gout' and her 'scurvy':

As to my Lady Sunderland, I can say nothing of my own knowledge, but she has very different characters given her. Some people say she is simple, ill-bred and knows nothing of right behaviour. Others that she has a termagant spirit and is ill-natured. And some say she has a great deal of sense and that she will disappoint my Lady Bateman as to her design in this marriage, which was to govern her brother and all his finances. Nothing but time can show who judges rightest, but for my own part I do believe that Lord Sunderland is a very weak man, who will always be governed by his sister. And as he does not love his wife, Lady Bateman's artifices will get the better, and she will keep her post at the expense of making her brother in a little time live ill with his wife ... my Lady Bateman took her sister [in law] by the hand several times in that great assembly like a fond lover; which looks as if she intends to manage her as long as she can.[18]

The conciliator Diana wrote back bravely defending her new sister-in-law, and Sarah quickly replied:

I wonder how she comes to have so easy and right a behaviour, who has always been used to low and ordinary company ... I am not at all surprised at her being pleased at the great change of her condition nor of his being so fond of her at first, who has certainly so nasty a constitution. I remember he was once so fond of Mrs Smith that some people fancied he would marry her. How long the honeymoon of this match will last nobody can tell ... his letter and behaviour to me has given a full proof that he has no nature nor true principles of honour. And since he had money in his power, he has never disposed of any, that I have heard of, with any judgement; nor has he governed himself in any one action by the rules of reason. He seems to be very fond of his person, though not a very pleasing one, and to bestow a good deal of time upon dress ... and if one could see an account of the money he has spent and taken up in a short time and how he has disposed of it, it would appear very ridiculous to anybody of sense. In short he is so weak a man that even those who have no good characters and very indifferent understandings can impose upon him . . . if he were my only son, I would not love a simple nor an ungrateful man, both which he certainly is.

At the same time, she was venting greater malice in a letter to an old friend, Mrs Strangways Horner:

I think it a very improper match for a man that might have had anybody, without being at all in love with the person, to marry a woman whose father is a mighty ridiculous man, a family of beggars and all very odd people. The woman herself (as they say for I have never seen her) has been bred in a very low way and don't know how to behave herself on any occasion; not at all pretty, and has a mean ordinary look. As to the behaviour, if she has any sense, that may mend. But they say she has very bad teeth, which I think is an objection alone in a wife, and they will be sure to grow worse with time.

This criticism of poor Elizabeth's appearance and bearing from one who has never seen her is typical of Sarah's unreasonableness; the fastidious Hervey had found her 'pretty'. She went on to blame Lady Bateman – 'very false and covetous, and has made this match purely to be her brother's Prime Minister and to manage his finances' – although this also was unreasonable because it was all too clear that Charles' finances certainly needed managing, but unfortunately for him, Lady Bateman never had a chance to do so. And she continued with a tirade against Charles: 'he has not sense enough to know what a principle is . . . has a great deal of pride and vanity and weakness in letting himself be cheated by everybody, the present Lord Sunderland is called by many a mighty generous man.' And she prophesied gloomily that 'he is so much pleased with that character that even when I am dead, his debts will be so much increased by his extravagance of all sorts, that till his aunt dies, who may live for these thirty years, he will be always taking up money upon hard terms'. Sarah was wrong only in her prediction of the sequence of deaths.[19]

Henry Fox was impelled to come to the defence of his friend, and wrote to Sarah to say that Charles was 'neither foolish nor worthless', as Sarah had described him. This launched a massive response whose length and obsessive repetition of her prejudices demonstrate her inflexible self-righteousness. She went right back to her favours to Charles' grandfather 'for whom I got £2000 a year pension from Queen Anne', father – 'what I did for his father and what I suffered from his madness I won't dwell upon', older sister – 'I got a portion and settlement for that vile woman Lady Bateman', younger sister – 'I will say nothing of my care and kindness to Di Spencer' – as mere preliminaries to Charles' own bad character and deception over his marriage, and finally Johnny's ingratitude in remaining loyal to his brother, for which she again blamed Lady Bateman. She concluded 'this is a very exact account of the whole matter, without the least flourish on my own account or aggravation of their crimes'.[20]

She became even more obsessively concerned with securing the loyalty of Diana, now the Duchess of Bedford, by trying to detach her from all her siblings. Since leaving Sarah (with whom she had lived for the past fifteen years), Diana had been the recipient of a constant stream of lengthy letters from her 'Mama Duchess'. In November 1732 Sarah referred to

the monstrous treatment I have had from your family, which I do believe you were very sorry for, though I have often observed you were partial to them . . . you must choose one of two things: which is to live with me as I have proposed [i.e. to take Sarah's side in the dispute], or to distinguish yourself by shewing how far you are from having any of Lady Bateman's principles. I don't mean by this that you should not see your brothers, but she is a disgrace to be anybody's sister . . . as to my two grandsons, they cannot help their weakness . . . John Spencer likes it better to depend on a vain extravagant brother than to have had a great estate from me.

This letter was written to Diana two weeks after the death of her newly born son.

Diana did cease contact with her sister Lady Bateman, which provoked a series of malicious anonymous letters to Sarah, apparently written at Lady Bateman's instigation. One summed up the younger family members' attitude: 'All your family wish for your death because that is the only time they hope to have anything but orders and direction from you.' And in another: 'Is it not enough for you to exercise your pretty temper yourself and for some atonement to your family, intaile your money without your wickedness and die as soon as you can'.[21]

Sarah continued to harangue Diana about Lady Bateman's dangerous influence: 'She is a great favourite at Court, and that must be from the hopes the ministers have of dividing a family, who, if they were wise would be strong enough to make any ministry afraid of disobliging them. But they certainly think that by her means they will get Lord

Sunderland. And I believe they will. And at the same time he will think himself a man of great honour and understanding.'

There was now however some reconciliation with Johnny, and even reluctant contact with Charles; when she learned that Johnny had loaned him several thousand pounds she demanded the return of his grandfather's diamond-hilted sword, presented to Marlborough by the Holy Roman Emperor, for fear, as she put it, that Lady Bateman would steal the diamonds.

Fate again smiled on Charles in October 1733, when his aunt Henrietta died and he thus became the third Duke of Marlborough. Happy and secure in his marriage, perhaps even sorry for Sarah in the loss of another daughter, already with grave financial problems which jeopardized his inheritance, he wrote to her making a gracious apology for their past differences. Surprised and touched, she responded warmly. Two days after receiving her letter he turned up unannounced at Windsor Lodge, and they had a reconciliation which moved her to tears. As she described it to Diana:

the Duke of Marlborough has been with me this morning, though I endeavoured in my letter to save him that trouble. It is not easy for me to describe, without lessening it, the goodness of his behaviour in every respect. All that he said was so extremely good natured, and with good sense. And I do really believe, he is very sincere and that I have now a prospect for the future of enjoying a great deal of happiness from the three children of your most beloved mother . . . before he went away, he desired that his wife might come to me, just as I was going to speak to him of her: which, I told him, I was that moment going to do, and that I should be glad to see her, when I came to London. For I never had anything to say against her. And that, as everybody gives her a good character, I hope she will always behave to him in the manner I wish. This is a very surprising turn . . .

Sarah's self-delusion in her attitude to the new Duchess is breath-taking.

Diana quickly applauded the reconciliation and put in more good words for Charles and his wife (with whom, unknown to Sarah, she had managed to establish a friendly relationship), for just four days later Sarah was still making a great effort to be charitable, while at the same time justifying her previous stance: 'Though I must ever be of the opinion that it was not a natural match for him to have made, without being in love, which is some excuse for anything, yet if he continues to like her, as you say he now does, and that her behaviour and temper is agreeable to him, I think he will be happier than if he had married one that in appearance had been more proper for him.' She was stubbornly determined to believe that Charles had not married for love, despite what he himself had told her. The marriage was to be a very happy one, as evidenced by Charles' letters to his wife for the rest of his life, in which he found the love and stability Sarah had not been able to provide. Sarah's alleged view that being in love might be an excuse for an unwise match would actually have provided her with cause for much greater opposition – love matches were certainly not the order of the day in her plans for the family. She preferred to cast the blame on Lady Bateman. The letter continued more perceptively: 'I wish him as well as I did before any disagreeable thing happened. I will take all occasions to shew the value which I have for him. At the same time I do really think that what he has done is yet better for himself than for me, though he had not so much good nature as I hope and believe he has because, without the least partiality and self-interest, nothing did ever give so great a wound to his character in all respects as that proceeding.'

The glow of self-justification and virtue was reaffirmed to Diana the very next day: 'You express so much satisfaction at the thoughts of my happiness in being reconciled with the Duke of Marlborough, that I cannot help assuring you, my dear Angel, that I think I love him better than ever I did in my life, which is saying a great deal.'

Lord Hervey commented to Henry Fox on this change of climate but was more cynically aware that Charles' motivation in the rapprochement was mainly triggered by his extravagance:

Your friend Lord Sunderland, new Duke of Marlborough, will certainly be ruined by succession to his new title. For as he thinks he must increase his expenses with his grandeur and the eclat of his way of living with that of his appellations, he is, without the addition of one thousand pounds a year to his income, doubling the charges of his disbursements, which were before so extravagant that, without these supplemental new drains, he was the beginning of this year threescore thousand pounds in debt. So that, paradoxical as it may sound to have the ruin of a man completed by becoming the Duke of Marlborough, it will, if his grandmother lives seven years, certainly be his case. By the bye, he is reconciled to her; he and his Duchess have both been at Marlborough House. The Batemans are now the only people that remain in disgrace at the Court; and there is even a flying report that secret orders are given for Lady Bateman's picture to be white-washed.[22]

Charles now had to vacate Althorp for Johnny, in compliance with his grandfather's will. As Sarah retained the use of Blenheim in her lifetime, the young Duke and Duchess were therefore homeless. As a mark of the new rapport, Sarah let them move into the Little Lodge in the Home Park at Windsor, which was in her gift as Park Ranger and not so far from her own Lodge in the Great Park. She imposed the condition that he make no alterations to this property: she had seen what he did and spent at Althorp, including the erection of an elegant stable block to the design of the distinguished Palladian architect Roger Morris, even though he knew that his occupation of Althorp was short-term. She also set about sorting out some of the complications of the marriage settlement (for which she blamed the Batemans as much as the Trevors) to secure Johnny's entitlement to the Sunderland estates as established in the will, which it was her duty as chief trustee to clarify. His estate secured, she now negotiated a desirable marriage for Johnny, with Georgiana, daughter of Lord Carteret, an able politician on the opposition side, who she felt would be a steadying influence on both her grandsons. As she wrote to Diana in December 1733:

Your brother John has good nature, sense, frankness in his temper (which I love) and in short a great many desirable things in him; but still wants a great deal to get through this world in the manner that I wish he would do . . . I know of nothing so desirable in the present case as the kindness and assistance of a father-in-law who, I think, must always make a considerable figure whatever way the world turns. And I think too that it is possible that this alliance may be an advantage even to your elder brother, who has been so miserably thrown away.

She is drawing painful contrasts between the characters of the brothers, between their fathers-in-law Lord Carteret and Baron Trevor, and between their wives. Now that she had got to know the new Duchess of Marlborough, the Dowager decided that she was 'extremely ill-bred, simple and pert'.

Hervey seemed to be agreeing with Sarah on the character of the new duchess, keeping Henry Fox, still abroad, up to date: 'The reconciliation of the Duke of Marlborough to his grandmother happened naturally and without being negotiated, upon the death of his aunt; but I hear it is not likely to last . . . it is certain that he is, by his own confession, £30,000 in debt and others say much more. His wife is grown tall, fat, coarse and proud.'

Charles began to take his place in public life. In January 1734 he was introduced into the House of Lords by his brother-in-law the Duke of Bedford and cousin-in-law the Duke of Manchester. He made his maiden speech in support of the proposal to make army commissions tenable for life, a measure opposed by the King. This was a topical issue, inspired by the recent case of Lord Cobham, who had been dismissed from his regiment because of his vote on the Excise Bill. Hervey reported to Henry Fox how the Duke 'was extremely frightened, said but little and what he did say was neither remarkably well or ill'. However his stance served to annoy the King and Walpole, and therefore pleased Sarah considerably, as did his membership of the Liberty Club, formed by and for opponents of Walpole. Over the next three years, he and Bedford, despite their contrasting characters ('the Duke of Marlborough was profuse and never looked into his affairs, the Duke of Bedford covetous and the best economist in the world ... the one in company, conscious of his ignorance was generally diffident and silent, the other was always assured talkative and decisive' – this was Hervey's view), supported the opposition; and Charles, despite his natural diffidence, played a regular part in the Lords' proceedings.

So for the moment relationships were tolerable, although Sarah was becoming increasingly concerned about Charles' uncontrollable spending habits (such as commissioning a pleasure launch), failure to understand the relationship between capital and interest, and resentment of the fact that, under the contentious will, he only received the residue of the income after substantial jointures had been paid to Sarah and other heirs. As she pointed out bitterly to Diana: 'It is necessary for me to die to support the Duke of Marlborough'. And she realized that even after her death, he would never cope: 'I fear nature is too strong for my wishes to have any effect. And that great as his fortune is, he will never be easy in money matters. For at a time that he saw that his extravagance obliged him to retrench and did put away some very useless horses, he has made a much greater expense in building a ship. Where there must be a captain and seamen. And this I cannot help thinking is a very odd thing when he owed so much money and cannot live in a decent way, without borrowing more.' And she complained to Diana how he failed to reply to the various letters of instruction or unsolicited advice which she was constantly sending him.

It was at this time that she commissioned a series of family portraits, including one of Charles, to be installed as a contribution to her latest project, the building and furnishing of a grand house for herself in an estate she had bought at Wimbledon. This was in addition to Blenheim, where she never went, the Lodge in Windsor Great Park, Marlborough House and her own old family home at St Albans. She wrote sarcastically to Johnny about Charles' image: 'Whood the Painter has drawn your brother's picture in the figure of an old Roman consul with a truncheon in one hand and one arm drawn quite naked; I suppose going to do some great execution . . . I think it would have been as well if he had deferred drawing this graceful figure till he had been in some battle'. And her disillusionment with Charles was continuing to grow, particularly when Johnny's wife became pregnant very soon after the wedding, unlike the young Duchess of Marlborough, who was still failing to breed in her third year of marriage. Sarah pointed up the contrast to Diana: 'Your dear brother Johnny and Mrs Spencer appear to be very happy. And I never saw anybody in my life better behaved than she is. And in a mighty easy and agreeable way. She certainly has very good sense, which is the thing in the world most to be wished for in anybody . . . she is bigger than she was but not quick [i.e. had not yet felt the baby move]. I hope no accident will happen to her, for I do not hear yet that the Duchess of Marlborough is with child'.

That summer of 1734 she was able to keep Charles and his wife under close surveillance, since she was spending a lot of time in her own house in Windsor. Johnny was now not only master of Althorp, but was also renting a house in Hanover Square. The Marlboroughs by contrast were dependent upon Sarah for their country house, although not permanently excluded from London, since Charles bought from his brother Sunderland House in Piccadilly, which had gone to Johnny as part of the Sunderland estate. But in Windsor there was no escape. Sarah reported to Diana how 'I was yesterday at your brother Marlborough's Lodge, which is extremely pretty and as convenient a house to live in as I ever saw. And I think it is as well furnished as any place need to be of that sort, and without any expense. For I see nothing new; and your brother has only bought one suite of crimson damask and some old field beds and upon the whole it is all done as I would have liked it for myself, excepting some pictures of horses and dogs and some old sort of Dutch pictures, with vast heavy carved frames . . . I daresay they cost a great deal more of money than the pictures that are in them, most of which I believe are very indifferent paintings'.

Charles was now buying pictures, some through the agency of Arthur Pond, a minor artist but versatile entrepreneur, and trusted dealer and connoisseur, whose range of activities in the 1730s included authenticating, arranging the purchase and importing works of art for high-spending clients such as the Duke of Marlborough. The 'Dutch pictures' so scorned by Sarah were in fact a shrewd investment in a newly fashionable genre.[23]

While Charles had to put up with Sarah's disapproval of his taste in paintings, his wife had to endure her continuing criticism and scrutiny, together with the scarcely concealed resentment that Charles had chosen the wrong woman. Sarah brooded about this to Diana, writing enthusiastically about the virtues of Johnny's sister-in-law, Lady Weymouth: 'If I had a son of my own, I should have bespoke just such a woman for him. And I could not help thinking all the time I was there, what a delightful thing it would have been if she had been married to your brother Marlborough. She looks like a woman of quality and by what I saw, I am persuaded, she knows what is to be done and said upon every occasion'. How could the poor, nervous Duchess hope to compete with this?

Sarah was now becoming increasingly querulous about Charles' inadequate business sense and lack of efficiency. In a dispute about the cost of hay-making at the Little Lodge in July, she was horrified to find that Charles was paying well above the going rate to a Mr Dodd, totalling £46 instead of the £20 that she thought reasonable. Diana was again meant to mediate: 'I do not care for writing to the Duke of Marlborough myself about it because I do see that he seldom makes answers in a long time, and when he does they are not full ones. However you may perhaps be able to do him some service. I am labouring like a packhorse every day to save him from the cheats . . . though his revenue will be considerable when I am dead, you will be able to judge whether it is not necessary for him to retrench in all reasonable things on account of the vast loads of his own debts . . . it is very unpleasant to go through so much drudgery for one that will not trouble to write ten lines in answer to things that only concern himself'. The lack of communication between them meant that when at last the Duchess became pregnant it was kept a secret from Sarah, as well as from Johnny and Georgiana, until it was quite well advanced. This was not unusual; the first suspicions were seldom made public until the dangers of the early months were past. But it must also have been a source of pleasure that this was the only area of their life that could for the moment be concealed from the terrifying dowager.

Rumours that the Duchess was breeding began to surface towards the end of 1734. Hervey wrote in November to Henry Fox: 'the Duchess of Marlborough is reported be five months gone of that desirable pregnancy that everybody is so proud of at first and so peevish with at last. But Mrs Spencer says this report is entirely without foundation; and at the same time flirts her fan over her own great belly with an air of sufficiency and satisfaction, as if she had obtained a grant from Heaven of the monopoly of making children for the Marlborough family'.[24]

And this satisfaction was justified when Mrs Johnny Spencer gave birth to a boy on 8 December 1734, a mere ten months after her wedding. This infant became the heir presumptive to the title until the Duke and Duchess of Marlborough could produce a son of their own. The Duchess now publicly confirmed her pregnancy, and so the brothers and their wives were officially in competition.

TWO

The Duke's Daughter

(1735–56)

'The ultimate end of your education was to make you a good wife'

LADY MARY WORTLEY MONTAGU TO HER DAUGHTER

The birth of a daughter on 24 March 1735 was further confirmation for Sarah of Elizabeth Trevor's failure as ducal wife and mother of heirs; and it was possibly even a source of satisfaction that Johnny's line was for the moment ensured for the succession. The Duke and Duchess might have preferred their baby to be a boy, but there is no reason why the young couple were not delighted. They loved each other, her fertility and stamina had been proved, there would certainly be many more to come. The baby was named Diana, after the only person in the family with whom Sarah had not quarrelled and who was loyal and supportive to them behind her grandmother's back – a charming letter from the Duchess of Bedford (herself desperately anxious for another baby) to her sister-in-law, written two months after the birth, refers to commissions she is undertaking for the new mother, ordering mineral water, a hat and the copying of a miniature painting, while a subsequent letter sends a desired recipe for a hair thickener and conditioner. Inviting Charles and his wife to stay at Woburn, she promises 'an extream good Nursery for Dear Lady Dye'. But this naming, a precaution and an indication of their continuing dependence on Sarah, who was occasionally promising to consider making over Blenheim to them (although the first Duke's will gave her the lifetime use of it), did nothing to allay her growing anger over

Charles' general incompetence and obvious lack of affection towards her.[1]

There was another petty dispute in August 1735 which demonstrated how rapidly he was falling out of favour. As Ranger of Windsor Park, Sarah was responsible for monitoring access to the Park through the distribution of keys, but Charles had secretly had more cut and distributed them to his friends. As a result, the Duke of St Albans was grazing unauthorized cows there. Sarah was concerned to establish use of the Park as a privilege, not an automatic right for anyone who asked, particularly not the upstart grandson of Charles II and his mistress Nell Gwynn. She laid all the blame on Charles, who wrote sarcastically back asking whether she wanted to padlock all the gates to keep him out as well. Sarah then accused him of lying about who had or had not keys, and of giving them to the wrong sort of people, including

his gamekeeper, a man that has been very impudent to me . . . those that have been so publicly rude to me as the Duke of St Albans has been and his brother Lord Sydney . . . such people should make a right use of such civilities and not turn it into an abuse by making more keys for their acquaintance . . . I do not complain of the Duke of Marlborough's not answering my letters because I have been so long used to it and from my experience I see that it is impossible for me to do anything to oblige him, tho my endeavours have been to do it upon all occasions, but in vain, for he never writes to me but as one would do to an enemy or at least to one that was mad and that he wanted to get rid of the trouble of hearing from as soon as he possibly could.

Clearly, the existence of baby Diana had not improved matters at all.[2]

In the autumn of 1735, the family suffered another of those unpredictable blows of fate in the death of the young Duchess of Bedford. Diana had inherited her mother's fragile constitution and had, as revealed in her constant correspondence with Sarah, mistaken the symptoms of rapid consumption for those of the longed-for pregnancy. Her charm and subtle tact had enabled her to mediate between Sarah and Charles and to keep some balance between the rest of her warring family. Deprived of this calming influence and almost maddened with grief, Sarah quarrelled irrevocably with the widower Bedford, and then with Charles, when she found out that, despite her instructions and his debts, he had begun elaborate land- and water-scaping at Windsor Lodge, works which included an artificial lake and island, gardens and an orangery. As described by an impressed Duchess of Portland: 'he has made very great improvements there and great plantations – a canal and a serpentine river and a mount that has cost a vast deal of money'. Sarah now took physical revenge on him by getting in a team of men to destroy his earthworks and uproot his trees, one of which she was alleged to have torn up herself, her rage apparently overcoming her crippling gout.[3]

Charles' debts were mounting but he was incapable of economy. Hervey mentions, in December 1736, how the Duke was 'ruining himself at play at the Bath, though he won £4600 on one card at basset'; less than a month later the Countess of Hertford, a retired court lady, reported how 'the Duke of Marlborough lost £700 on Twelfth Night, which was all that was considerable'. In desperation he tried to challenge the complicated trust set up by his grandfather and still administered by Sarah, in order to obtain more income to pay off his creditors. He was supported by his brother-in-law the Duke of Bedford, who had turned against Sarah in retaliation to her attitude towards him, and who offered to loan Charles money so that he could 'go to law and torment the old dowager'. Matters dragged on, with Sarah and Charles barely on speaking terms. Johnny Spencer and his wife had another baby, barely a year after the first one, a daughter whom they also named Diana, in sad homage to the late Duchess of Bedford. But the Marlboroughs did not produce another baby until 1737, and this was another girl, named Elizabeth, whose sex may have been a little less welcome than that of her sister Diana. Sarah bought the young Spencers a fine London house in Grosvenor Street.[4]

As well as becoming a family man, Charles was also active in court and political circles. He was now an intimate of the Prince of Wales, who 'liked to pass the evening with six or seven others over a glass of wine and hear them talk of a variety of things'. But these innocuous sounding amusements were read differently by the Prince's mother, Queen Caroline, who complained to Hervey how her son was 'induced by knaves and fools that blow him up to do things that are as unlike an honest man as a wise one. I wonder what lengths these monsters wish to carry him'. Establishing a Hanoverian tradition, Frederick Prince of Wales was at odds with his father George II and became a focal point for opposition to the court. Charles played a prominent part in the ceremonials of the Royal Wedding in 1736, being one of those who formally put the Prince and new Princess of Wales, Augusta of Saxe-Gotha, to bed. Following his marriage, the Prince demanded a settlement of £100,000 a year from Parliament in order to clear his outstanding debts and enable him and his wife to live in the style to which he thought he was entitled, a scheme firmly opposed by the King and Prime Minister Walpole. Charles acted as the Prince's go-between, putting his friend Henry Fox in an awkward position by asking him to support this proposal in the House of Commons; Fox temporized by saying that he would do whatever Stephen Fox did. Hervey and Fox privately discussed the matter, and Hervey discreetly reported matters to the Queen, although not mentioning Marlborough's name. There was greater public support for the Prince's cause than the King or Queen liked, and had Charles' name come out it would have done him no good in their eyes, although it would have won him Sarah's favour. However, the motion was defeated.[5]

He was in close attendance on the Prince when the Queen was dying, a terrible protracted occasion described in agonizing detail by Hervey, in his memoirs of the court, since he had attended the deathbed. The Prince was reported to take pleasure in the account of her long drawn-out suffering, sending messengers daily from his court in Pall Mall to the Queen's apartments in St James's Palace. The Duke of Marlborough was with the Prince at this time and told Henry Fox and Hervey how the Prince was longing for the good news of her death. Perhaps Charles was thinking of Sarah.

It was through his burgeoning public presence that Sarah soon had further reasons for grave displeasure. They had up to now been on the same side politically, since he supported the opposition in the House of Lords. But in March 1738 he changed sides and accepted office from Government and court, the two institutions of which Sarah so passionately disapproved, quite apart from her personal antagonism to the Prime Minister. Charles' main motivation was financial, but it also indicated his growing political maturity and independence from Sarah. The father of a young family was making a career move, a course of action seen as perfectly normal to anyone except his grandmother. Horatio Walpole (brother of Sir Robert) wrote to Charles' brother-in-law about 'what I am persuaded will be as agreeable a surprise to you as it has been to the whole town, of the Duke of Marlborough's having kissed his Majesty's hand yesterday and accepted a regiment. This was kept a secret from his nearest relations', i.e. Sarah. He was appointed Colonel of the 38th Regiment of Foot, and also a Lord of the Bedchamber, 'kissing hands' for this post in August 1738. Such court positions were now salaried, and were beginning to be seen as a useful source of income. Lady Suffolk, a former lady in waiting, commented grumpily to Horace Walpole in 1765 that such posts 'had no salaries before King William's reign . . . the salaries of the present great offices were formerly very small . . . it is plain that salaries were not the great object as now.' These were posts from which Charles could advance, gaining access to further lucrative appointments and the military career structure to which someone of his rank should aspire; but they also committed him firmly to supporting King and Government by no longer voting against them in the House of Lords. Prime Minister Walpole gloated: 'You see I know the way to get everybody I have a Mind to.'[6]

Sarah was shattered. The Marlboroughs' complex relationship with Walpole and his government was tortuously linked to the family trust funds, which provided a regular and safe source of income from the interest they earned on substantial loans to the Exchequer. Walpole had simply threatened to cease renewing these loans, and had thus virtually blackmailed the needy Charles into publicly supporting him by accepting the positions offered. Once he had agreed, the loans were renewed on a greater scale than before. The political influence of Henry Fox, then aged thirty-four, a recent and ambitious Member of Parliament, was also a factor in Charles' conversion. It was to Fox's influence rather than Walpole's persuasion that Horace Walpole later ascribed his change of sides: 'what an object would it be to Fox to convert to the Court so great a subject as the Duke'. And it was certainly Fox whom Sarah blamed bitterly for the defection, calling him 'the Fox that stole my Goose'. But she also blamed another betrayer, Lady Bateman, at that time well in with the court ('there is a report that my Lady Bateman is to be made Lady of the Bedchamber to some or other of the royal family', as Lady Hertford, who had just quit court service, reported in 1737). Anne Bateman may have wished to advance herself further through obtaining such a prize as her converted brother the Duke of Marlborough. But it was Sarah herself who was the ultimate source of his actions because of her own refusal, following their earlier estrangement in 1736, to advance him any more money. As a result, Charles was now deeply in debt to Matthew Lamb, the moneylender, at exorbitant rates of interest, against the expectation of Sarah's death. She was by then, in 1738, aged seventy-eight.

Sarah now took the familiar course of altering her will again. This time she took away from Charles not only the expectation of Marlborough House – her own property but one which her husband had always wished to go with the title – but also the Little Lodge in Windsor Park, which he was not only prevented from inheriting, but from which, in the summer of 1738, she evicted him and his young family. Diana was three, Betty one, and their mother was again pregnant. The loss of a comfortable home was vigorously resisted by the Duke, who tried to delay their departure as long as possible. He also took deliberate revenge by vindictively destroying some of his own improvements and removing what he could of the fixtures and fittings, even, allegedly, the chicken run. In Horace Walpole's version: 'The Duke she turned out of the Little Lodge and then pretending that the new Duchess and her female cousins, eight Trevors, had stripped the house and garden, she had a puppet-show made with waxen figures representing the Trevors tearing up the shrubs, and the Duchess carrying off the chicken coop under her arm'. Walpole was certainly prone to exaggeration, and loved passing on a piece of gossip, but wax modelling was a common medium at the time, and the anecdote does have parallels with Sarah's earlier blackening out of Lady Bateman's portrait.[7]

If the three-year-old Diana was aware of her parents' distress and anger, or confused by the sudden removal from the setting in which her short life had been spent, stability was resumed when the Duke found them a new home, Langley Park, in Buckinghamshire. This was ironically and perhaps even deliberately acquired from the widower of another of Sarah's mortal enemies. Lord Masham had married the former Abigail Hill, Sarah's cousin and former protégée, who had become her rival and then supplanted her in the affections and service of Queen Anne. Sarah had therefore hated Abigail just as much as she hated Robert Walpole and Lady Bateman.

It was at Langley Park, the first place that he had chosen for himself and which would remain his favourite home for the rest of his life, that Charles was able to develop properly those interests in architecture and landscape design that Sarah had tried to ban from his education and forbid him from practising at Althorp and Windsor. He ordered the replacement of the original, early seventeenth-century house by a square Palladian-style villa, with a grand colonnaded entrance hall, elegant central staircase and oval light well. He gradually added to it outbuildings consisting of dovecote, stables, orangery, walled garden and even a brewery. In the grounds, he was able to indulge his passion for earth- and water-works, creating a lake, woodland and parkland, and paths and drives, employing at one stage over one hundred workmen. The medievalist Walpole punned disapprovingly: 'We called at Langley but did not like it, nor the Grecian temple at all; it is by no means gracious' .

His Grace the Duke also acquired an enchanting and more informal retreat a few miles away, Monkey Island, on the Thames at Bray. Here there was 'a small house whose outside represents a farm, the inside what you please; for in the parlour, which is the only room in it except a kitchen, is painted upon the ceiling in grotesque, with monkeys, fishing, shooting etc'. These paintings had been commissioned by the Duke from the fashionable decorator Clermont (who also worked for the Prince of Wales) in the chinoiserie style, and with the popular *singerie* motifs, which were the height of fashion. There were also 'six or eight walnut trees and a few orange trees in tubs . . . there is another building which I think is called a temple'. The island was widely admired and regarded as a spot to be visited by elite tourists. One lady liked the island but commented on the Duke's lack of privacy from passing river traffic: 'for he cannot move on the island without being seen by the bargemen who pass; neither can he get out of the reach of their conversation, if they are disposed to talk'. Lady Jane Coke, who visited in 1751, was more enthusiastic: the island 'pleases me extremely from its singularity . . . several flowering shrubs and about ten old walnut trees, which are shade enough . . . an extreme good room with a delightful prospect on the river'.[8]

Diana and her little siblings played and picnicked on this magical island; a young child would have read with fascination the details of the wall paintings (and many years later she would paint murals for her own riverside villas). These early happy associations with the Thames, its meadows and islands, had an impact on the rest of her life; this was a part of the world to which she and Betty would return as an escape from London and their problems within it. Eventually, freed from husbands, they would both choose to settle by the Thames in rural Richmond.

The Duke's architectural activities were entirely appropriate to one of his rank, but reckless for someone who was still living on expectations. Sarah was determined to prevent Johnny from ever following his brother's dependence on court favour; she now redrafted her will to make his inheritance from her, and that of his heirs, conditional on their never accepting any post or pension from the Government. As if to add insult to injury, Charles was now openly associating with her sworn enemies, for example accepting an invitation from Sir Robert Walpole to visit his grand property at Houghton Hall in Norfolk, the home of a magnificent art collection, where Charles stayed, together with Lord Hervey, in the summer of 1738. (Hervey's mother complained to Sarah about the way that Hervey and his wife dumped the grandchildren – 'the young Vermin' – on her at Ickworth during the tedious summer holidays.) And in September that year Charles and Hervey went to visit Walpole when he was ill and spent an hour at the sickbed.

That autumn the Duke's allegiances, both political and personal, were recorded by William Hogarth in the painting known as *The Holland House group* or *The Hervey Conversation Piece*. This was commissioned by Hervey to commemorate his dearest friends and their concerns during a visit to Stephen Fox's estate at Maddington in Wiltshire. Charles and another Walpole man, Thomas Winnington MP, are shown in the company of Lord Hervey and the Fox brothers. Hervey is drawing their attention to an architectural plan held up by Henry Fox. Hervey's lover, Stephen Fox, seated, is slyly about to tip over with his cane the chair being uneasily stood upon by a clerical figure in black, who has his telescope trained on a distant church spire; whether this depicts Parson Willemin, who officiated in the previous year at Stephen's very secret wedding to a thirteen-year-old heiress, or the physicist Dr Desaguliers, a fellow Mason (Charles and Stephen were admitted to their Lodge on the same date), the whole work, with its subtle references, symbols and in-jokes, celebrates a specific stage in the long association of these cultivated gentlemen, amongst whom Charles was an enthusiastic participant.[9]

A long and complex lawsuit began between the Duke and the Dowager over the management of the trust, he determined to wrest control over it through proving her mismanagement, she equally determined to defend her life work and protect it from him. His own family line had at last become more secure through the birth of a son, in January 1739, whose name, George, recorded the Duke's new loyalty to the King (rather than the John which would have paid homage to his grandfather – Johnny's son had been named John). This was probably yet another source of grievance to Sarah. To maintain the outward courtesies, he took the pleasure of calling in person at Marlborough House to leave a message informing her of the birth of this male heir; her reply was 'that to complete his joy she was very ill'.

In the same month, his public career advanced further, through his appointment as Lord-Lieutenant of the counties of Oxford and Buckingham, followed by promotion to Colonel of the First Dragoons and then to the Second Horse. Most people now saw the young Duke in a more kindly light than his prejudiced grandmother, and were more sympathetic to his inability to live within his currently restricted means. Horace Walpole thought that 'he had good sense, infinite generosity, and not more economy than was to be expected of a young man of warm passions and such vast expectations. He was modest and diffident too, but could not digest total dependence on a capricious and avaricious grandmother'. However, he felt that both Charles and Johnny lacked the parts and ambitions of their parents, family and deceased eldest brother.

Charles had grown up. He was content in his marriage, in love with his wife and delighted by his children, creating for them the happy family life that he had not experienced himself. Gambling for high stakes was a normal activity for one of his class; he was not recorded as running expensive mistresses or drinking heavily, perhaps warned off by the dreadful case of his cousin Blandford which had gained him the title. Elizabeth was a force for good and a stabilizing influence; despite Sarah's fears, and because he had chosen for himself, he seemed to have married the right woman. An aristocratic heiress with aspirations to improve him would only have added to his insecurity and the pressures on him, but this woman, who, from the tone of his supportive and reassuring letters to her, seems always to have been anxious and very dependent upon him, looked up to him and adored him. His letters to her when they were apart show how content they were with each other, and how his own self-confidence had grown through looking after her. And this domestic security provided a safe and loving environment for their children, whose relationships with each other and with their parents continued to show a powerful family bond, with none of the quarrels or estrangements which marked so many of their contemporaries, and were the norm for Sarah.

Di, like all first daughters, had the strongest claim on her father's affections. The constant little mentions in his letters to his wife – a PS, 'kiss Di for me', 'kiss Di and the rest often for me', 'remember me to the dear little children' – suggest an affectionate man. His passion for his wife was strong enough for him to try to overcome her apparently depressive personality (which cannot have been helped by Sarah's attitude to her, even worse than having a hostile mother-in-law). A letter to Elizabeth expressed the 'hope to God by this time you have recovered your spirits . . . when you see the child, kiss her for me and be assured that nobody ever loved another as I do you'. Attempts to alleviate her health worries were made through various visits to Bath, though her resulting absence from the family caused her to worry more. Looking after the children at Langley, he wrote: 'as you say nothing of yourself, I conclude from my natural sanguine hope that you are well. I wish to God your opinion inclined you to the same way of thinking . . . the children are all well, Di is just come in from riding'. Another time, from Langley, he expressed uxorious hopes: 'your two boys are well and at breakfast with me . . . I shall set off for Bath for I long (I won't say any more) but as much to be there as you do to have me there.' Another time, when he was in London, she was in Bath with the youngest, Bob, and the other children were at Blenheim, after expressing the usual concerns for her health he added 'I have received a letter from Di, the girls are both well, and I left the boys so'.[10]

As the trust dispute dragged on, Charles came to realize that his salaries had not alleviated his financial problems at all; things seemed to have got even worse. In May 1740, when Elizabeth had produced a fourth child, he forced himself to make overtures of friendship to his grandmother; but Sarah refused to consider resuming contact until he had repaid to Johnny a long-standing loan. This was a vicious circle – he said he could not do this 'because I am really just now more in want of money than I ever have or perhaps shall ever be again'. Later that year when the judgement in their dispute was thought to be on the verge of finding in Charles' favour, Sarah dismissed her lawyers and caused further delay by pleading her own case in person. At the same time, she was writing her memoirs, with the aid of the historian Nicholas Hooke. This was ostensibly to justify her conduct during the reign of Queen Anne, when she ceased to be the Queen's favourite, and lost her influential position at court as Mistress of the Robes and

Groom of the Stole, followed by accusations that she had misused the royal purse for personal gain. But there was also a forty-seven-page appendix detailing her disputes with Charles; however, at the last moment, she decided to withdraw the latter from publication. The birth of a second son to the Marlboroughs in 1740 reinforced the family's succession and further diminished the chances of Johnny Spencer's heirs inheriting the title.

In 1742, Charles had the opportunity to become a real soldier when he was sent with his regiment to the Netherlands, as part of the British intervention in the complex War of the Austrian Succession. From his letters to Elizabeth we learn how much she and the family were missing him, and he them, and that Di, then aged seven, was also sending little notes: 'David Morris is just come aboard and has brought me your dear letter with Di's at the bottom' . . . 'Thank Di for her line in your letter'. Despite deprecating his own inarticulacy – 'the real reason for my writing short is that I am not capable of writing or talking in a prolix way more than some are of being laconic' – his letters show wit, fluency and a cheerful adaptation to what must have been utterly unfamiliar surroundings. When Di had written to him, sweetly, that she loved her mother and father just the same, he commented: 'Thank my dear little Di for her letter and goodness in loving me equal with you though I don't doubt that as she grows up she will have sense enough to find out more reasons for loving you than there can be for me'.

In his absence, Sarah announced a visit to the family at Langley. Elizabeth coped with this alarming prospect by using the children as pawns in the dispute and refusing Sarah access to them. Charles approved of her behaviour: 'I am glad you kept the children out of the way when the old Duchess was there; if she wants to see 'em for any good purpose she will contrive to bring about a reconciliation, if it is only curiosity I hope she will always be equally disappointed. As for the question she asked about my building at Blenheim, that depends on her: if she will be so good as to die soon that I may be able to clear my debts I believe I shall build; but if she is spiteful enough to live much longer, I fear I shall not build'.

As well as his involvement in the campaign, he was also under pressure from a wife who was coping badly with his absence. Charles had to soothe her: 'I beg you, for the sake of your children, for the sake of him that loves you, that you will not fret yourself sick' . . .

'pray my love, try to keep your spirits up' . . . 'for God's sake my dear, don't afflict yourself'. The Duchess also played the hypochondria card, and tried to make him feel guilty with complaints about her eyes, as well as general accusations that the worry was destroying her health. An occasional note of desperation creeps into his stream of brisk, cheerful letters, but he realized what a life-line they were to her, and wrote every two or three days. Considering the logistics of their letters having to cross the Channel, with the many delays from the unpredictable winds, quite apart from the problems of battlefield delivery, their correspondence was regular and prolific. He hints at his workload: 'Thank dear Di for her letter which I'll answer next but have a vast deal to write today'. He is longing to come home, to peace and quiet and an end of responsibilities, writing in November 1742: 'As for myself, I shall have more pleasure in seeing you and the children at Langley, where I need not so much as speak to anybody else'.

Military activities ceased for the winter months and he came home safely. In the following year, when he was due to return to his regiment, the Duchess insisted that she and the children should accompany him. This was a mark both of her inconsiderate dependency and of his timid devotion in agreeing to the idea. For the idea of taking the three oldest children, Di, aged eight, Betty, five, and George, four (baby Charles was left at home) if not actually onto the battlefield, at least to the wrong side of the Channel in a period of war, is evidence of the clinging nature of the Duchess – who however had got her own way in this matter, although the family's presence would clearly add to Charles' problems rather than easing them. The Duke travelled with his regiment; the Duchess and children, plus entourage of servants and nursemaids, after a long wait for favourable winds, eventually crossed the Channel in May 1743, in bad weather but in the same ship as the King. This caused Charles to write: 'the thoughts of your being at sea in a storm makes me more unhappy than is possible to be expressed. There is no torture I would not cheerfully undergo to hear of your safe arrival in Holland'.

For the children, this was an amazing adventure, a long sea voyage, a sense of danger from the elements as well as from their enemies, travelling aboard a ship with a royal passenger – though for this bedraggled and seasick family there would be no social niceties, nor the luxury of separate cabins. With a panic-stricken mother, it would have been the eldest daughter's responsibility to comfort her little brother and sister. Safely landed, the family stayed at The Hague, a fairly stable base once the Dutch had come into the war on the side of the allies; Charles and the army, however, were campaigning in Germany, just as separated from them as if they had stayed safely in England. The weather was terrible that spring, Charles warning, before they had even arrived, 'it has not ceased raining since I arrived in Flanders'.

As Duchess of Marlborough, Elizabeth was seen as an esteemed visitor to The Hague, and was obliged to take part in the formal social life of the town, which she did not enjoy. Charles' letters that summer continue to show his concern for them. He refers to Di's learning French, to his becoming so sunburnt 'that you may disown your once fair but now tawny husband'. He served in the front line at the Battle of Dettingen, the famous but ultimately indecisive victory for the British over the French, when he had 'a beard three inches long, which I am just going to cut off in order to see what colour my face is now'. His letters to her constantly make light of the hardship and dangers, and express his love and longing to see her, as well as promising never to go on active service again. This feeling was also inspired by his growing disillusionment with the conduct of the campaign by the King and the Hanoverian forces, and therefore with his position as a supporter of the court. He needed a pretext to resign, and found one in the King's action in promoting Hanoverian generals over British ones; he and a group of fellow officers resigned, and he also gave up his post of Lord of the Bedchamber. He eventually joined Elizabeth and the children in The Hague in September 1743, and they travelled together back to Britain.

His actions for once incurred Sarah's approval, for it meant his return to supporting the opposition. As she put it: 'It is very natural, he 'listed as soldiers do when they are drunk and repented when he was sober'. And she even stood up for him soon afterwards to the Duke of St Albans, who was trying to seek Charles' support on an election issue, saying tartly that Charles might be a fool but 'he should not be everybody's fool.' Further satisfaction was expressed in a letter to Johnny: 'I am pleased to think that your Brother is free from being influenced by such vile people as never thought of influencing him in anything that did not regard some private interest of their own'.[11]

Horace Walpole more cynically interpreted these resignations as being in order 'to reinstate himself in the old Duchess's will'. Charles' financial situation in 1744 led Sarah to comment that 'I am sure the Duke of Marlborough don't know what he owes but I am pretty sure that his debts and what he has thrown away is not much less than half a million.' By today's terms, this is a staggering figure. (A very rough modern equivalent of mid-eighteenth-century prices can be obtained by multiplying the sums by sixty.) This total had been reached because Charles not only spent very much more than he earned (although his income was now generous enough) but also borrowed at exorbitant rates of interest on the strength of claiming that Sarah's long-awaited death was imminent. And, as she well knew, in addition to the large sums owing to his major lenders, he had also borrowed smaller sums 'of several people, giving vast interest for them. But these people did not think it enough, so he told them I was dying and that he would give them a bond to pay double the sum when I was dead. This contented the lenders but I unluckily recovered'.

Charles continued to develop his public profile through cultural and philanthropic activities; he was elected a Fellow of the Royal Society and became a Governor of the Foundling Hospital. But his grandmother was still attempting to run his life: even when he offered his services again to the King in February 1744, in response to fears of a Jacobite invasion, she complained because he had not consulted her over this. Johnny Spencer (Jack Spencer to his friends) was proving an increasing disappointment to Sarah, although he still charmed her infinitely more than his brother. But his own debts, gambling, and drinking were public knowledge, while rumours had long been circulating about his murky private life and dangerous patronage of the London brothels: 'he was only twenty-five, but you would think he was sixty'. One among many was the courtesan Fanny Murray (so desired that her slipper did not merely serve champagne but was allegedly stewed and eaten by admirers), who began her career in Bath by being seduced, in her very early teens, by Johnny 'by a few tawdry gifts' before abandoning her. Years later she would obtain revenge and an annuity from his son by threatening to tell her story to the world.[12]

With such expensive hobbies, Johnny was just as dependent on Sarah and as anxious for her death as Charles. They were now men now well into their thirties, who had had a long wait for their inheritance, not just for the properties and money they so badly needed but, above all, for the independence which they sought from their domineering and capricious grandmother: although she had dedicated almost her entire life to the advancement of the family, they felt that this had now lasted far too long. The brothers would indeed be cited as monumental exemplars of family ingratitude sixteen years later, by Mary Wortley Montagu, at a difficult time when her own son was contesting his father's will: 'I am now told the young people understand each other and have a mind to get rid of an old woman, like J.S. and his brother the Duke.'[13]

Freedom was approaching. In the summer of 1744, Sarah, at eighty-four, recognized that her time really was running out and decided to rewrite her will for the twenty-sixth time, still trying to keep the family under control. Recognizing Johnny's weaknesses, and the ominous decline in his health (attributable to self-indulgence and syphilis), she protected the bequest of her fortune to him by appointing trustees to ensure that the capital should pass intact to his son. As a last act of malevolence to Charles, she sought to prevent him from having the use of Marlborough House, but complied with her husband's intentions by enabling it to pass to the next Duke of Marlborough, Charles' son George. In the meantime it should be occupied by one of her trustees, James Stephens. The legacies of £5,000 to Diana and the younger children were conditional on obedience to the terms of their great-grandfather's will, and were also tied up to prevent Charles getting his hands on them; this was in order to 'keep them at least from being beggars' through their father's 'madness and folly'.[14]

She died on 18 October 1744, with Johnny, but not Charles, at her bedside. For nine-year-old Di, and her little brothers and sister, the death of this legendary and hated figure, whom she had barely met but who had dominated her father's and mother's lives, represented the start of a new way of life which encompassed Blenheim Palace.

Di was old enough to remember the previous dislocation from Windsor Little Lodge to Langley Park, but these two properties were at least on the same scale, rural, domestic and suitable for a young family. Blenheim was a folly, vast, bleak and forbidding, a property which had never been lived in properly by anyone. When still unfinished, it was occupied briefly by the first Duke, by then incapacitated by a stroke, and it was grudgingly finished off and furnished by Sarah, who had never cared for the place, as a last token of her love and duty to her late husband. Even the epic scale of the decorations, the heavy tapestries and archaic murals, provided a total contrast with the light-hearted wall paintings at Bray, causing an open-mouthed child to wonder at the difference in styles. A meticulous inventory of the contents had been made by Sarah in 1740 as an element of her dispute with Charles and the realization that she could not prevent him from living there – although not until after her death. In this inventory, she deliberately indicated which were her own possessions 'because the house is now complete and to take them away would lessen the Beauty of it, which I have no mind to do so. For perhaps I may alter my mind and leave the things at death that are indisputably my own'. This was yet another threat to Charles, although he might well have been relieved if some of the huge, formally furnished rooms had been depleted of some of their archaic contents.[15]

These daunting lists of heavy furniture, crimson damask hangings, curtains and bedspreads, walnut tables and looking glasses in the chilly suites suggest the rich but sombre fashions of the early years of the century, far distanced from the lighter tones and elegant slender curves of the Frenchified tastes of the 1740s and '50s. Only the bedrooms on the second floor sound welcoming to a family with young children; there is mention of a nursery maid's room, and an apartment with white hangings with floral decoration, white Indian gauze curtains, a white marble table, a walnut stand for a tea-kettle, its adjacent bedchamber and bed covered with Indian calico, chairs of red and white velvet. Another room has a white Indian stitched bedcover with a fringe worked by Sarah herself, there are suites of white mohair hangings, embroidered curtains and firescreens. These lighter colours and softer fabrics make a striking contrast with the dark colour schemes of the state bedchambers below. And some sense of the scale of this great building, which had never yet served any role, is implied by the extent of the linen supplies: sixty-seven dozen damask napkins, ninety-three best tablecloths, eighteen pairs of fine sheets, forty-five pairs of servants' sheets. As the house had stood virtually empty between Marlborough's death in 1722 and Sarah's in 1744, it can be assumed that this linen was musty, mildewed and reeking of damp.

Visitors were not impressed. The chilly nature of the whole house was felt by Mary Wortley Montagu, recalling to her daughter how 'the Duchess of Marlborough built the most ridiculous house I ever saw, since it really is not habitable from the excessive damps'. Another critical visitor was Lady Northumberland, who regarded it as 'an immense Pile which has still a greater Air (in my opinion) of heaviness than Grandeur'. She went on to mention the 'prodigious size' of the Hall and the fact that the 'place is so dark one can scarce see' the Titian cartoons hanging in the Gallery. 'The furniture of the House in general is both old-fashioned and shabby. There is an immense number of rooms'. Mrs Boscawen was equally underwhelmed, a surly porter refusing to admit visitors until well after the appointed opening time: 'at length a dirty lad appeared and led us through the Hall and Saloon to the two rooms hung with tapestry; thence into the Gallery from whence the fine Titians are taken away, so there we were disappointed. We likewise went into the Chapel, and then he told us we had seen all we could see'. Horace Walpole condemned it as 'execrable within, without and almost all around', and 'one of the ugliest places in England'. On a visit in 1760, he noted 'all the old flock chairs, wainscot tables, and gowns and petticoats of Queen Anne that old Sarah could crowd among blocks of marble. It looks like the palace of an auctioneer who has been chosen King of Poland and furnished his apartments with obsolete trophies, rubbish that nobody bid for and a dozen pictures that he had stolen from the inventories of different families'.[16]

This state was because Charles never had the money to make Blenheim more comfortable and convenient, having already spent far too lavishly on Langley Park. He now looked for support from the court again, tempering his opposition stance in the Lords and expressing his loyalty to the crown during the threat to the nation of the Jacobite invasion in 1745 by offering, together with Bedford and other colleagues who had earlier resigned, to raise at their own expense thirteen regiments to support the King. Walpole reported how 'the Duke of Marlborough, who most handsomely and seasonably had come to town on purpose, moved for an address to assure the King of their standing by him with lives and fortunes'. As a result of such renewed loyalty, Charles was promoted to the rank of major-general.

Henry Fox, who once described Charles as his 'most intimate and dear friend from childhood', was a rising star in the Commons. It was earlier in 1744 that Charles had been one of the two witnesses of

Fox's secret wedding to Caroline Lennox, the eldest daughter of the Duke of Richmond, Fox then aged thirty-nine, she twenty-one. Following her parents' implacable refusal to consider Fox's proposal of marriage, Caroline, unobserved, left the family's London house in Whitehall on 2 May, and made her way to Conduit Street, the home of Fox's friend Sir Charles Hanbury-Williams (a fellow old Etonian), where Fox and Charles were waiting for her. A wedding ceremony was conducted by an unsuspecting clergyman in the presence only of Charles and Hanbury-Williams. The bride then went home to break the news to her parents, who responded by banishing her from the family; she returned to Fox in Conduit Street. This event created a great scandal, with Charles being accused of gross disloyalty to his old family friends the Richmonds. As Hanbury-Williams wrote to Fox the day after the elopement: 'The rage of his and her Grace is very high and I hear they intend making a point that nobody that visits them should visit you . . . they are very angry with the Duke of Marlborough and me'.[17]

Rather unfairly, Charles had not made a good impression on Caroline, isolated from her own loved family and therefore entirely dependent on her husband's rather older circle, who was inevitably jealous of the long-established friendship between Charles and Fox. She regarded Charles as a bad influence, 'excessively wild and given to women'. And she found Elizabeth 'a weak capricious woman fond of governing, knowing nothing of the world'. This is an unusually hostile note and the allegation of womanizing seems unfounded.[18]

They remained close politically, however, Marlborough in the Lords, Fox in the Commons; he entered the Cabinet as Secretary at War in 1746. Charles however maintained a rather more half-hearted role, dutiful and in some ways ambitious, but described by Horace Walpole as having 'virtues and sense enough to deserve esteem but always lost it by forfeiting respect . . . capable of giving the most judicious advice and of following the worst . . . a variety of changes in his political conduct . . . [his indistinct speech] confirmed the world in a very mean opinion of his understanding'. In 1749 he became Lord Steward of the Household, and in 1755 Lord Privy Seal, which he then relinquished to become Master General of the Ordnance. He involved himself in the parliamentary elections for Oxfordshire, and the family spent more time at Blenheim.[19]

The income from these posts made no impression on the Duke's debts. Living in the huge, cold palace, while also maintaining Langley Park and Marlborough House, was costing a lot of money. The Duke had no concept of economy and the Duchess did not have the spirit to take control of such matters. Amongst the Blenheim papers, there is evidence of an attempted economy drive in 1755. The household budget for the previous two years was reviewed by an anxious steward, who neatly listed each area of expenditure under six separate column headings – paid, still due, total cost over two years, one year's costs, proposed sum to be reduced, how this can be achieved. The latter section did not sound very convincing. To reduce the wine bill of £1,690 a year, it was proposed to spend all of £50 less and to consider 'buying French wines only when wanted'. For furniture, great savings could be made 'by having no more furniture for one or two years but what is necessary'. For household repairs, it was hoped to shave £100 from the not very significant (considering the scale of the property) total of £424 per annum 'by not having done but what is absolutely necessary, and proper orders given and amounts taken.' Real savings of £400 a year were identified by the prospect of sacking several servants. By contrast, there was not even an attempt to suggest reducing the sums spent on the family's wardrobe (clothiers and mercers £288 a year, hatters and hosiers £72, tailors £373). With a wife, two daughters and three sons to maintain in the public eye, this was clearly not an area for discussion.[20]

And the bills incurred during the family's frequent stays in London, particularly for Di's and Betty's clothes, soared above the separate figures for Blenheim; they did not even come under the eye of the careful steward since they were London bills, paid directly by the Duchess, who was investing in her daughters' outer- and underwear in order to secure the returns of a good marriage. Given the scale of the Duke's expenditure, these girls needed to marry money in order to keep them in the style to which they had become accustomed; it was unlikely that their father would ever be able to make them large settlements. The Duchess's London bills for the period 1756–57 show some of the outlay on her daughters as she launched them into their own careers as marriageable women and prospective breeders of heirs. For Lady Betty and herself, the Duchess bought from her staymaker white stays for 'fashion', 'furniture' and 'riding', made of the imported silk known as tabby. These garments were not merely underwear, but were the actual and frequently visible made-to-measure supports upon which the rest of the gown was structured. She also patronized a range of suppliers of fabrics, both luxurious and practical, in order to buy the materials which were then made up by various specialist needle-women. Many of these stockists to the nobility were based at this time in Covent Garden, such as the mercers Hinchcliffe & Croft of Henrietta Street, from whom Lady Di purchased in February 1756 the eighteen yards of rich brocade, gold-patterned on a pink ground, to make the grand dress almost certainly worn to celebrate her sister's marriage in March that year. The perilous nature of supplying prestigious clients who were too often short of ready cash is shown by the fact that the account, of which this was the first item, was not paid until the December of the following year. For 1757 alone, the clothing bills paid by the Duchess included the sums of £205 (mercer), and £124 and £252 for two separate dressmakers. But the prosperity of many such stockists at this time is indicated by a foreign visitor's 1755 description of London shops: 'a most brilliant and agreeable show . . . that we do not see in any other city – the custom has been introduced of dressing the front of their shops, particularly the mercers, with some order of architecture. The columns, the pilasters, the frieze, the cornice, every part . . . bears as great a resemblance to the gate of a little temple as to that of a warehouse'.[21]

While the girls were being groomed for prospective husbands, their brothers were being educated. There survive from this period a series of brief and dutiful letters from the two older boys, George, Marquess of Blandford, and Lord Charles Spencer, written from Eton to their sister Betty. (Another little brother, Robert, had been born in 1747.) These letters provide touching evidence of the close-knit family, notes preserved by Betty amongst the more eventful correspondence of the Pembroke family, into which she was to marry.[22]

They start in 1747, when Charles was seven and George was eight.

4 October 1747

Dear Sister Betty,

I hope you will excuse me for not writing before but I had not time to write to you last Tuesday as I promised you. I hope you and Papa and Mama and Sister Di and Mrs Trevor are all very well and pray give my Duty to all of them. Pray excuse me for writing so short a letter.

I am Dear Sister Betty your most affectionate brother, Charles Spencer

The same sort of thing was being written by his elder brother.

13 November 1747

Dear Sister Betty

I received your kind letter and am very glad to hear you are all very well. I forgot to tell you the Canary-bird desires his love to his Brother, pray mine to Mama and Papa and Sister Di & Brother Robert and Mrs Trevor etc.

I am Dear Sister Betty your most affectionate brother Blandford

So they continue. In 1752, Diana's health had apparently given rise to anxiety: 'I am vastly glad to hear that Sister Di is so well, and hope to hear that she continues so; pray write us word as soon as possible how she does. I have thank God done taking Physick and am very well after, so is Brother Charles'.

The education of girls of good families was of course different from that of their brothers. There is a sad little comment from Mary Dewes, the privileged and relatively well-educated niece of the cultivated, intelligent and industrious Mrs Delany: 'It is rather a hardship upon our sex that we have in general our own education to seek after we are grown up, I mean as to mental qualifications. In our childhood, writing, dancing and music is what is most attended to'. These were the female accomplishments, taught mainly at home, or more unusually at girls' schools, which ranged from charity foundations to those for the better born. Boys, however, like Lady Di's brothers, started with tutors at home but were then generally sent away to boarding school, Eton or Westminster for the elite, to be followed probably by Oxford or Cambridge, and definitely by the Grand Tour. This was meant to provide both an education and a cultural experience for young gentlemen through spending a couple of years on the Continent, learning not only to appreciate but also to acquire works of classical antiquity together with examples of Italian and French painting.[23]

The Blenheim accounts for the time of Di's girlhood do not provide any direct information about her own education. But comparisons can be made with the fuller records of the Bedford family, of the same high status and aspirations as the Marlboroughs, and linked to them by friendship and marriage. Lady Caroline Russell, the Duke of Bedford's daughter (by his second wife), eight years younger than Lady Di, was taught at home by a French mademoiselle, who lived in and whose job was to look after as well as to educate the young lady. Real teaching was done by outside tutors, who, when Caroline was aged between ten and twelve, included a writing master (who had previously taught her brother), a music master for singing and harpsi-chord lessons, a dancing master, who also taught her brother when he was home from Westminster School, a French master who also taught geography, and an Italian master. The employment of these various part-timers contrasts with the appointment of the more serious schol-ars who were appointed to teach boys. Lady Di's brothers attended Eton but were also taught at home by a succession of able and ambitious men, for whom responsibility for the heirs of the peerage was one rung on a career ladder. George's tutor, Jacob Bryant, was a classical scholar from King's College, Cambridge, who also served for a while as the Duke's secretary and would become a distinguished authority on mythology, religion and antiquities. Charles' and Bob's tutor, John Moore, would progress up the ecclesiastical ladder to become Archbishop of Canterbury. But Lady Di, as the eldest, would have been at a different stage from her brothers anyway. She was well taught: her letters are beautifully phrased and grammatically written, her handwriting neatly elegant. The Duke, in one of his letters, refers to her speaking French at the age of eight.[24]

Attitudes to well-born women's education were confused as to its purpose. Even the strikingly independent and intellectual Lady Mary Wortley Montagu, writing to her daughter in 1753 about the edu-cation of a granddaughter, stressed the ambiguities:

she should be permitted to learn the Languages. I have heard it lamented that boys lose so many years in mere learning of words. This is no objection in a girl, whose time is not so precious. She cannot advance herself in any profession, and has therefore many hours to spare . . . the second caution to be given her (and which is most absolutely necessary) is to conceal whatever learning she attains, with as much solicitude as she would hide crookedness or lameness. The parade of it can only serve to draw on her the envy and consequently the most inveterate hatred of all he and she fools . . . the ultimate end of your education was to make you a good wife. Hers ought to be to keep her happy in a virgin state.

Education in a girl is therefore dangerously subversive, since it may become a rival attraction to marriage. Lady Mary comments, in another letter, that 'there is no part of the world where our sex is treated with so much contempt as in England . . . I think it the highest injustice to be debarred the entertainment of my closet, and that the same studies which raise the character of a man should hurt that of a woman. We are educated in the grossest ignorance and no art omitted to stifle our natural reason; if some few get above their Nurse's instruction, our knowledge must rest concealed and be as useless to the world as gold in the mine'. Yet women must be educated in order to behave correctly: 'Learning is necessary to the happiness of women, and ignorance the common foundation of their errors, both in morals and conduct'.[25]

One enlightened parent was Charles' friend Lord Hervey, who in the early 1740s arranged to have his two eldest daughters taught the sciences; this was so effective that their grandmother complained to Sarah of these 'most learned ladies [doing] algebra; and studying the globes and all the stars in the firmament, besides measuring my Lord's land. All these things occasioned so many hard words at dinner that I begged to have a dictionary lie upon the table to help my understanding in explaining of them'.[26]

There is no mention of a drawing master for Caro Russell (although a witty sketch by her of 'Mademoiselle' was preserved), nor is art mentioned at all by Mary Dewes, for she obviously did not regard it as a 'mental qualification'. Lady Mary Wortley Montagu did, however, see drawing as an important part of a girl's education: 'At the same time I recommend books, I neither exclude [needle]work or drawing . . . I was once extream fond of my pencil and it was a great mortification to me when my father turn'd off my Master, having made a considerable progress for the short time I learnt. My over eagerness in the pursuit of it had brought a weakness on my eyes that made it necessary to leave it off, and all the advantage I got was the improvement of my hand'. Lady Di must have been taught drawing from quite an early age in order to achieve the degree of competence shown in the copies which she made of works at Blenheim: imitating the great masters was seen as a key form of art training.[27]

Her father, like his fellow aristocrats, had already been collecting pictures and other works of art before he inherited the treasure house of Blenheim. For a girl with a good eye, an interest and a talent, the acquisition of Blenheim, and the chilly times spent in the richly hung rooms, must have been a powerful stimulus in the development of a visual sensibility. From the inventory drawn up by Sarah in 1740, it is possible to realize the epic scale of the art works in the palace as well as in Marlborough House in London: Sarah boasts of the 'one hundred and twenty-six pictures by Great Masters' in the Long Closet alone. In the Great Hall there were seven huge paintings on leather of the gods and goddesses, attributed by Sarah to Titian, while looming above were massive ceiling paintings by James Thornhill, baroque visions of the first Duke surrounded by allegorical figures and Olympian gods. The thirty-seven pictures in the Grand Cabinet included several by Rubens, and elsewhere there were works by Veronese, Lorraine, Salvator Rosa, Raphael and Van Dyck, plus the Brussels tapestries which commemorated the first Duke's victories. Lavished throughout were the statues and ornaments which he and Sarah had acquired, with no expense spared, from all over Europe. A later visitor, the artist Joseph Farington, would describe the fame and extent of the Blenheim art collection: 'At 20 minutes before 3 we got to the Marlborough Arms at Woodstock, and immediately proceeded to see Blenheim. We were three quarters of an hour in the House and 5 companies arrived to see it before we left it – the Drunken Silenus by Rubens – the whole lengths of himself, His wife and child – the portrait of Mary of Medicis, also by Him, were with many others extraordinary pictures – the portraits of the Earl of Strafford and his Secretary by Vandyke is one of the finest pictures I ever saw'.[28]

So Lady Di had no shortage of models at hand to obtain that better understanding and appreciation of art which was fundamental for the commissioning classes, a process in which women fully participated. Queen Caroline, the wife of George II, was regarded as a talented amateur artist as well as a collector and patron; her daughter Anne, the Princess Royal, received a thorough training in drawing, which she continued to practise after her marriage in 1734 to the Prince of Orange – when the Dutch artist Heromen Vandermijn was summoned to St James's Palace to make portraits of the young couple, the Princess drew Vandermijn's face in return (although it was reported he had to finish off the rest). George II's other daughters were taught drawing by the miniature painter Bernard Lens, who specialized in copying the works of Rubens and Van Dyck and who also had opened an art school in St Paul's Churchyard. (Another distinguished patron of Lens was Sarah, who had commissioned him to paint the three little Spencers, Charles, and his brother and sister, in the happier days of 1720.)[29]

With such royal exemplars, the daily lives of many aristocratic women were now beginning to include a wide range of artistic activities. The industry and versatility during the 1750s of, for example, the Duchess of Portland and her daughters is lovingly recorded by their friend and frequent house guest Mrs Delany, a person who was never idle either: 'Lady Betty entreated the Duchess to let her stay at home and paint' in preference to paying a social call; 'Lady B and Lady H turn and carve in ivory to the utmost perfection; I did not before know they had ever attempted it'; 'the Duchess has just finished a bunch of barberries turned in amber, that are beautiful, and she is finishing an ear of barley – the corns amber, the stalk ivory, the beards tortoiseshell'; 'the Duchess has in hand twelve toilettes, a carpet to go round her bed, knotting of various kinds, besides turning, which goes on successfully'.[30]

Fascinating evidence for women's artistic practice and for some of the reasons behind it is provided by Mary Delany herself, who during her long life turned her clever hands to almost every artistic medium, and in her seventies would virtually invent a new art form of flower collages showing botanically correct specimens meticulously created from layers of thin paper. She produced ten volumes of these *Flora Delanica* during the 1770s, containing 980 examples which were so accurate that they were described by the botanist Joseph Banks as 'the only imitations of nature I have ever seen from which I would venture to describe botanically any plant without the least fear of committing an error'. But before this she had tackled crayon drawing, oil and watercolour painting, frescoes, woolwork, tapestry, quilting and embroidery as well as furniture design and decoration, and architectural appliqué ornament from paper and card, twigs and other organic materials. She noted the time spent on just one picture – 'it cost me 46 days of 5 hours at a sitting' – and she frequently copied from old masters: 'Wednesday morning, painted and repaired Guido's Madonna and Sleeping Child, and shall then finish the copy of the Salvator Rosa I began in London; it belongs to the Bishop of Derry – it is for the chapel'.[31]

She – and her friends – had a particular fascination with shells, which were not merely collected, admired and categorized, in accordance with Enlightenment principles, but used as artistic symbols of God's Universe: 'the beauties of shells are as infinite as flowers, and to consider how they are inhabited enlarges a field of wonder that leads one insensibly to the great Director and authour of these wonders'. Among her creations were the ceiling of her chapel in Wales 'done with cards and shells in imitation of stucco. In the chancel are four Gothick arches, two on each side, made also of shells'. These were in addition to 'the vines made of cards, the grapes, nuts and large periwinkles, the corn, real wheat, all to look like stucco'. This was nothing new by the 1750s – the Duke of Richmond's wife and daughters Caroline and Emily Lennox had created a shell grotto at Goodwood in 1735. The Duchess of Portland would follow suit at her country estate of Bulstrode in 1760. Mrs Delany also used shells for a wide range of small-scale decorations, including a shell-embossed chandelier, picture frames and bunches of flowers: 'I am making festoons with shell flowers, chained up with silver shells' ... 'Lady Andover and I have entered on a piece of work to surprise the Duchess of Portland ... it is the frame of a picture, with shell-work, and we are as eager in sorting our shells, placing them in their proper degrees, making lines, platoons, ramparts as the King of Prussia in the midst of his army, and as fond of our own compositions'.[32]

Yet despite this undoubtedly wholehearted commitment to artistic practice, she also stressed the moral element, for example writing to her sister in 1753: 'I think it prudent in a moderate degree to encourage in young people an inclination to any innocent amusement, and am happy when I find they have a turn for any art or science ... too often bad company and bad ways are the relaxations sought; to guard against that, nothing is so likely as any amusement that will not tire and must prevent that idleness ... an immoderate love of music may draw young people into many inconveniences; I would therefore confine it as much as I could to an amusement and never allow it to be their business. Painting has *fewer objections* and generally *leads people into much better company*'.[33]

So the practice of art is approved because it encourages moral restraint and self-control, as well as keeping ladies busy. They must not be seen to be idle, relaxation must contain a measurable ingredient of self-improvement and indeed home improvement in the making of these picture frames, hangings and ceiling ornaments. For young girls, learning these skills was not a device to catch a husband, but the demonstration of the virtuous industry and powers of concentration of a woman after marriage.

What their brothers did however was slightly different, in that although they practised art to gain enhanced understanding, boys did not learn to work in the wider decorative areas of shellwork, textiles, découpage and all the rest. Like their sisters and mothers, they were taught by drawing masters, professional artists who found this a useful source of income. Frederick, Prince of Wales, had as his drawing master the painter Joseph Goupy, who was subsequently awarded a pension by his later pupil, George III. When still Prince of Wales, during the 1750s George was also taught drawing by Joshua Kirby, and was allowed to contribute one of his own drawings as an illustration to Kirby's book on perspective: it was also said that Kirby exhibited under his own name two landscapes painted by the Prince in an exhibition held in the Gallery of Incorporated Artists. In the Royal Library at Windsor there are still many of George's landscape, architectural and perspective drawings. Another of his teachers was the eminent William Chambers, appointed his tutor in architecture. George's brother, the Duke of Cumberland, was taught drawing by the artist Bernard Lens the Younger. Boys at Eton College, like Lady Di's brothers, were offered drawing lessons, while Oxford undergraduates could study art with John Malchair, as skilled in music as in art teaching. But it can be argued that aristocratic men received the drawing and architectural training that they would require when it came to commissioning professional architects to work for them, while younger sons might receive drawing lessons in their naval or military academies to improve their plan- and map-making skills, and to illustrate reports. Therefore, it was no sign of effeteness for a man to be a skilled artist since it contributed to his role in public or professional life, as well as being a way of recording the natural world. As defined by George Turnbull in his *Treatise on Ancient Painting* (1740), the study of painting was an integral contribution to instilling 'in young minds the love of true knowledge and the love of society, mankind and virtue', with drawing widely regarded from the early years of the century as a morally improving and virtuous activity for men. And Mrs Delany provides evidence for privileged boys' art education: 'the two young Hamiltons are busily employed in the library in copying part of the pictures I am copying; they have not applied themselves to drawing above six months, and it would surprise you to see what progress they have made'.[34]

The difference between the ease of aristocratic access to art training and the difficulties of less genteel people is emphasized by the experience of Joshua Reynolds, whose father was an impoverished schoolteacher; his earliest efforts were drawing with charcoal on whitewashed walls, in lieu of expensive pencil and paper. After an apprenticeship with the portrait painter Thomas Hudson, Reynolds then achieved his own sort of Grand Tour by working for two years in Rome while studying the great masters.

The practice of art by leisured amateurs, both male and female, would increase enormously during the second half of the century. Even in Lady Di's youth, there was an alternative to being taught by an established artist, through a range of self-tuition manuals such as *The Art of Drawing and Painting in Watercolour* (1731), *The Art of Drawing in Perspective* (1755), and *The Complete Drawing Book* (1755), which 'made easier to the Comprehension of Beginners than any Book of this kind hitherto made public'. For those who wished to copy from classical sculptures without having to visit Rome or own the originals, the benevolent Duke of Richmond opened a gallery of antique casts in 1758 in his London home, Richmond House in Whitehall. Private drawing masters were allowed to send their pupils there, and teaching in the latest Italianate style was later provided in situ by Richard Wilson and Giovanni Battista Cipriani, who was also art tutor to the royal family. Another crucial impetus for learning was the widening availability of the print, which provided access to famous works for those who might not otherwise be able to experience them. There was even an early version of painting by numbers, through the production of prints prepared and marked up for colouring in.

With such a climate of encouragement, it would not be unexpected for a duke's daughter to have a genuine involvement in and enthusiasm for practising art, as well as receiving the appropriate training for one of her class (although there is little evidence to suggest that her younger sister Betty had any such interests). The earliest surviving examples of Lady Di's art demonstrate the impact of her privileged surroundings. Amongst the Blenheim collection were three works by Rubens, extracted by great-grandfather Marlborough from a reluctant city of Brussels in 1706. The family group, of Peter Paul, Hélène Fourment and their little daughter Clara, provided a more accessible and domestic model than the remote and imposing images of gods and rulers; it was also copied by professional artists such as Bernard Lens the Younger (who was permitted to copy several of the first Duke's acquisitions of Rubens and Van Dyck in the early 1720s, the period when he was commissioned by Sarah to paint the Spencer grand-children), Thomas Hudson and Joshua Reynolds. Lady Di produced a very competent pastel copy of the baby, and the Rubens images would remain a preoccupation beyond her childhood. Hudson visited Blenheim in 1754 to paint the Marlborough family (his own opportunity to view the Rubens); his massive portrait of the Duke and Duchess and their children groups them like a triptych under a colonnaded portico, with Blenheim shimmering in the background; to the right Lady Di, in an elegant blue gown, supports her little brother Bob. She then combined the Hudson and the Rubens in a large pastel which copied Hudson's version of her own figure, but clothed herself in the dress of Rubens' wife. This double exercise in copying involved an interesting strategy of self-presentation – she shows herself as historical personage, artist's model and at the same time a modern young lady wearing highly fashionable fancy dress. Versions of seventeenth-century costume, loosely described as 'Van Dyck' or 'Rubens', were characterized by squared necklines, slashed sleeves, the contrasts of black and white, fichus or ruffs and the feathered straw hat in which Rubens often showed Hélène, and were extremely popular wear at the masked balls and fancy dress parties of the day. Horace Walpole spotted Betty at the Russian Ambassador's masquerade in 1755: 'Lady Betty Spencer, like Rubens' wife (not the common one with the hat) had all the bloom and bashfulness and wildness of youth'. But this was not so much homage to the family Rubens as keeping up with fashion.[35]

Another self-portrait, again in pastel and of ambitious, life-size scale, shows Lady Di's unflattering vision of herself, but it is one which gives an impression of underlying strength and determination. Wearing a severely simple brown flower-sprigged dress, she gazes critically at the spectator/self. She has not spared the little bump on her nose, which is also present on the reworked Rubens/Hudson image, and which, many years later, she would still decry as 'the Spencer nose'.

But the main function of a young aristocratic woman was marriage and the production of heirs, not the production of art. This was the undoubted future of the eldest daughter of a duke – her artistic skills were merely an adjunct to the role of attracting suitors. One early fling was ungallantly reported by Lord Newbattle, who 'used to boast afterwards that he had been the first man who attracted the notice of two ladies so famed in the annals of gallantry as Lady Sarah Bunbury and Lady Di Beauclerk, for the latter and he had flirted when boy and girl'.[36]

There was gossip about one match for her which would have totally undermined Sarah's will through linking together the Blenheim and Althorp Spencers – in 1754 there were rumours that she might marry her first cousin John Spencer. Johnny's son had inherited Sarah's vast estate worth £750,000 (which has been calculated at around £45 million in today's terms) at the age of eleven, after his father died of alcoholism, fatally cursed, like his late cousin Blandford, by Sarah's generosity. This would have been a most lucrative match and a satisfying way for Charles' daughter to get back what Sarah had deliberately willed away from her father; but the fabulously wealthy young John could marry whom he chose and did not have to settle for an already probably too familiar cousin with a wary mother. In fact, he had fallen in love with a girl he had recently met, the unwealthy, untitled Margaret Georgiana Poyntz, daughter of a self-made man who had been a privy counsellor to George II. Mary Wortley Montagu, then living in Italy, was kept up to date with London gossip by her daughter, the well-placed Lady Bute, whose husband, the third Earl, was by then a Lord of the Bedchamber to George, Prince of Wales, and an intimate political adviser to the Prince's recently widowed mother. She commented drily: 'I am not surprised at Mr Spencer's choice. I guess some accident has occasioned a familiar acquaintance with the girl, and that is sufficient to make a conquest of a boy of his age, while perhaps the Duchess of Marlborough's prudence kept him at an awful distance from her fair daughter'. No doubt the Duchess felt she had received enough insults from that side of the family, including a long-standing antagonism with the boy's mother, who had flaunted her pregnancy and had temporarily beaten the Duchess in the race for a male heir. But the Spencer bride's jewellery, as described by Mrs Delany, must have caused some pangs: 'the diamonds were worth £12,000, her ear-rings three drops, all diamonds, no paltry scrolls of silver. Her necklace most perfect brilliants, the middle stone worth a thousand pounds'.[37]

A more serious relationship foundered through lack of money on both sides. As a grandson of the third Duke of Hamilton, William Hamilton was well enough born (although his mother was rumoured to have been a former mistress of Frederick, Prince of Wales), but as the younger son of a younger son, he had no hope of an inheritance and so had to earn his living. Hamilton's prominent Roman nose and bony face prevented him from being conventionally handsome but his exquisite taste, bawdy wit and passion for collecting works of art (not forgetting great talent on the violin) made him an entertaining and attractive companion. Military service was a socially acceptable career for those in his position, and he had enlisted in the 3rd Guards where he was soon promoted captain and served as aide-de-camp to Colonel Henry Conway, a cousin, friend and lifelong correspondent of Horace Walpole. Hamilton's involvement with Lady Di was doomed from the start because both of them were too well aware of the financial problems. Despite falling in love with her, Hamilton realized that he had to marry an heiress in order to be able to develop a career with an intellectual and cultural rather than military basis; she and her parents knew that she could do better than him in terms of title and fortune. They became attracted to each other early in 1754, but Hamilton quickly realized that the match was not being encouraged by the Marlboroughs, despite Lady Di's interest in him. He wrote unhappily to his friend, the urbane Earl of Huntingdon: 'London is to me at present very disagreeable for I must say I am fool enough to make myself uneasy about Lady D- S--. They are gone to the country for the summer and I am plotting how I can contrive to see her in the summer and I believe I shall bring it about. En amour si on crains tout on se flatte de tout aussi.' [Just as love inspires fear, it also inspires delight.] He then describes a visit to the seductive Swan sisters, who were 'on the catch', rousing him to such a pitch of excitement that he had to seek recourse to a prostitute in Temple Bar. By December, it was all over; he told Huntingdon that he was trying to get Lady Di out of his mind. Having 'worked myself up to the highest pitch of misery' he was determined never to suffer like that again.[38]

Huntingdon set out on the Grand Tour in 1755, but another correspondent, Theophilus Lindsey, kept him in touch with the London match-making scene, noting the exceptional range of eligible young bachelors coming on the market: 'our young ladies are said to be all of them brightening up for such a number of noble titles, fortunes and accomplishments as have scarce ever been seen single all at once . . . Lord Pembroke they say is engaged already to a daughter of the Duke of Marlborough'. Two weeks later, Lindsey reports: 'Lord Pembroke not yet married to Lady Di Spencer but soon to be'. The Earl of Pembroke's rank, lineage, finances and country seat, Wilton House in Wiltshire, were all impeccable. But he was known as an exuberant young man with unpredictable behaviour. He and Lady Di developed an easy friendship that would survive many years, but the rumours of their impending marriage had probably been exaggerated.[39]

The prospects of her eighteen-year-old sister Betty were also being analysed during the 1755 season. Lord Harcourt, governor to George, Prince of Wales, described the masquerade in February 1755 when Betty, in her Rubens-wife fancy dress, 'danced with Sir James Lowther, which makes people conjecture that she is not disagreeable to him'. Betty may well have found Lowther 'not disagreeable' for he had recently inherited from different relations an estate worth £2,000,000, although his own parents had been neither titled nor wealthy. One sympathetic and slightly involved spectator was Caroline Fox's younger sister, Emily. Happily married to the Earl of Kildare, with a family home in Ireland, she made regular visits to London to stay with Caroline and Henry. She wrote frequently to her husband, to whom she described Lowther's passion:

By the by, 'tis a secret, but Sir James Lowther has desired Mr Fox to propose him for Lady Betty Spencer. He is violently in love, poor man, and they don't behave quite well to him and are for putting it off for two years. Mr Fox and my sister and I pity him vastly, for he seems a modest good sort of man. It is a vast match for her but the Duchess is odd about it; the Duke would be reasonable enough if it was not for her . . . poor Sir James hardly dares speak to her, and she is vastly ashamed. Mr Fox thinks she rather likes him, but has not so much impudence as me to tell her Mother so, as I did. I long to know how it will end.

Two weeks later, the Earl of Huntingdon was being informed that 'it is thought that Sir James Lowther is to be married to Lady Betty Spencer'. But Lord Harcourt was more sceptical: 'I very much doubt whether it will be a match, the Duke and Duchess being very cautious to whom they dispose of her. Indeed they are greatly to be commended for it, for 'tis universally argued that she is one of the most amiable young women that ever was born, and I am afraid Sir James is a little wild.'[40]

Harcourt and the Marlboroughs were more perceptive than Emily Kildare, for Lowther's wildness would lead to his reputation as 'the bad earl', another commentator described him as 'truly a madman though too rich to be confined', while Horace Walpole regarded him as 'equally unamiable in public and in private'. And Betty let her parents' influence prevail, for in March the following year she married Lord Pembroke, whom they may already have approved for Lady Di.

The unmarried older sister's name continued to be linked with potential suitors. One was the Duke of Richmond, younger brother of Caroline Fox and Emily Kildare, who had returned from his Grand Tour in January 1756. But this scenario came to nothing, and he married Lady Mary Bruce in 1757. Another 1756 match which failed to ignite was with the Duke of Kingston, if Theophilus Lindsey, writing from the depths of Dorset to the Earl of Huntingdon, can be believed: 'The Duke of Kingston's marriage with the Duke of Marlborough's eldest daughter ceases to be talked of and his mistress is said once more to have resumed her ascendant'. An unmarried duke, Kingston was already in his mid-forties and had managed to resist all previous attempts to ensnare him. Walpole thought him 'a very weak man [although] of the greatest beauty and finest person in England'. (It was ironic that when he eventually did marry, at the age of fifty-eight, it was to the bigamous Elizabeth Chudleigh, as a result of which she notoriously stood trial in the House of Lords.)[41]

Lady Di's next reported relationship was with the Honourable George West, like Hamilton, a younger son (of Baron, later first Earl de la Warr) who had to earn his living as a soldier, and who succeeded Hamilton as General Conway's aide-de-camp. These dashing young men in their military uniforms were far more interesting and attractive than most languid court beaux; but it was the fact that they had to work for a living that made them far less eligible. Hamilton had now largely got over his broken heart and, according to Conway, who reported to Walpole (sympathetic to Hamilton's artistic interests and later describing him as 'picture-mad'), was not too upset on learning about her romance with West. Hamilton settled for an heiress, as he was the first to admit, whom he married in January 1758. That marriage was contented enough. But he would always retain a special feeling for Lady Di, which extended to the admiration of her art. His own reputation, as collector, connoisseur and influential patron would unfortunately be overshadowed by that of his greatest acquisition, Emma Hart, whose famous Attitudes Lady Di herself would witness thirty-four years later.

THREE
The Viscountess
(1757–61)

'You can do nothing at all without being married;
a single woman is a thousand times more shackled than a wife'

FANNY BURNEY, *Cecilia*

'I think that woman is a fool who risks her contentment
with one of a light disposition. Marriage will not change men's
natures and it is not everyone who has virtue or prudence
enough to be reclaimed'

FRANCES SHERIDAN, *Memoirs of Miss Sidney Biddulph*

By 1757, Lady Diana Spencer had been on the marriage market for a while; to have had her name linked with so many suitors without any engagement being finalized suggested a lack of commitment (even a reluctance to settle down) as well as a pleasing absence of parental pressure. At twenty-two, she was hardly on the shelf, for daughters of the aristocracy did not have to take the first offer that came along. Yet her younger sister Betty was already Countess of Pembroke and chatelaine of Wilton, and it was obvious that the independence of a married woman was greater than that of a daughter. So when Lady Di did agree to marry, it was casual in the extreme, apparently the result of a sudden whim and a chance moment. The proposal, in this very public world of polite society, was described by Mrs Delany in a letter to her sister:

Miss Egerton [a maid of honour] told me that the match between Lady Diana Spencer and Lord Bolingbroke is certainly true and not against the lady's consent, as was reported. They were together at a party at Vauxhall with the Duchess of Bedford; the company was teasing Lord Bolingbroke to marry, and he turned quick to Lady Diana and said, Will you have me? Yes, to be sure, she replied. It passed off that night as a joke, but with consideration on his side of the lady's merit (which they say is a great deal) and the persuasion of his friends, he made a serious affair of it and was accepted.[1]

This romantic, Georgette Heyer-style conversation was inspired by its exotic backdrop, the subversive setting of the raffish Vauxhall Gardens, whose intimate supper booths, twinkling illumination, maze-like pathways leading from the light into the darkness, and general atmosphere of underlying sexual licence attracted the ton to rub shoulders dangerously with the mob. The hostess and chaperone of the party, the Duchess of Bedford (the second wife of Lady Di's uncle-by-marriage the Duke), was like an aunt to the family, and would certainly have seen it as her duty to find a suitable match for the flighty girl: the inclusion of Frederick St John, second Viscount Bolingbroke, in the group was part of this strategy.

The news spread rapidly. General Conway wrote to Horace Walpole: 'You have heard of Lady Di Spencer's match with Lord Bolingbroke, which should break three or four hearts of our acquaintance . . . it was ridiculous enough that, the morning before we heard this news, Hamilton said that he was sure she would soon forget George West and that he would lay a wager she married within a year from *inclination* which I believe is quite the case'. This stress on inclination shows that her determined spirit was well recognized, and that her delay in marrying and future prospects generally had been the topic of an entertaining conversation between Conway and his junior officer Hamilton. Conway added that he thought 'the marriage would break the heart of my poor aide-de-camp and George West's; at least the latter, for Hamilton's indeed, stood its trial when she changed to him'. Walpole quickly broadcast the match, unkindly giving the young couple the surnames of their previous amours: 'Frederick Clinton-Maynard-Nevil-Douglas Viscount Bolingbroke is to be married to Lady Diana Hamilton West'.[2]

Her great-granddaughter's choice of husband would have made Sarah Churchill incandescent with rage, for the name of Bolingbroke was anathema to the first Duke and Duchess of Marlborough. Frederick's uncle was the statesman Henry St John, created first Viscount Bolingbroke in 1712, following his appointment as Secretary of State for the North to Queen Anne in 1710. He had been responsible for the sacking of his enemy, Marlborough, and the stopping of the Treasury funds which had been pouring into the insatiable building programme at Blenheim. But following Marlborough's reinstatement in royal favour and attachment to the Hanoverian cause after the accession of George I, the tables were turned. Bolingbroke was attainted for treason and fled into exile in France, to the delight of Sarah and her husband. Eventually pardoned in 1723, he returned to England. As he had no children, his nephew Frederick, eldest son of his half-brother John, second Viscount St John, became the heir to his estates and title.

The St Johns were an old Wiltshire family whose country seat was at Lydiard Tregoze, and who also owned an estate and manor house in Battersea village. Frederick's father had served as Member of Parliament for Wootton Bassett before inheriting the St John title; the constituency was later represented by his younger son Henry (nick-named 'the Baptist'). Frederick was born in 1732, and educated at Eton. His mother died when he was only fourteen, and his concerned uncle Bolingbroke offered to help look after the motherless children, whose father had 'left the two eldest sons at Richmond with somebody who belongs to his office at the Custom house'; this kindness was despite the fact that Bolingbroke had never met anyone 'so avaricious, more selfish or more false' than their late mother. John St John quickly married again, but died only a few months later: Frederick therefore became third Viscount St John at the age of fifteen. His uncle kept an anxious eye on his prospective heir, who, he believed, had already 'contracted habits that are not of the best, and for that are less corrigible by that sullen obstinacy and constant cause of dissimulation and falsehood which are derived from his parents and have taken the deepest root I ever observed in him . . . he not only has the Vices of a young fellow, that may be overcome [but also] those of a good for nothing fellow of forty . . . he has been a great disappointment to me. I expected to make him the comfort and he has been the plague of my life.' The sulky teenager was packed off to a tutor in Caen (who at one stage, in desperation, gave him twenty-four hours to reform his behaviour or be sent home).[3]

Many years later, the writer of Frederick's obituary, one F.P., would paint a very different picture, presenting the image that his subject clearly wished to project for posterity. This was allegedly 'based on a long intimacy and frequent conversations'. Frederick's version of his youth was that 'his uncle was enraptured with him and from his childhood delighted in his conversation', believing that he 'would infallibly become one of the greatest ornaments to this country [owing to his] brilliancy of parts, ready wit and extensive classical knowledge'. And the exasperated tutor was surprised 'by his Lordship's early genius'.[4]

Bolingbroke died in 1751 and Frederick became the second Viscount Bolingbroke, which gave rise to his nickname Bully. The Battersea estate was now added to that at Lydiard Tregoze but he seemed in no danger of inheriting his uncle's gravitas or political inclinations. The Earl of Chesterfield, an old friend of the first Viscount Bolingbroke, now tried to take some responsibility for the difficult young man, and wrote letters of introduction to friends in Paris, where the Viscount intended to pass a year or two as an acceptable alternative to spending most of his Grand Tour in Italy. Chesterfield was more charitable than Bolingbroke, but his accounts of Frederick at this time damn with faint praise: 'a very promising youth ... he is desirous of improvement, and he will improve ... his letters are such that would not be disowned by our late friend [Bolingbroke] ... what he still wants is a knowledge of the world, and the graces ... I dare say it will be possible, as he ardently wishes to please'. What the Viscount mainly acquired in Paris, if he needed any encouragement, was an addiction to spending money on luxury products. Over the next few years, he built up a fine collection of porcelain, laying out some 13,800 louis on that alone between 1755 and 1758. (To put this vast figure in context, in Paris in the 1750s the average month's wage for a working woman was one louis.) And his later letters to friends in France include commissions for suits, lace, and fine foodstuffs; he would also become a connoisseur of silver. He did manage to visit Florence, where Sir Horace Mann, the British Ambassador, complained to Walpole in July 1753 of 'the sudden arrival of my Lord Bolingbroke with three others' whom he had to add to that day's twelve invited dinner guests, although 'I don't think I have dishes and plates for so many'.[5]

At the age of twenty-four, Bully already had an impressive reputation as rake, drinker and gambler, and he was just launching into another extravagant career as an owner and breeder of racehorses.

His particular group of friends included the amiable socialite Gilly Williams, and the languid wit, the bachelor George Selwyn. Selwyn, rather older than Bully, had been expelled from Oxford for blasphemy, and spent much of his time in Paris, although he was a Member of Parliament. His reputation for necrophilia was probably exaggerated, in an age when executions were a popular public spectacle (though he was also accused of attending them 'in order to elude notice disguised in a female dress'). He had a very close relationship with another of Bully's set, the Earl of March, described in 1754 as 'the most brilliant, most fashionable, most dissipated young man in London, the leading character at Newmarket, the support of the gaming table, the supreme dictator of the Opera-House, the pattern whose dress and equipage were to be copied by all who aimed at distinction'. (March would later inherit the title of Duke of Queensberry, and become notorious as Old Q, the Piccadilly lecher.) He was involved at this time with the courtesan La Rena, an Italian woman originally married to a wine merchant of Florence, but acquired, like any other souvenir of the Grand Tour, by Lady Di's brother-in-law the Earl of Pembroke, who brought her to England in 1757. She was then protected by Lord March for eight years ('You never drove into the Park or through St James Street without meeting him with the Rena in his chariot, the Rena sat at the head of his table, the Rena hung on his arm at Ranelagh'), until March fell for a fifteen-year-old opera dancer, La Zamparini, and abandoned his older mistress. The loyal friend who had to break the news to the Rena that she had been dumped was George Selwyn. Racing, gambling, opera, mistresses, these were the activities of Bully and his friends.[6]

In the various intersecting social circles, Selwyn was also a friend of Horace Walpole, whom he had known since their schooldays at Eton; they stayed close for many years. In the way that we express different aspects of ourselves through different friends, Selwyn's artistic taste and style kept him in contact with the sensitive and highly cultured Walpole, while his love of more material pleasures made him a part of the Bolingbroke circle. During the 1750s, Walpole was immersed in the creation of his Gothic fantasy castle at Strawberry Hill, where Selwyn and Williams often stayed, calling themselves the 'Out of Town Party'. Walpole commissioned Joshua Reynolds to commemorate their friendship in 1761 in the painting *A Conversation Piece* which shows these leisured gentlemen relaxing in a book-lined study.

Although the projected image is tastefully intellectual, one of their main activities was observing and gossiping about their friends and acquaintances. It is their letters which provide a crucial backdrop to the political and social events of the day, including the course of the Bolingbroke marriage.

Spending large sums of money on high-status possessions, horses and women was a perfectly acceptable activity for a young man of Bully's background, and one which would not particularly tarnish the family name. However, he was already thoroughly familiar with London's sleazier side, and would become the subject, in 1772, of the raunchy Tête-à-Tête section of the recently founded *Town and Country Magazine*, which devoted one of its scurrilous articles to the goings on of 'The Battersea Baron'. As a forerunner of tabloid journalism, this gossip section was the most popular item in the new monthly, and ensured its regional as well as metropolitan circulation (some 14,000 copies per issue): in Goldsmith's *She Stoops to Conquer* (1774), the pretentious Mrs Hardcastle, who longs to be in the capital, consoles herself with its gossip. 'All I can do is to enjoy London at second-hand. I take care to know every Tête-à-Tête from the Scandalous Magazine'. According to the article, Bully's aims in life, unlike those of his eminent uncle, 'were all directed to explore new sources of pleasure, which he considered as the only philosophy worthy of attention'. He 'was early initiated into all the mysteries of Venus' by a range of Covent Garden ladies; one of these was Charlotte Hayes, who mingled with society names during the 1750s and '60s and was married to a Newmarket owner, but who also ran a 'house of convenience' in Great Marlborough Street in which she groomed ambitious young girls for careers as courtesans.[7]

Relationships with these sorts of women were not taken too seriously, but there was a real risk of scandal through being named in a divorce action. By 1757, Bully's long-standing association with a married woman was giving cause for concern. Maria Coventry was the elder of the famous Gunning sisters who had taken the town by storm in 1750 through their legendary good looks and numbers of illustrious suitors. Their fame was analysed by Horace Walpole. 'They are two Irish girls, of no fortune, who are declared the handsomest women alive. I think there being two, so handsome and both such perfect figures, is their chief excellence, for singly I have seen handsomer women than either. However, they can't walk in the park or go to Vauxhall, but such mobs follow them that they are generally driven away. There are mobs at their doors to see them get into their chairs; and people go early to get places at the theatres when it is known they will be there.' Henry Harris, another young man about town, was equally fascinated by the fame of these 'two most transcendent nymphs' and described to Henry Fox, then out of touch on the Continent, how 'all English beauty withers before them. Ten of our top toasts fell into fits upon their first appearance at Ranelagh; and such is the present *fureur* that if they happen to be at Vauxhall, the whole Round House at Chelsea immediately embark; and the poor cripples who do not love taking the water lye upon the shore all gasping with Priapism'. A few months later 'the King desired Lady Fawkener to bring them to court. They went, they looked, they conquered'.[8]

Their social ambitions were fulfilled by marriage into the aristocracy. Maria landed Lord Coventry, Elizabeth not one duke but two, first marrying the Duke of Hamilton, then, after his death, the heir to the Duke of Argyll. Maria was frivolous and flirtatious, with a reputation for promiscuity. Her affair with Bully was conducted, according to the *Town and Country Magazine*, 'at the Opera House on the nights of performance in one of the upper boxes, as soon as the doors were opened and long before the music began.' Even when her suspicious husband banished her to their country estate in Worcestershire, Bully managed to send her letters via an innocent intermediary clergyman, called by Selwyn, who knew all about it, 'Giles the postman'. But Maria was also unfaithful to her lover, as reported by Walpole in April 1756: 'the Duke [of Cumberland] had appeared in form on the causeway in Hyde Park with my Lady Coventry; it is the new office, where all lovers now are entered. How happy she must be with Billy and Bully. I hope she will not mistake and call the former by the nickname of the latter.' And she continued to keep the two in tandem, as the Earl of Huntingdon was informed a month later: 'His Royal Highness the Duke is the professed admirer of my Lady Coventry, but my Lord Bolingbroke does not give out for all that'.[9]

Bully's family and friends started to fear that Lord Coventry would decide to divorce his wife for her infidelity with Bolingbroke, who would then be forced to marry her. Walpole was kept up to date by Gilly Williams: 'Mr Williams is just come from his niece . . . he tells me that the plump Countess is in terrors lest Lord Coventry should get a divorce from his wife and Lord Bolingbroke should marry her. 'Tis a well-imagined panic.' Another alarming option occurred in June 1757, when Lord Coventry became gravely ill; the prospect of Bully marrying the widow was almost as bad as his marrying the divorcee. Emily Kildare, on one of her London visits, wrote to her husband in Ireland: 'Lord Coventry has been dying and Lord Bolingbroke frightened out of his wits lest he should die'.[10]

Walpole relished passing on further gossip to the Earl of Strafford about Bully's bad conduct in July 1757: 'For that of the pretty Countess, I fear there is too much truth in all that you have heard; but you don't seem to know that Lord Corydon and Captain Corydon his brother [Bully and the Baptist] have been most abominable. I don't care to write scandal; but when I see you, I will tell you how much the chits deserve to be whipped.'

So this was the desirable husband for whom the Duke's daughter had been saving herself. For him, marriage with the eligible Lady Diana Spencer was obviously the best way of getting out of the clutches of an older married woman, rescuing the family from potential shame and securing its future through the production of heirs. Mrs Delany's reference to the 'persuasion of his friends' suggests that his was a rational and not an emotional choice; his 'consideration of the lady's merit' was made more positive through his own need for money. And the letter to her sister went on to emphasize how '£1,500 a year jointure and £500 a year pin money have cast a veil over the past. If he has sense, he may be happy for he must then see the absurd figure he has hitherto made and know how to value a woman of worth, though no longer the dupe of beauty and folly.' The fulsome obituary written by the loyal F.P. shows that Bully was anxious to counteract this image; he wished to be remembered at the time of his marriage as 'the wonder of our sex and the admiration of the other; a gaieté de cœur distinguished him everywhere, whilst his politeness and good sense charmed the circle'.

Lady Di's motivation was equally practical. She was doing what she was meant to do, making a marriage within her caste and one which would not disgrace the name of Marlborough (although a viscount ranked lower than Betty's earl). The marriage had not been formally arranged or forced upon her by her father (whose own successful marriage had resulted from his making his own choice) and she may well have believed that she had followed her own inclinations. But the choice itself had been constrained by the restricted circles in which the daughter of a duke and a young viscount publicly moved, combined with their acceptance of society's powerful requirement to make a suitable match. And although their subsequent patterns of behaviour were initially those of an earlier generation who accepted and manipulated the structures of the arranged marriage, it has been argued that there was a shift in attitudes to marriage during the later decades of the century. The ideal of the companionate marriage, as a new and romantic alternative to the family-arranged model, tended to lead to more tension and unhappiness which actually resulted in higher rates of divorce, since the expectations of the participants were unreasonably high.

Whatever her hopes for the future, Lady Di's immediate concern was the acquisition of a fine trousseau, whose bills are still filed in the Blenheim archives. For the period 28 August to 6 October, between engagement and wedding, the bride's mother ran up a substantial account of £252 15s 3d with her dressmaker Mary Sleech; this bill was settled quite promptly, on 19 October. It included the making up of frills and ruffles, plus tuckers, tippets and caps. Lady Di made substantial purchases during those crucial weeks from the top people's mercer Hinchcliffe & Croft (whose many other aristocratic patrons included Lord Bristol and his daughters, and Lady Jane Coke – 'if you write to Mr Hinchcliffe . . . and say I recommended you, he will send you some patterns') which were paid for by her mother after the wedding. She bought quantities of sumptuous silks and brocades, luxury products imported from France, Italy and the Near East – silks made in Spitalfields by Huguenot weavers had less cachet, as had English-made lace, despite the high duties which were levied on such luxury imports to try and make the high spenders buy British. Attempts to smuggle in French-made products were frequent. Horace Walpole reported how customs officials had seized one hundred and fourteen French gowns and silks from Lady Holdernesse in July 1764 and there are frequent contemporary references to attempts being made to avoid paying duties.[11]

Two weeks after the engagement, she bought four yards of pink lustring (or 'lutestring', a taffeta silk with a particularly glossy texture), and twenty-three yards of pink tabby, at only 8s and 10s per yard respectively, being intended for everyday rather than special wear. The day before the wedding, she bought nineteen yards of black ribbon, to be used for trimming. There was a six-week lull during the honeymoon period, but serious shopping was resumed at Hinchcliffe's between 21 October and 4 November, when she was acquiring the materials for a whole new wardrobe – eighteen and a quarter yards of silver pink brocade, at £5 per yard, totalling a massive £91 5s 0d; eighteen and a half yards of gold ground brocade with purple, slightly cheaper at £4 per yard, but still totalling £74. Less costly were eighteen yards of marron, blue and silver satin at 12s a yard, thirteen yards of pompadour satin (9s a yard) and twenty-nine yards of rich black satin (10s 6d). The popularity of the colour pink from the mid-1750s was regarded as another example of the influence of French fashion; Lady Jane Coke, writing in 1754, disapproved of the dangerous foreign emphasis on youth culture: 'There is not such a thing as a decent old woman left. Everybody curls their hair, shews their neck and wears pink ... trying to outdo the French in every ridiculous vanity'.[12]

Lady Di also had a pre-wedding shopping session at the establishment of William and Elizabeth Gresham, who not only sold silks and satins by the yard but also made them to order, and who sold some ready-made garments such as hoods and cloaks, petticoats and hoops. Four days before the marriage ceremony, she bought three fine calico quilted bedgowns (an informal garment for casual indoor wear, rather than actually for sleeping in), quite reasonably priced at £5 8s for the three, a white lustring quilted coat lined with persian (another thin silk, generally made in Italy rather than the East its name implied) at £2 15s, the same in green, at £2 1s, and a more luxurious version in white satin at £4 10s. Other essentials included a figured à-la-mode cloak (a thin, shiny black silk), a fine screen basket, for which she ordered a quilted lining, two and a half yards of rose-coloured mantua, plus ribbons and 'fine stuff'. The total bill came to £27 5s 9d, which she paid herself on 18 October on her return to London; her mother paid the three much larger bills, to the dressmaker, to Hinchcliffe, and to a specialist lace-supplier with the fashionably French name of Catherine Giberne, who put in on 14 October a bill of £124 15s for the purchase and making up of lace and ruffles. Mrs Giberne ran a profitable business in Parliament Street providing fine lace ruffles, which were an important part of the mid-century costume; attached to a gown whose sleeves terminated at the elbow were deep double or treble layers of ruffle extending as far as the wrist, and made of different sorts of lace, preferably French. Mrs Giberne was making 'upwards of four hundred pounds a year' as early as 1742, despite attempts at shop-lifting made, as she complained, by people like a 'lady of ten thousand pounds' fortune. I found a piece of lace of £3 10s a yard in her glove, as she "put it in by accident" so by accident I thought it proper to shake it out'. [13]

While the women shopped, the men and their lawyers set to business. A marriage settlement was negotiated between Marlborough and Bolingbroke, in which the still cash-strapped Duke tried to reconcile not giving away too much of his modest capital while securing his daughter's future as wife, mother and widow. He handed over £10,000, which would be supplemented by Sarah's bequest of £5,000, due in 1761. In return, Lady Di would receive £500 a year 'pin-money' to spend as she chose – given the rate of consumption suggested by her clothes bills, this meant that she would be dependent upon Bully, another reckless spender, for most purchases. On his death, she would receive £2,000 a year jointure, and any younger children would be provided for out of a capital sum of £15,000.

Brocaded, ruffled and beribboned, Lady Di now joined her sister, friends and cousins as a married woman: the Annual Register recorded for the month of September 1757 the marriage of 'Lord Viscount Bolingbroke to the Right Honourable Lady Diana Spencer, elder daughter to the Duke of Marlborough'. The wedding took place on 8 September, just one month after the mock proposal, at Harbledown in Kent, another little country property of the Duke, in the presence of members of both families. Engagements were rarely long for fear of a change of mind by either party if something better cropped up, or of the deaths that could strike so suddenly and inexplicably. Both families were no doubt relieved that two such dangerously single people were now tied together. The newly-weds spent October in London and went to Paris in December, where Bully took the opportunity of adding to his Sèvres collection.

The new Viscountess Bolingbroke found herself the mistress of an estate which included the Manor House at Battersea, a rambling, many-roomed wainscotted Elizabethan house which had been lived in and loved as their London home by many generations of St Johns; a nearby dower house had been built more recently by Wren. The gardens of the Manor ran right down to the Thames, where the widening river curved and gave misty views of Chelsea village on the opposite bank, accessible by private ferry. The first Viscount Bolingbroke was buried in the adjacent medieval parish church of St Mary (whose living was in the family's gift and where even the stained glass of the east window boasted the Tudor connections of the St Johns), where he had been commemorated in marble by Roubiliac with an epitaph composed by himself. But for a modern, fashionable young couple, this ancient family property was inconvenient and remote from central London. The village was surrounded by marshlands, and travellers had to cross the notorious Battersea Fields at a time when highwaymen and robbers were confident enough even to prey on victims in the heart of the city. The first Viscount had written during the depressing winter of 1749: 'Battersea is much further from London than it was before; we have four feet of snow, the wind howls round the house and no-one ever comes near us.' And his wife complained about 'this old decaying house . . . as fast as we build it up on one side, it falls down on the other'.[14]

So the young Bolingbrokes preferred to begin their marriage in a rented house in one of the most desirable and central spots of the day, at 7 St James's Square. This gracious and elegant development, begun in the late seventeenth century as a piece of speculative building, spanned the area which ran between the old palace of St James's and the latest expansions north of Piccadilly, as new London's focus shifted from the City, the Strand and Bloomsbury to the cleaner air of the west. Living in the parish of St James's was equally convenient for court, for social life, and for getting out of London. Their house was on the north-east side of the Square, whose occupants in the late 1750s were mainly titled people – as well as the Pembrokes, there were the Earls of Bathurst, Hardwick, Strafford, Dartmouth and Macclesfield, the Dukes of Leeds and Cleveland, and a clutch of viscounts. There was also the ancient and hospitable Lady Betty Germain, whose card parties were attended by the best gossips of the day, Lady Mary Coke and Horace Walpole. Number 7 was rented by the Bolingbrokes from a Member of Parliament, Thomas Scawen, for £216 per annum.[15]

Despite having fine town houses, most English noble families had their real roots in the country: they stayed in London for the social season, and while Parliament was sitting, during autumn and spring, but spent the summer months in the ancestral home. The St John family had been at Lydiard Tregoze, in Wiltshire, since the early fifteenth century. The little church of St Mary, adjacent to Lydiard

House, was redolent of its medieval past; its glowing wall paintings and luminous stained glass powerfully recalled previous generations. As the new Viscountess took her place in the high-walled family pew, she could see earlier St Johns all around in their proud monuments – the brightly painted wooden triptych boasting a family tree of some thirty-two ancestors, the effigies of happy couples, together in death as in life, the thirteen children of the second baronet, the gleaming and life-size Golden Cavalier (a seventeenth-century St John in full armour): even the stained glass of the east window had St John heraldry arranged as a family tree. The family eternally inspected its descendants and their brides. For a new wife, the message was powerful; she was reinforced in her role as the vessel to carry on her husband's line. There was also a stark contrast with the ostentatiously modern chapel at Blenheim, whose earliest monuments were those of that self-made couple Sarah and John Churchill.

The most recent effigy in the church, by Roubiliac, was another commemoration of the first Viscount Bolingbroke, who had made over the house in the 1740s to his half-brother. Bully's father had then remodelled it and turned a seventeenth-century manor into an up-to-date, light-hearted Palladian villa of delightful proportions and non-daunting scale – again a very definite contrast to forbidding Blenheim, although not dissimilar to Langley. Lady Di had probably not even seen Lydiard before her wedding. The first view of the house was from the south, from the drive which led through the park, which Bully was then restructuring, towards the main entrance. This was crowned by a classical pediment, and the whole facade ornamented with balustrades and corner turrets. Inside, the stylish decoration included ornate stucco ceilings and garlands carved of wood. The formal rooms, grand entrance hall, library, dining and drawing rooms, were everything that could be expected. Off the master bedroom there was a dressing room that would have driven the medievalist Walpole wild with envy, for it contained a large stained-glass window, just the sort of thing that he was buying up avidly for Strawberry Hill. This did not depict the subject matter of saints or Bible stories appropriate for churches and chapels, but showed, in over one hundred diamond-shaped panels, vividly coloured and minutely detailed designs of flowers, animals, birds and human figures, including classical motifs such as cherubs, centaurs and fauns playing pan pipes. These were themes which would recur constantly in Lady Di's own work. The maker of this window was the Flemish glazier Abraham van Linge, who was working in England in the 1630s and had been commissioned to paint the east window of the church; his St John patron had been so satisfied that he was then asked to do something for the house, as well as for the church in Battersea.

Another source of encouragement for a young woman who enjoyed drawing and painting was provided by the portraits of Bully's great-grandfather and great-grandmother, Sir Walter and Lady St John – the house, like the church, recorded the past for the present generation. These imposing, ancestral images had been painted in oils by Mary Beale, a successful professional artist of the late seventeenth century, a rare role model in an age when painting was a masculine profession.

In addition to the church and the house, Lady Di had hundreds of acres of estate grounds to explore, set in the gently rolling Wiltshire downs. There was a great park, in which Bully was carrying on his father's scheme of transforming the earlier formal gardens into something more relaxed and closer to nature. He was creating a great lake to enhance the views of the house, just as her father had played with his earthworks and waterworks at Langley. There were stables and paddocks where grazing horses posed for her sketchbook. Other features included a magnificent avenue and a massively walled flower garden, which provided a sunny and fragrant haven as well as the fresh fruit and vegetables which were not just consumed at the house but also sent up to London when the family were there. And there was an ice house, to maintain the luxurious standards of cuisine required. Nearby was the little village of Lydiard Tregoze, through which the lady of the manor and the grand visitors to the house would drive and watch the goings-on of country folk – the village school-room, the travelling menagerie, pretty peasant girls carrying goods to market, all subjects that would appear in Lady Di's sketchbooks.

Although Lydiard was not as impressive as her sister's Wilton, and of course diminutive when compared to Blenheim, this was a home and estate of high enough status, comfort and convenience, within reasonable travelling distance of her parents and sister. As to the husband, he would do; he was not old, not ugly, not poor, but an inhabitant of the same select world with its shared codes of conduct, in his enthusiasms and extravagances like her own loved father. This was what she was meant to be doing.

The first year of her marriage was the last year of her father's life.

In 1756, the Duke of Marlborough had resumed active military service in response to the renewed threat of invasion from France. In a masterstroke of patriotic propaganda, he exhumed his grandfather's famous triumphal chariot, which was stored at Blenheim, to serve as the culmination of a grand morale-boosting military parade. Horace Walpole noted the prematurity of this action: 'What would his grandame if she were alive say to this pageant? If the war lasts, I think well enough of him to believe he will earn a sprig; but I have no notion of trying on a crown of laurel before I had acquired it'. That particular emergency abated but the nation remained in a state of alert, and the Duke was put in charge of the artillery at Byfleet, where he mishandled the accounts. Despite his resulting unpopularity with the King – 'His Majesty is still very severe in his opinion of the Duke of Marlborough: he will not consider him as in the Army', wrote Henry Fox to the Duke of Cumberland – the Duke was given the opportunity he sought. William Pitt, who had recently been called upon by the King to lead the government in the Commons following Fox's failure to create a ministry, involved the Duke in a preliminary expedition against the French at Rochefort. This campaign was not successful but Pitt was sufficiently impressed by Marlborough's conduct to involve him, as a premier duke with a famous name, in the renewed struggle with France in the late spring of 1758.[16]

His first job was to take part in the proposed naval attack on the key port of St Malo. For the Duchess, this was a repeat of the traumatic separations she had endured ten years earlier. She wrote anxiously from Blenheim to London: 'If you love me as you say, you will take care of your dear self when you reflect how absolutely necessary you are to my happiness'. The Duke was not the only member of the Marlborough family now contributing to their country's good. His son and heir George, Marquess of Blandford, aged nineteen, was serving with him, while his daughter, the Viscountess Bolingbroke, lent another distinguished name and played her own patriotic role by accompanying her father and brother to make them a public farewell from Spithead as the fleet set sail for victory. Her association with the launching of the St Malo campaign was just one example of the extensive aristocratic commitment to King and Country at this time of danger; the huge expedition fleet carried some 20,000 men, amongst whom, according to Walpole, were 'half the purplest blood in England'.

The Duke's letters to the Duchess that summer describe the journey to the coast, and Lady Di's presence as the daughter of the regiment. He had to make the usual reassurances to his neurotic wife. Having reached the Isle of Wight on 23 May 1758, he writes from Cowes: 'I am vastly glad to hear you endeavour to keep up your spirits . . . the weather here very fine and warm. Di is now with me very well and wrote to you yesterday but the post here is very uncertain'. The family was at that moment awaiting the birth of the Pembrokes' first baby, another source of worry for the Duchess, and he adds: 'If I should set sail before Betty is brought to bed, Di begs you will send her a letter when it happens, tho' I believe she sets out for London when we sail'. (Sadly, the baby was stillborn on 9 June.) A couple of days later: 'PS. Di dined with me yesterday'. As so often, the wind was contrary, but at last it changed, and the fleet set sail for France on 1 June. This had been a rare time together for father and daughter, marked by the emotional intensity of the imminent danger. For him a brief chance to reclaim his own daughter, his first child, who now belonged to another man, for her a rare opportunity to have her father to herself, away from the fretting presence of her mother, which would provide poignant memories of sunny, salt-tinged days.[17]

The letters which he wrote to his wife over the next few months, as he campaigned on sea and then on land against the French, continued to reinforce his loving, intimate and protective role: 'I shall now sail a little along the French coast; and I hope soon to see you, which is infinitely the greatest happiness of my life' (12 June 1758). He also manages to retain a sense of humour in circumstances almost unimaginable for people brought up to luxury: 'The ship now rolls too much to write plain but I don't believe I shall ever be sea-sick again. As for money I want none, for I don't know what to do with it. Every time I open my box I see a purse of guineas I am quite tired of, and tempted to throw it overboard; I would give it all for a dozen of clean shirts, as we can't spare any water on board to wash. Blan and I are in perfect health but rather dirty. I won't attempt to say how much I long to see you.' (24 June 1758.)

But after a few weeks of this, he had had enough of life on shipboard, and he abandoned the so far ineffectual St Malo campaign to lead the British troops to Germany, following promotion by Pitt to become Commander-in-Chief of the British forces there, fighting in support of the Hanoverian ally Ferdinand of Brunswick against the combined enemies France, Austria, Russia, Sweden and Saxony. In September Charles was made a general. His letters continued to detail his life and his love for his wife: 'We have had hot and long marches, a prodigious heavy rain of eight-and-fourty hours. The Foot have marched the last day almost up to their middle in water . . . you may depend on my missing no opportunity of writing, as that and hearing from you during my absence are by far the greatest comforts I have. Col Brown is not yet arrived. I long to see him and ask a thousand questions about you' (3 August 1758). 'I long most excessively to join Prince Ferdinand, chiefly because I hope to find a letter there from you. It is terrible to be so long without a chance of hearing from you. I shall have no opportunities of writing until I cross the Rhine, which will be about five days hence' (9 August 1758).

His frequent concern to allay her worries and her unreasonable complaints when she felt that he was not writing frequently enough, given these extremely difficult circumstances, suggest that he was still in some awe of her after twenty-six years of marriage. He wrote every two or three days, often just a couple of sentences, but always concerned with her feelings, which she was volubly expressing in her letters back. He always ends with a little postscript sending his love to 'Di, Be, Cha, and Bo'. Blandford was also learning the need to calm this most anxious of mothers, for he too wrote in an equally reassuring tone (his calm and orderly character expressed in his handwriting, far neater than that of his father).

By August 22, Charles was in Germany ('I hope your next letter will tell me you are better'); in early September, he insisted that because there would soon be peace and there was very little danger: 'I should not only be a foolish but a very bad man not to avoid action . . . I must do my duty as a General'. On 14 September he thanked her for her latest letter 'which appears tolerably cheerful and has of course more effect upon my spirits than can be imagined'. But this cunning ploy did not work and two weeks later: 'I must again beg you not to torment yourself unnecessarily . . . the campaign is very near over – why will you always look on the black side?'

But at last her pessimism was justified, for in October Charles succumbed to the dysentery which was posing as great a threat to the British forces as their combined enemies. He died on 20 October 1758, a sad, squalid and pointless death. But he might not have achieved a great longevity, for it was reported after his death that his lungs were quite far advanced with the consumption that had finished off his mother and sister: this was something which had apparently not been passed on to his own children (a useful inheritance from the robust Trevor blood so disapproved of by Sarah). His body was shipped back to Britain and buried in the chapel at Blenheim on 21 November to lie for eternity beside his hostile grandmother and the inimitable role model of the first Duke.

The sudden and genuinely unexpected death of this pleasant man, loyal husband and loving father was widely mourned – the heir was not yet of age and the widow had two dependent younger sons. But reservations were also expressed. A guarded epitaph was provided by the Earl of Shelburne (who had campaigned with Charles): 'an easy good-natured man who took a strange fancy for serving, to get rid of the ennui attending a private life, without any military experience or the common habits of a man of business, or indeed any capacity for either, and no force of character whatever'. And Lady Mary Wortley Montagu also emphasized the late Duke's notorious incompetence with money, writing ironically to her son-in-law about the eulogies in the press:

I read the news of the Duke of Marlborough's death with all the sentiments of a true Briton touched with the misfortunes of his country ... his dowager and children have cried bitterly and both his sons in law and many other people of the first quality will wear mourning on this sad occasion ... more sincere tears shed for his loss than for all the heroes departed for this last century. God knows how many tradespeople and honest scriveners and usurers are breaking their hearts for this untimely fall ... she gives me such an account of the late Duke of Marlborough's affairs as takes away all doubt of his well-being in the next world. He is certainly eminently distinguished amongst babes and sucklings; to say truth, I never could perceive ('tho I was well acquainted with him) that he had the least tincture of original sin.

Horace Walpole was also interested in the financial implications of the Duke's death, and the fortunate fact that he had died before he had been able to get his hands on the inheritance due to his son on majority: 'The estate is forty-five thousand pounds a year – nine of which are jointured out. He paid but eighteen thousand pounds a year in joint lives. This Duke and the estate save greatly by his death, as the present wants a year of being of age, and would certainly have accommodated his father in agreeing to sell and pay'.[18]

The succession of George, Marquess of Blandford, to the Marlborough title at the age of nearly twenty meant that he inherited the capital of around half a million pounds which had been protected from his father, thanks to Sarah's manoeuvres. He resigned his position in the Coldstream Guards and became a prime target for the matchmakers. Among these were Caroline Fox, seeking a husband for her plump pretty young sister Sal Lennox, who had recently come to live with the Foxes at Holland House after a childhood spent with Emily in Ireland. Despite Caroline's disapproving account to Emily of the widow's reaction – 'The Duchess of Marlborough, by all accounts, was not from the beginning in any great affliction for the poor Duke, which is very surprising and one of those unaccountable things that happen in this world' – she did not scruple to launch a campaign for the son. 'My ball was pretty and went off very well. Sal seemed much delighted. The Duke of Marlborough admires her of all things; my brother is vastly anxious to have it come to something. I'm grown too much of a philosopher to feel eager, at least to allow myself to be so on such occasions. In the first place he is so very averse to the thoughts of marrying yet . . . secondly, I think that a woman who marries so young a man as the Duke of Marlborough runs great risk of being unhappy very often . . . then the Duchess of Marlborough would be the most troublesome of all mothers in law'.[19]

Three weeks later, poor George is clearly trying to distance himself from the Foxes, causing Caroline to complain that 'he is scarcely ever in town, has not been since the ball one day, is not likely to see her three times these next six months, and a young man extremely determined not to marry young'. However, things seemed to have improved four weeks later: 'the Duke of Marlborough sat by her and talked to her at the last ridotto, I hear. For him, you have no notion how extraordinary it seems, 'twould be clever to be sure, but I'm determined not to think about it, all appearances of desiring it would do harm. He must be infinitely amiable; he has settled upon each of his brothers £2000 a year for their life, given his mother Langley for her life, and to the man that was his tutor £600 a year; these are noble things and shew a great and good mind'.[20]

Lady Di may have been starting to compare the noble mind of her brother with the rather less elevated character of her husband. For a start, despite his marriage to an impeccable young bride, he had not given up his feelings for Lady Coventry, whose health was now

causing concern. Horace Walpole kept his eye on them, as in a letter
to Selwyn in the spring of 1760, describing the trial of the fourth Earl
Ferrers for shooting his own steward, with the defence being a plea of
'occasional insanity' – attending elite trials was one of the amusements
of the London season, as popular among women as men. 'To the
amazement of everybody, Lady Coventry was there; and what surprised me much more, looked as well as ever. I sat next but one to
her, and should not have asked her if she had been ill, yet they are
positive she has few weeks to live. She and Lord Bolingbroke seemed
to have different thoughts and were acting over all the old comedy of
eyes'. Ferrers (whose wife had earlier obtained a much needed separation on the grounds of his cruelty) was found guilty and hanged at
Tyburn in May 1760.

Caroline Fox unkindly described the famous beauty's decline to
Emily in her usual moralizing tone: 'Poor Lady Coventry is going, I
hear, at Bristol. One is less sorry for her, I think, because she must
have been unhappy when old age came on and beauty went'. Old age,
in this case, was the late twenties. A few months later it was over:
'poor Lady Coventry for the last fortnight would not let her curtains
be opened, not to be look'd at by any mortal but her nurse; she would
let no light but a lamp burn in her room; she was grown quite
disfigured and could not bear to have that once beautiful face seen
when it was no more, so there is something very shocking in seeing
youth and beauty go off in its full bloom'.[21]

Lady Coventry was hailed as a genuine martyr to fashion, since her
long and painful death was attributed by many to poisoning from the
make-up which she wore: the desirably fashionable white skin could
be achieved by the application of mercury water or of white lead. This
was a danger of which smart women were aware but frequently chose
to ignore. Lady Coventry's husband had prophetically disapproved of
her use of cosmetics from the beginning. As reported by Walpole, at a
dinner party on their honeymoon in Paris: 'Maria arrived in full make-
up whereupon her husband had coursed her round the table . . . seized
her . . . and scrubbed it off by force with a napkin'. However, she was
perhaps being made a scapegoat for this unpopular French fashion,
for two months before her death, her doctor described symptoms
which sounded more like consumption – 'oppression on her breast
and the sickness at her stomach . . . pain in her side and across the
breast'. After her death, in October 1760, Walpole drily reported her

former lover's reaction: 'Lord Bolingbroke on hearing the name of Lady Coventry at Newmarket affected to burst into tears and left the room, not to hide his crying but his *not* crying'.[22]

There are glimpses of the Bolingbrokes' social life in London during these first years of marriage. Selwyn's friendship with Bully now extended to his wife. A cheerful note written by her to Selwyn reports that: 'Lady Bolingbroke is *actuellement à sa toilette*, and will be very glad to see Mr Selwyn, particularly as she goes out of town tomorrow. Lord Bolingbroke intends being at home also, in order to see Mr Selwyn, and to prevent any mischief that might happen from Mr Selwyn's inclination this morning to that *posture horizontale*'. They attended the grand events, such as one of the balls, 'numerous and magnificent' according to Walpole, given at Bedford House by the Duke and Duchess in April 1759, who borrowed two of the Boling-broke footmen to help wait on the guests during supper. This was not infrequent practice between elite households – for an earlier ball in 1757, Bolingbroke had loaned them some of his plate, which his chairman had carried to Bedford House.[23]

While Lady Di's life had changed radically on marriage, Bully's had not. He simply continued with the pursuits, friends and lifestyle of his bachelorhood, adding to them his new grand passion, the Turf. To the amenities of Lydiard, he now added an extensive stable range to accommodate some of the horses which he owned and bred, such as the eminent Arabian sires, the Bolingbroke Grey and the Bolingbroke Bay. He also had a stable at Newmarket. In the first five years of his new hobby, it has been calculated that he owned around seventy horses. Some of these horses, the ultimate status symbol for his class, were exquisitely portrayed by George Stubbs, whose commissions from such aristocratic owners at an early stage in his career contrib-uted extensively to his later success and fame. Works were com-missioned to be hung and admired at Lydiard; the centrepiece of the exquisite library, with its pedimented bookshelves and ornate ceiling, was Stubbs' portrait of 'Viscount Bolingbroke's favourite hunter', depicted with a background of the house and church, enshrining the properties of an English gentleman.[24]

One of Bully's first acquisitions was Lustre, which he bought from another addict, the Duke of Ancaster, and which won important races for him at Winchester and Newmarket in 1760; he commemorated these successes by his first commission from 'Mr Stubbs the Horse

Painter'. The next to be painted was Molly Long-legs, bought from Fulke Greville, and raced from 1761-2 (unusually, after she had foaled); this work was exhibited in 1762 in one of the annual exhibitions organized by the Society of Artists (of which Stubbs was elected Fellow in 1765), a chance for the wider public to admire the fame of the owner as well as the skill of the painter. Then there was the magnificent Gimcrack, one of the most famous horses of the day, which he bought after seeing it win in its very first race at Newmarket in the spring of 1765. On 10 July, Gimcrack provided Bully with his greatest triumph, by beating Sir James Lowther's Ascham in a competition in which the betting was reported to exceed £100,000, and which was the major news item on a day on which there was also a parliamentary reshuffle. The former Sal Lennox, now married to another racing addict, was one of the spectators, admiring 'the sweetest little horse that ever was. His name is Gimcrack, he is delightful ... I must say, I was more interested in the horse than the ministry'.[25] Bully commissioned Stubbs to record this epic victory in a painting which shows Gimcrack in front of the Rubbing Down stand at Newmarket, accompanied by trainer, stablelad and jockey wearing the Bolingbroke black colours; in the background the race itself is being run. The celebrated horse was then beaten for the first time, in October 1765, a bad month for Bully in other ways, as we shall see. In a fit of pique, inspired perhaps as much by a sense of personal as well as by professional failure, he promptly sold it to the Comte de Lauragais, a friend of the Earl of Pembroke. The new owner entered the horse in a beat-the-clock competition to see how far it could run in an hour – it allegedly managed twenty-two and a half miles. And it was then bought by Sir Charles Bunbury, Sal's husband.[26]

Turf was another of Bully's prized possessions painted by Stubbs in 1765, again in front of the Rubbing Down shed, with the jockey in the Bolingbroke black. One famous race was commemorated by another artist, Francis Sartorius, *The Race over the Beacon Course*, in which Turf was one of the four horses competing for 500 guinea stakes. This took place on 20 April 1767; Lord Rockingham's Melton and Sir John Moore's Herod put Turf into third place. Then there was Hollyhock, which Bully bought from the Duke of Cumberland, commissioning its portrait from Stubbs in 1766; he then sold the horse to Lord Rockingham and the portrait to a M. Monet, who had it embellished by no less than two fashionable French painters, Vernet and Boucher, to provide a more tasteful background of trees, sheep and shepherdesses.

Stubbs' reputation was growing amongst the racing set, and Lord Rockingham was another early and significant patron. Stubbs' artistic development is marked by his sensitive images of brood mares and their foals, versions of which were commissioned by a number of owners, including Bully, to provide elegant references to their cherished investments. Incorporating repeated but changing permutations in a frieze-like format, the group was originally composed as an exhibition piece for display by the Society of Artists in 1762. Lady Di copied one of these groups in pen and wash, one mare rubbing its muzzle affectionately over the neck of another. Bully named one of these prize fillies, bred by Squirrel out of Cypron, Lady Bolingbroke in honour of his wife. But other mares, Polly and Kitty, were named after his mistresses.

One of the many fascinations the Newmarket world held for young men like Bully was the relaxation of the tight boundaries of London society. Here they could be with people of very different backgrounds, who were measured by skill and enthusiasm rather than just rank and money. At the same time, it provided a great opportunity for those not born with such privileges to acquire them. A prime example was William Wildman (Gimcrack's previous owner), who was Bully's racing partner during the 1760s, providing necessary capital and sharing the profits. Wildman was originally a butcher, then a prosperous meat salesman at Smithfield, acting as middleman between landowners selling their livestock and London consumers. His growing prosperity meant that he could afford to indulge his interests in racing, and, eventually, collecting works of art. He commissioned a number of works from Stubbs, including a portrait of Gimcrack, in Wildman's racing colours of red, to celebrate its earlier victory for him before he sold it to Bully. The respected Newmarket trainer Mr Panton obtained a post at court and became the father-in-law of the Duke of Ancaster. Another success story was that of John Pratt, Bully's riding groom, who progressed upwards from being a stablehand, then jockey (he had ridden Gimcrack for Wildman) to owning racehorses and becoming the first man of humble birth to be elected a member of the exclusive Jockey Club.

Founded in the early 1750s as a London rendezvous for those who regularly attended the races at Newmarket (and, for Bully, conveniently based in the Star and Garter in Pall Mall, just round the corner from St James's Square), the Jockey Club was an example of the specialist and non-specialist societies and associations which marked the sociability and potentially fluid nature of Georgian society. It served to reinforce the exclusivity of those who ran the racing world yet could open its doors to a wider community through election on the grounds of merit alone. Members had to be proposed and elected by ballot, the majority wealthy or extravagant young aristocrats like Bully, who bred and raced their horses as a superior form of gambling but who seldom made a profit. Many of the members were professed Macaronis, or dandies; others in the 1760s included George III's brothers the Duke of Cumberland and the Duke of York, whose own dubious reputation was attributed to his following of a 'motley tribe of gamblers, jockeys, boon companions, fiddlers, singers and writers of good songs'. There was also Charles Bunbury, MP for Bury St Edmunds, an early steward of the Jockey Club (Bully would also become a steward in 1770) and by 1768 its virtual president. His passion for horse-racing, as well as his dullness, was beginning to put some strain on his wife, the former Sal Lennox. The Jockey Club's official aim was to regulate and control the burgeoning leisure pursuit of horse racing, to establish standards for lineage, distance, weight and age – Bunbury was credited with introducing the racing of two-year-olds. He and Bully bought and sold horses from each other for over twenty years; this shared obsession may well have contributed to their later reputation as famous cuckolds.[27]

If some men could rise, others could get dragged down in the racing world. Lady Northumberland, with the security of an old name and old money (despite her own husband's meteoric rise as a direct result of his marriage to her), would write scathingly of the dangers facing people like Bully and Bunbury: 'Men that are fond of horses generally prefer the stable to good company and occupied with the conversations of jockeys, coachmen, grooms and postilions, they contract in such company a rude coarse manner of speaking which destroys that politeness so necessary in the society of ladies, by which means they come to neglect them and often become swearers and brutes'. It was this perceived corruption of polite behaviour that had resulted in the extremely low status of sporting art, ranked at the very bottom in the academic hierarchy of subject matter for art, as defined by Jonathan Richardson in 1715 in his *Essay on the Theory of Painting* – the summit was 'history painting', the idealized depiction of noble deeds, while any form of the mere copying of nature, whether portraiture, scenery or still life, was believed to involve inferior talents. However, this view was being challenged by some English painters and their patrons, causing the Swiss visitor Rouquet to sneer in 1755 at what was becoming a popular genre: 'as soon as a racehorse has acquired some fame, they have him immediately drawn to the life ... they generally clap the figure of some jockey or other on his back, which is but poorly done'. Stubbs was taking this further: his precision and meticulous detail, the almost frozen figures of horses and jockeys, the restraint and calm, all produced an effect both classical and eternal, which encouraged viewers to forgive or forget the privileged, spoilt, bankrupt or fabulously wealthy participants in this rowdy, mercenary pursuit – art as usual reinforcing the ideology of the ruling class. For Stubbs, painting these thoroughbreds was a chance to turn the skills acquired from his earlier anatomical studies into a highly marketable form of art (a skill such that he was later commissioned by Joseph Banks to reconstruct a kangaroo from the skin he had brought back from his voyage to Australia with Captain Cook). And there was also the opportunity for him to practise landscape painting, a slightly more acceptable subject than the four-legged possessions of gentlemen, through the backgrounds which he incorporated into many of his works, such as the image of Lydiard Park.[28]

While a bachelor might behave in an extravagant or irresponsible way, the risks Bully took through his public passion were rather less attractive in a married man. Overall, he lost far more than he ever won, for although the prize for winning could be four or five hundred guineas per race, the costs of horse maintenance remained constant and high. Lord March described such Newmarket dilemmas to Selwyn at the end of a typical season: 'The Meeting has ended very ill and I am now a *mille* lower in cash than when we parted ... Bully, Lord Wilmington and myself are left here to reflect coolly on our losses and the nonsense of keeping running horses.' There were swings and roundabouts: in October 1764, Williams reported that 'Bully is victorious'.[29]

And he took the further risk of riding his own racehorses; this reckless behaviour resulted in at least one serious fall which got into the newspapers. 'On Wednesday last, the Lord Viscount Bolingbroke had the misfortune to be thrown from his horse on the heath at

Newmarket, by which he received a violent contusion in his leg; but by the immediate assistance of a Surgeon, his Lordship is in a fair way of recovery', reported the *London Chronicle* on 15 July 1765.

Incidents such as these all contributed towards the erosion of his wife's trust and confidence, particularly after she became a successful brood mare herself in March 1761, when her first child, George Richard, was born. This was three and a half years after their marriage, enough delay to have put some little strain between them, since she was clearly failing to perform her side of the bargain, yet not quite long enough to provoke gossip about their relationship. And there was a precedent in her own mother, who had not become pregnant until the third year of marriage.

The later stages of pregnancy were made more stressful by growing anxiety about money and their future prospects. Lady Di was now well aware of Bully's resemblance to her late father, in the way he lavished sums he could not afford on the house and estate, as well as on his stables. There was also the time-consuming involvement with his horses and racing cronies, hardly desirable in a man about to become responsible for a family, and one who had little ambition for public office. At this time, she appeared to be devoted to him, and concerned to work for his success and stability. Two letters survive, written to her mother early in the year 1761, during the tedious final weeks before the birth ('I hope you will be at Langley by the time I am well again. I shall never be brought to bed, which is a terrible thing'). She was trying to obtain for Bully a lucrative sinecure in the round of appointments being made by the new King, George III, and his advisers – George II had died, unglamorously, on his close-stool on 25 October 1760 and his twenty-two-year-old grandson, eldest son of the late Frederick, Prince of Wales, now succeeded to the throne.

What is striking in Lady Di's support of her extravagant husband is her attitude of responsibility towards Bully – she is the stronger character, trying, like Sarah, to negotiate and fix things, despite her advanced pregnancy. She tries to use the power of family obligation, although seeming in some awe of her brother George, five years her junior: theirs was a relationship which was always dutiful rather than close. The Dowager Duchess of Marlborough was then in Bath; the young Duke, about to return from the Continent, had already been favoured by the new King by being appointed a lord of the bedchamber. It was a mark of Bully's indolence, lack of ambition and perhaps slightly tarnished reputation that he had not been included in the first round of handouts.

She asked for her mother's support in bringing additional pressure to bear on George to do something for Bully; this apparently followed a letter she had already written to George 'to ask a great favour of him, which he is certainly able to do for us, and by doing it will make Lord Bolingbroke, consequently me, happy.' She mentioned their 'exceeding bad circumstances' and the strain of 'perpetually seeing Lord B. uneasy' because as 'he endeavours always to make me happy, I can have no wish so strong as to relieve him from the uneasiness I know he is under'. As the Trevor family, her mother's kin, had already helped one son-in-law, Lord Pembroke, so should the house of Marlborough be prepared to help her husband. 'Without that assistance he will get nothing, and with it he may get anything . . . I shall think it hard if we, for want of assistance, should, in this year of Plenty, get nothing, who really and especially are in want of something.' George only had to ask because 'I may say that I positively know the King has taken an almost unaccountable partiality to him . . . the King and channel to him, Lord Bute, are in a very different style from their predecessors'. The preferred post would have been that of the King's Master of Foxhounds, fairly appropriate in the light of Bully's interests, but that had already been allocated because George was not there to speak up for them. This 'would have repaired Lord Bolingbroke's circumstances as to have made him easy forever, the salary is no less than £2000 a year. Good things which alone are worth asking for are as easily got, I observe, as little ones'. Failing Foxhounds, Bully would settle, at the same salary, for one of the posts connected with Ireland – 'more than one have been granted lately and I believe are not difficult to obtain . . . were my brother to say that it was a thing he *really* and *earnestly* wished, it would be done'. Ireland had long been seen as the ultimate sinecure: when Lord Hervey had accepted with great reluctance his dismissal from the post of Privy Seal by George II, he requested instead a position as Vice-Treasurer of Ireland at a pension of £2,000 a year.[30]

She felt that it was George's absolute duty to ask for this favour and tried emotional blackmail on her mother: 'these, Mama are my distresses and this is the only way I have to get Lord Bolingbroke and myself out of them'. But she realized that her brother needed a nudge from his mother, as well as his sister, to take any action, and that, as a diffident man, he could always write to the King if he was unwilling to speak directly. She concluded: 'I am really very miserable at present'. The Duchess must have written back, saying that she was sure George would help but that Di should have waited for him to return and ask in person, rather than urging him to write to the King, for this produced a slightly hysterical response: 'Writing may be disagreeable to him, nor would I have pressed him to do it but from the ever fullness of my heart when I wrote to him'.

For the stolid and taciturn Duke, these outbursts from an emotional sister on behalf of a man with whom he had little in common had no immediate effect. His reluctance to help Bully was fuelled by his awareness of the fact that the shy, unsure young King himself did not like this prospective attendant. By the summer of 1761, perhaps worn down by further complaints from his mother and sister, Marlborough did approach the King's mentor and 'Dearest Friend', Lord Bute, who promised to look into the matter. His discreet soundings produced a response from the King in August: 'Nothing can be more proper than the manner my Dearest Friend has wrote to the Duke of Marlborough. Indeed if Lord B coming into the Bedchamber can be of any utility, I will not object to it, though he is far from being a character agreeable to me'. This courteous but lukewarm reaction meant that Bully did not actually get a place until November 1762.[31]

For the birth of the Bolingbroke heir, Lady Di was attended by Dr William Hunter, a man who was another fine example of the success that could be achieved even by the unpopular Scots. Born and brought up in Glasgow, Hunter had come to London to advance his medical career; he studied and lodged with a fellow Scot, William Smellie, whose influential *Treatise on the Theory and Practice of Midwifery* (first published in 1752) was providing a revolutionary approach to childbirth. Hunter learned sufficiently fast to set up a profitable private academy of his own, where he taught anatomy and physiology, but he became best known for his obstetric skills. He obtained invaluable experience as Surgeon-Accoucheur at the recently founded Lying-In Hospital in London, itself an example of the better provision becoming available for mothers and babies – four maternity hospitals had been established in London since 1749 – and he began work on his definitive *Anatomy of the Gravid Uterus*, eventually published in 1775. Both he and his younger brother, the equally respected surgeon John Hunter, were pioneers in the remarkable developments in medicine and surgery which were taking place from the middle years of the century – John would even carry out an attempt at artificial insemination, in 1776. Their professional and financial success was commemorated in William's acquisition of works of art, rare books, coins and medals, the foundation of the Hunterian collection in Glasgow (on which it has been calculated that he spent around £100,000) and by John's extensive anatomical and scientific collections, together with two menageries in London (where Stubbs was commissioned to paint the rhinoceros).[32]

It was a significant change of procedure, that births were coming to be supervised by men rather than women, and the former dominance of the midwife was undermined by new, rational attitudes to childbirth. These included the setting of professional standards through the study of anatomy and the medical education and training available to men but not to women. A new breed of 'men-midwives' was replacing the all-female support system for pregnancy and birth, their role heralded by William Cadogan, in his *An Essay Upon Nursing* (1748): 'the Preservation of Children should become the Care of Men of Sense because the business has been too long fatally left to the Management of Women'; one element in this care was the use of forceps, which only a clinically trained man was permitted to use. The new profession was attacked not only by female midwives for gravely undermining their own status, but also by male commentators during the 1760s and '70s on the grounds of the 'hands-on' nature of the job, involving physical and therefore genital intervention. Conventional doctors hardly undertook any form of physical examination, and indeed the role of the doctor itself was socially ambiguous, transgressing class boundaries let alone those of the body. The terms 'Man-midwife' or the equally derogatory 'Nightman' were used to imply the dubious status and propriety of the role, and it is significant that Hunter described himself as a Doctor of Physic while others referred to him as the man-midwife, and Horace Walpole, in a double insult, as the 'Scotch Nightman'. Scottishness was a grave hurdle at a time when the whole nation was still resented for its perceived support of the Young Pretender during the 'Forty-Five. And there was an additional focus in specific hostility to the most influential Scotsman of the day, the Earl of Bute, who was seen as a sinister power behind the throne through his rumoured affair with the young King's mother. (James Boswell's first words on meeting his hero Dr Johnson in 1763 were: 'I do indeed come from Scotland but I cannot help it', to which Johnson unkindly responded: 'That, Sir, I find is what a very great number of your countrymen cannot help'.)[33]

By 1761, Hunter, then aged forty-one, was in great demand as accoucheur to polite society and was the obvious choice for the Bolingbrokes, undoubtedly recommended by other satisfied clients not only for his medical reputation but also for his urbane and polished manner: his contemporary biographer commented on how 'he had such an appearance of attention to his patients when he was making his enquiries as could hardly fail to conciliate their confidence and esteem'. For a doctor, the care of the aristocracy through attachment to a great family and subsequent recommendation to others was a crucial stage in a career in which a successful man might earn £10,000 a year, a measure of considerable success. His approach to childbirth was as non-interventionist as possible – 'labour is not a disease' he said – while still justifying the substantial fee of ten guineas which he charged to people of fashion. His 'treatment' might include the recommendation of blood-letting in the final month of pregnancy (which would not be undertaken by the great man himself, but by a surgeon under his supervision), his selection of a reliable midwife to perform the actual delivery (in which he would not be directly involved unless there were complications) and the prescription of appropriate medicines and advice during the four-week lying-in period, which included his innovatory recommendation that the new mother should get up as soon as she was able.[34]

For Lady Di, his support was entirely successful, and she gave birth to a healthy boy on 5 March 1761, who was baptized George Richard in St George's, Hanover Square. As she became pregnant again three or four months later, she was not breast-feeding the baby, nor would she have been expected to; women of her class employed a wet-nurse, and the recommendation of a reliable nurse might have been another of Dr Hunter's functions. As well as nursery staff, she was employing at this time a gentlewoman, Rachel Lloyd, who was more of a companion than a housekeeper, and who stayed until the end of 1764 when she left to become head housekeeper at Kensington Palace.[35]

FOUR

The Lady in Waiting

(1761–63)

*'The circle of our employments moves in such unchangeable
revolutions that you have but to look at your watch any hour
in the four & twenty and tell yourself what we are doing as
well as if you were here, for as it was in the beginning is now
& ever shall be, Court without End, Amen'*

LORD HERVEY

In that spring of 1761, as she recovered from the birth of her son and
continued to worry about money, Lady Di's name was on a speculative
list of new appointments to the royal household following King
George III's choice of bride and Queen-elect. As the daughter of a
duke and wife of a viscount, Lady Di was an entirely suitable
candidate, and was mentioned by Henry Fox when he reported the
rumours to Caroline in April: 'They talk very strongly about a white
Princess of Brunswick, about 15, to be our new Queen, & so strongly
that one can hardly help believing it, tho' with no good or particular
authority. They make the Dss of Portland her Groom of the Stole; Dss
of Hamilton, Dss of Ancaster, Lady Northumberland and Lady
Bolingbroke, 4 of her Ladys of the Bedchamber . . . not one of these
conjectures may be true for aught I know.'[1]

The whole issue was of considerable interest to Fox at this time,
because his sister-in-law Sal Lennox had been considered, by the Fox
family at least, as a prospective royal bride, or even for the more
influential post of prospective royal mistress. (The latter was certainly

the interpretation of the Earl of Bute's own daughter, Lady Louisa Stuart.) Two years earlier Sal had so caught the fancy of George, when Prince of Wales, that the virtuous young man had been forced to confess his feelings to his mentor Bute, and to ask whether she would realistically be acceptable as a future queen. With Bute's less than impartial guidance, he was encouraged to reach the mature conclusion that he had to make an appropriate dynastic marriage, and not one to an English girl descended from a Stuart king's mistress, with a devious opposition politician for a brother-in-law. It had to be a Protestant German princess, of whom there were a number available. George's search for a wife was given added urgency following his accession in October 1760. There had to be a coronation, sooner rather than later, but to achieve its full impact there had to be a Queen as well as a King.

Public conjecture over the bride's identity continued during May and June but George had been secretly researching and consulting since the previous autumn, anxious to find someone suitably born and capable of doing justice to the great role he was offering her, but whom he also found physically attractive (something which could only be ascertained by proxy). She should also be of a docile and domestic character: he had observed all too well the machinations of his own mother and felt very strongly that his wife should never seek to meddle in political matters.

Sowing his final, chaste wild oats through a renewed public flirtation with Sal Lennox, when he passed on laborious compliments via her best friend, made eyes at her and singled her out for attention repeatedly, in fact the devious King had already chosen a wife – Princess Sophie Charlotte of Mecklenburg-Strelitz, a girl of barely seventeen, agreed by those who had inspected and those who knew her to be of pleasant character, musical, healthy, and mercifully unmarked by the smallpox which she had survived (and which destroyed the looks of so many women). The only reservation was whether her upbringing in this very small and obscure provincial court had provided her with sufficient social skills and confidence for successful transformation into the Queen of Great Britain; it was hoped that, given her obliging and courteous nature, this could be overcome. Although 'not a Beauty', according to Colonel Graeme, sent by Bute as bearer of the official proposal of marriage, 'what is little inferior, she is Amiable'.

The King informed the Privy Council of his choice on 8 July 1761, describing Charlotte as 'a Princess distinguished by every eminent virtue and amiable endowment, whose illustrious line has constantly shown the firmest zeal for the Protestant religion and a particular attachment to my family'. Walpole reported this statement, and renewed the speculation about the royal household: 'The solemn manner of summoning the Council was very extraordinary: people little imagined that *the urgent and important business* in the rescript was to acquaint them that His Majesty was going to lose his maidenhead. You may choose what complexion you like for the new Queen: every colour under the sun is given to her' ... 'Lists there are in abundance; I don't know the authentic; these most talked of are Lady Bute, groom of the stole, the Duchesses of Hamilton and Ancaster, Lady Northumberland, Bolingbroke, Weymouth, Scarborough, Abergavenny, Effingham for Ladies; you may choose any six you please, the four first are most probable'.[2]

By 23 July, Walpole was proved correct: the Queen's household was announced, with Viscountess Bolingbroke confirmed as a lady of the bedchamber, together with the Duchess of Hamilton, Lady Effingham, Lady Northumberland, Lady Egremont and Lady Weymouth, under the Duchess of Ancaster in the senior post of Mistress of the Robes. Their appointments officially commenced on 1 August 1761.

The selection of the members of the Queen's household had to reconcile satisfying the ambitions of the various, and sometimes rival, noble families at the same time as choosing women who would be worthy of the honour of the Queen's confidence and company. The Queen's attendants consisted of Maids of Honour and Ladies of the Bedchamber. Maids were recruited from the unmarried daughters of peers, Ladies were the wives or married daughters of peers. The posts were an honour and a mark of rank, but also a source of income, perquisites and patronage through the receipt and donation of favours as a result of being thought to have the ear of the monarch. Sarah Churchill, the chief attendant to Queen Anne as Mistress of the Robes, was a prime example of what could be achieved through the power which she had wielded and money which she had amassed. The salary of Mistress of the Robes was £800 per annum, a bedchamber lady received £500, and a maid of honour £300. One additional benefit was the acquisition of royal cast-offs, garments made at vast expense and hardly worn – Queen Charlotte was later to complain that 'I give away lace and gowns which I never did wear but once'. There were also gifts of presents and money, sometimes in the form of dowries or pensions, as well as sinecures for friends and family.[3]

Charlotte's Ladies were selected by Lord Bute, the King's most trusted adviser; his intention was not to provide friendship and support for a very young Queen completely unfamiliar with the ways of the English court or the English language, but to demonstrate his own powers of patronage and reinforce the obligations of those families for whom he had provided this sought-after honour and source of income. A fulsome letter written by Bully to Lord Bute just before the public announcement of the posts shows how these things were fixed: 'Lady Bolingbroke tells me she has just learn't from Lady Bute, by your Lordship's service, that she may depend upon having the honour to be one of the Ladys of the Bedchamber to the Queen, and though it is not yet made public, I feel myself impatient to return your Lordship a great many thanks both from her and myself for your goodness upon this occasion, and to assure your Lordship that you have obliged no one more sensible of an obligation, and less likely to forget it, than I am, who have the honour to be with great respect, Your Lordship's most obedient and obliged humble servant, Boling-broke.' This also implies the significant role of Lady Bute, who, despite having no official status whatever, was, as the wife of a great man, able to wield her own backstage patronage. Her mother, Lady Mary Wortley Montagu, had achieved her own independence through deciding to live apart from her husband, but this was at the price of having to live abroad. Lady Bute obtained her satisfaction through working from the centre.[4]

The new Bedchamber Ladies were all well known to each other from the elite circles in which they moved. They were all somewhat older than their new Queen, with Lady Di, at twenty-six, the youngest. Lady Weymouth was twenty-seven; she was the daughter of the Duke and Duchess of Portland, Mrs Delany's artistic 'Lady Betty', someone who would later be described by a fellow royal attendant as 'hard and unpleasant in her manners and so inferior to her charming mother the Duchess of Portland . . . that I cannot see her without surprise as well as disappointment'. This critical comment was made by Fanny Burney, the shy but sharp-eyed novelist, who had an unhappy stint attending the Queen in the 1780s, and whose journals provide the most painful insights into the true nature of court service. Lady Weymouth's husband, who shared Bully's general interests, had been appointed the Queen's Master of Horse. The Mistress of the Robes was the Duchess of Ancaster, now in her thirties. Although qualified for the position through marriage to a peer, she was an interesting example of how a woman could improve her status through the fluidity of the racing world, for her father was no peer but Thomas Panton of Newmarket, 'a disreputable horse jockey' according to Walpole. He was exaggerating as usual (as when he claimed that the last three Duchesses of Ancaster 'were never sober') for Panton was the trainer whose daughter had become the second wife of the Duke of Ancaster. The Duke, an ultra-loyal Hanoverian, was rewarded by Bute not only through his wife's prestigious appointment but also by her father being made Master of the King's running horses, and her brother one of the King's equerries. She had produced four children and was currently expecting a fifth. Fanny Burney would award her rare praise as being 'easy, obliging, unaffected and well-bred'.[5]

The next senior post, that of First Lady of the Bedchamber, also went to a woman distinguished by marriage rather than birth. The Duchess of Hamilton, two years older than Lady Di, was the former Elizabeth Gunning, a statuesque beauty, and the younger sister of the late Lady Coventry, Bully's former love. Elizabeth's impressive marriage to the Duke of Hamilton had left her a widow in 1757; two years later she married John Campbell, prospective heir to the Duke of Argyll, but she retained the more prestigious title of Duchess of Hamilton. At the time of the royal wedding, she was embroiled in a long-running court case defending her son's inheritance of the estates of the Duke of Douglas against an allegedly bogus claimant. The oldest Bedchamber Lady was Lady Northumberland, aged forty-five. She was the granddaughter of another Mistress of the Robes to Queen Anne; to emphasize the family links with the court, her husband was appointed Lord Chamberlain to Queen Charlotte.

The actual function of these Ladies of the Bedchamber, despite their title, was that of public not private attendance. Earlier in the century, the post had entailed duties in the royal bedchamber, supervising the Queen's getting up and being dressed at the hands of the lower rank of Bedchamber Women. Now the Ladies had no official reason to go near the bedchamber or dressing-room, since the Queen was actually dressed by her Wardrobe Woman under the supervision of one of the two Keepers of the Robes (whose job was defined by that later incumbent, Fanny Burney, as having 'nothing to do but *attend*'). On days when the Queen made public appearances, the Bedchamber Woman on duty was responsible for putting on the Queen's necklace, handing over her fan and gloves, and carrying her train to the ante-room; here the higher-ranking Bedchamber Lady was summoned to take over at the moment of transition as the Queen moved into public view.

Many of these duties were rituals which had fossilized since the reign of Queen Anne (and which would still be rigidly adhered to in the 1780s and '90s). In 1728, Abigail Masham, who had been appointed Bedchamber Woman to Queen Anne by Sarah Churchill (and who then supplanted Sarah in the Queen's affections), was approached for guidance over the demarcation lines between Woman and Lady by Henrietta Howard, a newly appointed Bedchamber Lady to Queen Caroline. Henrietta, as an ex-mistress of Caroline's husband George II, was clearly concerned to establish the superior nature of the Lady's duties. As defined by Abigail, 'The Bedchamber-woman came into waiting before the Queen dressed . . . the Bedchamber-woman gave the [Queen's] shift to the Bedchamber-lady and the Bedchamber-lady put it on. Sometimes the Bedchamber-woman gave the fan to the Bedchamber-lady. This was all that the Bedchamber-lady did about the Queen at her dressing. When the Queen washed her hands, the page of the back-stairs brought basin and ewer on a side table. The Bedchamber-woman set it before the Queen; the Bedchamber-lady only looked on . . . when the Queen dined in public, the page reached her glass to the Bedchamber-woman, and she to the Lady in waiting . . . in general the Bedchamber-woman had no dependence on the Lady of the Bedchamber'.[6]

The attitude of Queen Charlotte's Ladies to their new mistress was probably more than a little contemptuous and patronizing – a seventeen-year-old from a remote foreign court which no one had ever heard of (Walpole hoped that Lord Harcourt, the King's emissary sent to escort the bride to England, could find it), an unsophisticated, plain girl who spoke no English, a German (like the rest of the unpopular royal family) when all the standards of fashion and taste were set by France and Italy – but they all hoped to get something out of it. Lady Di's earlier anxiety to arrange a place for Bully was now alleviated by her own appointment, for which he too was profoundly grateful, both for the salary and for the influence which she might wield. Lady

Northumberland later defined her own motivation in soliciting the post as having 'no other view than as a demonstration of my respect for your Majesty and as an honour and pleasure to myself' but this was only half the story.[7]

The Ladies were meant to begin their duties on 1 August 1761; this reflected the King's intention of holding the wedding ceremony as soon as possible after the announcement of his betrothal on 8 July. However Charlotte's journey to England was delayed until early September because she had to go into mourning for her mother, who died suddenly in the middle of July. The Coronation itself was irrevocably fixed for 22 September.

Lady Di was lucky not to be one of the Ladies selected to cross the North Sea as part of the Queen-elect's retinue sent to escort her back to England. The most fitting were the two Duchesses, as Mistress of the Robes and First Lady of the Bedchamber. The details of their journey spread: one noble lady wrote to another, 'I suppose you know the two duchesses appointed to convey her intended majesty. That of Hamilton has made great interest to take her ass with her, which she has done and it is hoped may come back alive. The Duchess of Ancaster only takes a surgeon and midwife, as she is breeding and subject to hysteric fits'. There are no further references to the presence of the ass in the various accounts of the fetching of the bride, so perhaps this story was a wild invention. (However, asses' milk was a fashionable and therapeutic product at this time, available from London tradesmen, such as James Jones at the Ass and Foal, who was advertising supplies of milk or asses to rent on a monthly basis.)[8]

It was a gruelling expedition for all. The bridal fleet sailed to the mouth of the Elbe, from where the two Ladies and other members of the welcoming party were taken up river to the port of Stade, in Hanover, to meet Charlotte's triumphal carriage procession from her home in Strelitz, further up the Baltic coast. The duchesses sailed out in the *Mary*, and returned with their new mistress in the luxuriously refitted royal yacht the *Royal Charlotte*. It had been planned that after the return crossing the fleet should sail up the Thames to London, so that Charlotte and her retinue could disembark at Greenwich then drive to St James's Palace in a grand public display. Although the outward journey passed without incident, the return was a nightmare for all, as early autumn storms whipped up the North Sea, turning the expected three-day crossing into a nine-day ordeal. The duchesses were both reported to be extremely seasick, while the plucky Charlotte was presented as a fine sailor. The battered fleet was eventually forced to land at Harwich, and the planned Thames route to London had to be abandoned. The bridal party then spent nearly another two days on the road. The Princess, accompanied by the two Duchesses, at last entered London in the hastily redirected royal coach on the afternoon of 8 September.

The stamina of Charlotte and her Ladies has to be admired, for the Royal Wedding was to take place that very evening. When they neared the Palace of St James's, where she was to have her first meeting with the King, Walpole records (presumably reported to him by one of the Duchesses present) how the Princess grew frightened and turned pale at the thought of her imminent marriage. 'The Duchess of Hamilton smiled – the Princess said, "My dear Duchess, you may laugh, you have been married twice but it is no joke to me".' Lady Northumberland was also informed by the Duchess how 'the Princess was a good deal agitated and when she came into the Parks was almost ready to faint'. Having survived her first encounter with the King, Charlotte had to sit down to dinner with other members of the royal family, this break providing just enough time for the Duchesses to change out of their travelling clothes. The bride was then dressed for her wedding, on one of the hottest nights of the year, in a silver-stiffened gown with a purple velvet train lined with ermine, weighed down with diamonds and pearls – Walpole noted that this was so heavy, what with the pearls, that it 'dragged itself and almost the rest of her clothes, half way down her waist'. The trembling figure was now introduced formally to the court; she greeted the peeresses, including Lady Di, with a kiss on the cheek. She then met the glittering procession of bridesmaids who were to bear her heavy train; the strain was beginning to show, for she murmured 'Mon Dieu, il y en a tant, il y en a tant'.[9]

Reactions to this brave little figure confirm that the bride was not beautiful but had a certain presence. Walpole's first impressions were that 'she is not tall nor a beauty but looks sensible and genteel . . . her nose very well except the nostrils spreading too wide. The mouth has the same fault but her teeth are good'. (Good teeth were regarded as crucial to looks, as shown by Sarah Churchill's comments on the allegedly poor teeth of the new Duchess of Marlborough.) A later observer, the daughter of Charlotte's page and hairdresser, who would herself serve in the royal wardrobe, confirmed that 'she was certainly not a beauty but her countenance was very expressive and showed extreme intelligence ... her eyes bright and sparkling with good humour and vivacity; her mouth large but filled with white and even teeth'. The Duchess of Hamilton, a superior beauty, ungenerously described her royal mistress as 'niggardly endowed by nature with any charms to render her desirable'. And the portrait painter Northcote referred to her having 'not a vulgar but an elegant plainness'. It was felt that her appearance improved as she became older – her Lord Chamberlain, Colonel Disbrowe, was later quoted as saying that 'the bloom of her ugliness is going off'.[10]

This first evening of public scrutiny was described in the diary of Lady Di's fellow attendant Lady Northumberland: 'At half an hour after Seven, everybody assembled at St James's. The Peers, Peeresses & Peers' Daughters waited in the King's levée room till the procession began and proceeded down the great stairs ... on her head a little cap of purple velvet quite covered with diamonds, a diamond aigrette in form of a crown, 3 dropt diamond ear rings, diamond necklace, diamond sprigs of flowers on her sleeves & to clasp back her robe, a diamond stomacher, her purple velvet mantle was laced with gold and lined with ermine. It was fastened on the shoulders with large tassells of pearls. It was carried by the 10 following young ladies, all dressed alike in stiffen'd bodied gowns of white silk, the stays and sleeves embroidered and their petticoats trimmed with silver and all adorn'd with a great number of jewells'. The leading bridesmaid was Sal Lennox, who had managed to overcome her sense of rejection in order to play her rightful part in such a grand ceremony. Amongst the others were her rival in the marriage market, Lady Caro Russell, and her best friend and cousin Lady Susan Fox-Strangways.[11]

The increasing pomp attached to royal weddings had already attracted the sarcasm of Sarah Churchill thirty years earlier, when the Princess Royal married the Prince of Orange in 1733: 'I have heard that the peers and peeresses are to be summoned to walk at this great ceremony ... the peeresses are to walk in gowns as they did at the coronation. This must put them to great expense, which is no matter since I think that none but simple people and sad wretches will do it'.[12]

Lady Di, who cannot have been very comfortable since she was in the early stages of her second pregnancy, and the other Bedchamber

Ladies formed part of the Queen's procession to the Chapel Royal on that sweltering evening, heralded by drummers and trumpeters. They stood on one side of the Chapel awaiting the arrival of the King, who, like Charlotte, was clad in silver. The marriage ceremony was performed by the Archbishop of Canterbury. When the King placed the ring on his wife's finger, gun salutes reverberated from the Park and from the Tower of London. The scene was recorded for posterity by the up and coming society painter Joshua Reynolds, who had already painted George when Prince of Wales (although that work had not impressed the King enough for him to buy it). Reynolds was allowed to sit up in the gallery sketching the actors in this drama; he produced a rough version in oils, but did not receive a commission to produce the final version. Perhaps it was not grandiose enough: the couple are off centre, there is an expanse of what looks like empty floor (actually a carpet of silver cloth) in the foreground, and indistinct clumps of bridesmaids and Bedchamber Ladies to left and right.

The ceremony lasted for about an hour. Then the King and Queen, followed by her Bedchamber Ladies, processed back to the Palace where there was a grand supper for the whole wedding party, and a private one for the royal family. Here, according to Walpole, Charlotte sang and played the harpsichord after she and the King had formally welcomed their guests. She was undressed by the two German women attendants who had accompanied her from Germany, although an unenthusiastic Duchess of Hamilton noted that 'she insisted on sleeping in her stiff stays, a German piece of prudery to which, I imagine, the king had no objection'. The King and Queen were eventually left alone at around three o'clock in the morning.[13]

The Bedchamber Ladies were all involved during the public celebrations of the Royal Wedding. On the day after the ceremony there was a Drawing Room, one of those formal afternoon receptions which required the wearing of the ostentatious and by now rather archaic court dress: the gown known as a mantua, with pleated back and long train, worn with stiffened stomacher over an underskirt which was extended sideways by a massive oblong whalebone hoop, a fashion which was otherwise virtually obsolete. The ensemble was topped off by ornamental head-gear of trailing lace lappets or feathers, and a lavish display of jewellery. The Drawing Room was followed by a ball in the evening. Lady Northumberland recorded that the Ladies attended her Majesty to the ball, where 'everything was vastly well conducted, nor was it too hot, notwithstanding there were a vast many people (all very magnificently dressed) ... His Majesty this evening shew'd the most engaging attention towards the Queen, even to the taking of Snuff (of which her Majesty is very fond) which he detests & it made him sneeze prodigiously.' On the next day, 10 September, the by now exhausted Ladies were still on duty at a second Drawing Room 'where the crowd was less than on the foregoing day ... when we attended her Majesty back to her Dressing Room, her train caught on the fender and drew it into the midst of the room. I disengaged her. She laughed very heartily and told me a droll story of the Princess of Prussia having drawn a lighted billet out of the chimney and carrying it through the apartment firing the mat all the way she went'.[14]

Four days later, there was a new treat for the Queen (although one familiar to her sophisticated Ladies) when she went to the theatre for the first time in her life: all dramatic entertainments were forbidden in puritanical Mecklenberg on the grounds that they would promote dissipation and idleness. The King had ordered a command performance at Drury Lane Theatre, starring England's greatest actor, David Garrick, in the comedy which he had also written, *The Rehearsal*. This was Charlotte's first public appearance as Queen outside the confines of the court. After the first shock of finding herself the focus of attention of so many people, she enjoyed the play, well chosen by the King for its slapstick, singing and dancing, easy to appreciate by someone not yet able to understand the dialogue. This was the first of many visits by the Queen to the theatre, and Walpole noted how 'the crowds at the Opera and play when the King and Queen go are a little greater than what I remember'. He added that 'the Queen is so gay that we shall not want sights; she has been at the Opera, *The Beggar's Opera* and *The Rehearsal*, and two nights ago carried the King to Ranelagh'. At *The Beggar's Opera*, the royal party plus Ladies had to squeeze seventeen in one box and were cheered outside the theatre by an excited crowd. Two months later, the Queen's enthusiasm had not waned: 'Diversions you know, Madam, are never at high-water mark before Christmas: yet operas flourish pretty well; those on Tuesdays are removed to Mondays, because the Queen likes the burlettas and the King cannot go on Tuesdays'.[15]

There was a lull before the Coronation, when the King and Queen, accompanied by the Ladies on duty, left London to visit their summer palace at Richmond; this was where his father had started to lay out gardens at Kew, and where the project was continued by his mother, under the encouragement of the botanically minded Lord Bute; the gardens had been recently embellished by an orangery and by the pagoda designed by the King's tutor in architecture, William Chambers.

The Coronation, on 22 September, was the final culmination of these hectic weeks, placing further strains on wardrobes and energies. This thoroughly choreographed but still chaotic spectacle – 'in the morning they had forgot the Sword of State, the chairs for the King and Queen and their canopies', according to Walpole – was an affirmation of the stability of the Hanoverian dynasty, marking at last the accession of a young king and one who had actually been born in England; there was also the opportunity of inspiring further patriotic support through the image of a fairytale young couple, crucial for a dynasty not too well established in the public's affection. There was such demand to see the Coronation that, Walpole reported, an apartment overlooking the route was rented out for three hundred and fifty guineas, while seats in the Abbey cost ten guineas. In order to claim their seats, spectators had to be there soon after dawn, and those lodging nearby were kept awake from midnight through the 'hammering of scaffolds, shouting of people, relieving guards and jangling bells'.

The day started very early for Ladies of the Bedchamber. Lady Northumberland rose at half-past four, in order to complete her own coiffure and elaborate toilette before setting off to wait for the Queen in the Painted Chamber at Westminster Hall, where the royal party arrived at nine. Here assembled all those who were to take part in the great procession to the Abbey, led by the medieval figures of the King's Herb Woman and her maidens strewing flowers. This gathering was described by Lady Northumberland as 'a glorious coup d'œil, 6000 well-dressed spectators'. The peeresses wore their state coronation robes – for Lady Di, as a viscountess, this was of crimson velvet, ermine trimmed, with the train a yard and a quarter long. She carried her coronet – sixteen pearls, crimson velvet cap lined with ermine, plus gold tassel – until permitted to place it on her head after the Queen had been crowned. Emily Kildare had been planning her outfit since early August, as usual hinting about the cost to her generous husband: 'I have got the same velvet and petticoat for the Coronation as Lady Harrington. She took all the trouble of it for me. Only think how dear everything is; the gold rope that is to go round our waists and tie the mantle on the shoulders, the Duchess of Richmond gave £18 for this morning! I have not got mine; I hope Mr Sanxey will let me have it cheaper; it looks not worth above two or three guineas. How can the poor Scotch peeresses afford to walk?'[16]

Lady Di appeared in public blatantly wearing make-up, with the active involvement of her husband. This daringly modern behaviour attracted the notice of Walpole: 'Lord Bolingbroke put on rouge upon his wife and the Duchess of Bedford in the Painted Chamber; the Duchess of Queensberry told me of the latter, that she looked like an orange-peach, half red and half yellow'. However, Lady Northumberland thought the Duchess much improved by the make-up, which 'became her vastly and made her look like Lady Caroline'. The use of rouge was another insidious French fashion creeping its way into acceptance – only ten years earlier a visitor from France had reported that in England 'the women use no paint'. And another critical Continental visitor writing in 1755 described the 'art which as yet is only in its infancy in England, the barbarous art of daubing one's cheeks with glaring red. Some English ladies begin to use it a little, but still with such moderation as to flatter themselves that they are not suspected'. In the 1750s and '60s imported cosmetics were luxuries which attracted high customs duties; some of the ingredients employed to redden the cheeks, such as red lead, sulphur or mercury, were as dangerous as those which whitened the skin. But there were also more innocuous types of rouge, which could be made from the cochineal dye from crushed insects, powdered wood shavings from Brazil boiled in red wine, or ready-prepared blushers of 'Spanish wool'.[17]

From the account books of the Bedford family, we learn that the Duke, Duchess and Lady Caroline all commissioned costly new robes for the occasion. The Duke had the important ceremonial role of Lord High Constable, which involved having to ride a fractious horse into Westminster Hall and then make it exit backwards, since neither man nor beast was allowed to turn its back on the King. His ladies wore hooped skirts decorated with silver embroideries, nets and tassels. The Spencers also had prominent positions at the Coronation: as well as Lady Di in the Queen's train, Lady Pembroke led the procession of countesses and the Duke of Marlborough marched as bearer of the sceptre and cross.

The very long ceremony in Westminster Abbey (where the Queen and, one hopes, her Ladies, particularly those who were breeding, had access to a close-stool hidden discreetly behind the altar) started so late that it was dusk before it finished. The spectators, many of whom had been in their places for twelve hours, were consequently unable to see properly the grand procession back to Westminster Hall for the coronation banquet. Lady Northumberland, exhausted by her early start and clearly having had enough of the day, crossly recounts how it was 'almost dark and very cold walking back; halted half an hour at angle of streets where blew a cutting wind'. When the King and Queen finally entered Westminster Hall, there was a magical moment when three thousand candles suddenly burst into light, showering hot wax to the alarm of those seated below. Considering the timber hammerbeam roof of the ancient hall, the whole gala could have ended in disaster. The nobility were seated at long tables, under the hungry eyes of spectators in especially constructed upper galleries who sent down baskets and slings to haul up food supplies from the table. Lady Di and her fellow peers and peeresses were offered three separate courses, each with a selection of one hundred dishes. As the feast did not even begin until after six in the evening, and as the various covers were interspersed by pageantry from the mounted earls, many more hours passed before the participants were able to escape. The leading performers, the King and Queen, returned to their palace for some light gruel.

Walpole provided copious descriptions of the ceremonies and entertainments to his various out-of-London correspondents:

Oh the buzz, the prattle, the noise, the hurry . . . the Hall was the most glorious, the blaze of lights, the richness and variety of habits, the ceremonial, the benches of peers and peeresses, frequent and full was as awful as a pageant can be . . . the habit of the peers is unbecoming to the last degree; but the peeresses made amends for all defects . . . Lady Kildare and Lady Pembroke were as handsome as the Graces. Lady Rochford, Lady Holderness and Lady Lyttleton look exceedingly well in that, their day; and for those of the day before, the Duchess of Queensbury, Lady Westmorland and Lady Albemarle were surprising. Lady Harrington was noble at a distance and so covered with diamonds, that you would have thought she had bid somebody or other, like Falstaff, *rob me the Exchequer*. Lady Northampton was very magnificent too, and looked prettier than I have seen her of late. Lady Spencer and Lady Bolingbroke were not the worst figures there . . . Well, it was all delightful, but not half so charming as its being over. The gabble one heard about it for six weeks before and the fatigue of the day, could not well be compensated by a mere puppet-show; for puppet-show it was, though it cost a million.

The next official engagement for the Queen and her Ladies was Lord Mayor's Day in the City of London on 9 November. The royal party watched the Lord Mayor's procession from the balcony of a house in Cheapside, the home of the Barclay family, which provided an excellent view. The Queen was attended by two of her Ladies, one of whom interpreted for her in French. A round-eyed young Barclay later described the events, including how the Queen drank tea, which had been brought on a silver salver delivered to the lady in waiting, who then kneeled to present it to the Queen. This was followed by a banquet in the Guildhall, as lavish as that of the coronation, where the Lords and Ladies in Waiting sat at their own table; then there was a great torchlit procession home to the palace at one in the morning.[18]

The growth of any close relationship between the Queen and her Ladies was inhibited by two factors already in evidence during those early weeks, which would established a permanent pattern. Charlotte had been allowed to bring from Mecklenberg two attendants, Mmes Schwellenberg and Hagedorn, as well as her young page, Frederick Albert (who was hastily compelled to marry his sweetheart before setting off for England, so that she could join him with propriety later on). The Queen inevitably felt closer to these familiars – promising Albert for example 'that he should be her constant and confidential attendant' – who spoke her own language and represented a link with her late mother. Juliana Elisabeth Schwellenberg, who was appointed Keeper of the Robes, was loyal to the extreme in the service of her young mistress, but became ever more protocol-minded as she got older. In the early days, she must almost have taken the place of a mother for Charlotte, who had so suddenly lost her own, with no time to mourn. Schwellenberg therefore provided a link with home and past.[19]

The best-known descriptions of her behaviour and character are the very biased ones provided by the ultra-sensitive and unhappy Fanny Burney, whose service at court was made a misery by Schwellenberg. But other commentators also believed that 'Schwelly' contributed to the Queen's isolation through her jealousy towards anyone who attracted her mistress's affection and attention. One of these was her fellow-countryman, Albert, the Queen's page, who suggested that her influence came to be so dominating that the King tried to have her sent back to Germany. This move was allegedly resisted by the Queen 'not so much from sorrow with parting from her, as from regret that so unpleasant a circumstance should have happened'. Albert certainly felt that 'the overbearing disposition of this woman did disturb the harmony of the circle'. The Lennox sisters recognized her power too, discussing this woman whom 'the Queen was vastly fond of, and who it is thought has vast influence with her'. From 1786, there are the accounts of Fanny Burney, appointed junior Keeper of the Robes following Hagedorn's retirement, of how Schwellenberg dominated the attendants of the royal household, controlled the Byzantine hierarchies of dining, tea-drinking and travelling, and had access to her mistress several times a day.[20]

A more detached witness who acknowledged Schwellenberg's power was Josiah Wedgwood. This ambitious entrepreneur, who had determined to change the status of the pottery produced by his old family firm in Staffordshire from a lowly craft to a high-status decorative art, had an alert sense of who were the useful contacts. When he and his smoother London partner, Thomas Bentley, wished to give a boost to ailing royal patronage, they realized that it was through Schwellenberg that they could get access to her mistress. Wedgwood wrote to Bentley how 'a little push further might be still made . . . though Mrs Shevel-inberg [sic] might not think it proper to mention the affair to the K or Q herself . . . I wish you would consult Mrs Sh-----g when you see her on Thursday with the Edged pattern about the propriety of its being mention'd to their Majestys'. He goes on to mention his hope of becoming Potter to the Prince of Wales at least, if not to the King: 'I think it would not be amiss just to mention that circumstance to Mrs Sh----g and hear what she says upon it.'[21]

The Bedchamber Ladies would have had little direct contact with Schwellenberg, since she was an element of the Queen's private life, but her backstage presence as the person whom Charlotte trusted was certainly a factor in the Queen's failure to develop closer relationships with her Ladies. The other main reason for the Queen's isolation was the King's determination to control his wife's behaviour. From the very beginning, he warned her that she should not 'attach herself strongly' to any of her Ladies; this expressed his firm belief that his Queen should concentrate her affections and interest entirely on himself and on their future family. She should look inward, and she should not risk putting herself into any form of potentially compromising relationship. His own miserable and lonely childhood had inspired his dream of an ideal family centred on a loyal and demure wife untainted by any court factions or decadent behaviour. The King would be later described by his own brother the Duke of Gloucester as 'delighted with having entirely under his own training a young innocent girl of 17 . . . and determined that she should be wholly devoted to him alone, and should have no other friend or society'. And the Duke went on to describe the Queen's 'miserably circumscribed life . . . except for the Ladies of the Bedchamber for half an hour a week in a funeral circle, she never had a soul to speak to except the King . . . and was hardly allowed to think without the leave of her husband'. This then became a habit: the Queen knew that she was not allowed to have close friends or favourites because of the damage this might inflict by making the royal family appear partial.[22]

So friendships with any of the Ladies were unlikely to be established, and there was a further handicap resulting from the rigid nature of court etiquette. After Charlotte's English had become fluent, she realized and regretted that people were inhibited from ever holding a dialogue with their sovereign. Mrs Delany, one of the very few people whose company Charlotte actively sought, would urge Fanny Burney not to reply to the King or Queen in monosyllables because 'the Queen often complains to me of the difficulty with which she can get any conversation, as she not only always has to start the subjects but commonly entirely to support them'. Duties for Lady Di and her colleagues were formal ones: attending the Queen at court and on public visits, and contributing to her official presence through their own rank and title. Some attendance was also required when the Queen was 'off duty', Lady Northumberland recording for example how she was requested to sit with the Queen while she was sewing, and during the weekly family concerts with her new brothers- and sisters-in law organized by the Queen in the early days of her marriage.[23]

Once the exceptional festivities celebrating the wedding and coronation were over, a routine was established which was in some ways faithful to the traditions of the earlier Hanoverians but at the same time reflected the aspirations of the King in presenting himself as an accessible modern ruler and the head of a family. There were the

Drawing Rooms at St James's Palace on Sundays and Thursdays, and additional court receptions to mark royal birthdays and New Year's Day. These all required new clothes for those attending, with appropriate head-dresses, jewellery and accessories, to impress one another and flaunt their loyalty to the Crown. Mrs Montague, the literary hostess, observed the Queen's Birthday reception in 1764: 'I never saw anything equal to the court on Wednesday. There was hardly a gentleman or gentlewoman in London who was not expiring under a load of finery. Indeed I was one of the fools myself'. There were royal visits, for duty and for pleasure, and trips to the more off-duty retreats of Richmond and Kew, where the King and Queen spent their summers until the refurbishment of Windsor Castle, which would become the King's favourite residence (its remoteness from London adding to the Queen's loneliness and depression), where he would publicly parade his wife and children in the grounds.[24]

Bedchamber Ladies served for periods of four weeks, arranged by rota. The fact that they were actually attended by their own maids was resented by the King. He described to his dearest friend a grave security breach in the royal household, when an intruder, whom he thought had been tipped off by one of these maids, had known where the key to the Queen's rooms was hidden: 'I wish to know what can be done to find out who acquainted him with the bedchamber woman's rooms and with the key being in the drawers, that makes me suspect that some of these Ladys' maids (for they always bring their own) must have instructed him'.[25]

For these sophisticated women, used to moving in the relative freedom obtained by marriage, aware of the foibles of drunken husbands, extravagant fathers, the thrill of flirtations and the fun of gossiping about the latest scandal, it must have been very difficult to endure the frozen nature of the Queen's circle. The court was never a happy place but always a hotbed of place-seeking and malice. Lord Bute's daughter, Lady Louisa Stuart, thought that things had not improved since the time of Queen Anne, whose Maids of Honour 'were as fond of spitefully teasing each other . . . as their successors in Queen Charlotte's train'.[26]

Waiting on the little doll-like Queen, stiff with diamonds, was made rigid by conventions both imposed and evolving. It was not permitted to sit in the presence of royalty, regardless of ill-health or pregnancy, the semi-permanent state of most women. Experienced attendants managed to find something to lean against secretly. If members of the royal family entered the room, everyone else had to back away towards the nearest wall. It was not permitted to turn one's back on royalty, nor could anyone leave a room before the royal person had left; if graciously dismissed the royal presence, one had to walk backwards out of the room. Twenty-five years on, Fanny Burney, after her first few weeks in royal service, described how 'I have come on prodigiously, by constant practice, in the power and skill of walking backwards, without tripping up my own heels, feeling my head giddy, or treading my train out of the pleats – accidents very frequent among novices'. And she describes a heroic backwards exit by the Duchess of Ancaster's daughter while suffering from a sprained ankle: 'backwards she went, perfectly upright, without one stumble, without ever looking once behind to see what she might encounter; and with as graceful a motion and as easy an air as I ever saw anybody enter a long room, she retreated, I am sure full twenty yards out of one'. Fanny was always torn between her genuine affection for the Queen, awareness of the ludicrous nature of the protocol, and terror at being found out doing the wrong thing. She was well aware that there was a limit to the Queen's charm and kindliness when faced with a breach of etiquette. It was rubbed in to Fanny, who had never solicited the job, what an honour a post in the Queen's household was, and how there were 'thousands of offered candidates, of high birth and rank, but small fortunes, who were waiting and supplicating for places'. Poor Fanny had simply been offered the position directly by the Queen because of her literary reputation and friendship with Mrs Delany, and did not have the courage to turn down such an honour without shaming her family.[27]

Some of the other hazards were listed by Fanny in the minutely detailed journal and letters which recorded for her family and fortunate posterity her stressful day to day life as a member of the royal household. Under *Directions for coughing, sneezing, or moving, before the King and Queen* ('I inquired into every particular, that no error might be committed') she satirically describes how it was more important to choke than let out an audible cough, better to break a blood vessel than sneeze out loud; and that you must not move an inch in the royal presence despite being in agony if, for example, you had been accidentally stabbed by a pin and were bleeding to death. Nor was it permitted, in the royal residences, for anyone to walk past the open door of a room occupied by a royal person; if you met them in the corridor, you had to back towards the nearest wall and stand stock-still. No one was allowed to speak in the presence of the King and Queen, except in response to something said by the royal couple. Eating in the royal presence was another forbidden activity. Fanny provides a hilarious account of a royal visit to Oxford, where, in the hall of Corpus Christi College, the King, Queen and Princesses sat down to a meal. But the famished and exhausted attendants, including two Bedchamber Ladies, who had not eaten since six in the morning, had to wolf down refreshments provided secretly by sympathetic dons, screened in turn by the other attendants. The Duchess of Ancaster, whose duties that day had included standing behind the Queen's chair while the latter ate her first course, 'was most happy to join our group and partake of our repast. The Duchess, extremely fatigued by standing, drew a small body of troops before her, that she might take a few minutes rest on a form'.[28]

The accounts of the first few months of the royal marriage suggest that before the annual childbearing began (although this admirable bride conceived less than two months after the wedding) the Queen did enjoy the gaiety of the London round, and her Ladies were, at the beginning, required to attend the visits to theatres and operas, receptions and balls. Within a very few years a different routine prevailed, which helped contribute to the Queen's later state of depression. They first moved from the central but cramped St James's Palace to the more spacious and rural Buckingham House, known as the Queen's House. As the family expanded, London ceased to be their focal point, the King preferring to detach his family from the metropolis. Walpole commented in the autumn of 1764 how 'the court, independent of politics, makes a strange figure. The recluse life led here at Richmond, which is carried to such an excess of privacy and economy that the Queen's *friseur* waits on them at dinner . . . disgusts all sorts of people. The Drawing-Rooms are abandoned: Lady Buckingham was the only woman there on Saturday se'nnight'. These must have proved dreary sessions for the Bedchamber Ladies on duty, since the court rapidly came to be seen as the epitome of dullness and dowdiness, the source of mocking laughter among smart circles: 'Buckingham House served as a byword – a signal for the onset of Ho! Ho! Ho! – and a mighty scope for satire was afforded by the Queen's wide mouth and occasionally imperfect English, as well as the King's trick of saying

What? What? his ill-made coats and general antipathy to the fashion'. And these followers of fashion were further annoyed by the Queen's support of the English clothing industry; in 1765 as a patriotic gesture of support for the weavers of Spitalfields, she 'not only herself wore gowns of English manufacture, but requested the ladies of her Court to do the same. This gave no small amount of dissatisfaction among a few, who prided themselves upon their French costumes'. This had little effect in smart circles, as Lady Sarah Bunbury implied in 1766: 'There is nobody but Lady Tavistock who does not dress French, who is at all genteel, for if they are not French they are so very ill-dressed it's terrible'.[29]

By 1768, Lady Northumberland was describing a puritanical regime, with the King and Queen in bed by eleven in the evening, so that he could get up soon after five, and get on with his papers. The Queen rose between six and seven, in order to join him for breakfast; she was washed and dressed, under the supervision of one of the Keepers of the Robes, by her wardrobe woman, for many years the German Mrs Thielky, described by Fanny Burney as 'the real acting person, though I am the apparent one'. For the Queen, there was a second more elaborate toilette in the middle of the day, which had to start earlier on Drawing Room and other public days, when the elaborate court dress was worn and her hairdresser attended for the complicated curling, craping and powdering. Once the Bedchamber Lady took over, the wardrobe woman and Keepers were released from duty. When the royal family stayed at Kew, they travelled in to St James's Palace for Drawing-Rooms; on these occasions the Queen had her hair done at Kew, but put on her massively hooped court dress at St James's. Those seeking to be presented to the King and Queen at one of the Drawing Rooms were meant to send in their names to the Lord Chamberlain's office in advance, in order to receive a ticket of admission; but for those who had omitted to do this, the wearing of appropriate dress generally provided entrée.

As well as being present in hoop and feathers at these public events, a Bedchamber Lady might also attend the Queen at private functions such as the ball described by Walpole: 'The night before last there was a private ball at court, which began at half an hour after six, lasted till one and finished without a supper. The King danced the whole time with the Queen, Lady Augusta with her four younger brothers. The other performers were the two Duchesses of Ancaster and Hamilton, who danced much . . . Lady Bolingbroke was there in waiting, but in black gloves and breeding, so did not dance'. The black gloves were the correct code of etiquette for marking the death of a parent – the Duchess of Marlborough had died on 7 October, after an autumn visit to Bath which had not provided the cure for her declining health. The King had rather disapprovingly noted this fact when inviting guests who would be willing to dance at his ball; he had intended including the Duke of Marlborough 'but I find from what Lady Bolingbroke said the other day none of that family chuse dancing, in their black gloves for their mother'.[30]

Her second pregnancy had hardly been restful; on 1 March 1762 she gave birth to a daughter loyally named Charlotte (to whom the Queen may have stood as godmother), whose baptism took place in St George's, Hanover Square on 25 March, the day after Lady Di's twenty-seventh birthday. But the baby died five months later, and was buried in the St John family vault at Battersea. Such frequent events had to be taken with the balance of stoicism and sadness expressed by Emily Kildare to her husband on the death of one of her babies in 1757: 'I did imagine you would be glad to hear that I was not too much affected with the death of the poor little child, which I have now quite got the better of, tho' I was much more grieved at first than I cou'd have thought it possible to have been for an infant that I cou'd know nothing of'. And that tough mother, Mrs Thrale, wrote unen-thusiastically about her fifth baby: 'a small weakly female Infant . . . she sucks well enough at present but is so very poor a Creature I can scarce bear to look on her'. But a baby aged five months is a very different creature from an unknown new-born, and a woman already neglected by her husband might have felt a deep sense of loss.[31]

Duties had to be resumed. Some idea of the stressful nature of royal service and the petty tensions between the Queen's attendants is suggested by Lady Northumberland, who, with a hint of satisfaction, recorded in her diary Lady Di's unpunctuality on one occasion: 'I went to court, the Queen called before Lady Bolingbroke who was the Lady in waiting, came. The Duchess of Ancaster going in, I step'd before her and said I was the Lady in waiting, which nettled her so that she would not speak to me after. The Queen was very gracious'. However, despite this blunder, and whatever mileage Lady Northumberland might have tried to make out of it, this did not affect the Queen's attitude to Lady Di; despite the King's jealous strictures, Charlotte

Self-portrait, c. 1755.
Lady Di shows herself in the fashionable
'Rubens' wife' fancy-dress outfit, copying
her costume directly from that in the
Rubens family group which hung
at Blenheim.

Francesco Bartolozzi:
Portrait of Lady Di, 1780s.
This drawing was owned
by Queen Charlotte.

Charles James Fox, probably early 1780s. This hung at Robert Spencer's house, Woolbeding.

Edward Gibbon, c. 1775. Gibbon as a Roman bust, wreathed with the victor's laurels, in reference to his recently published *Decline and Fall of the Roman Empire*.

Georgiana, Duchess of Devonshire, 1778.
This portrait was subsequently engraved by Bartolozzi in a limited edition of 200 copies, which were rapidly snapped up. Walpole admired its 'grace and simplicity' and compared it to great Greek sculpture.

Children watching birds, 1780s.
A typical work from her sketchbook –
wide-eyed, chubby little children at play,
fascinated by two flying birds.

Cupid with a mirror.
One of a series of cupids, this drawing is
accompanied by an Italian poem.

Musical faun (left) and
Satyr and fauns (below)

A Triumph of Bacchantes (*above*) and *The Drunken Silenus* (*below*).
Two wax sculptures in the form of classical friezes, probably late 1770s.

Wedgwood: Bacchanalian tablet.
This shows Lady Di's various Bacchanalian Boy designs, 'under arbours with
panthers' skins as festoons', as described in Wedgwood's 1787 Catalogue.

The Mysterious Mother, Act Two, Scene 3, 1776. Walpole especially admired in this scene 'the devotion of the Countess with the Porter'.

The Mysterious Mother, Act Five, Scene 6, 1776.
The dramatic climax of the play, showing 'the tenderness, despair and resolution of the Countess' and Edmund's 'stroke of double passion'.

The Faerie Queen, Book One, Canto 6,
1781. Una and the dancing satyrs.

The Faerie Queen, Book Three,
Canto 12, 1781. Britomart, in armour,
rescues Amoret, tied to the pillar.

Theodore and Honoria, c. 1791, the one
surviving original from her illustrations
for Dryden's *Fables,* to be engraved by
Bartolozzi. Theodore reveals the Phantom
Knight and his Hell-hounds to Honoria.

The Beauclerk cabinet, made to Walpole's specification in 1784
by Edward Edwards especially to display Lady Di's drawings 'of a gypsy girl,
and beautiful children', her Wedgwood plaques, and Walpole's gem
and stone collection. It took pride of place in the Great North
Bedchamber at Strawberry Hill.

was clearly being drawn to the personality of the youngest Bedchamber Lady. (Lady Northumberland remained hostile and, ten years later, was to make a comparison between Lady Di and a Parisienne of easy virtue spotted at Versailles: 'there were also very near us 3 Filles de Joye de la dernier Magnificence. I dare say the cheapest of their Gowns did not cost less than 7 Guineas a Yard . . . they had also many Diamonds, particularly the youngest (& I thought the prettiest of them), who was exactly like Lady Di Beauclerk'.)[32]

In August 1762, just three weeks after the death of her own baby on 25 July, Lady Di was involved in the compulsory duty of being present at the birth of the royal heir. The very public nature of this event, attended by representatives of church and state within earshot in an adjacent room, was to provide witness of the true succession (and quell any rumours of smuggled-in pretenders). Lady Northumberland's diary recorded the events of 12 August 1762: 'Called before 5. The Q being in Labour, the K called Chapman (Dry Nurse) between 2 and 3. Before 4 the Princess was sent for and immediately after, the Ladies and Cabinet Council. We assembled in our Waiting Room. The Queen's labour was short but severe. The persons present were the Princess, the Midwife, the 2 German women, Duchess of Hamilton, Lady Effingham, myself, Lady Egremont, Lady Bolingbroke, Duchess of Ancaster, Lord Bute, Archbishop of Canterbury, Lord Egremont, Duke of Devonshire, Duke of Rutland, Mr G. Grenville, Lord Talbot, Lord Halifax, Lord Huntingdon, Lord Cantelupe and Lord Masham. The Queen scarce cried out at all and at 24 minutes past 7 she was deliver'd. The Ladys then all went into the room, and soon after the Archbishop'. One person not permitted to be present was the obstetrician in charge of the birth, Dr William Hunter: however he earned his fee by making regular visits to the mother and baby over the next few weeks.[33]

The christening of the infant prince took place four weeks later, at St James's. This was another occasion of magnificent ostentation, with the attendants as well as the royal party in extravagant new clothes. Lady Northumberland

went to Court at half an hour after six. We waited in the presence chamber until the Queen ordered us to come in. It was the prettiest sight I ever saw. At the head of the Drawing Room was a Bed of State with crimson velvet trimm'd with Gold lined with White Satin and adorn'd with Carving, Gilding, & plumes of White

Feathers. The Queen was very finely adorned with Jewels of Diamonds & Emeralds, particularly a vast knot which almost covered her Stomacher. Her dress was White and Silver, the whole counterpain & Valens of the Bed was covered with Brussels Lace most extremely fine; it cost £3700 ... On the Right Hand nearest the Bed stood Ly Bolingbroke ... [after the christening] all present congratulated the Queen, after which, being left alone with her ladys, we assisted her in getting off the Bed & then attended her to her Apartment.[34]

The Queen's partiality to Lady Di was becoming obvious enough to attract comment and suggests that, for a while, Charlotte was minded to ignore her husband's disapproval of favourites. Walpole reported: 'The Duchess of Bedford has sent to Lady Bolingbroke a remarkably fine enamelled watch, to be shown to the Queen. The Queen desired her to put it on, that she might see how it looked – and then said it looked so well, it ought to remain by Lady Bolingbroke's side, and gave it her. Was not this done in a charming manner?' This might also have been the Queen's delicately oblique way of hinting at recurrent unpunctuality; the Duchess of Hamilton, who was once late for duty on the grounds of her watch being broken, was also presented by the Queen with a new timepiece. But the relationship was certainly noted by the Lennox sisters, Sal mentioning 'Lady Bolingbroke's being favourite to the Queen' and Caroline soon after writing to Emily: 'Lady Bolingbroke is the *bon ton favorite de la Reine*, all the men in love with her, Monsr de Nivernois, who is very agreeable, Lord Gower, Rigby etc. She wears rouge, and looks quite handsome. The other ladies, particularly Lady Egremont is so jealous of her favour with the Queen, which amounts to nothing, tho' that's serious. The Duchess of Grafton is head of the opposition ladies, which makes but a small figure'.[35]

Attracting married men, antagonizing women, wearing make-up; no wonder Lady Di fascinated the prim Queen, who was perhaps even trying to make a stand against the lifestyle that the King was imposing on her. The Lennox women obviously did not approve of make-up. Lord Gower, in his mid-thirties, was a first cousin of the Duke of Bedford, and was then serving at court as the King's Master of Horse. The Duc de Nivernois, 'a very polite sensible man with a great deal of good breeding and 'tis said much literature', according to Mrs Montague, was a significant arrival in London. He was the French envoy, subsequently appointed Ambassador, sent to negotiate the peace settlement ending the Seven Years War, and was currently renting the Pembrokes' London house.

This was available because the Earl of Pembroke was deliberately keeping a low profile at this time, having emerged from months of scandal after he had suddenly and spectacularly left his wife. Walpole, who had always regarded Betty as the greater beauty of the two sisters, wrote with glee to George Montagu in February 1762:

It is a week of wonders, and worthy the note of an almanac maker. In all your reading, true or false, have you ever heard of a young Earl, married to the most beautiful woman in the world, a Lord of the Bedchamber, a general officer, and with a great estate, quitting everything, resigning wife and world, and embarking for life in a packet-boat with a Miss?

And he spelt out the details a few days later to Horace Mann in Florence:

Lord Pembroke – Earl, Lord of the Bedchamber, Major-General, possessed of ten thousand pounds a year, master of Wilton, husband of one of the most beautiful creatures in England, father of an only son, and himself but eight-and-twenty to enjoy this assemblage of good fortune – is gone off with Miss Hunter, daughter to one of the Lords of the Admiralty, a handsome girl with a fine person, but silly and in no degree as lovely as his own wife, who has the face of a Madonna and, with all the modesty of that idea, is dotingly fond of him. He left letters resigning all his employments, and one to witness the virtue of Lady Pembroke, whom he says he has long tried in vain to make hate and dislike him. It is not yet known whither this foolish guilty couple have bent their course; but you may imagine the distress of the Earl's family and the resentment of the house of Marlborough who dote on their sister.[36]

On the very same day, he found time to update Montagu:

No news yet of the runaways but all that comes out antecedent to the escape is more and more extraordinary and absurd. The day of the elopement, he had invited his wife's family and other folk to dinner with her, but said he must himself dine at a tavern; but he dined privately in his own dressing-room, put on a sailor's habit and black wig that he had brought home with him in a bundle, and threatened the servants he would murder them if they mentioned it to his wife. He left a letter for her which the Duke of Marlborough was afraid to deliver her and opened. It desired she would not write to him as it would make him completely mad. He desired the King would preserve his rank of Major General, as some time or other he may serve again.[37]

This dinner party, worthy of Alan Ayckbourn, was unlikely to have been attended by Lady Di, who was then in the final stages of her second pregnancy, but the dreadful news and her sister's dismay cannot have helped her own condition.

Caroline Fox was quick to let Emily Kildare know about the affair:

What a shocking thing this is of Lord Pembroke and poor Kitty Hunter. Dowager Pembroke is miserable to the last degree, Mr Hunter quite distracted, and young Lady Pembroke very unhappy, but bears it better than expected; she is with her brothers at Blenheim, I believe, as Lord Pembroke says in his letter to Mr Stopford that he has for five years past taken so much pains to wean her from him that the shock is less to her than many people imagined. What an unhappy fate for so sweet a woman, as everybody says she is so domestic and so doatingly fond of him, as she was without the least thought of pleasing any other man, tho' so much liked and admired by them all as she is.

Caroline's emphasis on Betty's not being concerned to please other men suggests that this was rather unusual behaviour in a modern marriage.[38]

Two weeks later, Caroline was able to update her sister:

Lady Pembroke says she don't yet give up her Lord, she is sure he has a good heart. Did I tell you of his writing her a letter to beg her to come to him and Miss Hunter at Utrecht? Miss H was perfectly innocent, he assures her, and they might all live very happily together. The house in town might be let, which would save money. He desires her to bring with her the violincello and a fiddler he names with her. If she don't find them at Utrecht she will hear of them there, he says, and begins his letter "Dear Betty, follow the dictates of your tender heart, consult nobody but come to us"; he must be mad, I think.[39]

The respectable Mrs Montague was scathing about Lord Pembroke's intentions – 'his affections are as uncertain as they are unlawful and ungenerous' – and she blamed the modern French novel for undermining society: 'Miss Kitty Hunter was a great lover of French novels and much enamoured of M. Rousseau's *Julie*. How much have these writers to answer for who make vice into a regular system, gild it with specious colours and deceive the mind into guilt it would have startled at'.[40]

After a month, the scandal had died down, as Walpole told Mann: 'Lord Pembroke is quite forgotten. He and his nymph were brought back by a privateer, who had obligations to her father, but the father desired no such recovery, and they are again gone in quest of adventures. The Earl was so kind as to invite his wife to accompany them; and she, who is all gentleness and tenderness, was with difficulty withheld from acting as mad a part from goodness as he had done from guilt and folly'. Three weeks later, Pembroke was still trying to have his cake and eat it: 'It was very true that Miss Hunter was brought back by a privateer, but her father desired that she might be released; so they sailed again. Don't compassionate Lord Pembroke, he is a worthless young fellow. He does nothing but write tender and mournful letters to his charming wife, which distress her and are intended to draw money from her. He is forgotten here, which is the best thing that can happen to him'.[41]

Although living quietly abroad was the correct conduct for eloping or adulterous couples, Pembroke was reluctant to sacrifice his army career. He had served in Germany as a major-general commanding the Cavalry Brigade during the Seven Years War, and his cavalry skills were widely recognized: his book *Military Equitation* ran into several editions and remained a standard army text well into the nineteenth century. This was a decisive factor. Two weeks later, Walpole informed Mann: 'Poor Lady Pembroke has at last acted with spirit. Her lord, being ordered to the German army, wrote that he had a mind to come over first and ask her pardon. To the surprise of her family and without their instigation, she sent him word that she was surprised he could think of showing himself in England; and for her part she never wished to see him again till he should have retrieved his character.'[42]

Pembroke rejoined his regiment in May, a means of escaping from both the women in his life. As he wrote to a new friend, Lady Di's old love, William Hamilton, 'far from wishing, as some tired warriors do, a bad [peace] rather than none, my private affairs make me beast enough to wish for another campaign'. In November, Miss Hunter gave birth to their son, whose distinctive name of Augustus Retnuh Reebkomp included the reversal of her surname and the anagram of Pembroke.[43]

By the spring of 1763, Lady Pembroke appeared to have forgiven her husband, for she took him back. The status quo had been resumed; but this was simply the first instalment of a recurrent pattern of behaviour by Pembroke, which would result in Betty's eventual separation from him. Walpole to Montagu:

Lord and Lady Pembroke are reconciled and live together again. Mr Hunter would have taken his daughter back too, but upon condition she should give back her settlement to Lord Pembroke, and the child. She replied nobly that she did not trouble herself about fortune and would willingly depend upon her father; but for her child, she had nothing left to do but to take care of that and would not part with it. So she keeps both – and, I suppose, will soon have her lover again too, for my Lady Pembroke's beauty is not glutinous.[44]

Pembroke's generous allowance to mother and son continued until the boy reached the age of twenty, long after Kitty Hunter had married. He was a loyal and supportive father to Augustus, and his son Lord Herbert would maintain a friendly relationship with his illegitimate half-brother: such bastard siblings were frequently recognized and accepted in noble families, as long as they were the children of the husband. However, Pembroke's wish to change the boy's exotic surname to the family name, 'to be Herberted and unReebkomped', as he put it, was not acceptable to his wife or legitimate heir. Lady Pembroke preserved a discreet facade, but they did not have another child until 1773, when a daughter was born, to everyone's great surprise.

The young Duke of Marlborough was still being pursued by ambitious mothers. The Duchess of Bedford was working hard on behalf of her daughter, Lady Caroline Russell (described by her former rival Sal Lennox as 'the bouncing Lady Car'), who appeared to be the hot favourite. Emily Kildare described the campaign, at the time of the Coronation, when 'the Duchess of Bedford lives at Ranelagh now, where she seldom or never went before. It's taken great notice of, as it is since the Duke of Marlborough's arrival that their passion for it has begun. My sister carried Sal one night, but to no purpose'. Like Vauxhall, where Bully had been inspired to propose to Lady Di, the popular pleasure gardens at Ranelagh were another site for romance and transgression, where young men might get carried away by the moonlight and the alcohol. Sal was then still available but in February 1762 she became safely engaged to Charles Bunbury. However, she felt herself fated to be dogged by the Bedford heiress, as Caroline Fox described: 'Mr Bunbury admires Lady Elizabeth Keppel and Lady Caroline Russell vastly and wishes to encourage Sal to be intimate with them. He was in love with her when he first came to England and Sal is so jealous whenever he commends her . . . and says it's very hard Lady Car Russell must always interfere with her . . . the Duchess of Bedford, now that she thinks her safe out of the way, is so fond of her'.[45]

But the Duke of Marlborough continued to refuse to commit himself to Caro Russell; her mother then tried to ensnare his younger brother Charles Spencer, and unsuccessfully sought the help of Lady Di. 'That great lady [Duchess of Bedford] has made herself more ridiculous than ever, making a bustle about Lord Charles Spencer being so particular to Lady Caroline, which nobody but she ever found out, nor has that pretty boy the least thoughts of her. She went to Lady Bolingbroke about it, and there is a fine tracasserie between them, which has I hear ended in the Duke of Marlborough being vastly angry with her Grace. I don't understand what the meaning of all this is, but I find they are now courting the Duke of Bridgwater violently'.[46]

However, by the summer of 1762, the Bedfords had worn down the Duke of Marlborough. Caroline reported to Emily that 'Lady Car Russell's perseverance will do at last, for that there is the greatest reason to think the Duke of Marlborough now intends to marry her . . . I would not for the world have taken so much pains to bring about anything as the Bedfords have Lady Car's match'. And Henry Fox was equally scathing about the Duchess, although he and Caroline had taken just as much trouble to find a husband for Sal: 'The mean and unbecoming artifices the Duchess of Bedford made use of to bring this match on, and which she had so little pride as to use in publick too, exposing herself to the ridicule of the whole world, are not to be described. The D. of Marlboro saw through them, and spoke of her Grace always with the utmost scorn and derision, sometimes with detestation; and this too publickly for his own honour, as the event has happened'. The successful marrying off of a daughter, subtly or blatantly, signified the ambition, influence and power of women of rank, and, in these elevated circles at least, it was the mother who made the running. Yet the match was predictable. Lady Di's father and Bedford had remained friends and political allies after the death of Sarah's favourite, the late Diana, and following Bedford's remarriage to the energetic and determined Gertrude Leveson-Gower. There was also the dowry of £50,000. The young couple were married on 23 August 1762, in the chapel at Bedford House. One commentator noted the haste of the bride's family to clinch the deal, since the marriage took place 'eight and forty hours after His Grace declared himself a lover. The Duke of Bedford was always known to be a man of business, but he never despatched a matter quicker than this'.[47]

Unlike his father, who had invested so much money and time at Langley that there was not enough left for him to turn his attention to updating Blenheim, the new Duke of Marlborough had always loved the place and could not wait to live there. Over the next twenty years he transformed its bleak and old-fashioned interior into a relatively modern and comfortable family home. In character reticent and responsible, he impressed the young George III, although the King was maturing politically and realizing how people he thought were his friends were trying to use him. The Duke was still being pestered by his mother and Lady Di to ask for a place for Bully, and he made another request in November 1762. George III's letter to Bute about this matter showed his developing antennae: 'The Duke of Marlborough's letter would have caused me great surprise when I first mounted the throne, but I am now so used to find men wanting something more the day they are benefited that this only confirms me in my opinion of the greed that this age is cursed with'. However, this time the Duke's intervention was successful and Bully was made a Lord of the Bedchamber, on 22 November 1762, at a salary of £2,000 per annum. The Duke himself was appointed Lord Chamberlain, a surprisingly senior position for one so young and inexperienced, but then was moved to the post of Lord Privy Seal. He would have preferred to become Master of Horse, but this went to his sister's admirer, Lord Gower.[48]

Despite the additional salary, the Bolingbrokes continued to live beyond their resources. Rather than economize, Bully's policy was to continue selling off his assets. He introduced a Bill in the House of Lords in 1761 which would enable him to dispose of some family lands and clarify mortgage problems; he also sold the rights of advowson, or the presentation of the living, at Battersea, to one Charles Taylor for £420. In 1762, he introduced another Bill which would allow him to sell off the Battersea Manor itself (which had been rented out to Sir Charles Hanbury Williams, fellow conspirator at the Fox secret wedding, during the last, mad year of his life); and in 1763, the Manor House, owned and lived in by St Johns for six generations, was sold to the trustees of Lady Di's very rich cousin Lord Spencer, son of Johnny.[49]

But their glittering social round continued, carefully chronicled by Walpole, who spotted Lady Di at a typical evening:

The Lady in Waiting

Last night we had magnificent entertainment, at Richmond House . . . a masquerade and fireworks. The Duchesses of Richmond and Grafton, the first a Persian sultana, the latter as Cleopatra – and such a Cleopatra – were glorious figures in very different styles. Mrs Fitzroy in a Turkish dress, Lady George Lennox and Lady Bolingbroke as Grecian girls, and Lady Pembroke as a pilgrim were the principal beauties of the night. The whole garden was illuminated and the apartments. An encampment of barges decked with streamers in the middle of the Thames kept the people from danger, and formed a stage for the fireworks. The ground rooms lighted, with suppers spread, the house covered and filled with people . . . the bridge, the garden full of masks, Whitehall crowded with spectators to see the dresses pass, and the multitude of heads on the river who came to light by the splendour of the fireworks, composed the gayest and richest scene imaginable. The Dukes of York and Cumberland were there, and about six hundred masks.[50]

FIVE

The Amateur

(1763–64)

*'I would rather see the painting of a dog that I knew than
all the allegorical paintings they can shew me in the world'*

DR SAMUEL JOHNSON

Despite court duties, social life, family problems and motherhood, Lady Di made time to draw and paint. Her commitment to these pursuits was publicly recorded in the portrait of her completed by Joshua Reynolds in 1765; the porte-crayon (a metal device for gripping a chalk, a pastel crayon or a lead) which she is holding was a crucial tool – Reynolds would advise young artists, in the second Discourse which he delivered at the Royal Academy in 1769, that 'the porte-crayon forever ought to be in your hand'. For her to be depicted as a practising artist suggests that this role was already defined and accepted by her family: a portrait painter was paid to create the images his patrons required. Reynolds was the ambitious and able pupil who had rapidly surpassed his master, Thomas Hudson (whose own master and father-in-law Jonathan Richardson had tried to define the criteria by which the status of British painting might be improved), and who was elevating portrait painting to a higher plane. To depict a young aristocratic woman in this way not only referred to her commitment to drawing and painting, but also turned her into an eternal, allegorical figure, a Muse of Art. Such a strategy enabled Reynolds to show off his repertoire of visual quotations from the great art of the past, as well as flattering his patrons' learning. By the early

1760s, his portraits were in great demand by the noble, rich or social aspirant.[1]

She had the first of several sittings with him in March 1763. According to Reynolds' careful accounts, Lady Di's portrait was paid for in two instalments of £52 10s (a total cost of one hundred guineas, his standard fee for a three-quarter length), the first by 'The Duke of Marlborough for Lord Bolingbroke' in January 1764, and the second by (presumably meaning for) 'Lady Bolingbroke' in November 1764 – a year in which the Duke had also commissioned portraits of himself and his wife. The portrait took a while to complete because the sittings were interrupted by her third pregnancy, and had to be resumed in 1764 after the confinement. It was a mark of Reynolds' fame that his clients came to him rather than vice versa; it was rarely that he was prevailed upon to travel to them, and then only if they were sufficiently important. He did stay at Blenheim in July 1764 in order to complete his portraits of the Duke and Duchess (who had kept cancelling her appointments for London sittings) – the inconvenience of not being able to work at home no doubt far outweighed by being the guest of a duke. (He would stay there again for two weeks in 1777, to finish the imposing family group, when he allegedly annoyed the Duke and Duchess by spilling his snuff on the carpet and then forbidding the servant to sweep it up for fear of dust damaging the work in progress.) In the 1760s and '70s he was on sufficiently good terms with the Duke and with Lord Robert Spencer to dine with them occasionally.[2]

At the time when Reynolds started work on Lady Di's portrait, he had recently completed one of his paintings of the lovely courtesan Nelly O'Brien, a favourite model of his. Nelly had been one of Bully's mistresses after Lady Coventry's death in 1760, when he was perceived by society to have had a string of other women in his life (another expensive activity). Walpole referred to the unfortunate timing; although Reynolds had made 'a speaking picture' of Lady Di, 'Lord Bolingbroke said to him: "You must give the eyes something of Nelly O'Brien, or it will not do." As he has given Nelly something of his wife's, it was but fair to give her something of Nelly's; and my Lady will not throw away the present!' The portrait of Nelly, seated, cuddling a little dog and wearing a straw hat whose shadow turns her face into a subtle mixture of light and shade, was described by Walpole as 'a very pretty picture', when he saw it later in the 1763 Society of Artists' exhibition.[3]

Bully might well have visited both ladies while they were being painted. Sitters were frequently joined by their friends, and going to such a fashionable studio was a social event which would hardly be discouraged by the artist since it could generate more business, as could the admiration of recently completed works on display. The critical Rouquet noted in 1755 that 'the women especially must have their pictures exposed for some time in the house of that painter who is most in fashion'. For Lady Di, attending Reynolds' house for sittings in his purpose-built studio was a useful opportunity to study the equipment and techniques of the professional painter; her own amateurish attempts at portrait drawing could benefit from the experience. Another lady sitter found Reynolds' approach rather disconcerting: 'His plan was to walk away several feet, then take a long look at me and the picture as we stood side by side, then rush up to the portrait and dash at it in a kind of fury. I sometimes thought he would make a mistake and paint on me instead of the picture'.[4]

Reynolds' image of Lady Di shows her wearing the loose, vaguely classical dress that he advocated, in his written theory as well as his painterly practice, in his attempts to turn modern women into eternal beauties. The non-contemporary image is reinforced by his characteristic device of a richly textured curtain hanging in the background in a High Renaissance manner. An intriguingly prophetic and more time-specific object in the background is a massive vase decorated with bas-relief figures, of French seventeenth-century design. This epitomizes Bully's collecting policy (along with jackets, lace and fine foods) on his extravagant little jaunts to Paris, a time when Walpole was commenting to the Florence-based Mann on 'our passion for everything French'. The more commercially minded Josiah Wedgwood did not see why French rather than English craftsmen should profit from the profligacy of Bully and his kind: 'Mr Boulton tells me I should be surprised to know what a trade has lately been made out of Vases at Paris. The artists have even come over to London, picked up all the old whimsical ugly things they could meet with, carried them to Paris, where they have mounted and ornamented them with metal, and sold them to the virtuosi of every Nation, and particularly to Millords D'Anglaise, for the greatest raritys, and if you remember we saw such things at Lord Bolingbroke's, which he brought over with him from France.'[5]

Reynolds' portrait of Lady Di was sufficiently popular to merit wider distribution, in the engraving by W. Greatbach; and it would later be copied for Horace Walpole by Powell, who specialized in painting smaller versions of Reynolds' works. Reynolds continued to be commissioned by the family. In 1765, he painted the Duchess of Marlborough with her first child, Caroline, the Duchess bouncing the baby on her lap in a delightfully informal image. Then there was Charles Spencer's wife, Mary, who was painted in 1766, holding an affectionate black spaniel, and again in 1775, in an elegant black riding outfit, accompanied by her horse. The presentation of Lady Di as a maker of art, rather than a mother or a horsewoman, was not just an image created by Reynolds for her family. It was also recognized in the hothouse circle of the court, and it was one which provoked comment. Lady Craven (who would later abandon the pressures of aristocratic London society following adultery and divorce) described in her memoirs an incident which shows the Queen's appreciation of Lady Di's art, as well as the rigid nature of court etiquette: 'I will relate an anecdote, soon after I was married, which caused much conversation – Her Majesty expressed a desire to see a certain painting done by Lady Bolingbroke. As a Peeress of the realm, her Ladyship thought it proper to attend herself with the picture: and although a Lady of the Bedchamber, but not in waiting, she sent a page to say that she was solicitous to present the picture in person. Lord Bute, who was present with their Majesties at the time, came out and said, in a peremptory manner, that Lady Bolingbroke must deliver it to the lady in waiting.'[6]

Lady Craven's point was the ridiculous nature of an etiquette which always demanded an intermediary between the royal person and the outside world, which Lord Bute expected, but that given the reputation of the artist and her own relationship with the Queen, this was rather an insult. We do not know whether the Queen kept the work or merely wanted to see it. She had a considerable interest in the arts, and collected many paintings, drawings and prints; most of them were sold after her death, and in the current royal collection there is nothing attributed to Lady Di of this earlier period. The subject of the picture might have been a family member, one of her sketches of rural life, or an example of the classical figures of nymphs, fauns, cherubs and satyrs, of which she produced so many throughout her career.

She might have copied these fashionable antique motifs from some of the figures assembled by Bernard Lens (drawing master to many elite amateurs) in his *New and Complete Drawing Book for Curious Young Ladies and Gentlemen* of 1750. Compiled for his pupils at Christ's Hospital, where boys were trained for naval careers in which competent draughtsmanship was a requisite, the book was also described as being for 'other Young Gentlemen and Ladies that practice the noble and commendable art of drawing'. His models for copying included slender nymphs and humorous chubby cupids with bows and flowers – just the sort of subjects that most characterize her work. A broader source lay in the contemporary French art that was so frequently collected by the aristocracy on their visits to Paris, such as the precocious merry cherubs of Van Loo and Boucher, and the graceful classical motifs of Vien.

Lady Di's nymphs and cupids also echoed the fancy dress of the day, when balls and masquerades allowed the privileged to play in disguise. Dressing-up started in infancy, with the royal nursery establishing the classical mode as the norm. Lady Northumberland describes how the royal governess, Lady Charlotte Finch, arranged a birthday entertainment for the two eldest princes which involved dressing them all up, with Prince William (aged three) as Cupid and the Princess Royal (two) as Flora. A year later, the tableaux were recreated with the baby Prince Edward as Bacchus 'with vine leaves and tendrils twining round him and a chaplet of vine leaves and clusters finely interwoven among his little white curling locks ... he sat in a pavilion adorned with vines and bacchanalian figures of all sorts, bestriding a little tun, and holding a gilt goblet in one hand and a large cluster of real ripe grapes in the other'. This sounds exactly like a description of one of Lady Di's paintings.[7]

Other subjects she chose were sweet little children and charming moments from country life. She, and other artists, were being indirectly influenced by the advanced teachings of Rousseau, which were beginning to produce a shift in attitudes towards the family: there was an emphasis on more natural and informal child-rearing, and a newly sentimental yet moralizing view of the virtues of the simple life – rustic characters were no longer lovable buffoons but possessors of innocence and goodness. Such Arcadian visions, involving shepherds and shepherdesses, clean wholesome gypsies, and milkmaids and peasants, were popular themes for modern French painters, such as Greuze's images of childhood, and the rural idylls of Fragonard. Another fashionable style she adopted was that of the more dramatic, Italianate landscapes, epitomized by the works of Salvator Rosa. These were seen to express that awe-inspiring quality of the 'sublime' which had been defined by Edmund Burke in his 1757 *Enquiry into the Origin of our Ideas of the Sublime and the Beautiful.* Lady Di's treatment of landscape involved the placing of trees, with dense clumps of leaves, or jagged branch formations, to highlight and structure the essence of the scene, thus incorporating an almost theatrical element.

Her works therefore sought to combine the refined classical style and subject matter which had been stimulated by the recent excavations at Pompeii and Herculaneum (plus the appreciation of the many Greek antiquities surviving in Italy) with the more emotional taste which would later be defined as Romanticism. There was also conventional portraiture of family and friends, including Lady Di's sister and sons. She drew George in pastels, wearing the frock worn by both sexes when little; aged perhaps four, he sits on a chair and holds a pencil – he is learning to write, the docile child of a dutiful mother, a tender image looking shyly and sweetly at its creator. In another portrait, a year or two later, she showing him, now dressed as a miniature adult, stroking George Selwyn's adored pug dog, Raton; there was also a matching pair of pastels showing George and Frederick in formal dress. Inspired by the Reynolds' image of her as Muse of Art, she tackled in vivid pastels an allegorical self-portrait as Terpsichore, the Muse of Music and Dance: in classical dress with floating draperies, loose, curling hair held in place by a fillet, and holding a lyre, she seems to be dancing through the landscape.[8]

Although some elite women had been receiving training in art since the late seventeenth century, it was really from the 1760s that its practice became much easier for the non-professional, both through the increasing availability and commodification of equipment, and through widening access to various methods of studying and training. As a result, many more leisured women were able to become enthusiastic and competent artists, with role models in the ever-expanding royal family. Queen Charlotte and her daughters all practised art copiously; their tutors included the engraver Richard Cooper, the designer Giovanni Battista Cipriani and the painter John Gresse (art teacher to the princesses from 1777 to 1794). Gainsborough (who portrayed the royal family in the 1780s) was also recorded as having to make some simple oil paintings for Princess Mary to copy. The

Queen's efforts, as preserved in the albums at Windsor, consisted mainly of copies of religious works, the Princess Royal produced botanical drawings and copies of engravings, and Princess Elizabeth did landscapes. While in more informal mode at Kew Palace, the Queen was reported to spend some time each morning on drawing, music or embroidery – so perhaps, for her, art was simply one visibly industrious way of passing the time. However, Princess Elizabeth was seriously committed, and was known for her silhouette cutting, including a celebrated series, *The Birth and Triumph of Cupid*, which was engraved by Tomkins, a pupil of the distinguished engraver Francesco Bartolozzi; she produced etchings and mural paintings, and she even tackled interior design and architecture, including a tasteful garden bower known as the Hermitage, which was built at Frogmore, the royal family's rural retreat near Windsor Castle. The other princesses, equally hard-working (and possibly also bored and frustrated as a result of their father's reluctance to let them leave the parental home through marriage), undertook mural paintings and furniture decoration at Frogmore; Mary specialized in chalk, Sophia drew and embroidered. In 1787 the Princess Royal even established classes for drawing and painting held at Buckingham House, which were attended by her sisters and their friends. So for them, and for other young women in their position, art was perhaps a form of therapy against idleness and a way of reinforcing family links, as well as simply an appropriate recreation for the well born: their commitment survived long beyond childhood.[9]

Other aristocratic practitioners included Lady Lucan (hailed by Horace Walpole as one of three female geniuses of the age), who painted miniatures and spent sixteen years illustrating the historical plays of Shakespeare; Lady Buckinghamshire (later a friend and neighbour of Lady Di), society hostess and member of the group of learned ladies known as the Blue-stockings, who personally decorated some of the rooms in her house (the rear drawing room had rural scenes with real mirrors to represent water); the Countess of Carlisle, whose etchings were inspired by those of Rembrandt; Lady Louisa Greville, who made etchings after Salvator Rosa and Annibale Carracci, and who won three gold medals from the Society of Arts; Lady Andover, who worked in cut paper – Mrs Delany described one of her landscapes, set in an oval frame made of card, with embossed flowers imitating carving.[10]

Such amateur industry was now possible because artists' materials no longer had to be obtained from specialists or laboriously prepared in the professional's studio, but could be bought ready-made from stockists who offered a wide selection of goods. Changes in paper-production techniques meant that a wider range of good-quality paper for drawing and painting was being made in England after the 1740s, and pencils, chalks and paint brushes, as well as cakes of paint, could be bought directly over the counter. For example, the 1761 trade card of Dorothy Mercier, Print-seller and Stationer of Windmill Street, Gold Square, advertises not only Continental prints and flower paintings made by her own hand, together with a framing service, but also 'all sorts of paper for drawing, the best black lead pencils, black red and white chalk, variety of watercolours and camels' hair pencils [i.e. brushes for fine details], English, Dutch and French paper' as well as vellum and silk drawing paper, and writing paper of various sizes. The illustration on the card shows a genteel shop interior with well-dressed male and female customers. So in just one place (and one of many), Lady Di could buy the pencils, chalks and papers which she needed: ladies had no inhibitions about shopping and it was quite acceptable for a woman of her rank to visit such shops attended only by a servant.[11]

By the following decade, another supplier of artists' materials, John Middleton (whose customers included Joshua Reynolds), was advertising a range of goods which included camel-hair brushes, lead pencils and, most significantly, watercolours in cake form. These were made of ready-ground powder pigments already mixed with water-soluble gum arabic (to bind the colour to the surface of the paper), with the crucial addition of enough honey or glycerine to stop them from drying out. Such pigments had previously only been available from the colour-men who supplied professional artists, but in the 1770s, William Reeves, one of two colour-men brothers, pioneered the idea of ready-prepared cakes of watercolour. For this invention, he was awarded a Premium by the Society of Arts. (The next major break-through would not be until the 1840s, with the invention of ready-moistened pigments, available in squeezable metal tubes.)[12]

A dauntingly wide range of colours was being produced for the amateur to spend money on; by the end of the century, Brown's *New Treatise on Flower Painting, or Every Lady Her Own Drawing Master* (1799) was warning ladies against the excessive consumerism of buying the whole range – boxes containing eighteen, twenty-four, thirty or even forty cakes of colour – and advocated sticking to ten basic shades, from which a whole variety could be obtained by judicious mixing. Even some of the containers provided for these more accessible colours would become desirable commodities, such as Wedgwood's jasper-ware oval painting box, whose bottom tier held little pots for the separate colours, with an elegant palette above for mixing them. Such items were more attractive and tasteful than the economical but equally functional oyster shells which were often used as pots for mixing separate colours.

The new selection of easily prepared colours affected the nature of the end product. Watercolours had been used in the seventeenth century for colouring in details in prints and maps, and for making smaller copies of oil paintings, while gouache, the more opaque water-soluble pigment, was popular for miniature painting. Now, with the interest in Romantic and Picturesque nature, there was more emphasis on colour and less on the monochrome wash which had enhanced the outlines of pencil over chalk, or pen and ink – Lady Di's own works would show such a transition, from an early use of light wash to later confidence in colour.

As to subject matter, the stationers and print-sellers provided the artist with a range of models in the form of prints which were not only to be collected, framed and hung on walls (economical yet morally improving for those who could not afford original Great Masters) but were quite specifically for copying. Sayer & Bennett, Print-sellers of Fleet Street, included in their extensive 1775 Catalogue a set of twelve engravings of fruits and flowers 'the most useful for Ladies delighting in embroidery, painting, japanning etc', and there was another set of twenty flower prints 'extremely useful to Artists, Manufacturers etc'. Among other interesting sets of collectables were 'the most celebrated Beauties of the present time' such as the Duchess of Ancaster, the Gunning sisters and the Duchess of Marlborough; and a selection of great racehorses, which included Bully's own Gimcrack.

There were also books. *The Artists' Vade Mecum* (1764) included 'An Essay on Drawing, the introductory rules for learners . . . that it may be attained in a short time without a master'. This could be achieved by copying the engravings of old masters, landscapes, animals and flowers. The more ambitious amateur could soon tackle the human form without having to attend the life-drawing classes of the Royal Academy or other schools – *The Triumph of Painting* offered forty plates to copy which included parts of the human body, and the famous proportions from the antique and heads depicting the human passions as drawn by the seventeenth-century French Academician Le Brun. Cipriani's *Rudiments of Drawing* (1786, reprinted 1792) with engravings by Bartolozzi of various parts of the human body, provided a further home version of the life class. Another drawing book presented views for youths to copy and flowers for ladies, an ominous signalling of gender-specific subject matter. The intention seemed to be to make amateurs independent: many models were provided but little advice given.

So there was no problem for a committed artist like Lady Di to obtain her own equipment and training. The expansion in the number of drawing masters to the genteel also manifested the general enthusiasm for practising art during the second half of the century. Joseph Farington records in his diary a conversation in 1800 with the artist and musician John Malchair, then aged seventy-one, who had first taught drawing in London in 1754 when 'there were only five or six drawing-masters. . . . now, said He, there are hundreds'. It was often the drawing masters who sold equipment such as papers, chalks, pencils and brushes to their pupils, so this was another way the amateur could obtain supplies. And it was these masters who prepared the manuals for their pupils as a further teaching aid, and who defined the correct artists to emulate: Poussin, Claude and Salvator Rosa were especially recommended.[13]

There was already concern in the 1750s about the need for improvements in art training. The Society for the Encouragement of Arts, Manufacture and Commerce (more simply known as the Society of Arts) was founded in 1754 to improve standards of design. As well as furthering its aim of encouraging young professional talent, it recognized that amateur as well as professional women artists required training, and that their aspirations might also provide a source of income for the Society. Classes were offered not only for those boys and girls who would need to earn a living but also for the privileged young ladies for whom art was a leisure pursuit. William Shipley, Registrar to the Society, announced in an advertisement in *The Public Advertiser* for June 1757 that 'it will be Mr Shipley's endeavour to introduce Boys and Girls of Genius to Masters and Mistresses in such manufactures as require Fancy and Ornament, and for which the knowledge of drawing is absolutely necessary. . . . parents who have children of good natural abilities may here meet with opportunities for having them well instructed. . . . a genteel apartment is provided for the reception of Young Ladies of Fashion, who are attended every day from eleven to one'.[14]

And the growing consumer culture helped to increase the gender division (in tandem with the growth of journals targeted at the woman reader). By the 1780s Wedgwood, who was always one jump ahead of the market, was producing items of ready-to-decorate pottery with a completely matt exterior which could take watercolour decoration by genteel purchasers. The artists' manuals come to describe a range of practical activities suitable for ladies, including various decorative techniques and prescribed ways of ornamenting objects – women were perceived to be good at imitating and following instructions but lacking in the true creativity of the imagination: allegedly closer to nature, they worked with the ultimately natural ingredients of shells, twigs, feathers and so on, copying nature through flower paintings, working on the diminutive scales of miniatures, and ornamenting their domestic, feminine spaces. These decorative arts were seen as a lower hierarchy than the higher arts of oil painting and sculpture which men created with their minds, while women merely copied with their hands. Lady Di's nephew, young Lord Herbert, when on his Grand Tour, was found a drawing master who 'will teach him in the *Grand Style* and not in the trifling taste of small finished landscapes' – his tutor was stressing that art was an intellectual process, and not just a matter of reproducing nature. (Three months later, however, his tutor sadly concluded that 'as to drawing, he hardly has any inclination for it, and as he never practises but the twice a week with his master, I think he might almost as well have done with it'.)[15]

Those women who were achieving professional success in the 1760s and '70s were distinguished not just by what they did, but also by who they were. Being a woman was not necessarily a disadvantage: difference could be emphasized positively through the acceptance of alternative critical criteria. To be of foreign origin or training or to be connected with professional male artists was a definite bonus. One of the young beneficiaries of the Society of Arts' policy of 'bestowing premiums on a certain number of boys and girls under the age of sixteen, who shall produce the best pieces of drawing, and show themselves the most capable when properly examined' was Mary Moser, the daughter of George Michael Moser, an enamel painter and gold-chaser of Swiss origin (whose craftsmanship was of such fine quality that Lady Di's brother the Duke commissioned an enamel watch case from him). Moser had opened a drawing school in London, and taught his daughter so well that she won the Society's prizes in 1758 and 1759. She established a reputation as a flower painter – which, in professional hands, was rather more than the hobby of the leisured. Flowers were not only significant subjects for seventeenth-century Dutch and eighteenth-century French painters, but provided essential motifs for contemporary English embroidery and textile design. Mary Moser's work was admired and commissioned by Queen Charlotte, who paid her the very substantial figure of £900 for flower murals to decorate a room at Frogmore. Charlotte and her daughter the Princess Elizabeth were reported as visiting Moser while she was working on these. Moser also had the confidence to tackle the large-scale, moralizing history paintings which were regarded in some circles as the most prestigious and demanding form of painting. This view was the official policy of the Royal Academy, founded in 1768, with Joshua Reynolds as its President (newly knighted to signal the status of the body). An artist had to demonstrate historical and literary knowledge as well as having the technical skills to produce large oil canvases in a Renaissance manner. It was Moser's reputation in history painting as well as in flower painting, and certainly not tokenism, that earned her the distinction of being invited to become a founding member of the Royal Academy (where she later stood, unsuccessfully, for President).

Angelica Kauffman, the other woman founding member of the Academy, shared with Mary Moser the advantage of being seen as an outsider – Swiss-born, Italian-trained, her father an artist – who came to England with a well-established reputation and able to command high fees. This caused conventional judgements based on class and origin to be suspended. Kauffman became one of the most prosperous artists of the day, receiving plaudits for her history paintings but also making a good living from portraits, decorative designs, and the engravings taken from her works. Another successful outsider, not a member of the Royal Academy but able to exhibit her works there, was Maria Cosway, half Italian, trained in Rome and an elected member of the Florentine Academy, who was married to the miniatur-

ist Richard Cosway. Like the other two, she undertook history paintings as well as portraits because she had been trained in the life
drawing that was inaccessible to most of their gender, but which was
crucial for depicting dramatic narrative.

There were other professional women artists who achieved varying
degrees of success. Mrs Grace, self-taught, had a studio in Shorter's
Court, Throgmorton Street, where she produced portraits in oil and
history paintings. She exhibited in the 1766 exhibition of the Incorporated Society of Artists, and did so well that she left a fortune of
£20,000. The miniature painters Anna Louisa and Mary Lane were
sisters who specialized in hair portraits – they created the sitter's image
by sewing with needle and the subject's own hairs. Their works were
exhibited in the Society of Artists' gallery from 1770 to 1777, and
they gained excellent publicity through soliciting commissions from
famous people such as Lady Di's cousin Lady Spencer, her daughter
Georgiana, Duchess of Devonshire, and their friend the actor David
Garrick and his wife, eliciting the reply: 'Mr Garrick presents his
compliments to Miss Lane; he has sent a little of Mrs Garrick's and
his own hairs. He has but one lock left behind or he would have sent
more.' Another more modestly successful artist was Joshua Reynolds'
sister Frances, who managed to survive her brother's lack of support
– he was alleged to have said of her self-taught copies of his and other
masters' works 'They make other people laugh and me cry' – and
exhibited well-received domestic subjects at the Royal Academy in
1774 and 1775. She also painted miniature portraits on ivory. Dr
Samuel Johnson, despite his reservations about art and women painters generally, admired her work and had ten sittings while she painted
his portrait.[16]

For a woman to achieve artistic recognition and attract commissions
it was essential to be able to exhibit in public. One venue was the
Incorporated Society of Artists, to which women could be elected
Honorary Members from 1769 (although they were excluded from
voting). Such members included Catherine Read (described by Fanny
Burney as the Rosalba of Britain), Mrs Grace, and a Miss Black, who
copied the old masters and supplemented her income in the way that
male artists did, by teaching young ladies pastel painting. Women
could also exhibit at the Royal Academy, with their rank contributing
to their eligibility – early exhibitors included Lady Lyttleton, Lady
Beechey, the Hon. Miss Wilhemina King, the Hon. Miss Egerton, the

Hon. Mrs Vernon, the Hon. Mrs Harcourt, and Miss Georgiana Shipley, daughter of the Bishop of St Asaph and niece of the founder of the Society of Arts. Fanny Burney recorded 'her fame for painting and for scholarship' and reported indignantly that Miss Shipley had placed herself uninvited between Joshua Reynolds and Edmund Burke at a dinner party and monopolized them both. The respect given to such industrious women meant that Lady Di's own artistic works were created within a supportive climate; the production of art was an appropriate activity for a woman of her class.

The completion of Reynolds' portrait of Lady Di had been delayed by the birth of a second son, Frederick, on 20 December 1763. Like the young Queen, she had now fulfilled her dynastic function through the production of two sons, one for heir and one to spare. They had both secured the future of the families into which they had married. Their paths would now diverge.

SIX

The Adulteress

(1765–68)

'Although, in a political view, infidelity is much more criminal in the wife than in the husband, yet in every other respect the offence is as great in one as in the other; and no man has a right to complain that his wife does not love him if he disgusts and shocks her by an intimate association with abandoned women'

JAMES BOSWELL, *On Marriage*

Society permitted a married woman who had performed her main duty to indulge in other relationships, as long as they were reasonably discreet and free of consequences; the husband of course had been permitted to indulge from the beginning. Rifts had already been noted in the Bolingbroke marriage. There were hints of tensions – gossip about a quarrel, a reconciliation, Bully's ongoing infidelities. As early as September 1762, Fox wrote to Selwyn about 'Lady Bolingbroke and the quarrel', and Selwyn responded: 'I am just come from Sion [home of the Northumberlands] where we dined, Horry Walpole, Lord Coventry, Lord March etc. Lady Northumberland talked a great deal of the Queen and her way of life, or rather of not living, but not a word of Lady Bolingbroke. I am much impatient to find out that history'. Dullness at court had obviously set in just a year after the royal wedding; any gossip about a Bedchamber Lady would be a welcome relief.[1]

In June 1763, Gilly Williams tells Selwyn that, following another quarrel, the temporarily reconciled Bolingbrokes have 'gone lovingly to Lydiard' but how Bully had also rented a house in Windsor Forest for his mistress. This was when Lady Di was three months pregnant, and therefore facing her third confinement within three years. Two weeks later, Bully set off without his wife for more shopping and fun in Paris.[2]

His bachelor lifestyle also included much time spent in his London club, White's, where heavy drinking and gambling with high stakes were the norm. Newmarket was like a second home, where he entertained large parties of friends. Williams reports an uncharacteristically profitable season for Bully in 1764: 'Contrary to all expectations, his affairs thrive in the hands of Compton [his racing manager]. He wins so much at Newmarket, that he looks upon it as one of his best farms, and one indeed that will bear no price at market'. Men of fashion might also attend public executions. Bully's brother described one such event to Selwyn, who had been forced to miss it because of being in Paris: 'what served to encourage my writing was the curiosity which you expressed to hear of Waistcott's execution, which my brother and I went to see, at the risk of breaking our necks by climbing up an old rotten scaffolding, which I feared would tumble down before the cart drove off with the six malefactors. However we escaped, and had a full view of Mr Waistcott, who went to the gallows with a white cockade in his hat, as an emblem of his innocence, and died with the same hardness as appeared throughout his whole trial . . . my brother desires you would be so good as to send him some very good Provence oil, if you can find such a thing at Paris'.[3]

Bored with the court, neglected by her husband, Lady Di was also beginning to stretch her wings. The general discontents which had begun to surface had not been eased by Frederick's birth. In 1764, gossip recorded a flirtation which was clearly just a trial run for her, but also a significant indication of the restlessness which, when once felt in marriage, sets off an unstoppable fissure.

Lady Sarah Bunbury wrote to her best friend Lady Susan Fox-Strangways: 'Since I am on the subject of scandle, I'll tell it all at once: Lady B----ke and Lord G----r go on as usual; the Dss of Grafton, who is quite in retirement is supposed to affect it, & they won't allow her any merit for it: that's all the scandle I know of'. Sarah's confidante Lady Susan had provided a fine scandal of her own earlier in the year, through eloping with a glamorous young Irish actor, William O'Brien, whom she had admired on the London stage. The guilty couple had been banished to New York in order for her husband to establish a new career, and Sarah's letters to her provided a lifeline for both women.[4]

The names of Lady Di and Lord Gower had already been linked nearly two years earlier. The allegation that she was now having an affair with him would be made eight years later in the columns of the *Town and Country Magazine*, in the 1772 Tête-à-Tête article devoted to the doings of Bully, the Battersea Baron. Since the intended purpose of these pieces was to report 'the rapid progress of matrimonial infidelity', the Baron's wife was also cited, the article suggesting that Bully's 'irregularities excited her Ladyship to resolve upon retaliation, and the elegant and persuasive G---r proved too powerful a suitor to sigh in vain'. The gossip columnist went on to hint, although selflessly sparing readers detail so unpleasant 'that we are incapable of relating in its full latitude', that Bully, suspicious of his wife's fidelity, deliberately gave her a venereal infection so that she would pass it on to G----r – 'our hero deliberately sacrificed his own health to be revenged on his rival'. And she is accused of having a second lover, a Captain W---, to whom she also gave 'a kind of contagion', which he passed on to a 'woman of pleasure', who in turn, La Ronde style, gave it back to Bully. Considering that it was Bully who 'administered to his pleasures and promoted his success with the first-rate demi-reps of this kingdom' it would not be surprising if his own wife was not sporadically infected by him, another likely factor in their growing rift. However, this was also a literary device – the idea of testing a wife's fidelity in this way had already been explored by Henry Fielding in *Amelia* (1751). Whatever the causes, the article painted a plausible picture of the Bolingbrokes keeping up appearances and maintaining the requisite conventions of polite society: 'like people of fashion indeed, they lay separately; seldom met but at meals; conversed upon general topics; and seemed almost to have forgot that there was such a passion in love, at least in the marriage state'.

But the deteriorating relationship continued to attract the notice of those who knew them well. In the early summer of 1765, Gilly Williams wrote to Selwyn from Brighton, contrasting the unhappy couple with the apparently successfully reconciled Pembrokes: 'Poor Lady Bully would envy the extreme conjugal felicity her sister lives in if she had been witness of their life here; but fond as he [Pembroke] was, in the evening, he seemed to have his partiality in the grasshopper bagnio'. The bagnio, or elite brothel (with its origins in the alibi of the nudity and decadent heat of the bath-house), was a popular resort for the aristocracy, as available in Brighton as in London; Pembroke had always been, and would continue to be, particularly blatant in his sexuality and self-indulgence.[5]

By July things had become so bad that Lady Di was threatening to leave her husband. Selwyn was sufficiently concerned to involve Henry Fox, Lord Holland, whom she may have regarded as a father figure, since he had been one of her own father's dearest friends: 'I wish you was in town for so many reasons, but one is to give the Viscountess a little advice: she has a mind to separate. Bully, pour le coup, is extremely right-headed in this affair; has behaved very handsomely to her and to her whole family. I have told him, as the Duc of Rochefoucauld says, "les querelles ne dureroient pas long tems si le tort n'etoit que d'un cote" [sic: Quarrels should not last long if only one party is in the wrong]. He has promised to add no fresh matter.' Selwyn was clearly taking the side of his friend in a matter where he felt Lady Di was at fault.[6]

Separation was a serious step for a woman to consider, but it did not necessarily have to lead to the notoriety of divorce; couples who really did not get on could decide to live apart unofficially in a status recognized and accepted by society. (The Duke and Duchess of Grafton, for example, had separated in November 1764 after a series of violent quarrels provoked by her remorseless party-giving and gambling and his infidelities.) Lady Di's exasperation with her husband had been further increased by his reckless resignation from the post of Lord of the Bedchamber, so laboriously obtained for him through her brother's help, and the loss of salary entailed. 'Lord Bolingbroke, Seymour and Augustus Hervey have or are to resign, which I hear will shut up the list', as Walpole reported to Holland. This was part of the general fall-out following a cabinet crisis earlier in the summer, and George III's choice of the lightweight Marquis of Rockingham to lead the new administration. By the end of July, Bully had been replaced by Cornwallis – at a time when he was investing particularly heavily in his horses.[7]

Bully turned to Selwyn for guidance, and Selwyn tried to analyse to Holland the Bolingbrokes' problems and to apportion the blame: 'You are quite right about the Viscountess. Their case is, as I believe, full of

Reciprocity; I have only strongly recommended it to him, to be no more in the wrong, and she will be tired of being angry and of *other things* and then her good sense will dictate to her to make it up with him, if he desires it. But it affects him much at present, and as I love him extremely, it hurts me too'.[8]

Bully wrote two plaintive letters seeking Selwyn's help, which describe his sense of devastation and suggest a mind very slightly unhinged by the situation. On 31 August, he begged Selwyn to invoke the aid of Horace Walpole's niece, Maria, the widowed Lady Waldegrave ('the handsomest woman in England' according to her uncle), at that time a close friend of Lady Di's, to 'preach the doctrine of reconciliation rather than resentment and by degrees persuade Lady Di that what women call good spirit is only passion and absurdity, and that it would not be meanness in her but good sense and good nature to forgive me'. One major grievance was that Lady Di had been refusing him sex, hardly surprising if she had previously been infected by him (although also an ominous sign of attraction to another), and he demanded a 'total reinstatement and an entire restitution of Body as well as Mind . . . I know Lady Wal. will see the absurdity of their being separated'. Continuing to insult his wife, and thus potentially antagonize her friend, he wanted Selwyn to make Lady Waldegrave aware that 'Lady Di is stupidly or maliciously and for the sake of vengeance ignorant of the true full meaning of the word forgiveness'. But Selwyn must not let on that all this is coming from Bully: 'I hope you have not let Lady Waldegrave suspect that I desired you to speak to her upon this affair, for that would certainly reach Lady Di's ears and ruin all'. He is also prepared to blame Lady Waldegrave if his scheme does not work, for she shares 'the common stupid fundamental rule of not caring to intermeddle; the consequence of which is that many reconciliations are never brought about, which a third person frequently has it in his power to affect'. In short, it will be everyone's fault but his, this 'loss of a most amiable companion, the woman you really love, and of your home, which is the most essential thing upon earth to a man, who has once tasted what it was to have an agreeable one'. This very long letter was written in reply to the detached, unmarried Selwyn's response 'not to let this or anything affect one's spirits', advice which Bully agreed was 'certainly good but next to impossible to follow'.[9]

Selwyn agreed to speak to Lady Waldegrave, but insisted on telling her that it was Bully who had asked him to intervene. Bully's next letter, written on 11 September, pathetically thanked Selwyn for his support and sympathy, and accepted his conditions, as long as they remain discreet 'or else I am totally undone with Lady Di'; she is shortly going to stay with Lady Waldegrave, who must therefore speak 'as if it were of her own accord and that she had no other hint or notion of speaking but her own observations and what she accidentally heard'. Still trying to put the blame on others, 'I am determined to do everything in my power to put myself as much as possible in the right'. In the meantime he remains 'a man oppressed with the most disagreeable and tormenting thoughts'.

His prejudiced obituarist, writing with the hindsight of 1787, referred to the passion of both sides, and thought that the separation was 'a perpetual misery to him and probably still so to her, as their regard for each other was excessive and their feelings alike delicate and sensible; certainly that marriage laid a foundation for immediate happiness'. Therefore it was Lady Di's fault for destroying the foundation, which resulted in that 'general apathy' into which Bully fell, followed ultimately by the destruction of 'the noblest mind that ever man was endowed with'. And blame for the breakdown of the marriage was also laid on her by the *Town and Country Magazine* columnist, although for a different cause, that of blatant infidelity 'with a certain military gentleman. At length her conduct became so glaring that broad shame stared [Bully] in the face and he instantly resolved upon a separation'. But these were later accounts, the one written to vindicate Bully, the other to titillate readers and thus increase sales. Bully's letters show no awareness that there was another man in her life at that time, otherwise he would have had an even greater sense of grievance.

Selwyn's initial reaction, that Lady Di's good sense would lead to a reconciliation, was completely wrong. Her anger did not evaporate but hardened into a fixed determination never to return. Bolstered by Maria Waldegrave's support (Bully's and Selwyn's plan had had no effect at all) during her stay at Cholmondely Castle in Cheshire, the home of Maria's cousin, the Earl of Cholmondely, she decided to turn the temporary estrangement into a permanent separation, even though this would risk losing contact with her two sons (the children in such cases normally remained in the custody of their father). In October Bully went to stay with Lord Orford, the feckless and extravagant

nephew of Horace Walpole, at his country estate of Houghton in
Norfolk. Lady Di took advantage of his absence to move all her
possessions out of their London home, then in Lower Brook Street,
Mayfair. She left London, for the moment, and put herself under the
protection of the official head of the family, her brother the Duke of
Marlborough (just as Betty had done three years earlier when abandoned by Pembroke). The Duke and Duchess were then still living in
the old family home at Langley while he was refurbishing Blenheim.
This was an important part of Lady Di's strategy; although she was
the one who had walked out, she needed to be seen by society to have
the support of her family, who were thus condoning a justifiable
course of action. Her brother played his part by taking her under his
roof and lending her £1,000; she had no property or money of her
own, with the exception of her salary as a Bedchamber Lady.

Bully was shattered by this flight. Over the next few weeks he sent
many messages to her, and to her friends and family, begging her to
return. Having failed with Lady Waldegrave, he now persuaded his
aunt to talk to the Duchess of Marlborough in the hopes of bringing
some pressure to bear on her sister-in-law, all to no avail. It was also
at this time that he sold his celebrated horse, Gimcrack. The perma-
nence of her decision was recognized by their friends more rapidly
than by her husband. Williams wrote to Selwyn: 'Poor Bully! Though
I cannot pity him, yet I think he should in all his practice know so
much of the human heart as to despair of retrieving it when once it is
alienated and otherwise engaged'. Further evidence that the break was
final was the support of her brother in the negotiation of a private
deed of separation, by which Bully agreed to pay her £800 a year
maintenance, but in return retained the entire marriage portion, and
ceased to be responsible for any future debts she might incur. She also
lost her entitlement to her widow's allowance of £2,000. Any evidence
of sexual impropriety on her side might seriously jeopardize her
entitlement to support. There had been problems even getting the
figure of £800 out of him, which was not regarded as generous:
Williams thought that 'with what he offers, she will have less than the
Rena' – Lord March's cast-off mistress.[10]

Those who knew the couple less well found the separation difficult
to believe. Walpole's Grand Tour travelling companion, the poet
Thomas Gray, wrote to him in Paris: 'I would send you English
news but that I know you receive it from better hands . . . there are

three separations I hear talked of in the married world: the Boling-brokes, the Shelburnes and the Warkworths; the last I believe may be true'.[11]

As to her reasons for leaving, Lady Di had to safeguard her own reputation by putting the blame on Bully; she chose to emphasize the fact that their estrangement had been caused by his behaviour. The daughter of a duke and a member of the Royal Household could survive as a separated woman, and keep her maintenance, as long as she was above scandal. Given Bully's reputation, most people were quite prepared to accept her allegations of his constant drinking and violent behaviour. Lady Sarah gave the official line to Lady Susan:

I do not find that it's true that seventeen people are to be parted, as the newspapers said, but there have been as many reports to the full; however, I think none is fixed but Lord and Lady Bolingbroke, Mr Finch and Lady Charlotte, and Lord and Lady Fortescue: the two latter because the husbands are stark staring mad and have attempted to kill their wives and children; the former is because both sides are mad, I believe. But, seriously speaking, I believe Lord B is much the same as mad when he is drunk, and that he is generally. Lady B's reason for parting is that she cannot live with him with safety to her health. Lord B is very penitent and wants her to come back, but she won't trust him. Her reason is a very good one, but whether she ought to forgive him or not depends on circumstances and tempers, which nobody but themselves can be judge of. He says he is more in love with her than ever, and would marry her now if she was Lady Di Spencer. Everybody that don't love her pities him; but as I heard he had got a woman in the house already, I can't say I do. For if he was unhappy at the thought of having used her so cruelly as he has done, surely a man that had any feeling would not recover his spirits so easily. If he feels that at all, he must feel it very strongly. I own I am partial to her and have taken a great fancy to her lately; not but that I think she may be very much to blame too. She is in great spirits and seems to be very glad that she has got rid of him.[12]

These great spirits were inspired not just by ridding herself of a husband at best neglectful and at worst abusive, but by the fact, recognized by Gilly Williams, that her affections were 'otherwise engaged' – she had fallen in love for the first time. The object of her passion and the cause of her leaving her husband, home and children was a strikingly handsome young man, four years her junior, who was the great-grandson of Charles II and Nell Gwynn. Topham Beauclerk had inherited the brooding, dark good looks (such a contrast to Bully's fair complexion) of the Stuart king and the wit, charm and powers of seduction of the most famous of royal mistresses. The love child of the King and the orange-seller, Topham's grandfather was made the first Duke of St Albans; his portionless younger son, Topham's father, was Lord Sydney Beauclerk, the notorious fortune-hunter. Sarah Churchill called him 'Syd the Beggar' and his relations 'the family of the idiots'; others referred to him as 'Worthless Sydney'. He was described in 1727 by Lady Mary Wortley Montagu as 'a youth of royal blood, with all his grandmother's beauty, wit and good qualities. In short, he is Nell Gwynn in person with the sex altered, and occasions such fracas amongst the ladies of gallantry that it passes description'. Failing to become the heir of the Duchess of Cleveland, or to marry the aged Lady Betty Germain, from whom however he managed to extract £1,000 as compensation for her breach of promise, Sydney managed to inveigle Richard Topham MP, of Windsor, into leaving him his estates and works of art; gratitude would be publicly demonstrated by using his benefactor's surname as his son's Christian name. With this inheritance, he managed to attract an heiress (although a rather desperate one, aged thirty-six), from Speake, Lancaster, Mary Norris. Their son, duly named Topham, was born in 1739. Sydney Beauclerk died in 1744, and Topham therefore inherited what had been Richard Topham's property, consisting of extensive estates at Windsor and Clewer Brocas in Herefordshire, together with an annual income of £5,000.[13]

Educated at Trinity College, Oxford, followed by the Grand Tour, Topham appeared to be just another elegant young gentleman who drank, gambled, travelled and spent money abroad and at home; he was comfortably off, although hardly in the league of many of his companions in pleasure. His chosen public image was that of the avant-garde sophistication of the Macaroni (from the Italian *maccherone*, or coxcomb). As defined by Walpole in 1764, 'the Macaroni Club is composed of all the travelled young men who wear long curls and carrying spying glasses'. The initial reaction against the florid old styles of the earlier part of the century, under the inspiration of exotic Italianate fashion and behaviour, would turn into excess, with the Macaronis of the 1770s adopting for their tribal identity massive artificial coiffures capped by very small hats, extremely tightly cut clothes, make-up, perfume and two watches; they might carry huge canes with tassels or very small bunches of flowers, and critics would accuse them of effeminacy. But in the '60s this degree of extravagance had not been reached, and the Macaroni was perceived as a member of a stylish group rather than a fashion victim.

Yet underneath Topham's immaculate exterior, there was a very different person, whose demanding mind was not capable of being satisfied by the restricted social rituals of the court and aristocracy; being a Macaroni was a very minor way of reacting against the establishment. And he was already living two separate lives, for he was a close friend of Dr Samuel Johnson and a founding member of the Literary Club, whose masculine fellowship was founded upon intellect and talent, not birth and wealth. At the age of twenty, Topham had been introduced by a fellow Oxford undergraduate, Bennet Langton, to the eminent writer and journalist, then aged fifty. The publication of Johnson's great *Dictionary* in 1755 had contributed to the award of an honorary degree from the university which he had earlier had to quit through poverty; other literary distinctions included founding and being the main contributor to the periodical *The Rambler*, as well as much other journalism, the novel *Rasselas* and the tragedy *Irene*. Their mutual friend, the virtuous Langton (of whom Johnson said, 'I do not know who will go to Heaven if Langton does not'), had so admired Johnson's moral essays in *The Rambler* that he had gone to London in order to make the acquaintance of his hero. Their friendship flourished, and Johnson, always appreciative of new friends as weapons in his battle against loneliness and depression, came to visit him at Oxford; here he met Langton's companion Topham Beauclerk, 'so different [from Langton] that it seemed utterly improbable that they should agree', according to James Boswell.

Boswell, who would himself be dazzled by Beauclerk, tried later to account for the equally unlikely friendship which developed between the sage and the dandy:

Johnson at first thought it strange that Langton should associate so much with one who had the character of being loose, both in his principles and practice; but by degrees he himself was fascinated. Mr Beauclerk's being of the St Albans family and having in some particulars a resemblance to Charles II contributed, in Johnson's imagination, to throw a lustre on his other qualities; and in a short time, the moral, pious Johnson and the gay, dissipated Beauclerk were companions. Beauclerk was too polite and valued learning and wit too much to offend Johnson by sallies of infidelity or licentiousness; and Johnson delighted in the good qualities of Beauclerk, and hoped to correct the evil. Beauclerk would take more liberty with him than anybody with whom I ever saw him.

Johnson in his turn admired Beauclerk's wit and learning, and once remarked: 'Everything comes from Beauclerk so easily that it appears to me I labour if I say a good thing'.[14]

Mrs Thrale, another rival for Dr Johnson's attention and company, although on a rather lower social plane than Beauclerk, also attempted to analyse Johnson's friendships: 'Johnson & Boswell put me in mind of Cato & Juba; I told them so and both were pleased; Miss Reynolds said Johnson & Beauclerk put her in mind of Socrates & Alcibiades, and both of them were pleased'. Such comparisons also involved the ladies competing to show off their learning through citing the puritanical and censorious Cato, ultra-loyal Juba, the moralizing Socrates and cynical and sacrilegious Alcibiades.[15]

The ambiguities in Beauclerk's character would be later analysed by one of his closest friends, the cultivated Earl of Charlemont, whose contemporary biographer Hardy reported their discussions about Beauclerk:

Lord Charlemont often mentioned to me the pleasure which he derived from Mr Beauclerk's conversation, which could hardly be equalled . . . he possessed an exquisite taste, various accomplishments, and the most perfect good breeding. He was eccentric, often querulous, entertaining a contempt for the generality of the world, which the politeness of his manners could not always conceal; but to those whom he liked most generous and friendly. Devoted at one time to pleasure, at another to literature, sometimes absorbed in play, sometimes in books, he was, altogether, one of the most accomplished, and, when in good humour, and surrounded by those who suited his fancy, one of the most agreeable men that could possibly exist.[16]

Letters from Johnson refer affectionately and even possessively to 'Beau'. His reaction to Beauclerk's mother was less favourable, and the poor woman has been condemned for posterity by Johnson for not having a sense of humour: the three of them, together with Langton, had been on a coach journey during which Johnson had teased her with the ludicrous idea of buying a house in a notorious area of London, Cupar's Gardens. She indignantly said that 'an old man should not put such things in young people's heads'. Johnson later commented to Boswell: 'She had no notion of a joke, Sir, had come late into life and had a mightily unpliable understanding'.

Johnson stayed with Beauclerk in his house at Windsor; it was on this occasion that Johnson stretched out on a tombstone in the churchyard during divine service, and was compared by Beauclerk to Hogarth's Idle Apprentice. And it was with Beauclerk and Langton that Johnson shared the delightful escapade described by Boswell:

One night when Beauclerk and Langton had supped at a tavern in London and sat until three in the morning, it came into their heads to go and knock up Johnson and see if they could prevail on him to join them in a ramble. They rapped violently at the door of his chambers in the Temple, till at last he appeared in his shirt with his little black wig on the top of his head, imagining probably that some ruffians were coming to attack him. When he discovered who they were and was told their errand, he smiled and with great good humour agreed to their proposal.

JOHNSON: What, is it you, you dogs! I'll have a frisk with you.

He was soon dressed and they sallied forth together into Covent Garden where the greengrocers and fruiterers were beginning to arrange their hampers, just come in from the country. Johnson made some attempts to help them, but the honest gardeners stared so at his figure and manner and odd interference that he soon saw his services were not relished. They then repaired to one of the neighbouring taverns and made a bowl of that liquor called Bishop which Johnson had always liked; while in joyous contempt of sleep, from which he had been aroused, he repeated the festive lines:

> Short, O short then be thy reign
> And give us to the world again

They did not stay long but walked down to the Thames, took a boat and rowed to Billingsgate. Beauclerk and Johnson were so well pleased with their amusement that they resolved to persevere in dissipation for the rest of the day. But Langton deserted them, being engaged to breakfast with some young ladies. Johnson scolded him for 'Leaving your social friends to go and sit with a set of wretched unidea'd girls'. Garrick, being told of this ramble, said to him smartly: 'I heard of your frolic t'other night. You'll be in the Chronicle'. Upon which Johnson afterwards observed: 'He durst not do such a thing. His *wife* would not *let* him.'

David Garrick, the now phenomenally successful actor, had once been a pupil at Johnson's short-lived school in Lichfield, and had set off with him to London in order to make their fortunes. Their relationship remained one of teasing intimacy, with the shared knowledge of humble beginnings; but Johnson did not approve of the acting profession, and could not help contrasting Garrick's fame and success with his own long struggle for recognition and solvency.

Following his time at Oxford, Beauclerk did the Grand Tour, but remained in correspondence with Johnson. There was to be a meeting in Milan with Joseph Baretti, a fellow lexicographer and author with whom Johnson had become friendly a few years earlier when Baretti had been working in London and to whom Johnson had then introduced his young friend. Johnson wrote: 'I beg that you will shew Mr Beauclerk all the civilities which you have in your power; for he has always been kind to me'. However, Beauclerk did not get to Italy on that occasion, getting side-tracked by the pleasures of Paris. Johnson wrote disapprovingly to Baretti: 'You are not to suppose, with all your convictions of my idleness, that I have passed all this time without writing to my Baretti. I gave a letter to Mr Beauclerk, who, in my opinion, and in his own, was hastening to Naples for the recovery of his health; but he has stopped at Paris, and I know not when he will proceed'. While in Paris Beauclerk attended the famous salon of Mme de Boufflers, a long-standing royal mistress with a complaisant husband. (She 'does not appear ever to have been handsome but is one of the most agreeable and sensible women I ever saw' – Walpole.) He set off again in the following year, this time travelling with young Lord Ossory in the autumn of 1763. They went via Paris and Geneva to Florence, where they dined on 20 November with the Ambassador, Sir Horace Mann, Walpole's correspondent. This may have been Beauclerk's first meeting with another distinguished guest invited that day, David Garrick, who was giving himself an extended sabbatical from the strains of theatre management by touring Europe for a year. December to March were passed in Rome and Naples, spring and early summer in Venice. It was here that Beauclerk was painted by the expatriate artist Richard Brompton amongst a whole group of elegant young Grand Tourists, the wild Duke of York (also a Newmarket friend of Bully's) and his entourage, which included Bully's brother, Colonel Henry St John. This was the first visit to Italy by a member of the royal family as a mere 'cultural tourist', and it excited enormous interest in the English newspapers. Garrick was in Venice at the same time, and had to lend Brompton £80 when he was unable to extract immediate payment from the royal party for the group portrait and its three copies. (The work would be exhibited at the Society of Artists Exhibition in 1767.) It was also in Venice that Beauclerk was reported by Gilly Williams to have gambled away £10,000.[17]

Yet he also indulged in more serious pursuits, and discovered that Garrick shared his passion for collecting rare books. Having made the delayed contact with Baretti in Milan, he introduced the latter to Garrick, who bought some 180 books in Italian through Baretti (although with the intention, he claimed, of selling them on to the compulsive purchaser Beauclerk). During those two years, Johnson missed his young friend and commented sourly on his return: 'how little does travelling supply to the conversation of any man who has travelled? How little to Beauclerk?' Beauclerk was now qualified to become a member of the Society of Dilettanti, founded in 1734 to encourage taste and connoisseurship among those who travelled and purchased; the Society was sneered at by Walpole: 'the nominal qualification for membership is having been in Italy, and the real one being drunk'.

Despite Topham's relative youth and conventional, privileged upbringing, it was his demanding intellect and witty conversation that enabled him to become one of the ten founding members of a more demanding fraternity, the Club (later called the Literary Club), that diverse group of men from very varied backgrounds who, late in 1764, came together to provide a forum for their friendship and conversation. The chief qualification for membership was that they should be 'men of such talents, that if only two of them should meet for the evening, they should be able to entertain each other', according to the antiquarian and literary vicar Thomas Percy (later Bishop of Dromore) who was elected to the Club in 1768, in his life of another founding member, author Oliver Goldsmith. At the core were Samuel Johnson (who had set up a prototype, the Ivy Lane Club, years earlier in 1748) and Joshua Reynolds, and the writer and orator Edmund Burke. There was also Burke's father-in-law Dr Christopher Nugent, Bennet ('Lanky') Langton, lawyer and writer John Hawkins, politician Anthony Chamier (a prosperous but cultured businessman who would be controversially appointed to the Cabinet as Under-Secretary of State), and mathematician Samuel Dyer, most of them men at least in their forties, who had already achieved distinction in their various fields.

Yet the youthful Beauclerk held his own in this distinguished gathering. According to Hawkins, 'his conversation was of the most excellent kind; learned, witty, polite, and where the subject required it, serious, and over all his behaviour beamed such a sunshine of cheerfulness and good humour as communicated itself to all around him'. Another account of him at this time referred to 'the elegance and fascination of his manners, his inexhaustible fund of agreeable information, his delightful conversational powers, his love of literature, and his constant and enviable flow of animal spirits ... a universal favourite with the grave and wise as with the dissipated and gay'. And Johnson admired his deadpan delivery as well as the content: 'No man was ever so free when he was going to say a good thing, from a *look* that expressed that it was coming; or when he had said it, from a *look* that expressed that it had come'.[18]

The Club started off with weekly suppers on Monday evenings at seven, at the Turk's Head Tavern, described by Topham as 'our ale-house in Gerrard Street'. There was an informal rule that members should attend at least two out of every five sessions. Numbers gradually expanded, and there had to be a ballot before a new member could be admitted. Hawkins (whom no one really liked) was the first to resign, following inexcusable rudeness to Burke one evening. Johnson subsequently described him as 'a very unclubable man', the worst sort of insult in this gregarious world.

Beauclerk and Johnson also continued to meet outside the Club. In 1765, for example, they made an excursion to Cambridge, which gave rise to various memorable quotes, such as their discussion of the poet Kit Smart (who had recently been confined in a lunatic asylum), whom Johnson described as mad.

BEAUCLERK. What do you mean by mad, Sir?
JOHNSON. Why, Sir, he could not walk the streets without the boys running after him.
But Beauclerk later added: 'What he says of Smart is true of himself.'

They then went on to joke about the recent publication by the dangerously radical Mrs Macaulay of the first volume of her five-volume *History of England* which she had presented to Johnson but which he had not yet read – Beauclerk threatened to tell the authoress that 'it still remains in your study without one of the leaves being cut open, which is such a contempt of the lady's genius and abilities that, should I acquaint her with it, I wouldn't be in your place, Doctor, for a good deal, I assure you'.[19]

This was a side of Beauclerk's life unimaginable to the grand circles in which he would have encountered Lady Di, such as visits to the Duke and Duchess of Bedford, as a guest of their son, the Marquess of Tavistock. There was one such visit during Mme de Boufflers' visit to England in 1763. March reported to Selwyn in July: 'Since this letter was begun I have been at Madame de Boufflers, who returned last night from her expedition to Woburn and Wakefield, and seems perfectly satisfied with everything here. Beauclerk was at Woburn'. He did in fact seek to intersect his worlds on this occasion by taking the celebrated Frenchwoman to call upon Dr Johnson, and described Johnson's appearance for the occasion 'in a rusty-brown morning suit, a pair of old shoes by way of slippers, a little shrivelled wig on the top of his head and the sleeves of his shirt and the knees of his breeches hanging loose', as Johnson escorted his guest to her carriage.[20]

In the small world of London's elite, Beauclerk was already an acquaintance of Bully. They were both early members of Almack's in St James' Street, a club founded in 1764 by a Scotsman, Mr Mackal, who had spotted the niche for a socially exclusive venue for young men who gambled with high stakes. Beauclerk was proposed by the Marquess of Tavistock, one of the original founders, and was among the first wave of 140 elected members, amongst whom also were Bully, his brother Colonel St John, Lady Di's brother Charles, her brother-in-law the Earl of Pembroke and Charles Bunbury. Many of these new younger members were recognized as leading Macaronis, as Williams reported to Selwyn: 'the Macaronis have demolished Young Whites by admitting [to Almack's] almost the whole club . . . Mr Beauclerk has had that honour'. 'Young' Whites was an informal grouping of those on the waiting list for membership of White's proper, a slightly more sedate and old-established institution, whose members had included Lady Di's father, the Duke of Bedford and Horace Walpole.[21]

They may also have met as fellow members of the worthy institution founded ten years earlier as the Society for the Encouragement of the Arts, Manufacture and Commerce. Now generally known as the Society of Arts, it redistributed the annual subscriptions of its distinguished or rich members in the form of prizes to promising young artists and designers, and organized annual art exhibitions (a novel and exciting experience for artists and spectators) in its premises in the Strand. Public patronage of the arts was an appropriately moral duty of the privileged classes; other members at this time included Bedford, Pembroke and Lady Di's brother George, Duke of Marlborough; women could also join this enlightened body. There were also the inevitable marriage connections within this tight community: Lady Di's middle brother Charles married Topham's first cousin Mary, daughter of Lord Vere of Hanworth and half-sister of Aubrey, Duke of St Albans, in 1762. Another Beauclerk cousin, Diana de Vere, was a fellow court lady, serving as maid of honour to the Queen.

Like his father, Beauclerk had hoped to marry money and been briefly engaged to Miss Anna Maria Draycott, the heiress who was so stout that it was once unkindly noted that her tonnage had become the equal of her poundage. However, she broke off the affair after the marriage licence had been obtained, as recorded by Walpole: 'Miss Draycott, within two days of matrimony, has dismissed Mr Beauclerc'. She soon got better value for her money by marrying the Earl of Pomfret and becoming a countess rather than a mere Mrs.[22]

So the single Topham and the married Lady Di were known to each other through family and social circles, reputation and rank. At some stage their masks dropped briefly. Her own discontents, her interest in art, his friendship with Joshua Reynolds, his access to a wider world may all have been factors in their growing interest in one another, which had culminated in her flight from her husband. And the fact that she was able not merely to attract but to retain the attention of this brilliant, complex young man, who was prepared to devote himself increasingly obsessively to her, suggests the power of her sex appeal, intelligence and charm, quite apart from the guile that was needed to conduct a secret affair.

Therefore, as Lady Sarah Bunbury had realized, Bully was not entirely to blame for the separation. Fashionable London now took sides as rumours began to circulate about her true reasons for leaving. Walpole, temporarily out of touch in Paris, wrote to Lady Mary Coke on 17 November, begging to be kept up to date with the latest developments: 'I would be content to know what has turned things around so, that my Lady Bolingbroke is in disgrace at Bedford House and my Lord in favour there. These may be old stories in London, but would be very new to me. You see I am humble in my curiosity!' His correspondent, Lady Mary (whose ambiguous albino looks had once caused her to be compared to a white cat), kept a detailed journal recording the activities and preoccupations of polite society; she was in many ways a kindred spirit of Horace Walpole, both prone to exaggeration, gossip, and a great sense of their own importance (it was unkindly said of her by her niece Lady Louisa Stuart that 'nothing ever happened to her after the fashion of everyday life'). The sister of Lord Bute, she herself had been the centre of a great scandal in 1750, when she refused to consummate her marriage with an incompatible husband, the heir to the Earl of Leicester. She was virtually imprisoned by him for a year in remote Holkham Hall, Norfolk, followed by a messy public annulment. (She would later terrify Selwyn's friend Lord March by taking a polite remark of his to be a proposal of marriage.) Therefore despite her relishing Lady Di's situation, she was more sensitive than many to the dangers of a damaged reputation.[23]

Lord Holland, writing to George Selwyn, apparently did not know the full picture and believed, quoting poetically, that reconciliation was still possible:

Tell Lord Bolingbroke to take Jupiter's advice –
'Follow, and you'll find her soon appeased,
For I, who made her, know her in just state;
No woman, once well pleased, can truly hate.'
She has been well pleased, I hope; let him follow, court and prevail with her to be so again.[24]

But Lady Di had no intention of going back to her husband, nor of remaining in her brother's house. She returned to London in the middle of November 1765 to begin a new life as an independent and separated woman, responsible for her own household and finances and determined to maintain a spotless reputation in order to retain her salary as Lady of the Bedchamber and her maintenance from Bully. (The Duchess of Grafton, who had left her husband the previous year, was approvingly described as going 'nowhere except to church'.) Topham Beauclerk had taken himself off to Paris in late October, perhaps to defuse suspicion, or perhaps in a genuine attempt to detach himself from an involvement which had suddenly become too serious: it was acceptable to flirt with a safely married woman but one who had left her home, husband and children represented a far more serious commitment. In Paris he visited the as yet unsuspecting Horace Walpole, to whom he delivered a letter from Selwyn, and Walpole wrote to their mutual friend Mrs Pitt how 'the genteelness and slimness of [Beauclerk's] person' was admired there.[25]

It is not only from the comments of their fashionable friends and enemies, written to entertain, amuse and shock their own kind, that the end of the marriage and the course of the new relationship can be reconstructed, but from the cumulative accounts, detached yet partial, provided two years later by the witnesses summoned in the action brought by Viscount Bolingbroke against his wife's lover, Topham

Beauclerk, for criminal conversation with Lady Bolingbroke. From their different perspectives, the depositions of a dozen witnesses describe the same set of events to create a palimpsest of an eighteenth-century affair, which also provides a clear picture of the day-to-day arrangements and structures of a smart London household. These extras move around the two central characters, ostensibly their servants yet also their masters; it was virtually impossible for a member of the upper classes to be alone and unobserved, and even worse for two people who wanted to come together for illicit sex.[26]

Glimpses of Lady Di's new life and daily routine as a single woman are given through the testimony of her household. She took furnished lodgings in Clarges Street, Mayfair; this also meant having to hire servants. The most important and the most loyal was Mary Lees, aged thirty-three, who became her housekeeper and woman servant, and who was to remain with her for a number of years. At the same time William Flockton, aged twenty-eight, was hired as footman and living-in servant; he was dismissed eighteen months later. Elizabeth Thomas, twenty-three, became the living-in housemaid, to be dismissed shortly before Flockton. Samuel Miller was hired on 1 January 1766 as a chair-man, at 12s 6d a week. He had to come to the house every morning at eleven, where he remained in attendance all day until around eleven at night, in order to take her out in her chair or run errands as required. He would remain in her employment for one year, being discharged at the end of 1766, but then worked for her on an occasional basis during 1767, including a three-week period as a living-in house servant in September. Jane Morgan was hired as cook in March 1766, just before the move to a larger house, and she remained until August 1767. This was a small-scale household by any standards, reflecting Lady Di's much reduced circumstances. Even having a female cook rather than a male one was a mark of lower status. There was no question of running a carriage and horses any more – these were real luxuries which cost far more to acquire and maintain (through the costs of fodder and of coachmen's liveries) than the relatively low wages of house servants; at this time a footman earned between £10 and £12 a year, and a housemaid £6 or £7.[27]

There was no contact at all with Bully; her chair-man reported that on the embarrassing occasions when they came face to face in public places and promenades, when Lord Bolingbroke was out walking and she was being carried in her chair, they totally ignored each other.

And the footman Flockton noted how she would not keep the most trifling things belonging to her husband, but sent back any of his books or papers that she had found among her own things via him or the chair-man. When the housemaid was pressed, during the court hearing, as to whether Lord and Lady Bolingbroke had ever been together at this time, she said that if they had it would certainly have been commented on by the servants.

This watchful band gave totally conflicting evidence, with Flockton and Thomas having no doubt at all about the sexual nature of the relationship between Lady Di and Topham Beauclerk. It was not Elizabeth Thomas's job to open the door or wait upon Lady Di, and indeed she never even saw Topham in the early days, while they were still in Clarges Street; but Flockton would often come downstairs from the dining room and report, undoubtedly with nudges and winks, that Mr Beauclerk was with their mistress. On the other hand, Mary Lees, who was the only one to remain in Lady Di's service following the divorce, was apparently prepared to perjure herself by denying that any impropriety had ever taken place, and insisting that they had seldom been alone together, and were no more than just good friends. Lees' ambiguity is very interesting, for although she alleged that 'her place was such in Lady Bolingbroke's family that she very seldom knew who used to be with her or visit her in town', and described her job as being only to dress and undress Lady Di, and not normally attend her in the parlour or dining room, it is clear that it was she who ran the entire household. And, during later events, she was taken completely into Lady Di's confidence. Her evidence contains a series of denials and evasions – she 'cannot say', she 'does not know'. The cook Morgan was similarly noncommittal about the relationship, so the household seems to have been split into two cautious allies and two prurient spies.

The servants first became aware of Topham's existence on his return from Paris in December; the friendship appeared not to give any particular cause for comment, since he called only two or three times a week, and he and Lady Di occasionally sent each other notes. In April 1766, Lady Di and her household moved to a house in Charles Street, at the south-west corner of Berkeley Square. This was a modern terraced house in a convenient and fashionable location which combined genteel residents with useful shops – in 1766, Berkeley Square contained a coffee house, tavern, wax chandler, hosier, tailor, fishmonger and Gunters the confectioner, and Charles Street itself had a baker, shoemaker, grocer and chandler. Although such squares could be dangerous at night – the caretaker of Lansdowne House in the Square (built by the Adam brothers for Lord Bute) was murdered that very year – security in the area had been recently tightened up, with watch-boxes being provided and the centre of the square paved and lit.[28]

In addition to hiring and managing servants, another new responsibility was that of paying unfamiliar types of bill. Instead of dressmakers' accounts, she was faced with the rates: London householders were charged a national tax (land and window tax) and a parish rate, the latter contributing towards poor relief, the watch, and street lighting, cleansing and repairs. There were also water bills. By the 1760s, Londoners prepared to pay the necessary fee were supplied by one of the water companies with water piped under the streets through elm-trunk pipes into domestic cisterns in the front basement area. The New River Company, based at Sadlers Wells, used a steam pump to supply local mains. Households could have their own supplies even pumped to an upper floor, and many had a flushing lavatory. (Not for the use of the servants, however, who had to use a hut in the back yard, whose cesspool was emptied by the night-soil men.)[29]

Topham now began to call more often; the housemaid saw him for the first time, and was informed by Mary Lees that this was indeed Mr Beauclerk. The cook confirmed that although Topham at first did not visit so frequently as he did later on, he was certainly coming regularly for breakfast, dinner or a late supper; and the notes and messages increased. The attraction between them was evidently growing powerfully, although at this stage still chaste – had it been otherwise the servants would have known.

The next stage was the consummation of their passion, which required some advance planning. In July 1766 Lady Di went to stay at the house taken by her sister, Lady Pembroke, in Tunbridge Wells. The Wells was at this time a rather more elite spa resort than overcrowded Bath. It was felt to combine tasteful entertainment, excellent shopping, coffee houses under a covered arcade and good company with the beneficial drinking of and bathing in the local waters. Sarah Churchill had approved of the place sufficiently to be a regular visitor, and it was now frequented by the great and good, including the members of the royal family. George Selwyn gave a rather qualified approval: 'Tunbridge is, in my opinion, for a little time in the summer, with a family, and for people who do not find a great deal of occupation at their country houses, one of the prettiest places in the world'. A later visitor, Betsy Sheridan, described the typical routine: 'Rise at seven, go down in a Habit to the Wells, walk on the Pantiles, saunter into the library, look at the shops, say good morning to your acquaintances' followed by afternoon walks to picturesque spots (including the Rocks where tea was served by a 'poor woman' in a little cottage) and evening card parties, concerts or balls. 'Tho a large village we have no streets here but each house lies separate and has a garden and often a field or two belonging to it'. Lady Di stayed for six or seven weeks, taking with her Flockton and Mary Lees. Two days later, Topham Beauclerk arrived in Tunbridge Wells, where he also stayed for several weeks. As a friend of fellow club member Lord Pembroke, he naturally came to visit the family. However, as Pembroke was only there once, for three days, and as Topham most frequently came to call when Lady Pembroke happened to be out, William Flockton concluded that Lady Di was the main target.[30]

And it would appear that in the more neutral and, they hoped (wrongly), less closely observed setting of someone else's house, they intended to make love for the first time – no easy task given sharp-eyed servants, and the public nature of grand families who lived and moved about in inter-connecting downstairs rooms, not forgetting the elaborate clothes which required the assistance of maids and valets to put on and take off. Spontaneity was simply not an option.

She had instructed Flockton to hire a couch by the week for her use while at Tunbridge Wells. This was placed in a smaller parlour across the passage from the main parlour where guests were received. One might ask why it should have been Lady Di's servant rather than that of her hostess Lady Pembroke who was responsible for obtaining the extra piece, but plausible reasons must have been provided – and as the sisters were always very close, the truth may even have been told.

One day, when the Pembrokes and most of the servants were out, Topham came to call. He and Lady Di first sat in the main parlour, alone. She rang the servants' bell – perhaps to check who was within earshot – and it was answered by William Flockton, whom she asked to bring her a glass of water. She drank this and he took the glass from the room. But, aware of their palpable tension, he lurked in the hall instead of returning to the servants' quarters; he then observed

Topham and Lady Di leave the larger room and cross the passage into the back parlour, which contained the recently installed couch. Here they stayed for about ten minutes. This is an alarmingly short period of time for such a long-planned event but they knew that any longer absence was dangerous. After they had returned to the public room, the suspicious Flockton entered the smaller parlour and noticed firstly that the previously open shutters were now closed, and secondly that the couch looked 'rumpled and used'.

Perhaps they felt that the risks, even although out of London, were too great, for this appears to have been a one-off event during the Tunbridge Wells visit – or at least the only one observed by Flockton in the Pembrokes' house. She returned to London at the end of August, accompanied by Flockton and Lees, spending the night en route at Farnborough. Here she was joined by Topham the following morning, and they travelled to London together, although in separate chaises; this was in any case a normal security precaution, given the prevalence of highwaymen on the western approaches to London.

Soon after their return, Topham was taken ill and had to stay in his house for about a week, during which time she sent messages to him every day. As soon as he recovered, a honeymoon period began during which they were constantly together. Topham now came to Lady Di's house several times a day, beginning at nine or ten in the morning, then two in the afternoon, five in the evening, and sometimes later as well. He had supper there almost every evening, often staying until around eleven. On one occasion, clearly painfully remembered by Flockton, who would have had to wait up, he had stayed until three in the morning. He and Lady Di had been playing cards with her former companion and housekeeper, Rachel Lloyd – although, as Flockton stressed, the latter had left at midnight.

When they were alone together they generally sat in the first-floor dining room, or in a small room which led off this but also had its own door at the top of the stairs. And there was a couch, which was moved by Flockton, on Lady Di's orders, between these two rooms. Mary Lees acknowledged the existence of the couch, but firmly denied that it had flaps or sides which could be let down to turn it into a sort of bed, in direct contradiction to the housemaid's claim that it did and could. Flockton said that Lady Di often ordered him, when Topham was visiting or expected, to tell other callers that she was not at home, but only to admit Topham; these instructions were relayed to Flockton by Mary Lees, who, as a superior grade of servant, came downstairs to the basement to relay her mistress's orders to Flockton and the housemaid. As a result, many callers were told that Lady Bolingbroke was not at home. Lees however denied firmly that any such orders had been given, and said that no one had ever been refused admittance.

Since they were upstairs and the servants were downstairs, there was no further reason for them to be interrupted. But one evening, when Topham's chair-man had brought his chair around at nine, Flockton went upstairs to tell him it was ready. On trying the door to the little room at the top of the stairs, he was much surprised to find that it was locked. Instead of knocking, he waited, listening, for about two minutes, and heard the couch move and creak 'as if there were persons on it' and the rustling of clothes. He then tiptoed downstairs, for fear of discovery, and waited in the passage, talking to the chair-man, until he heard the door open and then shut again. When he went upstairs again, to announce the arrival of the chair-man, the door was not locked, and Lady Di and Topham were sitting on the couch looking 'a little flurried and confused'. After that occasion, Flockton started going into whichever room contained the couch immediately after they had been in it alone together, and frequently found it 'tumbled and rumpled', with hair powder at the top, and clots of dirt 'of the type that would have come from a man's shoes or boots' at the other end. (One of these clues was the result of the current fashion for dense hair powdering.) Mary Lees, however, denied that the door was ever locked; she confirmed that she had heard Flockton telling the housemaid about the couch being dirtied with shoe marks, but said that when she had inspected the couch herself she had seen nothing suspicious.

Flockton must have made it clear to Lady Di that he was well aware of what was going on, but it was in her interest to keep employing him for the moment since servants were hard enough to get hold of. A mark of her dependence on his discretion was an incident in December 1766, when she sent a twenty-pound bank note to Topham in order for him to obtain change for her; he came for dinner, bringing the change, and after he left at midnight and Flockton came upstairs to clear the dining room, Lady Di gave him one guinea out of the money – a sum worth several weeks' wages.

Elizabeth Thomas, the housemaid, also observed the lovers during their early passion. She too was keeping an eye on the couch, which, she confirmed, was often moved from the dining room to the adjoining back room, and she noticed that the couple were often alone in that room together, sometimes in the morning, around eleven or twelve, and sometimes in the evening. After they had left the room, she went in to put it to rights, and would find one or both of the shutters closed, and the curtains let down. There were clots of dirt on the couch, its pillows were on the ground or shoved behind it, the whole couch was tumbled, as if someone had been lying on it, and the arms and pillows were covered with hair powder. Thomas was so shocked by its state one evening that she even fetched up the cook, Jane Morgan, who normally remained below stairs, to examine the dirt. And the cook had to agree that it did look as if it had come from a man's boots.

Whatever her private life, Lady Di was anxious to retain her public position at court; the separation itself was providing no bar to the continuation of her duties as official attendant to the Queen. Lady Mary Coke, for example, noted that on 22 September 1766 'at one o-clock I went to court and found Lady Bolingbroke and Lady Effingham in the drawing room. Soon after there came in several ladies, and among the rest the Duchess of Hamilton. She placed herself at a great distance from me, which gave me no concern; I think her beauty is much gone off'.[31]

By the autumn of 1766, a year after she had left him, Lady Di had finally made her husband accept that there was not going to be a reconciliation. Bully had remained in charge of the two boys, living temporarily in a house near Hyde Park Corner, and then in Queen Street, Mayfair. Although this was very close to Charles Street, the servants never mentioned Lady Di's sons being in her house, and being free for Topham's visits was her main priority. But there is a touching account by Selwyn to Holland of how 'Lord Bolingbroke carried his son [George, aged five and a half] to Wandsworth School yesterday and very pathetically recommended him to Harry's protection [the youngest Fox]. I believe he went so far as a bribe. The little "Bully" was very glad to go, but his father left him, les larmes aux yeux [with tears in his eyes]'. And a letter from Bully to Selwyn refers to the boys: 'the little gentleman is gone to dine with his brother but shall pay his respects to you to-morrow or the next day before his departure for Wandsworth'. Selwyn was clearly regarded as an honorary uncle. The letter carries on affectionately, Bully hoping to accept Selwyn's offer of dinner, but not if it is inconvenient: 'for God's sake, don't let your civil offers of yesterday be any hindrance to you. All I shall require will be the pleasure of dining with you some other day'.[32]

On another occasion that same autumn of 1766, he was wallowing in self-pity:

I intended to sup with you this evening, but I am so low, dejected and miserable that I cannot speak; I can only cry. The just parting with her whom I know (though she does not) I shall not see again this long while quite overcomes me; I shall therefore go and lie out of town this evening. . . . If ever you happen to talk of me to Lady Di, represent me as appearing to you altered and unhappy. Excuse me plaguing you with my nonsense. You know too well the comfort it affords to an afflicted man to talk to his friends of his affliction not to forgive me.[33]

Selwyn was sufficiently disturbed by this depressed mood to report it to Henry St John; the latter took a slightly more robust view of Bully's anguish and replied:

My brother, whom you inquire so kindly after, is not sunk into such low spirits as you seem to have heard. I think, on the contrary, though he laments the loss of a home, he does not whimper and whine after the object that has been these two years past the cause of his melancholy, and I fancy he at last sees that object in its true light. From a desponding lover and husband, as we have seen him, he is determined to become more a man of the world, and not to sacrifice his pleasure and interest in life to the indulgence of a grief brought on by an accident originally and afterward continued by the foolish obstinacy of a woman, and promoted by the unfeeling behaviour and indolence of her brother. I need not illustrate to you my meaning; you are master of that subject and I am sure was always much concerned at the rupture. As my brother is, as you style him, a vagabond, he eats every day his mutton at my house; for he parted with his cook, and all his establishment, together with his house.

And Bully was certainly not suffering alone, because the Earl of March reported to Selwyn that same November that 'Bully continues at Newmarket with his girl, though he is as much tired of her as of anything else'.[34]

By this time, Lady Di and Topham were still behaving with sufficient discretion to deceive some, although not all observers, and she moved confidently at court and in society. March continued in the same letter: 'Milady Bully came last Sunday to Guerchy's, where I dined with the Bedfords and Lord Gower. I suppose she was not invited on his account. Women are so much more impudent than men; I never saw anything like it. She came just after we had drunk coffee, handsomer than ever I saw her, and not the least abashed. Pauvre Milord Gower, il ne savoit que faire de sa personne [he didn't know where to put himself]. I was sorry for him, because I knew what he suffered'.

The far more perceptive Caroline Fox wrote to Emily that autumn, expressing her own dislike of Topham and probing beneath the veneer of his flirtatious behaviour with their unpopular sister-in-law, the Duchess of Richmond:

Lord Frederick is not I believe in such vast favour as he was; the Duchess at least has got another flirt whom she doesn't own to love as well as Lord Frederick, but whom it is suspected she does – Mr Beauclair [sic], the most self-sufficient coxcomb, in my opinion, I ever saw. He has the rage of being fine, and his following her is only because she is a Duchess. Lady Bolingbroke is his passion, if he has any passion but for himself, which is doubted. The Duchess laughs about it and says 'who would have thought I should ever flirt with a Macaroni?'[35]

The Earl of March continued to monitor his friend's progress: 'Bully is coming again into the world, and swears he will seduce some modest woman: I have no doubt he will'. There was financial disappointment following the death of Bully's aunt, from whose will he had great expectations, but from whom he only received £100. Williams confirmed the new mood to Selwyn, who was then in Paris: 'Bully says he intends to take to politics. He sits every night next to Lord Temple, and has a complete bore of two hours. What that arch-politician will make of him, I cannot determine. The Viscountess is shut up altogether with Topham. His mother is dead, by which he has some considerable moveables'.[36]

The moveables which Topham inherited from his mother were the Norris family's house of Speke Hall in Lancashire, a fine timber-framed manor house, and a further £3,000 a year. He thereupon sold his Windsor property to Sir Edward Walpole (Horace's elder brother), who was consolidating various local interests. Topham's mother had wanted him to live in Speke Hall, and to take the name of Norris rather than Beauclerk (the disgrace of a man having to change his surname for money was one moral dilemma posed in Fanny Burney's *Cecilia* of 1782). But the choice between living amongst rural gentry in the north of England and being in London with his mistress and Dr Johnson presented no dilemma at all. Nor had mother and son been particularly close, although he now did his duty by her, according to

Lady Mary Coke: 'Lady Sidney Beauclerk is dying; her son at present behaves decently and goes nowhere; he will get by her death near £3000 a year'. Lady Mary did not realize that 'going nowhere' was not the product of filial devotion but of lust. He went to Speke to wind up affairs that December, and managed to kill two birds with one stone by arranging a meeting on his return journey with the revolutionary thinker Jean-Jacques Rousseau. Rousseau, who had fled France to avoid persecution for his subversive views of society (*The Social Contract* and *Emile* had been published in 1762), was encouraged by the philosopher David Hume to come to England from his exile in Switzerland and was then travelling in England accompanied by a mistress and a badly behaved dog. Fascinated by the reputation of the sage, Topham got his friend Richard Davenport to provide a note of introduction: 'Mr Beauclerk, a gentleman of distinction and a friend of mine, who is well acquainted with the Prince of Conti and Madame Boufflers, having often heard them speak much in commendation of Mr Rousseau, had a vast desire of paying his compliments in passing to London and desired I would give him this little note of recommendation'.[37]

Bully, feeling some emptiness in his life (and purse) as well as great hostility to his wife's family, now attempted to reinstate himself in his position as Lord of the Bedchamber and placed the blame for his resignation on the Duke of Marlborough. He complained to the Duke of Grafton, in November 1766: 'I voluntarily gave it up to oblige a man for whom I have in return received the most unmerited behaviour. Any connection therefore with him, my Lord, is what my pride will forever make me avoid; the same pride, my Lord, makes me wish to owe it to his Majesty's goodness, without the shadow of owing it to the Duke of Marlborough the honour of being in his Majesty's family as I was before'. This was both hypocritical and ungrateful, since he had previously begged for his brother-in-law's influence, which had been reluctantly but effectively exercised.[38]

It was the recognition of a fait accompli (as long as it was not too blatant) that enabled Bully to come to terms with the loss of his wife. He wrote with dignity to the compassionate Selwyn, when the latter had tried to arrange for the motherless boys to visit their Spencer cousins at Althorp: 'I am infinitely obliged to you, and so are the boys, for your invitation. But they are not acquainted with, or even known to, Lord and Lady Spencer, and I cannot any longer pretend to intrude anything upon the Spencers'. A more cheerful letter seeks to put Selwyn in the wrong in regard to the latter's optimistic views on the morals of the Romans:

Lord Bolingbroke believes Mr Selwyn will allow that there was some degree of vice among the Romans during that period so wonderful for its virtues. If he will look into Lib. XL, cap. 43 of Livy, he will see that, between the first and the end of the second Punic War, the practice of poisoning was so common that during part of a season a praetor punished capitally for that crime above three thousand persons in one part of Italy and found information of this sort multiplying on him. In Lib. VIII, cap. 18 of Livy, Mr Selwyn will find a similar, or rather worse, instance of the more early times of that virtuous commonwealth. So depraved in their private life were that people whom in their histories we are taught so much to admire! Do not these facts seem to denote vice enough at that period for me to doubt a little the propriety of your observation – that so great was the virtue and so trifling the vice of it as to make the history of that age appear fabulous?[39]

As well as debating intellectually and showing off his classical learning, Bully was fantasizing about a career in politics. Williams wrote to Selwyn in December: 'Your friend Bully told me he writes to you by this post. He is quite altered; goes to every assembly; is clothed every day in purple and fine lace, and swears he will at last be minister through Lady Blank, to whom he professes amorous intentions. I think he begins to be diverting in his old way, and we know he has great capabilities'.[40]

Another letter from Bully to Selwyn, still in Paris, confirms his new mood:

Lord Bolingbroke is more like a gentleman than he has latterly been, and mixes more in the polite world. He not only thinks you better qualified than anybody to form and polish the mind of a fine gentleman, but also, by your present situation very much qualified to adorn and improve the outside, and has therefore a mind to desire you to bring him over two or three pair of lace ruffles and a suit of plain velvet. By plain is meant without gold and silver; as to the colours, pattern and design of it, he relies upon Mr Selwyn's taste. A small pattern seems to be the reigning taste amongst the Macaronis at Almack's and is therefore what Lord B. chooses. Le Duc, however, must be desired to make the clothes bigger than the generality of Macaronis, as Lord B's shoulders have lately grown very broad. As to the smallness of the sleeves and length of the waist, Lord B desires them to be outré, that he may exceed any Macaronis about town and become the object of their envy. . . . for God's sake, return home. Nature never meant you for a Frenchman . . . there is nothing Mr Selwyn can import from France that will give

Lord Bolingbroke half the satisfaction as the immediate importation of himself; for no-one, neither the Queen of France nor the President Henault can possibly admire Mr Selwyn more, or love him with half the sincerity and warmth of his obedient humble servant, B.[41]

The sarcastic references to Macaronis show that Bully was now just as aware as his friends were of the identity of his wife's lover; yet at this time he appeared to accept the situation – which was not after all an uncommon one amongst his circle of acquaintances. He continued with his other old pursuits, losing money on cards and racehorses. March to Selwyn: 'there are a great many people at White's every night. Bully has lost £700 at quinze'. By the summer of 1768, Bully had even decided to relinquish his membership of Almack's, following a loss of £300, but as his brother commented to Selwyn: 'I approve much of what he has done, providing Almack's is the only place where he is capable of committing follies; but you and I, who know him, know his indiscretions are not limited to one place'. But that season was a good one at Newmarket, so some of his losses were recouped.[42]

Despite his allegedly secret liaison with Lady Di, Topham retained his public role as Macaroni and trend-setter. Lady Sarah wrote to Lady Susan in May 1766: 'You must know that there is now a rage in London for grey equipages, and Mr Beauclerk came out in the most *fringant* equipage, all grey and silver, that ever was seen'. And Williams reported to Selwyn in September how 'Madam Pitt has sprained one leg and lies at full length on her couch. She met with the accident leaning on Topham as she was stepping out from her chaise, and swears she will trust the shoulder of no Macaroni for the future'.[43]

During 1766, Topham found it impossible to reconcile his three roles as secret lover, leader of fashion and member of the masculine world of the Club. The latter lost out; as a result of his failure to attend the weekly meetings, he was deemed a lapsed member (and would have to reapply for admission two years later). The absence of the favourite, and the cause of that favourite's absence, were ominously noted by Dr Johnson.

In December 1766 Lady Di rented a house in Taplow, Buckinghamshire, just a few miles from King's Langley and so a familiar area from childhood. Here she went to stay a few days before Christmas. She took Lees and Flockton but left the cook and housemaid behind in London (the latter to be given full details later by Flockton).

Topham joined her, hotfoot from his meeting with Rousseau and his mother's funeral; he spent a week at the nearby Orkney Arms, Maidenhead, then rented a house from Sir James Lowther at Cookham Ferry, about two miles from Taplow (in the lease giving his address as Charles Street, Berkeley Square, which was actually Lady Di's address).

During this period, he was constantly in her company; he would normally come over at about eleven or twelve in the morning, and stay until at least midnight, and even 2 a.m. on one occasion. At least this was Flockton's version; but Lees said he only stayed once even until midnight, and that was because the postboy who brought his chaise was dead drunk, so another one had to be ordered; meanwhile Lady Di had gone to bed and Topham waited alone in the parlour. She sometimes had other visitors, including her sister, who was staying with their brother at Langley, but was mainly with Topham. He put up his horses in her stables, kept his chaise in her carriage house, sometimes dressed in the house, and generally annoyed Flockton and the other servants by behaving as if he were the master of the house and ordering them around.

It was this treatment that turned Flockton into such a hostile witness, who had no hesitation in confirming the adultery of his employer, in complete contrast to the blind loyalty of Mary Lees. He repeated the same suggestive anecdotes about their behaviour. One afternoon he was attending Lady Di and Topham in the parlour, when Topham suggested that they play chess, ordering Flockton to shutter the windows and fetch candles a good hour and a half before it was due to get dark. (In Lees' version, the candles were fetched and windows shut because 'though it had not been quite dark, yet it was too dark to dine'.) At other times, Topham transgressed the rules of polite society by arriving at eight in the morning and going up a pair of stairs to Lady Di's bedroom before she had formally left it to come down to breakfast – although Flockton had to concede that he did not know whether she was up or still in bed, and that Topham did speak to Mary Lees first to ask how Lady Di was. Lees denied that he ever went into the bedchamber, saying that he could not have done so without her knowing it, except perhaps on one occasion, which she could not recollect. But Flockton was now definitely spying on them – again, there was a couch in a reception room, the 'great parlour' which overlooked the garden, and again a door was frequently locked so that Flockton, on whatever excuse, could not get in. In tones of injured innocence, Flockton described how, one day when her sister had sent a letter via the postboy, he had been unable to open the door to deliver it, but had to lie to the postboy and say that he had done so 'in order to prevent his knowing that the door was fastened'. When he eventually gained access, he found them both sitting on the couch, 'much flurried, and Lady Bolingbroke's clothes and hair were much rumpled and her cap was almost off'.

He continued to keep a close eye on the couch, and found, after they had been alone together almost every night, that it was always 'rumpled and tumbled'; and after one long session he discovered three shillings lying on it. Was this a sweetener, or merely proof that Topham had again been horizontal, with money falling from his pocket? Lees however stated that the parlour door was never locked, and the couch never rumpled.

By this time, knowledge of the liaison had spread beyond the bounds of immediate friends and relations, and Lady Di's family became increasingly concerned about the damage being done not only to her reputation but, by association, to theirs. Lady Mary Coke continued to revel in the scandal:

Lady Bolingbroke, I am told, is in a situation worthy of pity, her health extremely bad and her circumstances still worse. Her brother has wrote to her to desire that she will pay him the interest of the thousand pounds he lent her last year and I am told she says she has not five guineas. This conduct in the Duke appeared so shocking that I would not have mentioned it before or give credit to it, though I am still in amaze how it is possible that a man who was always looked on to be generous with fifty thousand pounds a year can think of asking forty or fifty pounds from a sister who is in distress.[44]

So living in the country was not just a romantic idyll and an extension of the honeymoon period, but part of an economy drive, with half the servants being left in London on board wages rather than eating and drinking her better quality provisions. It was at this time that her London chair-man, Samuel Miller, was dismissed. Being in town meant new gowns (especially for court occasions), entertaining, tips, fine wines, expensive beeswax candles and the hire of costly horse transport.

But things were to become more complicated. In late January Lady Di suspected that she might be pregnant; she decided to return immediately to London to consult her former obstetrician, Dr William Hunter (appointed Physician-in-Extraordinary to Queen Charlotte in 1762, and currently supervising the almost annual succession of healthy royal births, which would eventually total seven princes and four princesses). She sent Flockton in advance to order the housemaid to light the fires, while she travelled the next day with Mary Lees in Topham's postchaise.

Strict secrecy had to be observed. She sent a note to Hunter asking him to come to her house after dark – a sensible precaution since Charles Street was in a smart residential area full of enquiring eyes, and a separated lady should not be requiring the services of an obstetrician, especially such a well-known one. And she requested him not to give his name to the footman, in the light of the footman's character another wise move. The reason why she approached Hunter, who had not assisted at the births of her second or third babies, was not just for his gynaecological skills but for his reputation for discretion. One of the causes of the widespread hostility towards the new-fangled men-midwives was the suspicion that they colluded in the secret delivery and subsequent disappearance of illegitimate babies. Although the very secrecy entailed prevented any public acknowledgement of Hunter's involvement in such activities, his name was certainly passed from one embarrassed wealthy client to another, contributing almost as effectively to his fame and wealth as his high-profile public reputation as a distinguished doctor with a well-honed bedside manner acceptable to the highest in the land.

His attitude to pregnancy, not merely unwanted but capable of destroying a woman's or a family's reputation, was compassionate and supportive; his mission was to assist women in this position rather than uphold society's disapproving attitude which might result in infanticide, or even suicide. Among other women in this position who sought his help was the unmarried 'daughter of a peer', who found herself pregnant by an army colonel, who was then killed in the American War. Hunter attended her during the secret pregnancy and birth, which had to take place silently in her family home. He then immediately removed from the house not one baby but twins, and paid £100 for each to be looked after at the Foundling Hospital. Another aristocratic client was the Duchess of Grafton, in a case very similar to Lady Di's: Hunter had previously officially attended as man-midwife the birth of her legitimate children, but when she separated from her husband the Duke and became pregnant by her lover Lord Ossory (Topham's travelling companion on the Grand Tour) Hunter visited her, in conditions of the strictest secrecy, in the house in the country where she had gone to give birth. He carried away the newborn child to London and arranged for a wet-nurse. He also attended Martha Ray, the mistress of the Earl of Sandwich, on several occasions. Some aristocratic women chose to go abroad to give birth to their love children, like Lady Bess Foster, when having the Duke of Devonshire's babies, and the Duchess of Devonshire herself, when having a baby which was not the Duke's. But for those who could not afford this luxury and had to remain based in London, Dr Hunter was the man. By 1765, he had already amassed a fortune of £20,000, much of which had come from his fees for such services.

When he arrived at the house, the door was opened by Flockton, who confirmed that Lady Bolingbroke was at home, and asked his name; when Hunter said that it did not signify, Flockton replied that his lady would not see anybody unless she knew their name. Hunter persisted, and Flockton reluctantly reported his arrival to Lady Di, upstairs in the dining room with Topham, who had obviously been put in the picture from the moment of her first suspicions. Hunter was shown into the little room off the dining room, and noticed that Lady Di appeared to be flurried and almost fainting; he initially thought that she had suffered some great misfortune. However, after she had recovered a little, their conversation soon established that she was pregnant. He had quickly suspected that she was 'breeding' but at first told her not to tell him what she thought was wrong but let him guess, a form of heavy Scottish irony which she could probably have done without. A rational man, he did not regard pregnancy as requiring any particular form of treatment or unnecessary medicines but simply advised her to go back into the country, and remain in touch with him by letter. For greater discretion – this was a very tactful and experienced doctor – she should use the false name of Mrs Molineux when she wrote: this was the real name of one of the midwives with whom he worked.

Pregnancy and childbirth were viewed by the upper classes as a frequent and integral part of a woman's life, reinforcement of the function of marriage and the justification of the union of great families through the due production of heirs. The conception of an illegitimate child involved different rules for men and for women. The bastards of married men were often publicly acknowledged, and taken into or supported by the family, like Augustus Retnuh Reebkomp; there was not a lot of shame involved in the recognition of a husband's extra-marital relationship, apart from hurting a wife's feelings. But the tangible proof of a married woman's adultery did not merely imply her moral transgression but was a betrayal of the social structure and something which threatened the whole system of inheritance. This was not just the viewpoint of the aristocracy but also of any logical moralist: Dr Johnson attacked adultery because of 'the confusion of progeny which might result. All the property in the world depended on female chastity'.[45]

Lady Di's shocked reaction to her pregnancy confirmed the danger-ous position that she was now in – a woman of rank, long separated from her husband, should not be publicly seen to be with child. Any methods of birth control had clearly been unsuccessful. Various herbal mixtures were believed to be effective, particularly a compound of the bark of the poplar tree, which was thought to encourage barrenness in women, and Mary Lees did refer to the bark medicine which Lady Di took regularly. The condom was mainly used as protection against venereal infections from prostitutes, and could be purchased in broth-els for immediate use, at a vast mark-up, from the madames who bought them in bulk. They were made of linen and came in three different sizes – although Mrs Constantia Phillips, who ran a sex shop in Covent Garden in the 1750s, was pioneering one made of sheep-gut.[46]

It was possible that they may have considered abortion and dis-cussed this option with Dr Hunter. Abortion, or induced miscarriage, was indeed viewed as one of a range of methods of birth control. It did not become a statutory offence until 1803, and only then because the reform of the brutal laws which had previously made infanticide a capital offence meant that abortion was treated with greater severity. Nor was it even interpreted as the deliberate taking of life until after the baby could be felt moving, or 'quickening', at the end of the fourth month of pregnancy. This meant that the foetus now had a life of its own and often served as the definitive confirmation of pregnancy. Even the 1803 act made procuring an abortion a felony punishable by death only when applied to 'any woman then quick with child', therefore not a felony before the quickening. There were attempts by doctors at this time to demonstrate that life had begun at the moment of conception, and to change the outmoded attitudes of women that life was not truly present until movement could be felt. But in the 1760s and '70s, the law had a duty only to protect a foetus once it had quickened.

Conception had occurred in late November and pregnancy was confirmed in late January. As the quickening would not be expected until the end of March, there was still some time to take action. Hunter would probably not have recommended attempts at inducing abortion, since his particular skill was in midwifery, public or secret; yet he himself had stated that 'the life of the mother . . . is almost of an incomparably greater value than that of an unborn child; a being which we may suppose has no enjoyment, and has neither a desire to live nor fear to die'. There were a range of drugs and potions, based on plants and herbs, including pennyroyal, hellebore, savin, and ergot of rye, which were believed to be effective abortifacients. These domestic or kitchen-garden remedies were being increasingly supplemented in the expanding consumerism of the day by 'female pills' which were widely advertised as claiming to be able to regulate various women's disorders, by controlling or rather bringing on menstruation. So while the encouragement of pregnancy and protection against miscarriage were crucial elements in the medical well-being of a married woman, a more lateral interpretation could produce the opposite effect. Just as the man-midwife was replacing the female one in supervising childbirth, so even the practice of abortion was becoming more professionally regulated. Doctors, men-midwives, apothecaries and herbalists were regarded as the main practitioners, rather than the old crones who had been the only previous resort for supplies and advice, not only for seduced single girls but also by married women to whom yet another pregnancy was not convenient or safe. For example in the 1750s, the upright Caroline Fox, on suspecting her third pregnancy within three years, told her husband: 'I'm certainly breeding. I took a great deal of physic yesterday in hopes to send it away . . . [later] I am not breeding (is not that clever!)' Of course, for a married woman, whether the miscarriage was natural or encouraged was not significant; the latter could simply be interpreted as the former. But it was a different matter for a separated woman who was still legally married although meant to be living alone.[47]

Another method believed to be effective in encouraging miscarriage was the letting of blood. Lady Di was bled on two or three occasions by Mr Kimber, an apothecary and surgeon, but this was during the later stages of her pregnancy and may have been to alleviate the various other discomforts she was suffering. Earlier attempts at intervention are hinted at in the accounts of mysterious boxes of medicine ordered in London by Topham and sent twice a week by the London stagecoach; a small oval deal box, addressed to Topham, was delivered to the Maidenhead Bridge coach staging point, from where it was brought by Topham's servants to Taplow, and taken by Flockton to Topham in the parlour; it was not allowed to be opened or touched by anyone else. The box contained phials of medicine, but Topham tore off and burned the labels. He might give a phial to Flockton to carry to Mary Lees to prepare; or sometimes Flockton himself was ordered to take two of the phials and the cup out of which their contents were drunk, to Lady Di; or else the housemaid would take the medicine and a cup up to Lady Di when she was in bed. The housemaid then removed the empty phials. Mary Lees said that these medicines were sent by Mr Tuerdale, the apothecary who attended Lady Di in London, and that they contained bark, a medicine which she took twice a day – presumably as an acceptable although ineffective contraceptive. But this contradicts the apparent secrecy about the contents and the fact that the deliveries were organized by Topham. Other heavy hints of wrongdoing were given by Flockton in his particular emphasis on the rye loaves provided every week by Topham for Lady Di – ergot, a fungus growth produced in rye bread, was commonly regarded as the most successful abortifacient (as ergometrine, it is still used today to stimulate uterine contractions). But it was also recognized as an aphrodisiac, and as a hallucinogenic drug, so Flockton's allegations were wide-ranging.[48]

So it is possible that various attempts at abortion were made in the earlier stages of Lady Di's pregnancy. The servants reported her falling ill in February, allegedly with the measles, and being confined to bed for several days, under the care of a nurse, and it was another week before she could come downstairs. But if there had been signs of possible miscarriage, it did not take place. While she was ill in bed, Topham went upstairs to her room, again transgressing the normal boundaries; the housemaid was shocked to see him often sitting by the bedside. And after she was out of bed but still confined upstairs, he continued to go up to see her, often alone. Indeed, while she was recovering, the back drawing room couch was taken up another flight of stairs into the bedroom, and after Topham had spent the evening with her it was described as looking tumbled again. After she was better he would come for breakfast, dinner and supper, staying till midnight while they went on rumpling the couch, now restored to the dining room. Apart from the hair powder and the mud from the boots, the cushions were sometimes replaced upside down by the careless couple.

That the relationship was now known about in her closer circles is confirmed by Mary Lees' evidence: Lady Di was happy to receive visits, while in Topham's company, from her brothers and sister and other regular friends, but formal callers tended to be denied admittance, whether or not she was alone.

In early March she returned to Taplow, attended by Mary Lees, Flockton, and the housemaid Elizabeth Thomas, where they remained until after Easter. At the same time, Topham stayed in the house he had rented at Cookham but visited Taplow constantly. There were sometimes other visitors, including Mrs Pitt, who stayed for two or three days, and Lady Pembroke. Lady Di and Topham often went for walks together, or she would ride in his chaise while he rode on horseback beside her, and, perhaps as an attempt to escape the ever-watchful eyes of her own servants, she now spent many evenings with Topham at Cookham, going over in his chaise about five in the evening, and being brought back at ten by Topham, who would then stay with her for supper, sometimes not leaving till one in the morning. On one occasion, Flockton reported with relish, the cook had told him that she had heard them lock the parlour door, which Flockton had of course gone to check. And on the many other occasions when they had been alone in the parlour, the couch was very much tumbled and rumpled.

While staying in the country, Topham had hired horses and a driver from one Bright Hemmings, of Curzon Street; the driver, Abyen Rowley, took the horses to Cookham and remained there, working for Topham, and subsequently for Lady Di, who took over the same horses from July. Rowley confirmed how he would sometimes take them both to London, just for the day, and how Topham visited Taplow every day from Cookham, returning late at night, or Lady Di went to Cookham, to dine or to take tea, fetched either by Topham or by Rowley. Topham or Lady Di's groom always travelled with them.

Despite his obviously continuing fascination with Lady Di, enjoyment of her company and support for her in this dangerous situation, Topham did manage to maintain a little of his 'other' life by occasionally visiting London at this time. He would then bring back with him oil and vinegar for Lady Di, and also sent her other food and game, plus a hamper of wine, and a case of Dorset beer.

While at Taplow, she was attended not by Dr Hunter but by her own physician, Dr Turton (another rising man, later to become physician to the royal family), who saw her in company with Topham, and who ordered prescriptions which were prepared by her London apothecary; she was also seen by Mr Kimber, the local apothecary and surgeon from Windsor; she complained of toothache, and earache, and was often sick.

When the other servants commented to Mary Lees about Lady Di's state of health, she simply replied that her mistress was unwell, and described her as being ill and feverish. But the servants had also noticed that her size was increasing. Flockton even claimed to have been suspicious since late January; he said that he and his fellow-servants had realized that she was pregnant and frequently discussed the situation, although the loyal Mary Lees tried to deny it and said she had put on weight because of her poor health and because she was dropsical. But Flockton and his colleagues agreed that 'if she was not with child, they never saw a woman that was'; and despite Dr Hunter's celebrated discretion, Flockton claimed to be aware of his profession. To fit her mistress's widening waistline, Mary Lees had to order maternity underwear from London in the form of a new pair of 'jumps'. This was an unboned loose and comfortable undergarment, unlike the whalebone-stiffened stays normally worn, but still designed to minimize swelling stomachs ('when our grandmothers were pregnant they wore jumps to conceal it', wrote a lady in 1794); and it obviously should have been worn by the pregnant Miss Burchell – 'soon discovered by her shape (for she was without her stays) that it was high time for her to seek a place of concealment' – in Frances Sheridan's *Memoirs of Miss Sidney Biddulph* (1761).[49]

The sensitive task of ordering the jumps was entrusted to Morgan, the cook, who was still in London. Elizabeth Thomas, the housemaid, must occasionally have acted as lady's maid, for it was her job to lace up these jumps, and she noticed latterly that she could not do them up as tightly as she had previously managed. Mary Lees claimed unconvincingly that it was not until June or July that she noticed that Lady

Di's clothes were not fitting her as well as they used to so that she had to have her stays and gowns let out.

During April and May, Lady Di alternated between London and Taplow; she travelled in Topham's chaise, and they would stop for dinner at an inn at Cranford Bridge, an appropriate halting place halfway between Taplow and London. Their discretion was now such that, on one such occasion, they travelled together in Topham's chaise as far as Cranford Bridge, then came on to London separately, with Lady Di remaining in Topham's chaise, while he hired another one. When in London, she saw Dr Hunter regularly. He always came after dark, at around nine in the evening, and would walk to her house, even when it was raining, this rich, famous man, rather than taking his own chair or chaise, so that his own servants should not know where he was going. And when they wrote to each other, she continued to use the false name, in case the letters fell into the wrong hands. She was taking a lot of medicine at this time but now to relieve the various discomforts of her condition rather than possibly to terminate it.

As the pregnancy became more obvious, the presence of the gossiping, indiscreet servants was a major problem. Elizabeth Thomas was dismissed in early May, following a quarrel with Mary Lees, who had found out that she had been telling the whole neighbourhood about the pregnancy. William Flockton was dismissed a week later, ostensibly because he was not sufficiently obedient to Mary Lees but really because he was too well aware of what was going on. Lees said that he was dismissed on her mistress's orders.

In the middle of July, now eight months pregnant, Lady Di returned to London, and began to employ the driver Rowley on a regular basis; he either went daily to her house to find out if he was needed, or waited to be summoned. Rowley noted that she was now very secluded, seeing only Mr Beauclerk, and her brothers and sister, though she went out every day in a post-chaise to take the air (this being a part of Hunter's modern approach to healthy pregnancy), attended by Mary Lees and the driver, but no other manservant.

Mary Lees was now masterminding the arrangements for the approaching birth to take place in the maximum secrecy. A new footman, George Carpenter, was taken on, but was soon sent to the Taplow house. Rowley was regarded as trustworthy, for at this time he was asked by Mary Lees to come in the mornings and clean the knives and light the fires until a temporary girl could be found. He was then told he would not be needed for a week or two, was paid his outstanding wages and was given an extra guinea for his trouble. Morgan the cook was also dismissed in early August; she asked indignantly why she had been discharged, but Lees simply replied that it was on Lady Bolingbroke's orders and that there was no particular reason. However one factor was the cook's too thorough knowledge of Topham's involvement; he had made Lady Di the rather ostentatious gift of a fine new four-poster bed, to replace her tent-bed (a structure designed to be portable, and therefore appropriate for a lady living in temporary accommodation). This was installed at the beginning of August by an upholsterer's assistant, who told Morgan that his boss worked for Topham; the bed was later shown off by the cook to Topham's maidservant, who had come to visit, and the maidservant said that Topham had personally selected the design. While the two women were poking around upstairs, where they certainly should not have been, the cook also noticed in Lady Di's bedroom a mysterious box, which had not been there before – perhaps this contained a cradle which had been ordered from the same firm.[50]

The birth had been intended to take place at Taplow, since Carpenter, the footman, and a new housemaid were sent down there in early August. Another servant, Maria Alford, had been hired by Lees in late July, in order to look after the Charles Street house while Lady Di went to the country in about five weeks' time; Mary Lees had not been able to specify exactly when this event would take place, but told Alford to be ready whenever she was sent for. She was obviously not meant to be in the house until Lady Di had left it.

In the middle of August, Lady Di became increasingly unwell. The footman was sent urgently to the country home of the apothecary Mr Tuerdale, asking him to come back to London and see her. She was described by Dr Hunter as being very ill for the few days leading up to 20 August, when he understood she was planning to leave London for Taplow; in the house were only Mary Lees and Mary Molineux, the monthly nurse, who had been hired some time in advance. Nurse Molineux, then aged fifty-nine, had attended Lady Di at the birth of her first child, and was now recruited again by Hunter, with whom she regularly worked, as a general part of the service he offered during the accouchement and lying-in period. The role of the monthly nurse was to assist in the actual birth, attend the mother afterwards and generally carry out the doctor's orders. The nurse had moved into the house in early August and was hired for a month; she slept in a room adjacent to Lady Di's, and sat for company with Mary Lees downstairs.

On 20 August, Maria Alford, the new temporary housekeeper, was fetched to Charles Street at about six in the evening by a postilion belonging to Topham. Here she was greeted by Mary Lees, who seemed very confused and in a great hurry, and said that her mistress had been going to go out of town, but was now taken ill with a cold and could not go. At around nine that evening, Dr Hunter was summoned, and pronounced Lady Di to be in labour; at eleven, she gave birth to a daughter, in the presence of Mary Lees, Dr Hunter, and Nurse Molineux. Topham was in the house, waiting downstairs. Informed of the birth by Dr Hunter, he immediately went up to see Lady Di and their baby. Maria Alford knew nothing of this, but heard during the evening a lot of noise in the house, which went on until midnight, with the street door opening and shutting, and people going up and downstairs. Her only contact was with Mary Lees, who asked to be informed, next morning, when Mr Beauclerk's postilion arrived. Dr Hunter removed the baby from the house, and took it to a wet-nurse near Westminster; as Molineux claimed not to know where, this had been arranged and carried out by Dr Hunter himself as a part of the standard service expected by his clients.

In order to maintain the secrecy, the soiled linen and clothes were sent out to be washed not by the regular washing-woman but by another, a Mrs Coward. When the regular washerwoman called, she was told that Lady Bolingbroke was about to leave town, and that there would be linen to wash after she had gone.

Lady Di remained in seclusion for three weeks, attended daily by Topham, who visited her at first in her bedchamber, sometimes staying until ten in the evening, and there were some evening visits from Dr Hunter. During this time, she was cooked the foods appropriate for women who had just given birth, chicken broth and caudle, by Maria Alford, who did not normally see her mistress, but would carry the food upstairs, knock at the bedroom door and leave the tray outside for Mary Lees or the nurse to fetch in.

The preparation of 'caudle' (from the Latin *calidus*, warm) was a confusion of medical and social ritual and in this case was mainly medicinal; caudle itself was a mildly alcoholic but nourishing beverage, sweetened wine or ale mulled with herbs and spices, bread or eggs into a thin gruel that was meant to alleviate the discomforts of childbirth and afterwards, but was also shared in a ritual of female solidarity with the women attending the birth. Following legitimate, welcomed births in the eighteenth and early nineteenth centuries, communal caudle-drinking was enjoyed by the female members of a family when they came to see the new baby. Chicken broth was also part of the recommended very light diet, consisting mainly of liquids, that was recommended for a new mother (as prescribed, for example, by Dr Hunter for Queen Charlotte).

The suggestive presence of the monthly nurse was kept secret from Alford, who was initially told that Lady Di had an elderly female visitor in her bedchamber. On the second or third day after the birth, when Alford had taken a tray up, she noted that the bedroom door was opened by a woman who was not Mary Lees. Another time, Alford took the tea-kettle up, and overheard Lady Di calling 'nurse'. Alford had been instructed by Lees not to admit anyone, with the exception of Mr Beauclerk, since her mistress was 'not at home'.

Lady Di saw no one else for the first ten days, although her brother-in-law Lord Pembroke called during this period. She then came downstairs; Topham visited two or three times a day, staying for dinner and supper. As there was no proper cook in the house, the dinners were brought in from a tavern in Curzon Street. She began to see her friends again, including her brother Lord Charles Spencer, Lord Pembroke, and Lady Caroline Adair, a cousin of the Lennox sisters, who had already braved a scandal of her own by eloping with a mere surgeon ten years earlier.

As her servants had either been dismissed or sent to the Taplow house, Mary Lees, on 5 September, sent Maria Alford to Westminster to hire the former chair-man, Samuel Miller, to run errands and act as footman and living-in manservant for three weeks, until 27 September. Lady Di was attended during this period by Dr Turton, her own doctor, who continued to write prescriptions which were made up by the apothecary. One of Miller's errands for Mary Lees was to fetch some medicinal substance which was put into Lady Di's whey.

Despite all the precautions, news of the birth inevitably started to spread. Just a week after the event, Selwyn wrote to Holland:

The affair of Lord and Lady Bolingbroke is likely to become very serious, and a great amusement to the town when it fills, according as people's curiosity or sensibility is the most predominant. The *Chronique* says she is brought to bed. Servants are become evidencers, and the husband hopes by this imprudent management of her and her simple lover, to be freed *a vinculo matrimonii*, and in future times to marry a rich monster and retrieve his affairs. I hope you will not quote me. He made me his confident upon the first discovery, and I kept his secret, but I found he and his servants together had, in my absence from town of one day only, told it to a hundred people.

A few days later, Selwyn claimed, surely unconvincingly, that the news had died down: 'I hear no more of Lady Bolingbroke. Bully thinks he has sufficient grounds to go upon, so he will proceed with his civilians and deponents'.[51]

On 7 September, Bully sent a card, by the hand of his valet de chambre John Dupont, which read: 'Lord Bolingbroke is very sorry to hear Lady Bolingbroke is ill, and desires to know how she does.' This received the reply: 'Lady Bolingbroke is much obliged to Lord Bolingbroke, and is a little better'. While Dupont was delivering the note to Charles Street, he observed Topham approaching, in company with Dr Turton. The presence of Topham, and even the visit of the doctor, would not in themselves be startling news: but doubtless some kind friend had taken it upon himself to inform him of the real reason for their combined presence. Bully could accept being left, and even being cuckolded, but as he and society knew too well, his inheritance could go to Topham's bastard if the two legitimate sons were to die (a not unreasonable scenario given the prevalence of smallpox and the risks inherent in most medical treatments), as long as he remained married to Lady Di.

One week later, Lady Mary Coke reported his reaction:

Have you heard that Lady Bolingbroke is brought to bed of a son and that her lord is endeavouring to have a divorce? It is thought however that he will not be able to succeed, and the Duke of Bedford, I am told, has advised him to take no notice of this business; in answer to which his Lordship says he can't bear to think of Mr Beauclerk's son inheriting his estate and title, in case his own two sons should die, and that on that account he must try to procure the divorce. Lady Bolingbroke in the meantime braves the affair, and says that though she had been very ill, she was now so much better that she thought she would soon be well enough to go to the Queen. But is it possible her Majesty can keep her in the royal household after it is so publicly known she has lain in?[52]

It was not the adultery or the actual lying-in that was the scandal, but the fact that the child was not begotten by the husband. Although Lady Mary's source had got the sex wrong and the baby girl, for the moment, had been magicked away by Hunter to the dubious care of a commercial wet-nurse, the next might be a boy. Bully may even have chosen to claim that it was a son, in order to justify his subsequent course of action. There was also the interesting moral dimension recently expounded by Rousseau, whom Topham had been so anxious to meet, that the child born to an adulterous wife was already a thief because it violated the rights of inheritance. Divorce was now inevitable.

Before the establishment of the Divorce Courts set up by the Matrimonial Causes Act of 1857, obtaining a divorce was a complicated and very expensive legal process, a prerogative only of the wealthy and influential, and one which attracted a very great deal of publicity. By the early eighteenth century, there had only ever been three divorces granted to peers. The fourth, in 1740, was that of the Duke of Beaufort, who, in order to disprove his adulterous wife's counter-charge of his impotency, managed to demonstrate his virility to court officials and doctors, impressing also Horace Walpole on the grounds that he was able to perform behind a screen instead of demanding his ancient right to be accompanied to a brothel: 'His Grace's ---- is in everybody's mouth.' The fifth noble divorce was that of the Bolingbrokes.[53]

From the middle of the seventeenth century, divorce cases had become subject to civil as well as ecclesiastical law (those committing adultery had previously been tried by the Church in its 'bawdy courts'), since it was recognized that property as well as morality was involved. A husband was entitled to bring an action for damages against his wife's lover, if he could prove the accusation that the lover had committed what was described as criminal conversation (crim. con. for short) with the accuser's wife. It was necessary to prove crim. con. in both ecclesiastical and civil courts before a divorce could be granted, and it was only by Act of Parliament that permission to remarry could be conferred. So by the second half of the eighteenth century, obtaining a divorce involved three separate legal actions. There were proceedings in the Ecclesiastical (or Consistory) Court, for which witnesses were privately interrogated and their evidence recorded in the form of written depositions. On consideration of this evidence, the court could then grant a separation from bed and board on the grounds of cruelty and adultery by a husband, or adultery by a wife. The Church might approve the separation, but common law had also to be invoked through the civil courts, in order to consider the husband's claim for damages from the lover. By going to court rather than fighting a duel, the aggrieved husband at least obtained funds for the considerable costs involved in three lawsuits, which would have to cover not only lawyers' fees for their time, but also the administrative and secretarial expenses. (As the clerks and copyists were paid per page, they might write as little as ten words per page, and therefore the preparation of witness statements alone could run into hundreds of pounds when the costs of travel and maintenance were included.) The third and final stage was a Private Bill introduced in the House of Lords, during which witnesses had to appear before a Committee of the House; the Bill then had to go through the House of Commons before royal assent could be obtained for an Act which dissolved the marriage and gave to both parties the right to remarry.

This complicated, expensive and very public procedure meant that, although unhappiness and adultery were common enough and many couples informally lived apart, official separations were rare and very few seriously considered ending their marriages. The Bolingbroke divorce marked the thin end of a wedge and signalled the shifts in expectation and morality during the second half of the century. Only two years later the commentator on another aristocratic divorce, that of the Earl and Countess of Grosvenor, stated: 'Adultery is become so fashionable and Divorces so frequent, that it may admit of some debate in the polite world whether the first was criminal or the latter dishonourable'.[54]

On 20 September, Walpole, who had just returned from Paris, heard that 'it was reported in town that Lord Bolingbroke had got sufficient evidence to obtain a divorce, and had wrote to the Duke of Marlborough to acquaint him with his intention. This will put it past a possibility of her keeping her place at court; indeed it would have been shameful if she had'. Three weeks later, he was updating Selwyn, still in Paris: 'Lady Bolingbroke has declared she will come into waiting on Sunday se'nnight; but as the Queen is likely to be brought to bed before that time, this may be only a bravado. The report is that she intends to acknowledge all that my lord can desire'.[55]

Lady Mary Coke was also hovering like a vulture, but still getting her facts wrong: 'Mrs Berkeley said she heard the child Lady Boling-broke was brought to bed with is dead, since when it is said the Duke of Marlborough has prevailed with Lord Bolingbroke to stop the proceedings of the divorce'.[56]

It was too late. Lady Di was taking legal advice from Thomas Walker, the town clerk of Woodstock, and professional adviser to the Marlborough family on legal and administrative matters; he had worked on her father's will, and often visited London on her brother's service. She wrote him an anxious note, at eleven in the evening of 18 November 1767, on the verge of the opening of the official proceedings: 'Sir, I must beg you to call upon me tomorrow morning any time before eleven, as there are two or three questions I want to ask before you leave Town that are of great consequence. I hope this will be no inconvenience to you, for I shall be in great distress if I cannot be resolved these questions tomorrow.'[57]

On 21 November, Lady Mary recorded: 'Sir William Duncan told me that it was reported in town that Lady Bolingbroke had wrote to the Queen to say that she should not presume to pay her duty to her Majesty till she had cleared her character. It was said that Lady Delawar was immediately to be appointed in her place.' A few days later, there was competition to fill the favourite's place: 'Lady Ailes-bury told me the Duchess of Hamilton had said Lady Holdernesse, Lady Hertford and Lady Delawar had all asked to be Lady of the Bed Chamber in the room of Lady Bolingbroke, but that it was likely to be Lady Delawar.'[58]

The news, rippling outwards, spread to Mme de Boufflers' salon in Paris by David Hume (appointed Secretary to the British Ambassador in place of a reluctant Charles Bunbury): 'There is an affair broken out which makes a great noise, between Lady Bolingbroke and your friend Beauclerk. This lady was separated from her husband some time ago but, 'tis pretended, bore a child lately to Mr Beauclerk; and 'tis certain her husband has begun a process for a divorce, in which nobody doubts of his success. It is a great pity; she is handsome and agreeable and ingenious, far beyond the ordinary rate. I know not whether she was of your acquaintance.'[59]

And Walpole informed Florence, via Sir Horace Mann: 'This is all our public and private news, except the divorce of Lord and Lady Bolingbroke, which is determined; and by the consent of her family she is to marry Mr Beauclerk, the hero of the piece – an affair in which I suppose you interest yourself no more than I do!' A line has been inked out after 'hero of the piece' – Walpole has lapsed in bawdy language to his old friend.[60]

His assumption of the foregone conclusion – divorce and remarriage – suggests that the three parties, with the support of the Duke of Marlborough, were colluding in an uncontested divorce suit in order to speed up the proceedings, as well as saving money and hoping to limit press coverage. This would prevent a long drawn-out hearing in which Lady Di could, in theory, have brought a counter-suit citing Bully's alleged infidelities and cruelty. But as they all wanted a clean break, with the right to remarry as soon as possible – Bully needed an heiress, and Lady Di needed to secure the legitimate father of her love child – they and their legal advisers fixed a deal whereby Bully would settle for modest damages from Topham in return for being quickly freed from the marriage by Act of Parliament.

The content of these proceedings was being discussed in the south of France, where a select group wintering in Nice were kept in touch with London life by George Selwyn. Lord March wrote back salaciously: 'I hear the house of Hayes in Chamber Alley is to make its appearence at B---'s trial. Are they to prove that Beauclerk, etc. etc? – or has Bully called these witnesses to appear to his character?' This was a reference to Charlotte Hayes' tasteful brothel just off Covent Garden. And Lord Holland thanked Selwyn on 23 December for a letter written as recently as 8 December (evidence of an efficient postal distribution system): 'I think poor Lady Bolingbroke's folly is likely to end better than I thought it would, though, God knows, I am sorry for it, very badly.' Selwyn agreed in his next letter: 'Poor Lady Bol., quelle triste perspective pour elle! J'en suis veritablement touché. [What a sad prospect she faces! I'm truly affected for her.]'[61]

The first stage of the divorce was for Bully to sue Topham in the common law court of the King's Bench (tucked into a corner of Westminster Hall, separated only by a partition from the rest of that busy forum and attended by interested spectators). This procedure was brief and virtually a formality in an uncontested suit; neither participant had to appear in person, and damages were awarded to Bully of a modest £500 plus costs. This product of civilized collusion was actually cited as a precedent in the next celebrity divorce, just a year later, between the Duke and Duchess of Grafton; the Duke's legal adviser stated: 'in the case of Lord Bolingbroke, there was a verdict at law for £500, which he was to take no advantage of'.[62]

Far more detailed evidence was required by the London Diocesan Consistory Court, known as Doctors' Commons, 'an ugly unpleasant place in this Town where love causes are tried en dernier resort' according to Mrs Montague, when the husband of a friend of hers was being cited for adultery. She was aware of the press interest in such cases: 'I am quite vex'd to think how Lady V. will be mortified, how her Lord will be fined and all the unpleasant circumstances of this affair . . . not yet Publick but it will soon speed round the Country and through the Cities on paper wings'. Proceedings were not open to the public; the warring couples of the 1760 and '70s would have been horrified to know that every detail of their infidelity would later be sold in print.[63]

Here, on 5 December, Bully's proctor (a civil lawyer licensed to practice in an ecclesiastical court) launched Lord Bolingbroke's suit 'that he may be divorced from bed, board and mutual cohabitation' with his wife on the grounds of her adultery, and presented a summary of the case. The court then considered the written statements provided by the witnesses called by both sides, who included Dr Hunter and all the servants involved. These had all been interrogated privately; although there was no oral cross-examination, there could be a second interrogation of witnesses in order to respond to particular queries raised by the other side. Such evidence took several weeks to obtain and process. At the end of the third week of January 1768, there was a hearing in which the proctors spoke on behalf of their clients, and the judge had to weigh up the conflicting claims of Mary Lees and William Flockton as to whether or not Lady Di had committed adultery with Beauclerk (Lees' evidence confusingly conceding that Lady Di had given birth but that 'Mr Beauclerk could not have been the father'). The judge had no doubts: 'Lady Diana, Viscountess Bolingbroke, after the solemnisation and consummation of the marriage, being altogether unmindful of her conjugal vow and not having the fear of God before her eyes did commit the crime of adultery with Topham Beauclerk.' Bully's suit of crim. con. was allowed, and the court granted divorce on 9 February. The terms were that Lady Di should receive an annual allowance of £800, but lost her entitlement to £2,000 per annum as a widow, and neither were allowed to remarry as long as the other remained alive – that was a right that could only be conferred by Parliament.

These stages were of course the source of more excited gossip. Coke recorded:

Lady Waldegrave mentioned Lady Bolingbroke's divorce having passed Doctors' Commons, and that it was to come into the House of Lords after Christmas; that the Duke of Marlborough had shown himself a very kind brother and been to see her and assisted her with money. She added that Mr Beauclerk was to marry her as soon as the divorce had passed the House of Lords and that they were to go abroad. The Duke of Marlborough intended being very little in town till this talk of the town was over, and that Lord and Lady Pembroke had gone abroad on the same account. She said she understood Lady Bolingbroke had received her dismissal from court. Those who suffer have always a title to be treated with compassion, and 'tis said Lady Bolingbroke repents her bad conduct and is very miserable; yet I must say I think her family give great proof of their friendship in treating her with such kindness, considering the disgrace she had brought on them; the little friendship I have met with, who never gave offence either to my family or the world perhaps occasioned this reflection. I am really glad that friendship exists, though I don't meet with it.[64]

Confirmation of the Duke's generosity, as well of his participation in the collusion, came from Sir William Musgrave, writing to Lord Carlisle: 'It is said Lord Bolingbroke's proceedings against his Lady are compromised; that he takes a sum of money from the Duke of Marlborough, who is also to allow the lady £200 per annum and Lord Bolingbroke to do the same, and no more to be said about it.'[65]

That the relationship between the divorcing couple was fairly civil is also implied by Selwyn's role as intermediary in negotiating for Lady Di the rights of access to her two boys, which Bully, in theory, could have forbidden. 'Sat an hour with poor Lady Bol; she was very easy and cheerful, et avec une insensibilité qui m'en donneroit pour elle [and with an insensitivity which I ought to reciprocate]; but that cannot be. She told me she had a favour to ask of me, which was that I would use my endeavours that she might see her children. Bully is at present out of town, but to be sure I shall have no difficulty in that negotiation'.[66]

Dismissal from court was inevitable; her position as Lady of the Bedchamber was officially terminated on 5 January 1768. This was a blow, not least because of the loss of independent income but also because of the further public acknowledgement of her lowered status and presumed guilt. However, it did bring an end to the tedium and sycophancy of the routine. (When Lady Northumberland decided to resign in 1770, it was because she wished to become 'no longer a dependent, a state I ever detested and longing to enjoy my liberty entire'. This was her private diary entry but her resignation letter to the Queen cited, untruthfully, a decline in her health.)[67]

Selwyn reported to Carlisle how 'Lady Bolingbroke has sent her resignation to the Queen, who wrote her a very gracious letter upon it', adding that Bully had just kissed hands following his own long-sought reappointment to the King's Bedchamber. Another news item in this letter was the fact that Bully was seeing the notorious Polly Jones: 'The night robberies are very frequent. Polly Jones, my neighbour, was a few nights ago stopped, when the chair was set down at Bully's door, and she robbed of 12 guineas, which, I suppose, she had been out to earn with the sweat of her brow'. Polly Jones, sometimes known as Kennedy, was a part-time actress and full-time whore, who had a long and successful career in and around Covent Garden and beyond. Her lovers included the Duke of Cumberland, and her reputation was such that 'Louis XV would dissolve our parliament if Polly Jones did but say a word to him', according to Walpole, criticizing the instability of the French constitution. Her own opinion of Bully was as 'a profligate tawdry fellow . . . who boasted that he could seduce any innocent girl whatever'. Her assets and defects were described in the *List of Covent Garden Ladies, or the New Atlantis*, a sort of Michelin Guide to the tarts of the area. According to the 1773 list, she 'has a very snug annuity besides a number of pretty things . . . she never knew what love is – she has no heart susceptible to that Passion. When she holds you in her arms, she thinks she beholds a diamond ring, a necklace'.[68]

Despite the assumption that Lady Di was now a ruined woman and one who had disgraced her family too, she continued to be received in society. One evening in January, for example, she dined at Selwyn's and then went to the theatre in a party which included the Bunburys, Lord March and James Craufurd. But Lord Holland lamented from Nice: 'I do not know Mr Beauclerk; but be he what he will, the fate of my poor dear friend's daughter afflicts me. I cannot bear to think of the folly of it, nor do I see how all her relations, if they wished her as well as I do, can mend the matter'. And Lady Mary Coke confirmed this attitude: 'I went to Bedford House and found the Duchess at home. The Duchess of Marlborough had brought her two little girls to make her a visit. They are both very fine children and both pretty; the eldest is a very good resemblance of Ly Bolingbroke & the youngest is like the Duchess of Marlborough. I thought the Duchess of Bedford seems to admire them very much. She mentioned Lady Bolingbroke and said she was so agreeable that she thought her a loss to society, that she was very impatient for the Divorce passing the House of Lords, that there might be an end to the Affair'.[69]

Beauclerk was also being observed. Selwyn thought that he 'looks wretchedly and has been very ill', in contrast to the Duke of Grafton, whose own divorce suit was pending, who 'goes on very well'. Selwyn also meditated on Bully's character, recalling his affair with Lady Coventry, and wishing that he had employed 'sentiments of honour and delicacy in love affairs . . . instead of admiring his profligate uncle and Lord Chesterfield's affected systems . . . he has the wherewithal to make himself respectable on every account, but will find it very difficult, if possible, to wear out the first impressions. It is a pity; he has besides some very good parts, some very good qualities, and naturally no ill ones'. Horace Walpole's revolutionary thesis *Historic Doubts on the Life and Reign of King Richard the Third*, which proposed the King's innocence of the murder of his nephews, had just been published, and Selwyn said that he had advised Bully 'to pay his court to Horry' in order to brush up his own reputation'.[70]

The divorce proceedings at last reached Parliament. On 22 January 1768, the House of Lords received 'the petition of the Right Honourable Frederick Lord Viscount Bolingbroke to bring in a Bill to dissolve his marriage with Lady Diana Spencer his now wife'. The First Reading was on 11 February. Two weeks later, on 26 February, a packed House attended the second reading – there were twelve bishops, the royal Dukes of Gloucester and Cumberland, eight other dukes, twenty-nine earls, four viscounts and twenty-five lords, as well as many spectators, such as George Selwyn – ('the House was pretty full'). The proceedings took the form of a trial: counsel for both parties were present, and most of those who had already given evidence in the crim. con. stage at Doctors' Commons were called again as witnesses, but they now had to appear and speak in public. Since the statements made for the earlier hearing were written (without the intention of future publication), this was the first opportunity for society to hear the actual details of the affair. The Solicitor General opened in support of the Bill, and then the witnesses were called, starting with Dr John Moore, who confirmed that he officiated at the Bolingbroke marriage in September 1757.[71]

William Flockton was the key figure, 'called in order to prove the adultery'. This was a wonderful opportunity for Flockton to be the centre of attention and take his grand revenge for Topham's rudeness and Lady Di's giving him the sack. He now had the ultimate audience, the greatest men of the day, all listening in prurient fascination. He repeated his tales of Beauclerk's private visits, the locked door, his sudden entering of a room when 'Lady Bolingbroke looked as if she had been lying on the couch', the soiled couch, and the secret visits of doctors.

The other main witness was Dr Hunter, described as a man-midwife. He confirmed her first urgent summons, the emphasis on secrecy, the confirmation of pregnancy, the involvement of Beauclerk and the birth of a daughter. The main point was that 'he never saw Lord Bolingbroke with her', which was also confirmed by Mary Lees (presented in a minor role here rather than the organizer of events), the cook Jane Morgan, and Bully's valet, all agreeing that 'Lord Bolingbroke never visited her ladyship'. The baby could not therefore have been her husband's, indubitable proof that she had committed adultery. Then the decisions of the two previous courts were read out, the 'definitive sentence of Divorce of the Bishop of London's Court against the said Lady Bolingbroke' and 'the judgement given in the Court of King's Bench against the said Mr Beauclerk for Criminal Conversation with the said Lady Bolingbroke'. Thomas Walker, acting as counsel for Lady Di, stated that 'he was authorised by her Ladyship to give her consent to the Provision made for her in the said Bill'.

The Bill was ordered to be committed to a committee of the whole House, which sat on the following day, 27 February; the attendance sharply declined, since the spicy bits were finished, to four bishops, two dukes, six earls, two viscounts and eight lords. The *Lords Journal* for that day reports that 'after some time, the House was resumed and that the Lord Delawar reported from the Committee that they had gone through the Bill and made an amendment thereto'; this was read twice by the Clerk and was agreed by the House. The details simply concerned minor aspects of the financial provision: the Bill confirmed the Consistory Court terms that she forfeited the widow's jointure of £2,000 a year fixed by the marriage settlement together with her personal income of £500 pin-money. She renounced all claims to Boling-broke's estate following his death, and freed him from any responsi-bility for her debts. Bully kept the marriage portion of £15,000, in return for providing an annuity of £800 (to which the Duke of Marlborough may have continued to contribute at least £200). This was not a generous figure: in the following year, the divorced Duchess of Grafton would be awarded £2,000 a year.

The third reading took place on 29 February, and the Bill was then referred to the House of Commons, where it passed its three stages unopposed. Progress was closely monitored by Lady Mary Coke: 'You will hear from Ly Strafford that Ld Bolingbroke's divorce passed the House of Lords yesterday, and the House of Commons had the com-plaisance to sit today, to receive the Bill, that the business may be finished as soon as possible'. The Bill was returned to the Lords in time to receive the Royal Assent on the very last day of the session, 10 March. King George III was there to prorogue Parliament and had to listen to the reading out of the new Acts, whose names were sono-rously declaimed to the assembled peers. The nineteenth Act to be passed that day was the one that ended the Bolingbrokes' marriage and confirmed the adultery of his Queen's favourite Bedchamber Lady, the Queen whom he had sought to keep free from the dangerous influences of the world of intrigue and high society, and whose trust had been betrayed. Two years later, after more divorce acts had been passed, the King would encourage his Lord Chancellor to support legislation being proposed to stop divorced women from marrying their lovers, to 'prevent the very bad conduct among the ladies, of which there had been so many instances lately'.[72]

The Bolingbroke divorce had opened up a dangerous breach in the previously solid facade of marriage. The numbers of elite couples prepared to reveal their private miseries and infidelities in order to grab at a second chance of happiness, heirs or fortune became, if not a flood, at least a steady eroding trickle over the next twenty years. The Bolingbrokes were followed, in 1769 alone, by their friends the Duke and Duchess of Grafton, and Sir Charles and Lady Sarah Bunbury (although their divorce would not be finalized until 1776); and in the following year, there were the particularly scurrilous revelations of the Grosvenor divorce, with the Earl receiving £10,000 damages from the King's son, the Duke of Cumberland, as the price of his criminal conversations with the Countess. The Grafton affair had much in common with that of the Bolingbrokes, including a secret pregnancy in the country involving the services of Dr Hunter, and the reasons for the divorce were the same, that the unfaithful and disgraced wife would be free to marry the baby's father, Lord Ossory (which she did three days after the divorce Act was passed), and that the cuckolded husband might be able to find a better second wife. Bully's brother Henry St John commented to Selwyn: 'I was surprised to hear that Lord Ossory's prudence and discretion had not taken warning from the example that Lady Di and Beauclerk set him. Lord Ossory and the Duchess seem to have copied them, as you may observe, step by step, and I fancy the Duke will be very happy to follow my brother in the successful method he took of ridding himself of his wife. However, I cannot help feeling sorry for my friend Ossory who has got himself into a damnable scrape very early in life'.[73]

The most intimate details of the evidence by which such divorces were granted would soon become a source of entertainment and titillation in the popular press, legitimated through the moral lessons which were allegedly meant to be drawn from these revelations of bad behaviour by the upper classes, especially wives, who, above all others, were meant to be setting an example to the lower orders. Crim. con. hearings were not only reported in newspapers, but would provide the raw material for a new and highly popular literary genre. The *Trials for Adultery* series published the Doctors' Commons depositions of the witnesses in some of the more spectacular divorce suits of the day, including that of the Bolingbrokes. The editorial introduction to the first volume, in which their case was printed, shows the wonderfully hypocritical morality and the tones of innocent indignation which still ring true today: 'Conjugal infidelity is become so general that it is hardly considered criminal ... this publication may perhaps effect what the law cannot: the transactions of the adulterer and the adulteress will, by being thus *publickly circulated*, preserve others from the like crimes, from the fear of shame, when the fear of punishment may have but little force'. There were also the responsibilities that came with rank and gender: 'When a woman (especially of the superior class) has lost that inestimable jewel, virtue, alas! how is she fallen! Her nobility no longer claims our reverence; her coronet ceases to be enviable; her birth (which she has so disgraced) but adds to her offence; as, from her situation, it was incumbent upon her to have been an example of purity to the rest of her sex; she is indeed become the subject of the scorn, pity and derision of her relations, her former associates, and the public'.

But this tirade would not appear for another twelve years. For now the agonies of the divorce had been justified, and both parties were free. On 11 March, the day after the Act was passed, Topham obtained a marriage licence from the Archbishop of Canterbury, and on 12 March 1768 Lady Diana Spencer and Topham Beauclerk were married at St George's, Hanover Square. Her brother and sister-in-law Charles and Mary Spencer attended and signed their names as witnesses, but the Duke of Marlborough was not present, nor were the Pembrokes, who had taken themselves off to Paris for a very long visit. The evening after the wedding, Mary Coke describes how 'Lord Bolingbroke was at the Opera, very gay, seemingly well pleased that she was Mr Beauclerk's wife and no longer his'.[74]

Bully was enjoying his private as well as his public life at this time. In mid-February, as the Bill ground its way through Parliament, he had taken Polly Jones to Newmarket to join a party which included Selwyn, the Duke of Grafton and Charles Bunbury. But their affair was on its last legs for Williams soon told Selwyn that 'Bully and Jones are parted; she is gone to Mr Dillon. What a turbulent life does that wicked boy lead with rogues and profligates of all descriptions'. She later moved on from Mr Dillon to the Duke of Cumberland, and subsequently sued the Duke for £3,000 on the grounds that he had sold gifts of furniture that he had made to her. Although Bully gave evidence for her, she lost the case.[75]

It would have been correct etiquette for the newly-wed Beauclerks to expiate their shame and cease to embarrass their families by going abroad for a decent interval. They had briefly considered this option, but then decided to brazen it out; Lady Mary Coke wrote in her diary for 15 March: 'went to the Opera ... Mr Walpole went up to the Duchess of Bedford's box ... Mr Beauclerk *and* Lord Bolingbroke were both at the Opera, but not Lady Di. Though the scheme of their going abroad is over, they have taken Mrs Pitt's house in the country'. It was perhaps reluctance to encounter her immediate connections, such as the Duchess of Bedford, rather than the whole of society which had kept Lady Di at home that evening. Nor did they go to the country but flaunted their new, no longer secret status in London. As Williams described to Selwyn: 'They are in town, at Topham's house, and give dinners. Lord Ancram dined there yesterday, and called her nothing but Lady Bolingbroke the whole time'. And again, a few days later: 'Topham goes on with his dinners – James tells me he eats there today. Report says neither of them will live a twelvemonth, and if it is so short, their life ought to be a merry one'. Perhaps this was society's wishful thinking that some sort of retribution should fall on a couple who had so blatantly got away with it, and were now openly enjoying themselves; there were no further reports of illness for the immediate future. The merry life included attending the opera *La Schiava* at the King's Theatre in the Haymarket on 16 April, a very public appearance, when Lady Di had gained the confidence to appear in an assembly packed with the nobility.[76]

Walpole, who knew both first and second husbands, initially remained friendly with Bully: 'George Selwyn, Lord Bolingbroke and Sir William Musgrave, who had been at Hampton Court, came in at nine at night, to drink tea . . . Augustus Hervey, thinking it the *bel air*, is going to sue for a divorce from the Chudleigh. He asked Lord Bolingbroke t'other day, who was his proctor? as he would have asked for his tailor'. Hervey was secretly married to Elizabeth Chudleigh (once a maid of honour to Queen Caroline), who had famously attracted attention by appearing in a see-through dress at a masquerade. (It was the dubious legal status of this marriage which led her to think that she could get away with marrying the Duke of Kingston too. Her spectacular trial for bigamy would take place in 1776.)[77]

Mrs Thrale later recalled how the affairs of the elite were also discussed in wider circles: 'There came out books called Everyman his own Broker, Everyman his own Brewer and such trash; it was that year when Beauclerk married Lady Bolingbroke and Lord Ossory the Duchess of Grafton. Why have we not a book called Everyman his own Cuckold? says Mrs Montague'.[78]

The marital prospects of the cuckolded but liberated husband were attracting Lady Mary's attention: ''Tis reported, but I don't know with what foundation of truth, that Lord Bolingbroke is to marry Lady Downing'. This was at the beginning of March, even before the divorce had been finally granted. But, by December, 'Lord Bolingbroke is making his addresses to Miss Pelham, and 'tis said she encourages him because she says he amuses her, but declares she has no intention of marrying him, and that when he offers, she proposes telling him "Not after Lady Downing", that she cannot accept what She refused'.[79]

Courting Frances Pelham was an indication of Bully's desperation. The younger daughter of George II's Prime Minister, she was now aged forty and was addicted to gambling. She was rumoured recently to have lost over £70,000 at the table ('when she has lost what money she has about her, she will solicit a loan of a few guineas from any person near her, even from a stranger'). Of voluble temper, she is described as swearing, weeping and even physically attacking those who annoyed her in public places. 'Poor Miss Pelham . . . I myself have seen her at that villainous faro table with the tears running down her face, the wreck of what had been high-mindedness and generosity', observed Lady Louisa Stuart. And Carlisle asked Selwyn: 'Do you think it possible that it will be a match between Fanny and Bully; one all fire and sentiment, the other with as much fire but without a guess at what sentiment is'. But Bully was viewed as an even less attractive catch than Miss Pelham: Lady Mary and a friend 'talked of Miss Pelham's marriage with Lord Bolingbroke, which 'tis now said will certainly take place; if it does I fear she will be miserable'.[80]

Some of Bully's friends were in the same boat as himself, maritally if not financially. In the autumn of 1768, he raced three horses, Grildrig, Sejanus and Darling, in the October meeting at Newmarket, where his fellow-owners and gamblers included the Duke of Grafton, Lord Grosvenor and Sir Charles Bunbury, another unhappy man, whose wife Sal was now heavily pregnant with a baby which he knew could not be his. Having managed to get reinstated as a Lord of Bedchamber, Bully would retain the post until 1780: in court circles, his reputation remained unblemished.

SEVEN

The 'Femme du Monde'

(1768–75)

*'Nothing is so delicate as the reputation of a woman: it is
at once the most beautiful and most brittle of all human things'*

FANNY BURNEY, *Evelina*

Lady Di's life had now radically changed. Whether she had made the
right decision would remain to be seen. But she had abandoned and
been abandoned by many of her former acquaintances and now found
herself in a new circle based on the intellectual, literary and artistic
world in which Topham already moved. At a typical dinner party very
soon after their marriage, the guests included Joshua Reynolds,
Edmund Burke and Oliver Goldsmith, all, no doubt, fascinated to sit
at the table of the notorious woman who had seduced their young
friend, taken him away from their Club and got him into such a
'damnable scrape very early in life' – as had been said of Lord Ossory
when he was cited in the Grafton divorce (Topham was in fact twenty-
nine at the time of their marriage, but Lady Di was almost thirty-
three). Such gatherings must have been initially quite stressful. No
longer bound by the time-consuming social rituals of the court and
excluded for the moment from the company of the great families, she
may have felt more disorientated than triumphant. To maintain a
secret affair is one matter, but she was now committed for life to
a strong-minded individual, who, having done the decent thing by her,
began to resume his old life with his own set of friends and set routine
– just as her first husband had done.

However, within a year or two, she was able to re-establish many of her former social contacts and, although no longer welcome at court, remained in contact with her own immediate family, even the Duke and Duchess of Marlborough. Another source of solace was the discreet retrieval of the love child, named Mary (perhaps in affectionate recognition of Mary Lees' support), followed by the birth of another daughter, Elizabeth, in March 1769, a respectable twelve months after the wedding.

Topham's reintegration in the Johnson circle within his first year of married life is made manifest in the bizarre murder trial of 1769, in which key members of the Club were called as character witnesses for Giuseppe Baretti. This gentle, myopic scholar, whom Topham had first met in Milan through Johnson, had now moved permanently to London. In October 1769, Baretti got involved in an incident in the Haymarket when he was accosted by a prostitute whom he vigorously cast aside. He was then attacked by three men, including her pimp, drew a knife in self-defence and stabbed the pimp, who subsequently died. Baretti was arrested, committed to trial for murder at the Old Bailey by magistrate Sir John Fielding, and thrown into Newgate prison. His friends stood by him; at the trial 'never did such a constellation of genius enlighten the aweful Sessions House . . . Mr Burke, Mr Garrick, Mr Beauclerk and Dr Johnson', as Boswell put it. Other distinguished supporters included Oliver Goldsmith and Lord Charlemont, another Grand Tourist who had met Baretti in Turin and on whose advice Baretti had first visited London in 1751: Baretti would dedicate his *Manners and Customs of Italy* to Charlemont.

Boswell described how 'Dr Johnson gave his evidence in a slow, deliberate and distinct manner, which was uncommonly impressive . . . their favourable testimony had due weight with the Court and Jury'. This included Topham's statement: 'I have known him ten years. I was acquainted with him before I went abroad. Some time after that I went to Italy and he gave me letters to some of the first people abroad. I went to Italy the time the Duke of York did. Unless Mr Baretti had been a man of consequence, he could not have recommended me to such people as he did. He is a gentleman of letters and a studious man.' He also turned sociological detective and demonstrated that the murder weapon was not carried aggressively but was a signifier of cultural difference: 'In France they never lay anything upon the table but a fork, not only in the inns, but in public houses. It is usual for gentlemen and ladies to carry knives with them, without silver blades. I have seen those kind of knives in toy shops'. Thanks to this sort of character evidence, Baretti was acquitted with a mere reprimand.[1]

Charlemont, another important witness in the trial, became one of Topham's closest friends. As an Irish peer, he spent most of his time in Ireland, but was elected to the Club in 1773, and the two men regularly corresponded. Topham's attachment to Charlemont is expressed in extravagant language, such as his florid apology for not writing sooner: '. . . nothing else could have prevented me from writing to you and endeavouring thereby to keep up an intercourse with one for whom I shall always retain the greatest and tenderest regard; lessening in some measure the greatest of all human evils, the separation from those whom we love, but that insuperable idleness, which accompanies me through life, which not only prevents me from doing what I ought, but likewise enjoying my greatest pleasure, where any thing is to be done, has hitherto prevented me from writing to you'. Other letters project a blasé and cynical wit, often mocking himself as much as his friends and acquaintances.[2]

Despite becoming a family man, Topham continued to spend time seeking intellectual stimulation as well as maintaining the less demanding convivialities of being a man about town. He was a member of many London institutions, where his companions ranged from people like Bully to some of the finest minds of the day. At the more challenging level, he became in 1770 a Fellow of the Society of Antiquaries, the eminent body founded in 1717 'to cultivate the knowledge of the Antiquities of England'. During the second half of the century, its membership had extended from historically minded parsons to men distinguished in many different fields, who included Benjamin Franklin, Joseph Banks, William Chambers and Horace Walpole. Candidates were proposed and elected by ballot, and had to pay a joining and an annual membership fee. Their privileges included receipt of the annual journal *Archæologia*, access to an expanding library, weekly meetings at which learned papers were read, and, from 1774, a dining club.[3]

Further evidence of his intellectual reputation was his election as Fellow of the Royal Society, again in 1770. By 1771, Goldsmith was writing to Langton that Topham was 'going forward directly to become a second Boyle. Deep in Chemistry and Physics' – a high compliment, since Robert Boyle, distinguished seventeenth-century Fellow of the Society, was famous for his research into the chemical constituents of colour; his studies of light and colour preceded those of Sir Isaac Newton. The name, and the compliment, might also have been familiar to Lady Di, since Boyle's name was often linked with one of the key eighteenth-century works on painting, *The Art of Drawing and Painting in Water-Colours* (1731), an important treatise for artists. Topham had a long-held interest in the sciences, even as an undergraduate undertaking 'experiments in natural philosophy', and his reputation amongst his friends was such that he was appointed Professor of Natural Philosophy in the imaginary academy staffed by members of the Club which Johnson and Boswell devised during the Highland Tour. His technical understanding was also respected by Walpole, who bought himself a camera obscura but needed Topham to explain how the new toy worked. The sciences were another interest in common with Johnson who, in 1771, was trying to set up a laboratory for chemistry experiments in the villa at Streatham owned by the prosperous Thrales, whom Johnson had virtually adopted. Henry Thrale was a successful brewer, and his wife (a distant cousin of Topham's on his mother's side) a hyperactive and assertively learned woman, dissatisfied with her marriage and annual child-bearing, and trying to compensate through cultural pursuits. These included providing a second home for the often lonely and depressive Johnson, who had a permanent room reserved for him at Streatham; it was Johnson who persuaded Baretti to enter Mrs Thrale's employment, in 1773, as tutor to her precocious daughter Queenie.

Topham remained a member of the Society of Arts, which moved its premises from rooms in the Strand to the Adelphi in 1774. Membership offered few privileges beyond the pleasure of patriotic support for the arts, in the widest sense, and privileged access to the exhibitions, but the peerage rubbed shoulders with professionals and intellectuals, among whom were Dr Hunter, in addition to the Adam brothers, Johnson, Boswell and Garrick. Hunter was also a Fellow of the Royal Society and of the Society of Antiquaries (a whole room in his Great Windmill Street house was now furnished as a museum), and an acquaintance of Johnson and Walpole; he also shared Topham's interest in collecting rare books.

Topham's name appears amongst the list of scholars making use of the recently opened Reading Room in the British Museum. Fellow readers included several Club members (Johnson, Boswell, Burke and Hawkins), the scientists Banks and Solander, and a host of other eminent names of the day. The one body with which he did not seem to be involved, despite friends and fellow Club members who were, was the Royal Academy. This was founded in December 1768, with Reynolds newly knighted to honour his role as President, Baretti as Secretary for Foreign Affairs, Hunter as Professor of Anatomy, and Johnson as Professor of Ancient Literature and Goldsmith Professor of Ancient History.[4]

The Club also continued to reinforce the masculine bonds of friendship. Topham's membership had been withdrawn because of his failure to comply with the attendance requirements as a result of the evenings of passion spent with Lady Di during 1766. But he was reinstated just before his marriage, and his conversation was again welcomed: 'he is a man who has lived so much in the world that he has a short story for every occasion, he is always ready to talk and never exhausted'. After 1772, the meetings were shifted from Mondays to Fridays and the original ten members crept up to sixteen in 1773; by 1774 there were twenty, amongst whom were Charles James Fox, Charles Bunbury and the historian and Member of Parliament Edward Gibbon. The normally eloquent Fox was awed by Johnson; Boswell described how he had 'heard Gibbon say that Fox could not be afraid of Johnson, yet he certainly was very shy of saying anything in Dr Johnson's presence'. This was Johnson's effect on people. Despite more new members, who included playwright Richard Brinsley Sheridan and botanist Joseph Banks, attendance declined for a while during the mid-1770s, partly because so many of the members had other commitments elsewhere, and there were attempts to impose fines for non-attendance. Minutes were kept from 1775. The weekly drinking and supper sessions became fortnightly dinners, starting at 4.30 p.m., and the day changed again, in 1779, to Tuesdays. Those members who wanted to could go on afterwards to the soirées held by the Blue-stocking Mrs Vesey, wife of Club member Agmondesham Vesey, Irish politician and friend of Burke. By 1780, there were thirty members.[5]

Another evening of Topham's week might be spent at the Thursday-night Club, at the Star and Garter in Pall Mall, of which he had been a member since the mid-'60s. Here there was card-playing and drinking; this club was also attended by the gregarious and unmarried

Reynolds, but its other members belonged to a slightly different group who included Williams, Selwyn, March, Carlisle, and Bully.

Topham remained a member of Almack's, which changed its name to Brooks' in the early '70s. Topham put up Garrick for membership in 1773, and wrote to Charlemont that Reynolds was hoping to also be nominated, while Bully proposed Walpole's nephew, the unbalanced Lord Orford. As the originally youthful membership matured, Brooks' took on an increasingly political emphasis. Lady Di's name does not appear amongst the members of the rival ladies' establishment set up in 1770, which had taken over the name of Almack's Rooms and was modelled upon White's, although her sister was one of the founding members.

Apart from Topham's separate interests, the Beauclerks, as a couple, had a wide circle of friends and entertained lavishly. They spent the first few years of their married life, when in London, in Mayfair, territory both familiar and fashionable, then moved in 1773 into the newly completed Adelphi development, between the Strand and Thames, designed by the brothers Adam. These Scottish architects, whose career had been boosted by a powerful Scottish patron, Lord Bute, had been apparently inspired by the palace of Diocletian at Split to create an elegant scheme of streets and terraces overlooking the river and soaring above the complex of old warehouses below – Walpole compared the Adelphi to a soldier's frill on an old regimental coat. But for those who lived there, the views of the Thames were magnificent, and the proportions and decorations of the houses very fine (although rooms at the back were said to be dark and cold).

One of their neighbours was another old friend of Topham's, David Garrick (who was criticized by Johnson for living like a prince rather than an actor), and there also was their prosperous family doctor, Turton, who also looked after the Pembrokes and Garrick, and would soon be appointed Physician to the Queen's Household, and then to the royal couple. At the corner was a bookshop, permission for which had been granted as a result of Garrick's application. Garrick was so pleased by the appearance of the Adelphi that he commissioned Robert Adam to reconstruct the facade of his country riverside villa at Hampton. To celebrate the completion of this, there was a lavish Fête Champêtre with fireworks and music in August 1774, attended by the Beauclerks and dozens of other guests. As Garrick's fame grew, he was welcomed in aristocratic circles; he had become friends with the

Earl of Pembroke in Paris in the 1760s, and was able to purchase a commission for his nephew in Pembroke's regiment. He stayed with the Pembrokes at Wilton, and was also an intimate of Lady Spencer, the wife of Lady Di's cousin. Dr Johnson, of a similarly modest background to Garrick, took a less adulatory view of the actor, and was accused (unfairly) of threatening to blackball his proposed membership of the Club on the grounds that an actor's status was lower than that of a writer or painter. What Johnson really disapproved of was Garrick's assumption that he was entitled to belong to such an intellectual gathering; however he was safely elected in 1773, the first new member (together with Topham's other good friend the Earl of Charlemont) since its foundation.

Garrick made a striking first impression. For Fanny Burney, 'I never saw in my life such brilliant piercing eyes as are his. In looking at him, when I have chanced to meet them, I have not really been able to bear their lustre.' Another observer noted his mobile 'countenance never at ease and, indeed, seldom his person', and also felt that 'it is impossible that any two people, husband and wife, should live on better terms than Mr and Mrs Garrick'. Eva Maria Garrick had been better known as the celebrated dancer Violette, who came to England from Austria to perform at the Opera. But following marriage to the rising actor-manager in 1749, she gave up her own career and lived an exemplary life. The couple now extended their affection for Topham to Lady Di. A poem written by Garrick commemorates one of their dinner parties which her husband had forgotten to attend because of the greater attractions of the gaming table, even though the other guests included Reynolds and Goldsmith:

> Our choice British Raphael and rare Dean of Derry
> With Drury's Tom Fool to be wise and be merry
> By Beauclerk were asked, but the dice came between
> And quite were forgotten Painter, Player and Dean.
> Nor indeed did they want him, for sweet Lady Di
> Did more than the loss of ten Beauclerks supply.
> At nine of next morning I saw with these eyes
> His honour sneak home, neither merry nor wise.[6]

Walpole describes Topham and Garrick in collusion following the first night of Goldsmith's *She Stoops to Conquer* in 1773, when the playwright had overstepped the mark in satirizing Almack's Ladies'

Club which had been set up by, amongst others, Betty Pembroke, the heiress Miss Pelham and Lady Di's former housekeeper Rachel Lloyd. In the original performance of the play (which Goldsmith dedicated to Dr Johnson) their names were hardly changed; the bashful hero, young Marlow, reveals that he has another side 'as the loud confident creature that keeps it up with Mrs Mantrap and old Miss Rachel Buckskin till three o'clock in the morning', and another character mentioned is 'Lady Betty Blackleg'. Walpole mentioned how 'Miss Lloyd is in the new play, by the name of Rachel Buckskin, though he has altered it in the printed copies [to Miss Biddy Buckskin]. Somebody wrote for her a very sensible reproof to him, only it ended with an indecent grossierité. However the fool took it seriously, and wrote a most dull and scurrilous answer; but luckily for him, Mr Beauclerk and Mr Garrick intercepted it.'[7]

Lady Di soon acquired a reputation as an elegant and witty hostess with a distinguished guest list. She was increasingly admired by Horace Walpole, whose encomiums attracted the slightly jealous interest of one of his most assiduous correspondents, the blind Mme du Deffand, whose own Paris salon was a focal point for English as well as French wits. Mme du Deffand was half in love with Walpole, who for years maintained a flirtatious relationship with her. She first mentioned Lady Di in August 1773: 'J'avais beaucoup entendu parler de Mme Beauclerk; c'est, dit-on, la femme du monde qui a le plus d'esprit . . . elle a eu la gloire de vous amuser et cela me le prouve. [I had heard so much about Mme Beauclerk; they say she is the wittiest woman in society . . . as she has achieved the distinction of entertaining you, that must prove it.]'[8]

The better Walpole got to know Lady Di, the more enthusiastic he became. A year later Mme du Deffand responded politely to another glowing account: 'Milady Diane Beauclerk est une personne parfaite . . . Elle vous a fait retrouver toute votre vivacité . . . je savais déjà de ce petit Craufurd que cette Milady avait infiniment d'esprit et de talent; vous m'apprenez que sa coeur et son caractere sont pleins de franchise, de sensibilité et de compassion. [Lady Diane Beauclerk is perfection . . . she has restored your vital spirits . . . I had already learned from little Craufurd that this Lady had boundless wit and talent; you teach me that her heart and soul are full of frankness, sensibility and compassion.]' James Craufurd, nicknamed 'Fish' (his brother Quentin was 'Flesh'), was one of Selwyn's intimates; another clubman and heavy gambler, he spent much of his time in Paris, but when in London belonged to the Whig circle, and was a friend of Bob Spencer. Three years later, Mme du Deffand was still uneasily defining her rival's charms: 'Tout le monde s'accorde à dire qu'il n'y a point de femme aussi aimable et qui ait autant d'esprit et de talents. Elle doit vous être d'une grande ressource. [Everyone agrees that there is no other woman as charming as she, or with so much wit and skill. She must mean a lot to you.]'[9]

To cope with the demands of an ambitious social life and expanding family, and to provide an escape from noisy, noisome London, the Beauclerks also had a country house, The Grove, at Muswell Hill. Just as Garrick had his villa at Hampton and Walpole had Strawberry Hill, this was a rural base within convenient reach of the metropolis. The property was rented, not purchased, but was subject over the ten years of the tenancy, from 1769 to 1779, to considerable expenditure and refurbishment. The house was situated just off the road which ran down Muswell Hill, overlooking Muswell Hill Common.[10]

Here they entertained in grand style. Horace Walpole reported to the Countess of Ossory: 'Away to dine at Muswell Hill with the Beauclerks, and florists and natural historians, Bankses and Solanders'. Joseph Banks the botanist and Dr Solander, his secretary, librarian and fellow botanist, had been on Captain Cook's first voyage to the Pacific in the *Endeavour*, which returned in 1771. They were so famous that Josiah Wedgwood was about to add them to his range of jasper portrait medallions of celebrities past and present, which included another famous friend, David Garrick. Not that Banks made a good companion, later described by Fanny Burney as 'so exceedingly shy that we made no sort of acquaintance at all. If instead of going round the world he had only fallen from the moon, he could not appear less versed in the usual modes of a tea-drinking party'. However, she found Solander 'very sociable, full of talk, information and entertainment . . . a philosophical gossip'.[11]

On another occasion, Walpole 'dined and passed Saturday at the Beauclerks, with the Edgecumbes, the Garricks and Dr Goldsmith, and was most thoroughly tired as I knew I should be, I who hate the playing of a butt. Goldsmith is a fool, the more wearing for having some sense. It was the night of a new comedy called *The School for Wives*. Garrick has the chief hand in it – I never saw anybody in a greater fidget nor more vain when he returned'. Another visitor was

John Wilkes, the controversial politician, and popular Lord Mayor of London (despite establishment attempts to block his original candidature), whose diary records a visit to The Grove, with a chaplain as a fellow dinner guest. Another guest was Dr William Hunter, whose professional relationship with Lady Di had extended into something far more social and relaxed, as shown by the affectionate and jokey tone of a note she wrote: 'Lady Di Beauclerk sends her compliments to Doctor Hunter and is extreamly obliged to him for his offer of the venison which she will send for Saturday morning. Mr Beauclerk and Lady Di wish vastly to see Doctor Hunter at Muswell Hill and think that if he wish'd as much to come he might find a day. N.B. Doctor Hunter is desir'd to recollect that a note cannot be answer'd before it is receiv'd'.[12]

They lavished so much attention on The Grove that it attracted visitors who had to apply in advance for tickets, available on Sundays only. Viewing other people's houses was a popular leisure activity, already well organized by owners such as Horace Walpole at Strawberry Hill, who tightly restricted numbers and times of viewing. Amongst would-be visitors to The Grove was Mrs Boscawen, one of the ladies of the Blue-stocking circle; in 1776, she complained to Mrs Delany about the need to apply for admission, having been refused access when she turned up without giving notice. She refers to the unfriendly nature of 'our reception at Lady Di Beauclerk's on Muswell Hill; tho' we met her Ladyship taking an airing and Mr Beauclerk was in town, yet they wou'd not admit us to see the conservatory (which was all we aspir'd) without a ticket: resistance you know, always makes one more obstinate, so Mrs Leveson has wrote to Sir Joshua Reynolds to beg he will obtain the necessary passport'. But Sir Joshua could not, or would not, help and Mrs Boscawen did not get to see The Grove until 1782, when there were new owners.[13]

James Boswell was welcomed and provided a reverential description in 1775: 'This morning, Dr Johnson and I go with Mr Beauclerk to see his elegant villa and library, worth three thousand pounds, at Muswell Hill, and return to dine with him . . . it is delightful, just at Highgate. He has one of the most numerous and splendid private libraries that I ever saw; greenhouses, hothouses, observatory, laboratory for chemical experiments. In short, every-thing princely.' The observatory meant a lot to Topham: Walpole refers in 1777 to his owning the superior type of telescope made by Short, and his keeping an astronomer. The location of the house, high up on the slopes of the Hill, was ideal for viewing as well as for reception of light waves – it was the spot subsequently chosen for the great television transmitter of Alexandra Palace.[14]

This lifestyle had to be paid for, yet Topham had little wealth compared to the landed families of the day (although very much more than those Club members who had to earn their living by their intellectual skills). The property which he had inherited from his mother, the medieval timbered Speke Hall, was allowed to run into disgraceful decay. To subsidize his Enlightenment paradise at The Grove, the ancient manor house was divided up and rented out to farming tenants, the wainscotting and carved woodwork in the Great Hall were broken up, together with the fine inlaid oak floor of the Great Parlour, which was used as firewood, while its tapestry hangings were turned into horse-blankets.[15]

Financial problems again became a part of Lady Di's life, indeed they had never ceased. Topham even ran into arrears with the payment of the poor-rate at Muswell Hill in the autumn of 1774, and he borrowed £5,000 from her brother the Duke, using his growing book collection as security. This cannot have endeared him to his in-laws, but the Duke, another obsessive collector, was aware of the quality and range of these thirty thousand volumes, specializing in English and Continental plays and in history. Topham's collection, according to Walpole, 'has put the [British] Museum's nose quite out of joint'.

Such a glamorous and aristocratic couple acted like a magnet on the young Scot James Boswell, whose annual visits to London were detailed in his often painfully frank journals. By 1773, he was well established in the affections of Dr Johnson, whom he had met ten years earlier, but he was still unconfident in London society:

After breakfasting at Mr Dilly's, I walked down to the Adelphi and called on Mr Garrick. His coach was at the door to carry him to the country; so I just had time to shake hands with him and make a bow to Mrs Garrick, who was seated in the coach ... I then called on the Honourable Topham Beauclerk, who also has a house on the terrace of the Adelphi. I was shown into a very elegant parlour. I liked his large gilded lion, a cast from the antique, supporting his sideboard. He received me politely but not with so much ardour as I would wish to find. However, the truth is I was never in company with Beauclerk but twice – once dining at Sir Joshua Reynolds' and once supping at Garrick's when I was last in town. He then invited me to see him when I should return; and Langton told me that my open downright manners had pleased him and he said "I do love Boswell monstrously". Beauclerk's highbred behaviour may have been construed by me as distant coolness. His great veneration for Dr Johnson and Johnson's love for him are enough to make me value him; and from what I have seen of him, he appears to be a man of wit, literature and fashion in a distinguished degree.[16]

Boswell was always wistfully watching people of fashion, longing to be accepted by them and almost certainly being laughed at behind his back. Having, as he believed, obtained entrée to the Beauclerks, completely undeterred by Topham's obvious lack of 'ardour' and his 'distant coolness', he automatically included them in his social round. Two weeks later: 'Breakfast Garrick's . . . then Beauclerk's. Shown up to drawing room. Very elegant. Lady Di comely and well behaved . . . we talked of hanging'. The fact that he found her 'well behaved' as being worthy of comment perhaps suggests that the expectations of this highly sexed man towards such a notorious adulteress had been for something rather different.[17]

Three days later he was formally invited to the Beauclerks, on the evening that the Club was to vote on his admission to the desired circle:

I dined with Dr Johnson at Mr Beauclerk's, where there were Lord Charlemont, Sir Joshua Reynolds and some more members of the Literary Club whom he had obligingly invited to meet me, as I was this evening to be ballotted as candidate for admission into that distinguished society. Johnson had done me the honour to propose me and Beauclerk was very zealous for me. The gentlemen went away to their Club and I was left at Beauclerk's till the fate of my election should be announced to me. And as one black ball could exclude, I sat in a state of anxiety which even the charms of Lady Di Beauclerk's conversation could not entirely dissipate. Mr Beauclerk's coach returned for me in less than an hour with a note from him that I was chosen. I hastened to the place of meeting and was introduced to such a society as can seldom be found.[18]

This evidence of intimacy between the Beauclerks and Johnson – Topham's support for Johnson's protégé, commitment to the Club and entertainment of Dr Johnson for dinner in their elegant London residence – is then rudely undermined by Johnson's brutal remark about Lady Di, exactly one week after he had dined at her house. Boswell recounted, in the *Life*, the following conversation, which, according to his notes, took place during breakfast with the Thrales on Friday 7 May 1773:

I endeavoured as well as I could to apologise for a lady who had been divorced from her husband by Act of Parliament. I said that he had used her very ill, had behaved brutally to her, and that she could not continue to live with him without having her delicacy contaminated, that her affection for him was thus destroyed; that the essence of conjugal union being gone, there remained only a cold form, a mere civil obligation; that she was in the prime of life with qualities to produce happiness; that these ought not to be lost; and that the gentleman on whose account she was divorced had gained her heart while thus unhappily situated. Seduced perhaps by the charms of the lady in question, I thus attempted to palliate what I was sensible could not be justified; for when I had finished, my venerable friend gave me a proper check. JOHNSON: My dear Sir, never accustom your mind to mingle virtue and vice. The woman's a whore and there's an end on't.

The fact that Boswell did not record the name of 'the lady' was a mark of obvious discretion; the *Life* was published in 1791, when many of the people mentioned were still alive. Boswell did not record the actual term 'whore' in his original notes of the conversation nor did the published remark actually appear in these notes, where Johnson's response was recorded as 'Go to Scotland! I have never heard you talk so foolishly.' But while Boswell did not scruple to work up some of his immediate jottings into a more literary style, he is unlikely to have risked offending someone whom he admired so much by inventing such a cruel put-down. Although Johnson often had no compunction about hurting Boswell's feelings, this was also a very unpleasant slur on his other, older friend. The divorce had taken place five years earlier, and Topham had since resumed his attendance at the Club. But Johnson had lost one young disciple to marriage, and was jealous of Boswell's determined spreading of his own wings through a widening circle of acquaintances; in particular he may have been fed up with Boswell going on and on about the wonders of Lady Di, who had already won Topham from him. He was certainly making a strong moral case for the sanctity of marriage. A later conversation with Boswell turned on the dangerous effect that 'debauching a friend's wife' might have on a man's reputation, and Johnson implied that Topham had got away with it: 'Who thinks the worse of [Beauclerk] for it?' But Boswell pointed out that Bolingbroke and Beauclerk had not been friends. There must also have been some personal animosity: Boswell's own wife had little love for Johnson, and the remarriage of Mrs Thrale, who had already come to resent the many demands she felt that he made on her, would cause an irrevocable break between them – Johnson required his younger friends to make him the chief focus of their affection.[19]

Renewed attention had been drawn to the divorce and its causes in the previous year, when the uncompromising Tête-à-Tête section of the *Town and Country Magazine* had published its graphically unpleasant article about the goings-on of 'the Battersea Baron' and his ex-wife. The magazine was read nationwide, avidly seized upon by provincials to keep au fait with London gossip. Club member Oliver Goldsmith referred to its function in his latest play, *She Stoops to Conquer* (1774), through the pretentious Mrs Hardcastle, who longs to be in the capital city: 'All I can do, is to enjoy London at second-hand. I take care to know every Tête-à-Tête from the Scandalous Magazine'.

Johnson also showed his disapproval to poor Bully, whom he met and deliberately ignored at the Thrales. The honour of a visit from Viscount Bolingbroke to the brewer's family was considerable, and Mr Thrale afterwards reproached Johnson for his discourteous behaviour. Bully must have deliberately dressed rather informally, for Johnson replied: 'I am not obliged, Sir, to find reasons for respecting the rank of him who will not condescend to declare it by his dress or some other visible mark: what are stars and other signs of superiority made for?' On the next occasion, he sat next to Bolingbroke, and openly made an attack on divorce. When Mr Thrale again remonstrated, Johnson said: 'Why, Sir, I did not know the man. If he will put on no other mark of distinction, let us make him wear his horns!'[20]

If Johnson found Lady Di morally repugnant he would not have bothered to hide his feelings. For a woman trained to follow the correct conventions and social niceties, Dr Johnson's presence in her dining room cannot have been enjoyable. There were his physical tics – even someone as fond of him as Fanny Burney commented on his mouth 'continually opening and shutting as if he were chewing something . . . his vast body is in constant agitation, see-sawing backwards and forward; his feet are never a moment quiet'. And Boswell described how 'his head and sometimes also his body shook with a kind of motion like the effect of a palsy'. He muttered unpredictably under his breath, he puffed and panted, he wolfed his food and gulped down huge quantities of the tea which he adored.

His clothes were not merely shabby but dirty, and he rarely changed his undershirt; 'his wigs were a constant source of trouble, for they were not only dirty and unkempt, but generally burnt away in the front, for, being very near-sighted, he often put his head into the candle when poring over his books.' His real friends loved the man behind the flawed exterior, but for those whom he criticized, the physical rudeness reinforced the verbal one.[21]

There is a hint in Boswell's journal of Johnson's deliberately avoiding Lady Di's company. One busy day in the spring of 1775, Boswell breakfasted with Johnson, then they visited Reynolds, before attending Mrs Abington's benefit at Drury Lane. Then, 'I half persuaded him to go with me to Beauclerk's. But he suddenly took a resolution to go home, saying "but I don't love B. the less" or something quite to that effect'. Another incident shows Lady Di's precise understanding of Boswell's relationship with Johnson, as well as the latter's idiosyncrasies.

Dr Johnson reproved me for coming drunk to the Club, but he did not dwell on it for he soon made a transition to some of the manuscripts of Lord Hailes' Annals of Scotland, which he was going to revise. We went to his bedchamber to look for it, and there I won a bet of five shillings from Lady Di Beauclerk about one of his peculiarities. It seems he has been frequently observed at the Club to put into his pocket the peel of the oranges which he has squeezed into his drink which he makes for himself. Garrick and Beauclerk told me of it, and seemed to think that he did it with a wish not to be discovered. We could not divine what he does with these peels, and Lady Di laid me a crown that I durst not ask him. I was resolved to come out with it slapdash some day. But this morning I saw on his table in his bedchamber some fresh peels with all the pulp taken out of them, nicely scraped on the inside and cut into pieces. Oh Sir, said I, I see now what you do with the peels which you put into your pocket at the Club.
JOHNSON: I have a great love for them.
BOSWELL: And pray Sir, what do you do with them? You scrape them, I see, very neatly; and what next?
JOHNSON: I let them dry, Sir.
BOSWELL: And what next?
JOHNSON: Nay Sir, you shall know their fate no further.
BOSWELL: The world then must be left in the dark. 'He scraped them and let them dry, but what he did with them next, he never could be prevailed with to tell.'
JOHNSON: Nay Sir, you should say it more emphatically – 'he could not be prevailed with even by his nearest friends to tell'.[22]

Lady Di also threatened to draw a satirical picture of the pair on their unlikely Highland jaunt, which took place in the autumn of 1773. Beauclerk wrote to Charlemont, now in Dublin (where he had set up his own literary salon in imitation of the Club), 'Johnson has been confined for some weeks in the Isle of Skye. We hear that he was obliged to swim over to the mainland taking hold of a cow's tail. Be that as it may, Lady Di has promised to make a drawing of it. Our poor Club is in a miserable decay; unless you come and relieve it, it will certainly expire.' He goes on to refer to her current pregnancy:

I delayed writing to you, as I had flattered myself that I should have been able to pay you a visit at Dublin before this time, but I have been prevented, not by my own negligence, but by Lady D., who is so near her time that I could not, probably, have returned before she was brought to bed, and somebody had put it in her head that there was great danger in passing the Irish seas, which made it impossible for me to leave her under those apprehensions in her present situation. I am rejoiced to find by a hint in your letter that Lady Charlemont is in the same way.[23]

The baby was due at the end of the year, and Beauclerk later complained, from the Adelphi, in November 1773, that 'everybody, except myself, and about a million of vulgars, are in the country. I am closely confined, as Lady Di expects to be so every hour'. The baby, Charles George, was born in January 1774, and Beauclerk wrote to Charlemont: 'Lady Di has been brought to bed of a son three weeks ago. She and the child are both perfectly well; she desires me to propose a match between my son and your daughter, which she thinks ought to be resolved upon immediately.'[24]

Modern attitudes to childbirth, as pioneered by Hunter, included abandoning the old compulsory lying-in period of at least four weeks. Even in Staffordshire, the Wedgwood family observed the changing fashion. Wedgwood wrote on the day Mrs Wedgwood had given birth to another daughter that same year: 'Mrs W continues in a good way & I hope to see her below again in a few days; for it is becoming fashionable here for the Ladies in the straw to become well & leave it as soon as they are able; & even a Lady of Fashion may be seen in her Carriage again, without shame, in ten days or a fortnight after delivery.'[25]

Although Johnson could not overlook the divorce, much of high society had now managed to forgive her, and she and Topham participated in major social events such as the masquerades at the Pantheon. This was an exciting new venue for winter balls, the select nature of whose clientele was meant to be controlled by subscription requiring the personal recommendation of a peeress. (Attempts to exclude undesirable women were totally ineffective – Charlotte Hayes and her young ladies attended, and Mrs Phillips even managed to advertise her sex products there: 'if you turn away every woman who is no better than she should be, your Company would soon be reduced to a handful'.) The whole thing appealed highly to Walpole – 'so glorious a vision that I thought I was in the old Pantheon, or in the Temples of Delphi or Ephesus' – and one glittering event in February 1773 was attended by some 1,500 people including Lady Di and Topham, the Duke and Duchess of Marlborough, the Pembrokes, Bully and his brother, and David Garrick, who came dressed as the king of the gypsies. The press reported the difficulties of getting in: 'When we came to the doors of the Pantheon, we met with a crowd of spectators which it was no easy manner to penetrate. The low wit and ribaldry which we were saluted with were not very agreeable to persons of the finer feeling'.[26]

Their names are also recorded in March 1774 amongst a dazzling list of guests at a reception at Pembroke House in Whitehall, where other party-goers included the Bedchamber Ladies the Duchesses of Ancaster and Argyll, cousin Earl Spencer, his wife and sixteen-year-old daughter Georgiana, her betrothed the Duke of Devonshire, the Duchess of Bedford, the Marlboroughs, and of course the bachelors about town Selwyn and Walpole. She and Topham were even welcomed as occasional guests at Blenheim; they spent Christmas there in 1772, Walpole reporting alarmingly to the Countess of Ossory 'George Selwyn has just been here and told me twenty more dismal stories. Lady Di Beauclerk is given over at Blenheim from a black vomit'.[27]

On Boswell's visit to London in the spring of 1775, he regarded his entrée to the Beauclerks' salon as proof that he was now mingling with society's cream:

In the evening I called on Mr Beauclerk. I found him in his easy chair in the drawing room with a number of books all about him as if in a confused library. Lady Di and her two brothers, Lord Robert and Lord Charles Spencer were there. I was pleased with seeing people of high fashion who, though no doubt of the same clay of which we are all made, have it refined and are like figures of Indian earth. I had engaged to war a fowl with Langton. Beauclerk went for him that we might all be together. The two lords went away, and Langton and I supped with Beauclerk and Lady Di. After supper, Garrick came and pleasant as usual.

They went on tell ghost stories, and talked of religion.[28]
A few days later:

At Mr Beauclerk's was a Mr B----, a clergyman. Beauclerk without knowing that I had any serious intention, encouraged me in coming to the English bar by observing that a man who succeeds ever so well in Scotland cannot advance his family. Whereas here, a man may practise the law and get not only riches but arrive at a British peerage, and have his children marry into the greatest families. He roused my ambition. He said that now in England being of an old family was of no consequence. People did not enquire far back. If a man was rich and well-educated he was equally well received as the most ancient gentleman though if enquiry were to be made, his extraction might be found to be very mean. He instanced Langton, to whom he said the antiquity of his family was of no service. I said I hoped they were not such barbarians, and that all who had birth valued it; that a gentleman of old standing in a country should have more influence than an upstart; that *he* would not for £10,000 be the son of a linen draper. Lady Di told me afterwards that Mr B--- was a linen-draper's son. These unlucky circumstances will sometimes fall out. I drank port pretty heartily but not a whole bottle for ----- had his share. Garrick came in and said I was as drunk as much.[29]

The Earl of Pembroke was an earlier acquaintance of Boswell, and one with whom he had much more in common than the sarcastic Topham:

I then found Lord Pembroke and breakfasted with him on good chocolate. He was in his usual good humour and spirits; talked to me of all the fine people as if I had known them as well as he did, and it seemed to me that in hearing them talked of in so easy and so rapid a manner made me in some degree acquainted with them, at least with parts of their character. He told me that last year there was a black bawdy house in London, that Blank went there one evening and, finding himself sitting in a company all black, he thought he was in hell. He said there were no whites mixed with them; but if I had a mind to go and drink there any evening he would show me blacks enough. He said that one night he had drank and whored till he was quite exhausted. As he was coming home a great strong whore accosted him. My Lord told her he was incapable. 'Never fear' said she, 'I'll make it do'. In this way he rattled on quite freely. He assured me that he had never had the venereal disease in his life. 'Then' said I, 'My Lord, it is wonderful how people lie; for I have heard that you gave it twice to Lady Pembroke'. 'It is not true', he said. 'Lady Di had it.'[30]

This was merely one item of masculine gossip in a conversation so evidently bawdy that the far from reticent Boswell tore out the next page of his journal. Boswell was the last person to accuse other people of having venereal disease, for he was frequently infected himself. But the anecdote seems to provide confirmation of the earlier unpleasant hints about Lady Di in the *Town and Country Magazine*.

Another conversation at this time revealed her attitude to the serious ladies known as the Blue-stockings.

I was discussing with Lady Diana Beauclerk Mrs Vesey, the celebrated hostess and 'blue stocking'. Lady Diana said 'I understand that Mrs V. is an idiot'.

BOSWELL: She is so much less of an idiot than I had expected that I do not think she is an idiot at all.

LADY DI: I think that she is bad enough if all that a lawyer can find to say of her is that she is only less of an idiot than he imagined.

I then reflected upon the different species of idiots that are loose upon the world, the land idiots, water idiots and so on, and discoursed wittily to her on the subject.

LADY DI: I think that is worth writing down.

Poor Lady Di: it was just as well that Topham was not there as he would hardly have endured Boswell's heavy-handed humour. Lady Di's malice about Mrs Vesey, whom she appeared not to have met, suggests her exclusion from the society of those learned ladies whose discussions and writings were often concerned with morality.

EIGHT
The Artist
(1774–80)

'The public practice of any art, and staring in men's
faces is very indelicate in a female'

DR SAMUEL JOHNSON

Lady Di was now in the company of people who were concerned with ideas and whose work involved the practice of art, literature, theatre and music, not as hobbies but as professions. In this intellectually stimulating environment, she had the time and the inclination to resume with greater vigour the artistic activities which had inspired the earlier Reynolds image of her. There was something in her art which attracted the attention of Horace Walpole, an influential critic, connoisseur and collector; but there can be no doubt that he was also fascinated by her rank and by the ambiguity of her reputation. (He was also a most loyal friend and correspondent of Lady Ossory, the divorced Duchess of Grafton, who lived a far more secluded life than Lady Di following her second marriage.) Whatever his motivation, it was he who provided the critical support and impetus to her career as an artist by his commissions, acquisition and display of her works at Strawberry Hill, as well as praising her liberally in his various writings. As well as the frequent eulogies in his correspondence, he commended her in the fourth volume of his *Anecdotes of Painting in England*, in a foreword describing the modern British art which he had deliberately excluded from the main text. This volume was written and printed in 1771, but publication was deliberately delayed until 1780 'from motives of tenderness' because the author would not 'dispense universal panegyrics . . . on many incompetent artists' – he had not been impressed by the previous generation's work. In a newly written foreword, dated 10 October 1780, he expressed optimism about the future of English art, and stressed 'how painting has rekindled from its embers, the works of many living artists demonstrate'. Among distinguished living artists, he included Reynolds, Gainsborough and Zoffany, with a particular recommendation for the gentleman artist Henry Bunbury (whose works he collected as enthusiastically as Lady Di's), whom he described as 'the second Hogarth'.[1]

But his highest praise is reserved for that 'genius' which

can draw from the sources of nature with more spirit than from the ideas of another. Has any painter ever executed a scene, a character of Shakespeare that approached to the prototype as near as Shakespeare himself attained to nature? Yet there is a pencil in a living hand as capable of pronouncing the passions of our unequalled poet; a pencil not only inspired by his insight into nature, but by the graces and taste of Grecian artists; but it is not fair to excite the curiosity of the public, when both the rank and the bashful merit of the possessor, and a too rare exertion of superior talents are confined to the proof of a narrow circle. Whoever has seen the drawings and bas reliefs designed and executed by Lady Diana Beauclerk is sensible that these imperfect encomiums are far short of the excellence of her work.

By 1780 he knew her work very well indeed, for he had begun to acquire it soon after 1774, the date of the first edition of his catalogue of the contents of Strawberry Hill. Walpole's antiquarianism and recording skills were already honed by the earlier exercises of cataloguing his father's magnificent picture collection at Houghton Hall, his lists of English authors and of English engravers, and the earlier volumes of *Anecdotes of Painting*. He now turned to describing his own life's work, his great artistic creations Strawberry Hill and its contents, not through 'visions of self love' but for posterity. The collection, which eventually totalled over a thousand objects and pictures, plus a further thirteen thousand prints and engravings, would be dispersed in the early nineteenth century but still survives, room after room, in his detailed, loving lists. The 1774 edition of his *Description of Strawberry Hill* only mentions a gift *from* Lady Di, a dessert plate of faience painted with figures of goats by Pietro Cortona (the seventeenth-century baroque Roman artist) which was displayed in his China Closet; this marks her appreciation of the nature of his collection and indicates the maturing of their friendship. But in Walpole's subsequent annotations and updatings of the catalogue (which were so extensive that a revised version would be published in 1784) there are not just further treasured gifts from her – 'a toothpick case of gold, enamelled with cameos' – and from Topham – 'a catalogue of the pictures belonging to the crown in the time of Queen Anne' – but many works *by* her, which are singled out for attention in his introduction to the second edition.[2]

Her first and major commission from Walpole was requested because he had detected in her the ability and potential to express in art the emotional, dramatic, Gothick spirit that he was trying to create in his literary works. Despite the classical pretensions of her current drawing and modelling style – the pretty little fauns and cherubs (pencil and wash equivalent of the Adam brothers' swags and scrolls) in her charming sketchbooks and delicate classically themed wax sculptures, all the sort of things being produced by other ladies of leisure – he recognized her skill at graphic design and the simplicity, restraint and strength of her pencil drawings. In the autumn of 1775 he was enthusing to Sir William Hamilton about her 'drawing children in bistre. I will only tell you that Sir Joshua Reynolds – yes I will tell you on my own authority, [said] I have never seen anything like them. Albano's boys are fools to them – dull, jolter-headed cubs and all alike, as if they were the Countess of Haynault's three hundred and sixty-five children [a medieval legend of multiple births]. She has promised me one a day as long as I live, and did three the first day – I mean, Lady Di, not the Countess'. He also admired the medium: 'charming drawings of children in soot-water, tingeing the faces with carmine; nothing could be superior to them'. 'Soot-water', or bistre, was a dark pigment made from wood or peat soot, which when dissolved in water produced a warm brownish wash.[3]

Walpole was so impressed by her handling of this potentially difficult medium that he decided to commission from her a set of bistre wash drawings to illustrate his five-act tragedy *The Mysterious Mother*. This was a play he had written in 1768, printing fifty copies only at his private press at Strawberry Hill for distribution to a very restricted circle, a special, broad-minded audience, some of whom were already the recipients of his mildly pornographic poetry. The play was not intended for performance or, at this stage, for wider publication, because 'the subject is so horrid that I thought it would shock rather than give satisfaction to an audience'; he made this statement in his preface to the first properly published edition of 1781, rather unconvincingly adding that he had 'done everything in his power to suppress the publication – in vain'. The 'horrid subject' was the theme of double incest involving a son's unwitting intercourse with his guilty mother and his marriage to the unknowing product of that union, his daughter/sister. Walpole said that it was based on a story he had read when young, from the novels of the Queen of Navarre, and he accordingly set it in early sixteenth-century France.

Walpole's revival of enthusiasm in 1775 for a work he had completed seven years earlier was triggered by Topham, who, in the August of that year, sent to Walpole (then in Paris for a few weeks) the text of an epitaph referring to an incestuous family tragedy which he had come across while pursuing his own antiquarian researches. As Topham was one of the select band who had been allowed to read *The Mysterious Mother*, he knew that the parallels would be of interest. In gratitude, perhaps, Walpole bought a present for Topham in Paris, 'a blue and gold cup and saucer with garlands, which cost two pounds', because it was this reference, combined with his growing admiration of Lady Di's work, which gave him the idea of an exciting new project. He decided to create a virtual performance of his neglected secret masterpiece by making a shrine-room at Strawberry Hill in which the play could not only be read but brought to life by images of the stage performance which would never take place. These scenes were commissioned from Lady Di, in the form of seven large pen and wash illustrations, which she began in December 1775. Although he claimed later, in the 1784 *Description of Strawberry Hill*, that the whole series of seven drawings had been 'conceived and executed in a fortnight', this is rather an exaggeration, since it was more like two months.[4]

That Walpole should involve Lady Di in what he regarded as a highly prestigious project is extremely significant. It implies not just that he saw in her the potential to work in a new style and one that would do justice to his tragedy but also that he felt that her scandalous reputation gave her the necessary broad-mindedness to interpret (let alone read and understand) this erotic piece, which would continue to shock; he may also have hoped that the association of her own rank and status might even help legitimize it. This was her big opportunity:

it was Walpole's copious accounts of this project to his many correspondents, in an age when letters were intended for reading aloud or
passing from hand to hand, that created an audience for her subsequent works.

She had made a start in December 1775, when she wrote him a note
from Muswell Hill: 'I send you the drawings, but I find the bistre will
not take well on the old cards. The bistre I have now seems of a
browner tint also. I am going to town for the night [presumably to
stay at the Adelphi]. Have you any commands?' Walpole's first
glowing account was written to Lady Ossory two weeks later: 'Just at
present I suppose I am the vainest creature in the universe. Lady Di
has drawn three scenes of my tragedy, which if the subject were a
quarter as good as the drawings, would make me a greater genius
than Shakespeare, as she is superior to Guido and Salvator Rosa. Such
figures! Such dignity! Such simplicity! Then there is a cedar hanging
over the castle, that is more romantic than when it grew in Lebanon!'[5]

Comparisons with the seventeenth-century painters Guido Reni and
Salvator Rosa were high praise indeed. The Italianate taste of eighteenth-century connoisseurs, who admired Reni's graceful sentimental-
ity, had also discerned in Rosa's tumultuous landscapes and wild
characters that quality of imaginative response which had been defined
by Club member Edmund Burke in his *Philosophical Inquiry into the
Origins of our Ideas of the Sublime and Beautiful* (1757) as the most
elevating kind of artistic experience; this indicated the shift in taste
towards an appreciation of art and literature not founded upon
classical rationality, but on an immediate emotional reaction. It was
not the 'Grand Style', another seventeenth-century concept being
reformulated by Sir Joshua Reynolds as part of his attempts to improve
the standards of English art; yet Reynolds had conceded, in his fifth
Discourse to the Royal Academy, delivered in 1772, that Rosa's
interpretation of Nature 'has that sort of dignity which belongs to
savage and uncultivated nature . . . everything is of a piece: his Rocks,
Trees, Sky, even to his handling, have the same rude and wild
character which animated his figures'. Walpole knew Rosa's works
at first hand for there were several at Houghton Hall, and one at
Strawberry Hill; so did Lady Di, for they were also prominent in the
great collections owned by her friends and relations. They were also
used as models for copying by industrious practitioners such as Mrs
Delany.

Lady Di worked on throughout January, and had finished by the middle of February, when Walpole was able to boast:

Lady Di Beauclerk has made seven large drawings in sut-water (her first attempt of the kind) for scenes of my *Mysterious Mother*. Oh! such drawings, Guido's grace, Albano's children, Poussin's expression, Salvator's boldness in landscape and Andrea Sacchi's simplicity of composition might perhaps have equalled them had they wrought all together very fine. How an author's vanity can bestow bombast panegyric on his flatterers . . . seeing is believing, miracles are not ceased. I know how prejudiced I am apt to be; some time or other you will see whether I am so in this instance.[6]

The recipient of this letter, William Mason, had both practical and theoretical knowledge of art; a cultivated clergyman, he was also a poet, writer and linguist whose works included a new translation of the seminal seventeenth-century French tract, Du Fresnoy's *The Art of Painting*, which Reynolds was using extensively among the source material for his Discourses. Walpole respected Mason's judgement but always needed to stress his own superior connoisseurship: his discovery of a new genius had to be rubbed in. A few weeks later, he is still longing to show the drawings off to Mason: 'Don't you intend coming southward? Am I not to harbour you? . . . Lady Di's drawings alone are worth a pilgrimage.'[7]

Her recreation of the play demonstrates a minute study of the text and empathetic ability to absorb herself in the emotions of its characters – a first but accomplished essay in the field of literary illustration, which would preoccupy her for more than twenty years. In addition, her drawing of the scenes suggests her deliberate use of the conventions of contemporary theatre. These are not just illustrations of a story, but are the imaginative visualizations of the various scenes of a play as it is being performed by actors: the characters use dramatic gestures, their expressions are exaggerated, the backgrounds are deliberately restricted to the two settings defined in Walpole's original stage instructions: 'Scene – at the Castle of Narbonne: partly on a Platform before the Gate; partly in a Garden within the Walls.'

Walpole stressed the play's 'essential springs of *terror* and *pity*'. Part of its ability to shock arose from its frank recognition of sexual passion; the Countess of Narbonne (having disguised herself as a servant) had bedded her own son sixteen years earlier, frenzied not merely by grief at her husband's recent death but also by enforced abstinence: 'for eighteen months an embassy detained him from my bed . . . impatience grew almost to sickness'. The resulting pregnancy and birth of a daughter, Adeliza, forced her to banish her son and live a life of seclusion, devoted to remorse and charitable works; the play begins when Edmund returns to claim his inheritance. The other key theme is anti-Catholicism, and the real villain is the manipulative priest Benedict, who plots the family's downfall because of the Countess's alleged heresy. The Countess is intended to inspire pity because she has repented, but she is dreadfully punished on learning of the marriage of Edmund and Adeliza, which Benedict has cunningly arranged. As the play's climax, she stabs herself to death.

The six drawings show Lady Di's confidence with her medium: firm, clear foreground figures contrast with a delicate, hazy background wash. The scenes all include architectural and natural features, which are used to frame the actors with a well-constructed perspective background. In his account of these treasured drawings in the second edition of the *Description of Strawberry Hill*, Walpole emphasizes how 'the beauty and grace of the figures and of the children are inimitable; the expression of the passions most masterly'. The first scene she illustrates follows his stage instruction: 'a procession of children of both sexes, neatly clothed, issue from the castle, followed by Friar Martin' (Act II, Scene 2), while in the foreground are the figures of Edmund and his travelling companion Florian. This was one of Walpole's favourites: 'In the scene of the children, some are evidently vulgar, the others children of rank; and the first child, that pretends to look down and does leer upwards, is charming'. He also mentioned other favourites, her depiction of Act II, Scene 3, 'particularly in the devotion of the countess with the porter'; 'of Benedict in the scene with Martin' (Act IV, Scene 1), where the two monks scheme destruction; and 'the tenderness, despair and resolution of the countess in the last scene; in which is a new stroke of double passion in Edmund, whose right hand is clenched and ready to strike with anger, the left hand relents' (Act V, Scene 6). This is the terrible moment when the Countess has revealed the truth to her son, who has just wed Adeliza. Lady Di has thrown herself wholeheartedly into these melodramatic moments, and presents the doomed characters sympathetically and powerfully; whether she should be seen to be able to understand and express such passions was another matter.

Walpole was so enraptured with the illustrations that he decided to create a purpose-built setting for them through a further extension to Strawberry Hill:

I am to have Mr Essex to-morrow from Cambridge, to try if he can hang me on anywhere another room for Lady Di's drawings. I have turned the little yellow bedchamber below stairs into a beauty room, with the picture I bought, along with the Cowley, at Mr Lovibond's sale, but I could not place the drawings there, because I will have a sanctuary for them, not to be shown to all the profane that come to see the house, who in truth almost drive me out of my house.[8]

James Essex was an antiquarian and architect who was pioneering the revival of the English Gothic style. For this demanding client, he managed to squeeze in a little 'turret' between the Tribune Gallery and the Round Tower, described by Walpole with offhand modesty to Mason: 'My whole history consists in having built a new tower which is a vast deal higher, but very little larger in diameter than an extinguisher; however it fully answers the founder's intention, which is to hold Lady Di's drawings'. A year later, Mason had still not seen the marvel:

I don't know anybody so much in the wrong as you are for not coming to me this summer; you would see such a marvellous closet, so small, so perfect, so respectable . . . Lady Di's drawings are hung on Indian blue damask. The ceiling, door and surbase are gilt, and in the windows are two brave fleur de lis and the lion of England, all royally crowned and painted on glass, which as Queen Catherine never did happen to write a billet doux in this closet, signify Beauclerc, the denomination of the tower. This cabinet is to be sacred and not shown to the profane, as the drawings are not for the eyes of the vulgar. Miss Pope the actress, who is at Mrs Clive's, dined here yesterday, and literally shed tears, though she did not know the story. I think this is more to Lady Di's credit, than a tomtit pecking at painted fruit.

This was an extravagant compliment, recycling the old anecdote about the Greek painter Zeuxis, so distinguished in his realism that birds flew down to peck at his painted grapes; first reported by Pliny, this entered the canon of renaissance art-historical writing and was cited by the writers drawn upon by Sir Joshua Reynolds in his Discourses. The Strawberry Hill accounts reveal that he paid eighteen guineas for thirty-six yards of the blue damask wall coverings.[9]

Horace Mann in Florence had more excuses than Mason for not visiting Strawberry Hill, and so was given the full account. The play has indeed received greater honour than any of its superiors; for Lady Di Beauclerk has drawn seven scenes of it that would be fully worthy of the best of Shakespeare's plays – such drawings that Salvator Rosa and Guido could not surpass for their expression and beauty. I have built a closet on purpose for them here at Strawberry Hill. It is called the Beauclerk closet; and whoever sees the drawings allows that no description comes up to their merit and then, they do not shock and disgust, like their original, the tragedy.[10]

When Walpole was seriously considering publishing the play, Mason, who had at last seen and duly admired the drawings, made some suggestions for improvement to the text, to which Walpole replied: 'I think your alterations marvellous and it is favourable to the tragedy that it could produce your alterations and Lady Di's drawings . . . the alterations so little affect the plot and characters that it does not even affect Lady Di's drawings. If it did, I know you would reject it without mercy; for I firmly believe you value them more than the rest of the work they belong to.'[11]

The Beauclerk Closet and its contents were, for the rest of Walpole's life, reserved for special visitors only. In the Closet there was a writing table, whose drawer held a copy of the play bound in blue leather and gilt. One visitor recorded her impressions: 'He was also so obliging as to show me again (for I was here last year) the beautiful drawings of Lady Diana Beauclerk . . . the story is the most horrid to be conceived but these drawings, tho' they recall to mind the horrid subject, are most affectingly interesting'. And Lady Mary Coke's Journal recorded a dinner at Strawberry Hill followed by a visit to the Closet: 'the drawings . . . are finer than anything of the sort I ever saw; she is certainly the greatest genius in that way that has appeared for ages'. Lady Mary was also sufficiently unshockable to appreciate the play, which Walpole read aloud to her during a coach journey from Reading: 'It pleased me very much . . . you know how well he writes on all subjects'.[12]

Another appreciative visitor was the musician and Club member Dr Charles Burney, who stayed at Strawberry Hill for a few days in 1786, accompanied by his daughter Fanny. He viewed the drawings by 'the accomplished Lady Di . . . with the admiration that could not but be excited by the skill, sensibility, and refined expression of that eminent lady artist; and the pleasure of his admiration happily escaped the alloy by which it would have been adulterated had he previously read the horrific tragedy whence the subject had been chosen'. This was

Fanny's account; she had not read the play prior to their visit but unfortunately managed to do so soon after, when she borrowed a copy from her mistress Queen Charlotte. The Queen, an industrious reader and keen book collector, had bought a copy which she had not yet read but which she happily loaned to Fanny. This resulted in a deeply embarrassing evening when the play was read aloud in mixed company: 'Dreadful was the whole! truly dreadful! A story of so much horror, from atrocious and voluntary guilt, never did I hear! . . . I felt a sort of indignant aversion against the wilful author of a story so horrible . . . a lasting disgrace to Mr Walpole . . . such a painting of human wickedness . . . when I returned it to the Queen I professed myself earnest in my hopes that she would never deign to cast her eye upon it.'[13]

Ten years later the Royal Academician and diarist Joseph Farington was another privileged visitor to the Closet: 'Went with Mrs Farington and Mr Lysons . . . to Strawberry Hill. Lord Orford [Walpole] showed us the house, which we had sufficient time to view at our leisure. We saw the small room in which are Lady Di Beauclerk's designs for Lord Orford's play of the Mysterious Mother – also his China Closet, neither of which are shown but seldom.'[14]

It was the association of her gentility with the reputation of the play that shocked some spectators, such as Laetitia Hawkins, the daughter of the 'unclubable' Dr Hawkins, ex-Club member (although this had not inhibited him from publishing a memoir of Dr Johnson, in rivalry to Boswell's *Life*). Laetitia was therefore hostile to Boswell and his friends, matters not aided by the fact that Boswell had publicly described her father as the son of a carpenter who had married an old woman for her money. She provided an acid gloss on the masterpiece: 'Horace Walpole was a great admirer of Lady Di Beauclerk's talent, regarding which I may say that it might have remained undisputed, had her ladyship been content with attempting portraits of her daughters or wooded landscapes with gypsies and other elegant productions of the same rank. But admiration ended when the Beauclerk closet, as it was ostentatiously called, was allowed to be seen – unless the proportions of the human figure are of no importance in drawing.' An even stronger reason for her criticism was the nature of the subject matter. No respectable woman, in Laetitia's judgement, should have had anything to do with Walpole's disgusting play, of which 'it becomes not a female to speak otherwise than to say that merit in composition is no excuse for the abuse of talents . . . Mr Walpole was very sensible to the enormous indecency of which he had been guilty'. Therefore, she concluded, Lady Di's drawings, just as much as the play 'can only be looked on with disgust and contempt'.[15]

Hawkins and his daughter, neighbours of Walpole in Twickenham since 1760, had even set up a local committee to ban Walpole's rumoured attempt to have the play performed: 'I think it an honour to have been employed, even in writing merely notes of appointment for meetings to consider on the means of stopping it'. They were apparently successful, in that the play was not performed (if indeed Walpole had ever seriously considered such a thing). But the self-righteous Hawkins also managed to ban a local production of *The Beggar's Opera* 'in pure care of the morals of the town'. Laetitia also disapproved of Walpole's architectural creation, his 'bauble villa . . . his crazy bargain and the enormous folly into which it led him in patching up a house anything but palatable . . . his extreme decorations frequently provoked the wanton malice of the lower classes who, almost as certainly as new pinnacles were put in to a pretty Gothic entrance, broke them off'.

Walpole's delight with the *Mysterious Mother* drawings meant that he then collected other works by Lady Di, all of which received hyperbolic praise. This adulatory attitude needs to be contrasted with his sharp comments on works by male artists – with the exception of the well-born Henry Bunbury, younger brother of Bully's Jockey Club colleague Sir Charles. He was almost equally fulsome about the works of the sculptress Anne Damer (daughter of his cousin General Conway) and the miniaturist and Shakespeare illustrator Lady Lucan. He grouped the two latter with Lady Di in *Anecdotes of Painting* as the three contemporary female geniuses worthy of inclusion alongside Reynolds, Gainsborough and Zoffany. It has been suggested that his intimate friendships with women, and particularly ladies of dubious sexual reputation and therefore vulnerable in society (Lady Di and Lady Ossory were divorced; Mrs Damer's husband had committed suicide, and she often wore men's clothing and was rumoured to prefer her own sex), results from his own homosexuality and sympathetic understanding of failed relationships: publicly enthusing about their work might be a way of making these outcasts dependent upon his favour. However it is more likely that, in the context of the times, he simply judged women's art by different standards from that of men;

and also the art of genteel people as more wonderful than that of those who earned a living by it. His sudden passions and overblown prose style were certainly not restricted just to the appreciation of art, whether by man or by woman, but were a way of flaunting his own discriminating and avant-garde tastes generally.[16]

Finding her artistic feet through this first attempt at literary illustration, Lady Di was also working in a new medium, that of wax sculpture. Walpole described her 'bas-reliefs of boys as finely drawn and with more grace than the antique'. Modelling in wax was both an activity in its own right, and a preliminary stage for multiple reproduction in another medium. As Wedgwood's 1787 *Catalogue* promised, 'if Gentlemen or Ladies choose to have Models of themselves, Families or Friends, made in Wax . . . they may have as many durable Copies of those Models as they please, either in Cameo or Intaglio . . . the art of making *durable copies* at a small Expence, will thus promote the Art of *making originals*, and future ages may view the Productions of the Age of George III with the same Veneration that we now gaze upon those of Alexander and Augustus.' Wax sculptures often took the form of small-scale portrait medallions or bas-reliefs imitating classical marbles in miniature. The tractable nature of beeswax, the ease of adding pigment to it, if required, and the texture of its sheeny surfaces made it particularly appropriate for portraiture: images could be tinted to imitate the living flesh, or made as creamy as an antique cameo. They might even be three-dimensional. Sculpting in wax was a more accessible activity than carving stone or casting metal for a woman who had no training or workshop space.

Walpole had already acquired two of her wax sculptures before he commissioned the *Mysterious Mother* illustrations. In the autumn of 1775 he was boasting to William Hamilton, that connoisseur of antique art: 'Your old passion, Lady Di Beauclerk, has lately turned to modelling in wax and has executed some bas-reliefs that have infinitely more grace, yes, yes, than the antique, and ten times more nature and expression. Come and believe your eyes, I have two of them.'[17]

One of these sculptures was placed in the Great North Bedchamber – 'two bas-reliefs of boys in wax on glass, designed and modelled in the most graceful and perfect Roman taste', according to the 1784 *Description of Strawberry Hill* – greater, he believed, than the works of the greatest classical sculptors, whom he compares unfavourably to her in the verses, engraved on a plaque attached to the back of the work and undoubtedly also intended to be appreciated by spectators:

> Tho' taste and grace thro' all my limbs you see,
> And nature breathes her soft simplicity,
> Me nor Praxiteles not Phidias form'd;
> 'Twas Beauclerc's art the sweet creation warm'd,
> From Marlborough sprung – We in one heaven-born race
> Th'attemper'd rays of the same genius trace;
> As big with meteors from one cloud depart
> Majestic thunder and keen lightning's dart.

He is rather confusing his sources here, as Hamilton would have been the first to point out, since Praxiteles and Phidias were famously Greek rather than Roman.

Displayed in his Breakfast Room was a second piece: 'two beautiful bas-reliefs; set in frames with her arms and cameos by Wedgwood and Tassie in festoons'. This frame was based on her own design, which survives as a delicate, tiny watercolour which Walpole has lovingly preserved and pasted into his folio version of the 1784 *Description*. He dates it to 1776: a grey roundel containing two cherubs is set against a square frame filled with oval and circular cameo medallions, the whole thing contained by a dark blue border with gold stripes.

There was also family patronage from the Earl of Pembroke, who acquired one of her bas-reliefs for Wilton. Two of her surviving waxes imitate antique friezes, but on a miniature scale. Planned as a matching pair, no more than fifteen centimetres long, they show considerable accomplishment and meticulous attention to detail in the handling of complex, overlapping groups of figures, who appear to move and sway in their delicate drapery; there is a genuine sense of depth and perspective in the sharp but low relief. Their subjects, *A Triumph of Bacchantes* and *The Drunken Silenus*, were well-established classical themes, aspects of the triumphal procession of Bacchus, the god of wine, whose orgiastic followers celebrated sensual pleasures that were hardly compatible with the principles of the age of reason; yet the topic fascinated and was familiar to eighteenth-century audiences from interpretations by admired sixteenth- and seventeenth-century artists including Van Dyck and Titian. At least one was directly known to Lady Di, for Rubens' *Drunken Silenus* hung at Blenheim. Her bacchantes, the maenads, or female followers of Bacchus who played musical instruments and danced themselves into a frenzy, process sedately, bearing urns and accompanied by little cherubs, one playing a pipe, one garlanded and leading a goat, the symbol of Bacchus. Her Silenus lolls, supported by his companions, on a stubborn donkey, tugged along by a satyr; they are preceded by a girl with floating garments, balancing a basket of fruit on her head, towards an altar, where another nymph kneels and plays a flute. These are all the standard features of the scene, and would be expected and identified by an educated spectator. Another wax by her, on the same miniature scale, shows 'Four Amorini in a chariot drawn by swans', a further celebration of classical learning and passion; these winged cherubs were the followers of Cupid, the god of love, while swans traditionally pulled the chariot of Venus, goddess of love. Some of her watercolours and drawings of the '70s show further explorations of Rubens' florid classicism, and these followers of Bacchus – Silenus, satyrs and little fauns, dancing musical nymphs, chubby naked boys – all recur in her work with the smudged, soft colours and hazy outlines of the original source.[18]

Another new activity for Lady Di in this decade was that of providing patterns for painting on Wedgwood's tableware. The constantly inventive entrepreneur had been searching from the early 1770s for new themes to attract new patrons. (He targeted, for example, a niche market in 1771: 'for all country gentlemen who are sportsmen there is scarcely anything gives so much pleasure to look on as dead Game'. Also considered were shells and seawood as additional lines to the current floral designs.) One of the later appendices to Walpole's 1774 *Description* lists in the China Room 'twelve Wedgwood plates with cameos of blue and white and blue festoons – from a design of Lady Diana Beauclerc'. This is likely to have been the commission mentioned by Wedgwood in May 1777: 'Pray are Mr Horace Walpole's plates done? We sent you a box by the last coach'. This suggests that the undecorated plates were sent from Etruria to Wedgwood's London workshop to be painted there. Lady Di would not have been involved in painting directly on to the plates; her watercolour designs would have been copied by one of the painting team. Wedgwood was always prepared to undertake one-off projects for his more distinguished patrons, reckoning that the trouble and lack of profit involved were more than outweighed by the publicity value. This would be particularly true in the case of Mr Horace Walpole, with the work being displayed in such a famous house as Strawberry. The arbiter of Gothick taste was also revealed as an eclectic patron anxious to obtain a fashionable quality product; neo-classicism was perfectly acceptable when designed by Lady Di. Another of his Wedgwood products decorated by her was the pair of square jasper flower-tubs set with plaques made to her designs of 'antique cameos and masks in blue'.[19]

She continued to produce portraits of family and friends, in pencil and wash, and in pastels, which she handled with growing confidence. Mary and Elizabeth are presented in pencil as sturdy toddlers, and, in crisp firm pastels, with superb detail and highlighting, as two well-dressed little girls, Mary with pearls in her hair and a wide-eyed Elizabeth in a lace cap and déshabillée gown. Betty is drawn with her little son George, and there was more than one attempt to capture the essence of Charles James Fox in pencil and watercolour. Fox, a friend both of her brother Bob and of Topham, is shown in a loving and unflattering manner which poses a contradiction between his initially dignified pose, head resting on pensive finger, the arm supported by a plinth, with a Reynolds/Titian-inspired background of grand pillar and draped curtain; yet there is relaxed and intimate feeling. His legs are splayed, his plump belly swells over his waistband, the one button which manages to fasten his too-tight jacket strains at the fabric, and he holds a small book clumsily on his knee. He looks thoughtfully at the artist. The facial features are familiar from the many later carica-tures, the heavy quizzical eyebrows, the beginnings of a double chin, the sensuous lips, and fine details of the face contrast with the softer wash of the background. She has tried, not very neatly, to imitate a professional mount by pencil outlines to a wash frame, but has had problems getting the lines straight. The portrait may have been a pre-sent for Bob Spencer, for it was in his house at his death.[20]

Lady Di's artistic reputation was now recognized by others. Mme du Deffand wrote to Walpole from Paris: 'Je ne veux pas manquer de vous dire que Milady Lucan reconnait une de très grandes superiorités de talents de Mme Beauclerk à celui qu'elle a. Elle m'en fait des recit admirables. C'est la différence selon ce qu'elle me dit, de vrai genie, du genie createur à l'esprit, et l'art imitatif. [I mustn't forget to tell you that Lady Lucan thinks that Mme Beauclerk has much greater talent than herself. She has given me a wonderful account. It is the difference, according to her, between true and creative genius, and mere imitative wit and ability.]'[21] This was a great compliment from

Lady Lucan, herself one of Walpole's three 'female geniuses', who was ascribing to Lady Di the male artistic attribute of imagination rather than the female one of imitation.

Walpole and the Beauclerks saw a lot of each other in the mid-1770s, although it was clear that he found Topham a far less sympathetic character than his wife: 'Mr Beauclerk told me t'other day he wondered I received everybody that came to see me. I told him it was very little inconvenience, for those I was not glad to see found little encouragement to come often'. One lively visit was in June 1776: 'Mr Beauclerk and Lady Di have been here four or five days – so I had both content and exercise for my philosophy – the Pembrokes, Churchills, Le Texier and the Garricks have been with us.' And he visited them in return: 'I have dined at Muswell Hill, and the next day the Beauclerks, Miss Lloyd and I went to Old Windsor to see poor Mr Bateman's auction. It was a melancholy sight to me in more lights than one . . . I purchased a cargo of ancient chairs and they at least have found a resting-place in their old age. The Beauclerks and the Virgin returned and passed two days here.' The Virgin was their nickname for Rachel Lloyd.[22]

They also wrote to each other. When Walpole was in Paris in the summer of 1775 (when Topham sent him the epitaph about incest which inspired the *Mysterious Mother* project), Lady Di posted newspaper cuttings to keep him up to date about the current scandal, the alleged bigamy of the Duchess of Kingston – her letters accusing the satirical actor and playwright Samuel Foote of libel had just been published in the press. Walpole wrote back to Lady Di twice from Paris, on August 23 and September 10, but unlike so much of his correspondence these letters have not yet been retrieved. In December 1775, he reported a dinner party at the Beauclerks attended by Adam Smith, when the American War was discussed.

But these busy and exciting days of artistic achievement and recognition, and friendship with some of the liveliest minds in London, coincided with the beginnings of a decline in Topham's health that started to sour his temper and undermine their marriage. Even writing to Charlemont in 1774, Topham referred to what sounds like a pre-existing condition, perceptively relating healthy bodies to happy minds: 'Ill health produces bad spirits, and anything that revives them does great good to the body; nothing can do that more to me than hearing from you that you still honour me with the same friendship which you showed me formerly . . . I am so much better this year (by having left off all medicine except laudanum, of which I take 400 drops every day) that I shall be able sometimes to enjoy your company, which was not the case for these two years last past.'[23]

Laudanum was the all-purpose and almost only effective medicine of the day. Made by dissolving opium (the product of the seed capsule of the white poppy) in alcohol or syrup, it was used to cure, or at least alleviate, the painful symptoms of a whole range of conditions such as toothache, headache, insomnia, stomach complaints, aches and pains in the joints and the general disorders attributed to the nerves. One highly appreciated effect was that of producing an euphoric sense of well-being in the sufferer, 'reviving the spirits' as Topham put it. It was not only obtainable from doctors but was freely available at a low cost from shops and taverns, and Topham's generous dose would have cost less than 6d a day. Opium was believed to be so beneficial and potentially lucrative a medicinal product that by the end of the century the Society of Arts (of which Topham had been a member) awarded prizes to two successful British growers of the previously imported white poppy. The only negative quality recognized was the effectiveness of an overdose for those seeking to commit suicide. The problem for constant consumers like Topham was the resulting toler-ance and dependency, which meant that a dose would have to be steadily increased for it to remain effective. Four hundred drops a day (the equivalent of 102mg of morphine) was a substantial, although not an exceptionally high usage – Lady Holland was recorded by Walpole as taking six hundred drops, and Coleridge was alleged occasionally to take a pint, or over eleven thousand drops, in one day. Although Topham's dose may have been effective for him in 1774, the level would have had to rise. The fluctuations in his health and temper over the next few years suggest an increasing degree of dependency combined with periods of withdrawal.[24]

In July 1774, another letter to Charlemont explained why Topham has not yet made the promised visit: 'that it was my intention to visit you in Ireland, and that it still remains so, is as true, as that I love and esteem you more than any man upon the earth, but various accidents have hindered me, the last of which has been a violent disorder, which obliges me to a very severe discipline, and a constant attendance upon doctor Turton' (who was then conveniently living in the Adelphi terrace).[25]

Knowledge of his disorder spread through the network of corre-spondence; Mme du Deffand referred that same July to Lady Di's 'malheurs'. In January 1775 Johnson wrote to Boswell: 'Poor Beau-clerk is so ill that his life is thought to be in danger. Lady Di nurses him with very great assiduity'. In March Johnson informed Boswell that Beauclerk was in pain, but not now thought to be in danger, and that he was consulting a Dr Heberden, in the hopes of 'a new understanding'. And he seemed better in April, when he visited Dr Johnson in company with Boswell, then back in London. By May 'Beauclerk talks of going to Bath'.[26]

Bath and, to a lesser extent, Brighton were, sometimes literally, the last resort of the sick. The Beauclerks visited these places several times in an effort to find a cure when the laudanum was ceasing to be effective. Their life became an unsettling mixture of the familiar social round (which of course also took place in the health resorts) inter-spersed with intervals of illness, when Topham was overwhelmed by pain.

Walpole describes a typical light-hearted evening at the Beauclerks', in December 1775, when Garrick recited an elaborate poem composed by Mr Cumberland in honour of Gray's odes. Beauclerk said he could not understand it and asked Garrick to recite it backwards to see if was any better. 'He did, and it was.' But early in the following year Mme du Deffand, briefed by English visitors to Paris, referred maliciously to the potentially grave outcome, and gave evidence of the gossip about strain in their relationship: 'Mme Beauclerk ne serait-elle pas heureuse de perdre son mari? [Won't Mme Beauclerk be pleased to lose her husband?]'[27]

Topham's illness now worried the whole family. Lord Herbert wrote to his mother Lady Pembroke in April 1776: 'You mention Mr Beauclerk's being better, but I believe two or three times, but only for the space of one week or two. It seems that they have thought of Bath very late. Pray let me know in your next, where Lady Di is to be directed to'. However, the same letter refers to their attending a forthcoming dinner party at the Pembrokes', and it was perhaps not so much Topham's ill health as his normal acerbity that squashed Boswell, as reported in his diary for the same month: 'At this time in London I was wearing out as my dress suit an old crimson suit embroidered with silver, made at Dublin in 1769. It was now old-fashioned, though a good handsome dress. I said "I feel myself quite different in this suit from what I am in my frock [coat]" (meaning that I felt myself better). Said Beauclerk: "So should I feel myself quite different, but I should not feel agreeably" (meaning that I was ridiculous). He has a fine malignity about him.' A few days later Boswell called at the Adelphi but had a dull evening: 'I went to Beauclerk's and sat with him and Lady Di. I recollect nothing.'[28]

Walpole described some of their activities that summer to Lady Ossory: 'I called at Mr Beauclerk's in the evening, where I found Lord Pembroke, Lord Palmerston, Garrick, Burke, the Dean of Derry, Lord Robert Spencer, and Mr Gibbon; but they talked so loud (not the two last) and made such a noise, and Lord Palmerston so much more noise with trying to talk, that it was impossible to know what they said, under the distance of a mile from them ... on Sunday night I had dined at Lady Blandford's, and the Beauclerks with Mr Gibbon and Monsieur Le Texier had been to drink tea with me in the meantime.' The group was shown around Strawberry in Walpole's absence, and he reported how Le Texier dashed off some verses to commemorate the occasion. Le Texier was a smart new acquaintance, a French actor-manager who had come to work in London the previous winter and who was achieving considerable dramatic and social success. He was sought after by the hostesses of the day, including the Duchess of Devonshire, and his public and parlour one-man performances pleased even Walpole: 'I cannot decide to which part he did most justice, but I would go to the play every night if I could see it so acted.'[29]

Edward Gibbon was another recent acquaintance (also taken up at this time by the Duchess), who had been elected to the Club in 1774. Lady Di drew a stylish caricature of him in the form of a profile bust of a Roman emperor garlanded with laurels, to commemorate his epic *Decline and Fall of the Roman Empire*, the first volume of which had been published that February. Caricature was a new mode for her, and a fairly new genre in England, but one which was becoming rapidly appreciated.

That summer was a frantic round of activity, organized to keep their minds off Topham's condition and perhaps even the fact that they were ceasing to enjoy each other's company. They joined a house party in Cambridgeshire, where fellow guests included the Duchess of Devonshire and Lord Westmorland. Georgiana described their visit to a regatta at Whittlesea, where they admired the 'fleet' of Walpole's nephew, the eccentric and, by then, intermittently mad Lord Orford, in which he lived during the summer. Walpole had been planning to take the Beauclerks to Houghton, in Norfolk, to see the fine art collection amassed by his father: 'I shall not go to Brighthelmstone, but another journey that will at least vary the scene a little for Lady Di. I have asked my nephew's leave to show them Houghton and to Mr Conway and Lady Ailesbury.' Poor Walpole had been responsible, as a trustee, for trying to run the estate during his nephew's bouts of insanity during the 1770s – 'ruin, desolation, confusion, disorder, debts, mortgages, sales, pillage, villainy, waste, folly and madness' – although he conceded that the precious pictures 'were in the finest preservation'.[30]

The proposed trip did not take place (and it might have provided curious memories for Lady Di, since it was while Bully had been staying with his good friend Lord Orford at Houghton that she had made her bolt). But Walpole's reference about the need to vary the scene for her reinforces the general awareness of the strain that she was now under.

Later that summer the Beauclerks went to Bath. For Lady Di this was an opportunity for renewed contact with George Selwyn. Although still an intimate of Bully, Selwyn had not taken sides during the divorce and had, for example, dined with her and Sarah Bunbury in January 1768. They were now brought together again as a result of Selwyn's new role as the doting guardian of a little girl, Mie-Mie Fagniani, whose father was almost certainly the Earl of March, although it was rumoured that Selwyn thought he himself was responsible. Mie-Mie's mother, the Marchesa Fagniani, had cheerfully left her daughter in the care of these two rich English gentlemen and returned to Italy with her complaisant husband; she later reclaimed the child but, after long and expensive negotiations, allowed her to return to Selwyn's care.

The Beauclerk daughters, Mary and Elizabeth, aged nine and seven, went to the same London school as Mie-Mie, Campden House; it was now not unusual for genteel girls, as well as boys, to be sent away to school, as weekly or even termly boarders (Susan and Sophie, the unfortunate daughters of the unmaternal Mrs Thrale, were almost permanently boarded out at their school during the 1770s). Campden House was much favoured by the elite; one satisfied parent described it, earlier that year, to another prospective customer as 'a most healthy and desirable school' and the headmistress, Mrs Terry, 'very assiduous and watchful in case of sickness'. Mrs Terry's confidence in the orderly running of her school was such that parents were welcome to visit and inspect without appointment on Wednesdays and Fridays.[31]

When it came to Mie-Mie, Selwyn was a terrible worrier. He either visited or expected a letter from poor Mrs Terry every day. Two of these notes survive:

Mrs Terry presents her compliments to Mr Selwyn; is very sorry to find that he is so uneasy. The dear child's spirits *are not* depressed. She is very lively; ate a good dinner; and behaves just like other children. She hopes Mr Selwyn will make no scruple of coming to-morrow morning, or of staying his hour or more if he likes it: she will then talk to him about the head; but in the mean time begs he will not suppose that the dear child suffers by his absence, or that anything is neglected; for if Mrs Terry thought Mr Selwyn could suppose such a thing she would wish to resign the charge. Haste must plead Mrs Terry's excuse for such a scrawl. She begs he will come tomorrow.

On another occasion: 'Mrs Terry has the pleasure to assure him that dear Mlle Fagniani is as well today as her good friend could possibly wish her to be. She is this minute engaged in a party at high romps.'[32]

As the Beauclerks were already in Bath that autumn, Selwyn had agreed to escort the Beauclerk girls, together with Mie-Mie, from London to Bath in December. Lady Di wrote from 12 South Parade: 'Will you excuse my reminding you of your promise? I have not yet heard from Campden House, which perhaps may be one reason for my thinking this place detestable. The fog has been choking me all the morning and now the sun is blinding me. A thousand children are running by the windows; I should like to whip them for not being mine. I will not trouble you any longer with my ill humour. If you are so good as to write, pray let me know if your distresses about the Fagnianis are yet at an end. I am sir, your most obedient humble servant, D. Beauclerk.'[33]

The distresses were at an end, for the moment, for the Fagnianis had just agreed, in August 1776, to let Mie-Mie stay in Selwyn's charge for another year. He was now fussing about the travelling arrangements, and Lady Di wrote back to reassure him:

I am vastly obliged to you for your long letter. Indeed it was not at all a --- – I dare not write the word because you seem to have such an objection to it; and as I am quite ignorant of its *sens radical* it is better not to use it. I have wrote once more to Mrs Terry and I hope that nothing but the children not being perfectly well will prevent them coming with you. I am perfectly at ease about their journey, approve of the cavalcade and still more of the private orders. I must insist upon Mary's sitting backwards, at least part of the way. I would not have Mie-Mie crowded for the world, and should be quite unhappy if I thought my girls were the least trouble to you or her. Bob is here, and tired to death already. *Entre nous*, this a most detestable place; and to make it complete, the Princess Amelia is here poking about in every corner; it is impossible to stir without meeting her, and as I have no hopes of her being gracious enough to take notice of me, I am obliged to avoid her. Perhaps you think that her taking notice of one would be a still better reason for avoiding her. The Fawkeners are gone; I do not know where. Mr B sends his compliments to you. I think my signing my name is as unecessary as your doing it.[34]

The word she 'dare not write' was the slang term 'bore'. As explained by Lady Sarah to Lady Susan: 'I told you the word "boar" is a fashionable expression for tiresome people and conversations, and is a very good one and very useful, for one may tell anybody (Ld G Cavendish for example) "I am sure this will be a boar so I must leave you Ld George". If it was not the fashion it would be very rude, but I own I encourage the fashion vastly for it's delightful I think'. Mrs Thrale had also spotted it:

It has been the mode of late to call every thing that's tiresome or disagreeable a Bore, taking the Allusion from an ill bitted horse, who pulls without meaning and is heavy in your hand. Among the many people who *bore* their friends, as it is called, with tedious and futile talk, Mr Holford the Master in Chancery is most eminent; so that he is known now by the name of Bore Holford. Col. Bodens was to meet him somewhere at dinner – but I wish, says George, that he might be served up with an apple in his mouth like any other Boar and so be kept silent.[35]

It was now nearly nine years since the divorce, but Lady Di's comment about being cut by the Princess Amelia, George III's aunt, shows that she was still persona non grata in court circles. Her brother Bob was not yet married: as a younger son with no fortune but the usual extravagant habits of his class he was not a very desirable catch. His earlier relationships had included a liaison with Bully's ex-mistress, the courtesan Polly Jones, alias Kennedy, who had subsequently alternated Bob with Bully's youngest brother John St John. When her two brothers were accused of murder in 1770, St John spoke in their defence at the trial, while Bob persuaded the Duke of Marlborough to ask the King for a stay of execution. This resulted in one of the brothers receiving a MacHeath-like reprieve on the way to the gallows

– but also further bad publicity for the Spencer family. Bob was now involved with a married woman, the lovely Harriott Bouverie, a member of the Fawkener family who had just left Bath. Her father, Sir Everard Fawkener, had begun his career in business, then gained influential positions which included being Ambassador at Constantinople and Secretary to the Duke of Cumberland. As Post Master General in the 1740s, his gambling losses at White's had provoked the bon mot: 'See how he is robbing the mail.' His older son, William, was married to Georgiana Poyntz, a niece of Lady Di's cousin, Lady Spencer; his younger son, Everard, a friend of Bob Spencer and of Charles James Fox, was the subject of one of Lady Di's pastel portraits. Harriott had married, at the age of fourteen, the Honourable Edward Bouverie MP, and was now a prominent Whig hostess, as was her friend Mrs Frances Crewe (to whom Sheridan dedicated *The School for Scandal* in 1777). Harriott and Frances had been painted by Reynolds in a double portrait as elegant shepherdesses contemplating mortality (in homage to Poussin's *Et in Arcadia Ego*), which was exhibited at the Royal Academy in 1769, and Reynolds had recently painted Mrs Crewe's little boy in fancy dress as Henry VIII. The ladies were also friends with Bob's sisters; one spectator of the fancy dress ball celebrating the Shakespeare Jubilee which Garrick organized at Stratford in 1769 thought that 'even the fascinations of Lady Pembroke, the Honourable Mrs Crewe and Mrs Bouverie, who tripped as the Lancashire witches, could not charm dulness from her throne'. Despite her long-standing and publicly known affair with Bob – Selwyn crudely commented how Bob had 'the run of Mr Bouverie's kitchen', and Walpole would later compare Harriott to a street walker – Mrs Bouverie had no intention of leaving her husband; she had taken warning from her first-hand observation of Lady Di's ambiguous status, and she enjoyed her role as one of the circle forming around the stylish Georgiana, Duchess of Devonshire.[36]

It was customary to sneer at overpopular Bath, magnet for the impoverished and the fortune-hunter, for plain women in search of husbands, professional gamblers, courtesans, and a whole service industry devoted to fleecing the vulnerable, gullible sick. Walpole had gone to take the waters there a few years earlier and reacted typically:

I dislike the place exceedingly and am disappointed in it. Their new buildings that are so admired look like a collection of little hospitals; the rest is detestable and all crammed together and surrounded with perpendicular hills that have no beauty. The river is paltry enough to be the Seine or Tiber. Oh how unlike my lovely Thames. I am quite well again; and if I had not a mind to continue so, I would not remain here a day longer, for I am tired to death of the place . . . these watering places, that mimic a capital and add vulgarisms and familiarities of their own and like abigails in cast off gowns, and I am not young enough to take up with either. They may say what they will, but it does one ten times more good to leave Bath than to go to it.

This was also the opinion attributed to the grumpy Matthew Bramble in Smollett's *Humphry Clinker* (1771), who criticized its perceived decline:

You must know I find nothing but disappointment at Bath; which is so altered that I can scarcely believe it is the same place that I frequented about thirty years ago . . . this place, which Nature and Providence seem to have intended as a resource from distemper and disquiet is become the very centre of racket and dissipation . . . nothing but noise, tumult and hurry; with the fatigue and slavery of maintaining a ceremonial, more stiff, formal and oppressive than the etiquette of a German elector.[37]

To alleviate the tedium and distance herself from incompatible companions (as described by Bramble, Bath was where 'a very inconsiderable proportion of genteel people are lost in a mob of impudent plebeians'), Lady Di continued to observe and draw. Among the small drawings and paintings pasted by Walpole into his personalized copy of the *Description of Strawberry Hill*, there was one inscribed in his own hand 'Lady Diana Beauclerc', entitled 'Dr La Cour's wife and her sister and jew beau, drawn at Bath 1776'. The drawing shows two fat, ugly women, the doctor's wife trying to marry off her equally unattractive sister, being addressed by a slender gentleman with prominent nose, wearing an embroidered jacket and holding a tricorne hat under one arm. The frilly caps and beribboned frocks of the ladies contrast grotesquely with their beefy arms and inelegant postures, as does the skinny suitor, whom either could easily squash: this neat piece of social satire sums up the tawdriness of Bath and brings to life Bramble's scathing reference to 'the wives and daughters of low tradesmen who, like shovel-nosed sharks, prey upon the blubber of those uncouth whales of fortune'. Walpole's memory however may have been defective, for the figure of the sister, slumping in her chair, with legs akimbo, is practically identical to a figure by Henry Bunbury in a drawing published in 1772, depicting the dullness of 'A Sunday evening'. As Bunbury's speciality was caricatures of precisely this type (and as Lady Di's was not) and as Walpole collected Bunbury's works as well as hers, he may have confused his two favourites. If it really was by her, however uncharacteristic, the confident sketchy style, with wonderfully restrained outlines, shows an area that she should have taken further.

Dr La Cour was a local physician who made money out of people like Topham, who apparently had great faith in him, according to Edward Gibbon. A fellow patient was Gibbon's stepmother, whom Gibbon tried to put in touch with the Beauclerks:

Lady Dy tells me that she was once in your company at Dr Delacour's for whom both she and Beauclerk express a veneration almost equal to your own. As little or no conversation passed between you, she had only an opportunity of admiring the harmony of your voice and the beauty of your teeth, on which she bestows lavish encomiums. They mean to visit Bath again this spring, and I was very desirous that you should be acquainted with her. You will find her one of the most accomplished women in the world, and she will soon discover in you qualities more valuable than those which are now the objects of her encomiums.[38]

With no real improvement in Topham's health, they left Bath early in January 1777 but returned later in the spring. Selwyn also decided to spend more time in Bath, and Lady Di was charged with the responsibility of finding suitable accommodation for him. She wrote busily from 4 Russell Street:

I have just taken a house for you in one of the most airy situations here. It must be taken for a month certain, and as much longer as you please: I thought this would be no objection as it is so good a house and as it grows very difficult to get good houses. Mr Wade found it for me and is proud of having got it so cheap, (five guineas a week) which is at least a guinea cheaper than he could have got had it been let before. I have been too ill to go out today, therefore was obliged to trust to Mr Wade about the house; indeed he is a better judge than I am. There is another circumstance which I hope is no objection, that it is within a few doors of us, for we were obliged to leave the South Parade, it was too intolerably close and we are now in Russell Street, near the Circus; your house is in Bennett St, close by. The house consists below, of two rooms and a small one for a servant, two rooms over that; three very good bedchambers over that; and four garretts over all. Mr Wade says they are very good rooms and the cleanest best furnished house in the town. The offices also are good; they provide you with linen, remarkable good also, you paying for the washing. I am quite out of breath for I never did so much business in my life before or wrote so long a letter. If after all you should disapprove of what I have done, I shall be in a fine fidget. So my poor little girls have the chicken-pox? When do you come – pray let me know. Fires are ordered in your house that it may be quite aired, and it will be ready to receive you immediately. Part of this letter was dictated by Mr Wade, part by my footman, part by my maid, which makes an agreeable mixture of style. I hope you like it. Mr Beauclerk is not at all well; all his pains have returned. I am very disinterested, you must allow, in taking this house directly; for by that means I can have no hopes of Mary and Elizabeth coming here. You will be very ingenious if you can decipher this letter – I cannot myself.[39]

After Selwyn arrived, she expressed her concern about Topham's condition:

Dear Mr Selwyn,
    The girls shall wait upon Mie-Mie whenever you please to send for them. I have no servants but if it is not convenient for you to send for them, I can contrive it somehow or other; only let me know the day and the hour. Mr Beauclerk continues very ill. The doctors say they cannot pronounce one way or the other for some days to come. I am worried and agitated too much to have the pleasure of dining with you myself. I would you would come here sometimes; it will be a charity. Ever yours, D.B.

Johnson also confirmed to Boswell at this time that 'Poor Beauclerk continues very ill.' However, there was another remission in the summer and when they returned to London, Walpole was able to describe how 'Mr Beauclerk and Lady Di dined here today; he looks so much less ill than he did, that one need never despair of any recovery after his and Lazarus's.'[40]

For a change of scene and a different sort of treatment, they spent the autumn of that year in Brighton, another popular stopping place on society's annual circuit of leisure. The fishing village of Brighthelm-stone became a popular resort in the 1750s, when sea-bathing and sea-drinking were first believed to promote good health. By the 1770s, these activities had been incorporated into a whole social routine, and the town was a lively place, with its own theatre and assembly rooms. As Walpole wrote a couple of years later: 'All the watering places are thronged: one would think this was the most unhealthy country in Europe. On the contrary, this proves it is the most healthy, for nineteen go to amuse themselves for one that goes for illness'. One convalescent's regime at Brighton in the 1770s was a course of

Sarah Churchill, Duchess of Marlborough, c. 1710 (artist unknown). Lady Di's grandmother displaying her key of office as Keeper of the Privy Purse to Queen Anne.

William Hogarth: *The Hervey Conversation Piece,* c. 1740. Commissioned by Lord Hervey to depict his dearest friends, it shows Lady Di's father, Charles, wearing his red military uniform. Also included are (*left to right*) Stephen Fox (seated), Henry Fox, Hervey and Thomas Winnington.

Joshua Reynolds:
Viscountess Bolingbroke,
1763–65. Lady Di is
portrayed as an artist,
and as the epitome of
artistic inspiration,
a Muse of Art.

Joshua Reynolds: *The Marriage of George III,* 1761.
The ceremony in the gorgeously decorated Chapel Royal in St James's Palace.
Lady Di is amongst the group of Bedchamber Ladies on the right.

Frederick, second Viscount Bolingbroke and *Lady Di*, c. 1760 (artist unknown).

After Richard Brompton: *Topham Beauclerk*, c. 1764. Topham at the age of twenty-four, 'having, in some particulars, a resemblance to Charles II', according to Boswell.

Blenheim Palace, the Great
Court and North Front,
c. 1750. The Marlboroughs'
official family home.

St James's Square, c. 1773.
The Bolingbrokes lived
at No. 7, at the far side
on the right.

Lydiard House, Wiltshire.
The country house of the Bolingbrokes.

Stained-glass window,
Lydiard House. The themes
in the window of Lady Di's
dressing room may have
inspired her own work.

Diana Beauclerk: *George St John,* c. 1765. Her eldest son (wearing the typical dress of a four-year-old), learning to write. This sweet little boy would become the seducer of his half-sister, Mary (*below*).

Diana Beauclerk: *Mary and Elizabeth Beauclerk,* c. 1780. Mary, in profile, reads aloud to Elizabeth. Described by Walpole as 'another specimen of her singular genius and taste', it was turned by Bartolozzi into a sought-after engraving. Sir William Hamilton noted 'the grace and elegant simplicity' of the figures.

George Stubbs: *Gimcrack with John Pratt up on Newmarket Heath*, 1765.
Bully's greatest racehorse, which he bought from William Wildman, who probably
commissioned this painting, and sold in the month that Lady Di left him.

Joshua Reynolds: *A Conversation Piece*, 1759/61. This was commissioned by Horace
Walpole to record his friends, the 'Out of Town Party', in the library at Strawberry Hill.
George Selwyn is standing on the left, Lord Edgcumbe (another wit and socialite)
is drawing, with Gilly Williams looking over his shoulder. Walpole described
the work as 'by far one of the best things Reynolds has ever executed'.

Samuel Percy: *An Evening at the Turk's Head Tavern*, c. 1780.
This vividly coloured, deeply carved wax relief shows a typical session of the Club.
Dr Johnson takes the president's chair, on the left, and the members present
include Reynolds, Garrick, Boswell, Fox and Beauclerk.

Richard Brompton: *The Duke of York and Companions on the Grand Tour*, 1764.
Topham (in brown) and Lord Ossory (in green) accompany the Duke (seated) during
his visit to Venice. On the left is Bully's brother, Colonel St John. David Garrick
had to lend the artist £80 until his royal patron paid up.

Dr Johnson's ghost returns to haunt Mrs Thrale as punishment for her unauthorized publication of his biography.

Joshua Reynolds:
Horace Walpole, 1756. Walpole is shown holding a print of one of his treasures, an antique marble eagle bought from another great collector, Cardinal Albani.

Joshua Reynolds:
James Boswell, 1785.

treatment which included 'drinking sea-water on the beach every alternate day, beginning with less than half a pint before breakfast, and bathing three times in seven days'.[41]

Mrs Thrale owned a house there, where she and her family often stayed. Despite her intimacy with Dr Johnson, and acquaintance with other Club members such as Garrick, Boswell and Goldsmith, she was not a visitor to the Beauclerks despite her distant kinship to Topham's mother. Her attitude to them is a curious mixture of familiarity, unctuous respect and hostility. She gleefully reports in *Thraliana* a conversation at this time with Baretti: 'Of Lady Diana Beauclerk he was saying a thousand fine things. I mentioned her bad character – oh yes, says he, I know she is a strumpet; had she not been so she would have sat in Heaven next Jesus Christ'. And another entry, for August 1777, recorded a conversation with Joshua Reynolds, which still harked back to the legendary divorce: 'Sir Joshua Reynolds observed how much Lord Bolingbroke loved a lace coat – a gold one particularly: now says he I hate a Gilding – even upon Gingerbread, no surely replied Lord Mulgrave, a King, a Queen and a Cuckold should always be Gilt'.[42]

In the more louche atmosphere of Brighton, the Thrales found themselves in the company of people whom they perceived as decadent, and with whom they would probably not have mixed in London. Since their lavish lifestyle depended on earnings from the family brewery rather than inherited wealth or land, there was a greater concern for the proprieties and for behaving genteelly. Mrs Thrale wrote regularly from Brighton to Johnson, who refused to come because he genuinely disliked the place, 'a country so truly desolate, that one's only comfort is to think if one *had* a mind to hang oneself, no tree could be found on which to tye the rope'. This was an opinion shared by Lord Pembroke, who referred to his wife and daughter visiting 'nasty Brighthelmstone'.[43]

In October, Mrs Thrale announced to Johnson: 'I have seen the famous J. Wilkes, he came hither to wait on Murphy . . . he professed himself a Lyar and an Infidel . . . Mr Beauclerk is here, and is said to be a charming creature . . . Mr Thrale has come to my room and read so far of my letter – why, says he, these are the persons we are all running after – Ay quoth I, and old Satan is the person that even *they* are running after.' The friendly reference to Topham suggested that she had not yet met him; when she did so, introduced by Arthur

Murphy, playwright and colleague of Garrick, she would be severely disillusioned, her epitaph being 'Lord, How I did hate that horrid Beauclerk'. She certainly regarded John Wilkes, Member of Parliament for Middlesex, Lord Mayor of London, radical politician and scourge of the government as a very dangerous influence. Two days later, she was informing Johnson that

Wilkes has invited Mr Thrale to a Dinner of Rakes – Beauclerk, Lord Kelly, and the men of *worth and honour* that are here & here are plenty too: says Murphy looking at me – he *dares not go* – I would not have him go said I gravely; I am not fond of trying my power over my husband, nor wish to exert it at all for a new Topknot – but if I could keep him out of such Company – I should think I did him an act of real friendship – so who says I have no spirit Dr Johnson? I got severely rallied for my Prudery & at last lost my Labour for he does go, but I know I did right.[44]

Mme du Deffand continued to ask after the Beauclerks in her letters to Walpole written during 1777. That October, Walpole involved her in the complicated task of ordering a Paris-made gown for Lady Di, which was to be brought to England by Gibbon with the hopes of avoiding the high customs duties: 'Je dirai a M. Gibbon ce que vous me mandez. Il m'avait parlé de la commission de Mme Beauclerk; il ne l'a point faite a la cause de la difficulté de vos douanes . . . il vous verra les premiers jours du mois prochain. [I will put your request to Mr Gibbon. He had told me about Mme Beauclerk's errand; he was unable to comply because of the problems with your Customs. He will see you towards the beginning of next month.]'[45]

In December they were entertaining guests in London, but returned to Brighton in January 1778. This provoked a little jealous outburst from Mme du Deffand: 'Ce doit vous etre une privation, l'eloignement des Beauclerks, mais vous vous suffisez vous-même. [You will be deprived when the Beauclerks go away, but you will have to suffer on your own.]'[46]

In the spring of 1778, Lady Di's artistic reputation received an important boost when her work became available to a public beyond the confines of Strawberry Hill. This was through the engraving of one of the family portraits she had painted, that of her second cousin Georgiana, Duchess of Devonshire. The Duchess, then aged only twenty-one, was quickly rising into public prominence through the dazzling combination of youth, rank, wealth, striking appearance and convention-defying behaviour; her every move was attracting the attention of the burgeoning popular press. Lady Di would undoubtedly have been cited by Georgiana's domineering and moralizing mother Lady Spencer (whom John Spencer had married in preference to Lady Di herself) as a dreadful warning against bad behaviour. But the younger woman, out to shock, agreed to pose for her wicked cousin. The watercolour itself was competent and charming enough: Georgiana sits in profile, her hair piled high in the exaggerated style of the day, wearing loose, vaguely classical garments. She holds a book, for gravitas, but gazes out of the window at a tree: natural beauty contemplates nature. What really gave the portrait and its artist wider publicity was its mass production in an edition of two hundred prints: these were snapped up by society and rapidly sold out.

Walpole of course acquired one, and compared its beauty to an apparition of Venus, as described by Virgil:

Lady Di Beauclerk has drawn the portrait of the Duchess of Devonshire and it has been engraved by Bartolozzi. A Castalian nymph conceived by Sappho, and executed by Myron, would not have had more grace and simplicity; it is the divinity of Venus piercing the veil of immortality when:
rosea cervice refulsit
Ambrosiaeque comae divinum vertice odorem
spiravere.*
The likeness is perfectly preserved, except that the paintress has lent her own expression to the Duchess, which you will allow is very agreeable flattery. The nymph-like simplicity of the figure is equal to what a Grecian statuary would have formed for a dryad or goddess of a river. What should I go to the Royal Academy for? I shall see no such *chefs-d'oeuvre* there.[47]

William Mason wanted one too, but had left it rather late. He begged Walpole to use his influence with the artist: 'Pray, do you think it is possible to procure me one of the prints of Lady Di's drawing of the Duchess of Devonshire? I should think you might have interest enough with the designer to obtain it. I hear the plate is in the possession of the Duchess of Marlborough'. But the image was so popular that even Walpole could not immediately assist: 'I doubt very much whether I can get you a print of the Duchess of Devonshire: certainly not before winter, for Lady Di is at Brighthelmstone; but I will try then: she has not many proofs for herself, and I know had not

---

* 'She gleamed with rosy neck, and the lovely hair on her head breathed a divine perfume.'

one left. Everybody, from taste or fashion, tore them away. The Duke, her brother, paid for the plate, and would suffer, I think, but two hundred impressions to be taken. I promised the Duke of Gloucester to beg one for him, which perhaps would not be refused. If I can obtain two, the second is yours. I have set my own in a frame I trust you will like, as it harmonises with it amazingly, though rich.'[48]

The engraving had been commissioned by the Duke of Marlborough from the top practitioner of the day, Francesco Bartolozzi, Engraver to the King and a founding member of the Royal Academy, a man whose distinction and skill was helping to elevate the status of what was often regarded as a mere craft; his innovative stippled engraving style (the use of dots rather than lines) produced such soft and subtle copies of delicate chalk or pastel originals that it was known as the 'crayon' manner. The Duke had a high opinion of Bartolozzi, whom he had commissioned to produce illustrations for the publication of his collection of classical carved gemstones, intaglios and cameos, the passion of his life – he had already bought up three major collections, and possessed around seven hundred and fifty treasures, which he lovingly stored on velvet in red leather cases. Bartolozzi was making engravings of the hundred best gems, and the first volume would be privately printed in 1780. Walpole's reference to her brother paying Bartolozzi's fee perhaps suggests that the marital tensions or hardships were such that the canny Duke wished his sister to have some future, independent source of income. There is nothing to suggest that Lady Di received payment for giving permission for the reproduction of her original, beyond receiving a number of copies for distribution to her friends, but it was common practice for professional artists, such as Reynolds or Kauffmann, to sell such rights to the engravers of their works. The latter might also be print-sellers, or would deal directly with the publishers and sellers. The profits in this instance would have initially gone to Bartolozzi, on to a sure winner with the print-avid public, eager to acquire the image of one celebrity created by another; later versions of the portrait were acquired and published by other print-sellers.

After this summer of success, the Beauclerks remained in Brighton for much of the autumn, as did the Thrales. Henry Thrale, now suffering from depression as a result of a financial crisis at the brewery earlier in the year, was recorded as chatting with Beauclerk, while Mrs Thrale swam.

The year 1779 started sadly with the death, on 20 January, of their dear friend and neighbour David Garrick. The funeral was a great dramatic event, produced by Richard Brinsley Sheridan; it started with a huge procession which accompanied the coffin from the Adelphi to Westminster Abbey. (Walpole thought the pomp was 'perfectly ridiculous'.) The pall-bearers included the Duke of Devonshire, Earl Spencer and the Earl of Ossory, and among the thirty-three coaches which followed the bier, each drawn by six horses, were four holding the members of the Club: Topham was there, with Johnson, Reynolds, Burke, Gibbon and the rest, and the Club meeting that took place four days later must have been a solemn one.

Boswell managed a couple of months in London in the spring of 1779; his family commitments, father's poor health and career at the Scottish bar meant that such jaunts were now harder to arrange and had to be appreciated to the full. His journal for the period shows that he was continuing to see a lot of the Beauclerks, and that Topham was for the moment in better health.

Langton asked me to call with him at Beauclerk's door to ask for his son, who was ill. I at first refused. 'For', said I, 'Beauclerk does not care himself about his son, and surely I do not care. I'll not affect it'. 'But', said worthy Langton, 'should not one care? Should not one have kindly affection' (or some such expression), 'and should not one do what is right even when there is no inclination?' Beauclerk was just getting up, and sent us word he would be glad to see us. We sat above an hour while he breakfasted and talked very well indeed. He controverted Dr Johnson's statement that a man cannot have pleasure in spending money who does not spend it fast. 'Everything', said he, 'is comparative. Reduce the Duke of Bedford to £3,000 a year, which is in itself a very good fortune for a gentleman who has never had more, and you make him as completely miserable as I should be if reduced to £200 a year. Great people have a certain established rate of expense which they cannot retrench. The Duchess of Marlborough is very great and must have a great deal of show. She is very narrow, so as to be doing mean things every day; for example, she has a false back to a grate by which I suppose thirty shillings is saved, and she wants to save a great deal of money. She is very indolent and cannot take the trouble of managing her affairs, so must be continually cheated. These three circumstances make her very unhappy. They have a vast number of servants, and as they are every year wishing to retrench in order to save money, they once considered which of all their servants they could spare, and which do you think it was? Why, the confectioner – the servant whom they could do worst without except the cook.'[49]

Since Topham was a regular visitor to Blenheim, these criticisms of his in-laws' domestic arrangements were based on first-hand experience; such outspoken and sarcastic comments about her family (who had loaned him a large sum of money) would have been all too familiar to Lady Di, as well as his views on her honorary uncle the Duke of Bedford. The conversation then turned to Dr Johnson, and why no one had the courage to stand up to his 'way of saying rough and severe things to people in company. Beauclerk answered "at his age he should be thinking of better things than to abuse people". Here was a more religious sentiment than I ever heard Beauclerk express. This was the most agreeable interview I ever had with Beauclerk. I told him next day that he was not only lively (or clever, or some such word) but good'. The allegations of Boswell, and others, that Topham was an uncaring parent seem harsh but not improbable, given his declining health.

On 16 April, Boswell recorded in his journal: 'Quarrel between Johnson and Beauclerk'. As written up in the *Life*, this was an argument at the Club over the current cause célèbre, the trial of the Reverend James Hackman. Hackman had stalked and eventually shot the object of his obsession, Miss Ray, the long-term mistress of the Earl of Sandwich, when she was leaving Covent Garden, and had then turned the gun on himself. She died but he survived, to be tried and condemned to death. In his defence, it was claimed that he had only intended to shoot himself. Topham decided to take Hackman's side.

Dr Johnson abruptly said, 'Mr Beauclerk, how come you talk so petulantly to me as "this is what you don't know and I know?" One thing I know which you don't know: that you are very uncivil.' Mr Beauclerk said, 'Because you began by being uncivil (which you always are).' The words in parenthesis were, I believe, not heard by Dr Johnson . . . A little while after this, the conversation turned upon the violence of Hackman's temper. Dr Johnson then said, 'it was his business to *command* his temper, as my friend Mr Beauclerk should have done a little ago'. 'I should learn of you', said Mr Beauclerk. Dr Johnson answered, 'You have given *me* opportunities enough of learning, when I have been in your company. No man loves to be treated with contempt'. Beauclerk (with a polite inclination towards the Doctor) said, 'You have known me twenty years and however I may have treated others, you may be sure I would never mean to treat *you* with contempt'. 'Sir', said the Doctor, 'you have said more than was necessary'. Thus it ended . . . he and I din'd at Beauclerk's on the Saturday se'nnight following.[50]

Two days later, Boswell was talking to Edmund Burke: 'I told Burke of the contest between Johnson and Beauclerk. Said he, 'Between Fury and Malevolence'. I 'The bear and – what is a small animal that stands ground?' BURKE. 'A polecat'. BOSWELL. 'Is that spirited enough?' 'O yes' said Burke.'[51]

Boswell attended Hackman's execution; the body was later displayed to the public in the Surgeons' Hall at the Old Bailey. Over these few weeks, Boswell mixed happily with the great names of the day, recording conversations, dinners and meetings with General Paoli, the Earl of Pembroke, John Wilkes and many others, but centred on the close friends of the Literary Club. On 24 April, he noted 'Oglethorpe called in coach and carried me to Beauclerk's. Lady Di not with us. Johnson, Sir Joshua, Langton, Jones, Steevens. Paradise, Dr Higgins'. The fact that he mentioned Lady Di's absence on this occasion implies that she was normally present as hostess to such a gathering. That there was still some uneasiness between Topham and Johnson is suggested by the conversation later in the day: 'After coffee, Johnson and I were set down by Sir Joshua at his sister's. By the way, Johnson said there was in Beauclerk a predominance over his company that one did not like. But he was a man that lived so much in the world that he had a short story for everything, was always ready to begin and never exhausted.'

Although the public facade of the Beauclerk marriage was maintained, the private strains worsened. One of Pembroke's chatty letters to his son, written that same April, mentions 'as usual, really terribly, the Devil to pay betwixt Lady D & Beauclerk, who wins fifty Guineas regularly every night'. As if determined to ignore his health and plan for the future, they moved twice in 1779, first briefly to Piccadilly, then to Thanet House in Great Russell Street. Here Topham indulged his hobby, as described by Walpole to Lady Ossory: 'Mr Beauclerk has built a library in Great Russell St that reaches half way to Highgate'. The new house with its splendid library was adjacent to the British Museum, and attracted almost as many visitors as had Muswell Hill. Lady Pembroke wrote to her son that 'the Beauclerks are now settled in Great Russell St by Bloomsbury Square, where he has built a very fine library, for they never go to Muswell Hill now'. Topham's book collecting remained obsessive and he seemed to be burning the candle at both ends, aware that time was running out. Malone described to Charlemont in April of that year how Topham sent his servant to the booksellers by six or seven in the morning on the days of sales, and how he succeeded in making off with anything rare – this did not inconvenience his master, since it was the time he usually came home to bed.[52]

At this time, both Bully and Topham were rumoured to be dying. Walpole asked Selwyn for the latest news, revealing, with characteristic malice, his real feeling about Topham: 'I shall be much obliged to you for a true account of Lord Bolingbroke. It is not common curiosity that makes me anxious, though not particularly interested about him, nor is he *the husband* I most wish dead'. Bully's emotional instability had been increased by the continuing money problems which he had not been able to sort out. Failing to land an heiress, in 1774 he became involved in what he thought was a lucrative project. 'Bully has a scheme of enclosure which, if it succeeds, I am told, will free him from all his difficulties. It is to come into our House immediately. If I had this from a better judgement than one of our sanguine counsellors, I should have more hope from it. I am ready to allow that he has been very faulty but I cannot help wishing to see him once more on his legs'. The loyal Selwyn agreed to chair the Commons committee considering Bully's Bill, a speculative scheme to enclose, improve and profit from boggy moorland. But, despite its being studied by 'a committee absolutely of Almack's', it was outvoted. 'The cause was not bad but the Question was totally indigestible . . . this phantom of £30,000 clear in Bully's pocket to pay off his annuities vanishes.'[53]

Then there had been another shot at an heiress, in 1777. An old friend, Anthony Storer, met 'a lady of great fortune, but, not wanting her myself, I cannot do better than recommend her to Lord Bolingbroke. If he will give me something for pimping, he shall have her'. This was the reason why Bully 'went down to Bath in pursuit of a lady who he proposes should retrieve his fortunes. Her name is Curtis – she is about thirty years of age, and has a fortune of £43,000'. But Miss Curtis was another one who got away. 1777 was another bad financial year for Bully, when one of his horses, Highflyer, a magnificent performer, and claimed never to have been beaten, was taken in lieu of his debts: Richard Tattersall 'laid hold on Highflyer in order to repay himself' with a Bill of Sale for £2,500. The horse went on to win over £9,000 for Tattersall.[54]

At the end of June 1779, Lady Mary Coke recorded that 'Lord Bolingbroke has been dying, some say of a natural disorder, but more

are of opinion that he had taken something to put an end to his life
... the physician says there is every reason to suppose he had taken
laudanum, an opinion that will gain credit from his having distressed
his circumstances and being that sort of man, so void of all principles
that he was very likely to put an end to his existence the moment his
life was no longer agreeable.'[55]

Walpole passed the gossip on to Lady Ossory: 'Lord Bolingbroke, I
hear, will live. At first they thought he had taken laudanum. It would
have been a monstrous injustice in opium to kill him, when it will not
dispatch Beauclerk'. Lady Mary was also up to date: 'Lord Bolingbroke is still alive but never in his senses. The physicians now think
the miserable state he is in was not the effects of laudanum but a palsy
upon the brain'. Walpole reported back to Selwyn how 'Lady Di's
case is melancholy indeed. It is patched up for the present; but there is
an *affection upon the brain* in both husbands that I believe incurable.
It is a pity that one is not in as much danger as t'other'.[56]

Lord Pembroke informed his son on 9 July: 'Lord Bolingbroke is
vastly ill with the palsy on his brain. Should he live it is much to be
feared that he will never recover his senses'. And he continued gravely
ill: another correspondent of Selwyn's, the Revd Dr Warner, wrote: 'I
forgot to ask the Duke [of Queensberry] today if Lord Bolingbroke
was dead. The papers all killed him on Saturday, but one of them
contradicts it this morning'. On 26 July, Pembroke reported another
crisis: 'poor Bolingbroke's illness took a sudden turn. He became
raving mad & is confined'. (Six months later, according to Walpole,
he was still in a mad-house – although retaining his post as Lord of
the Bedchamber.) Lady Di's sons, George and Frederick St John, were
then aged eighteen and fifteen.[57]

Relations between Lady Di and Topham were now so bad that she
was seriously contemplating leaving him. Betty Pembroke wrote
anxiously to her son, still abroad on an extended Grand Tour: 'I have
been almost distracted these ten days with miseries of my poor Sister's,
they are patched up, & she has consented to bear a little longer ...
Husbands are dreadful and powerful animals. I have a most constant
headache at present, from what I have gone through about it all'.
Enduring Topham 'a little longer' was almost as stressful for Betty as
for Lady Di. A few weeks later Lady Pembroke wrote to her son from
Brighton, where the Beauclerks were spending their third autumn: 'So
here I am arrived at last; much did Sis want me, & much did I and

Charlotte want the sea, I for old nerves & she from having been let alone too long, & so was forc'd to take some pretty strong worm medicines, which got rid of a great number. We have been here just a week & intend staying the most part of next month'.[58]

Charlotte was then aged six, in constant poor health with the beginnings of the consumption that would take her life at the age of eleven. Her cousins Mary and Elizabeth are not mentioned, and had presumably been left in Mrs Terry's care at school. Nor does Charles Beauclerk make an appearance; if it was felt (as expressed by Boswell) that his father did not much care for him, he was best kept apart from an ill and unaffectionate parent.

Walpole, deeply sympathetic to Lady Di's plight, kept closely in touch and sounded a note of optimism to Selwyn: 'I hear matters go very smoothly at Brighthelmstone, though I believe the staircase is not very clean'. And a month later Betty confirmed that the couple were surviving as a result of seeing very little of each other: 'my Sister who is still at Brighton with Mr Beauclerk has just had the chickenpox & been very ill with it. I did not dare go to her for fear of bringing it to Charlotte, only one day I spent with her in washing cloaths, & lay at the Inn, for greater precaution. Mr B keeps such odd hours that she does not see him above a minute in the day, & she lyes in the next house, & there have been no disputes at all since they came here.'[59]

Mrs Thrale was again in Brighton; she recorded in *Thraliana* a Johnsonian incident:

Beauclerk tells a story of him [Johnson] that he [Beauclerk] had two large pointers brought into the parlour on some occasion to show his company and they immediately fastening on one another alarmed the people present not a little with their ferocity, till Johnson gravely laying hold on each dog by the scruff of the neck, held them asunder at arms length and said, Come gentlemen, where is your difficulty?, put one of them out at one door and t'other out of the other; & let us go on with our conversation – he confirmed these two stories himself to me before I would write them down.[60]

Fanny Burney was staying with Mrs Thrale that October, and her diary describes the round – strolling on the Steyn, visiting bookshops, and tea-drinking and card-playing in the public assembly rooms where, one evening, she was introduced to Mr Thrale's acquaintance, 'that celebrated libertine and wit, the Hon. Mr Beauclerk'. She did not record her opinion of him but found the whole evening 'pretty stupid'.

A day or two later, however, there was more distinguished company, for 'the folks of most consequence who were at the rooms this night were Lady Pembroke and Lady Di Beauclerk, both of whom have still very pleasing remains of the beauty for which they have been so much admired'. Fanny subsequently met Lady Pembroke at a tea-drinking party, and was suitably impressed by her looks and manner.[61]

One news item that autumn was the rumour of an inheritance for the Beauclerk girls, as reported by Walpole to Selwyn in October 1779; the letter included a reference to another notorious aspect of Beauclerk at this time – his lice-ridden person: 'I heard last night that an ancient maiden Trevor, sister of Lord Hampden [this was Lady Di's great aunt], has left some fortune to Lady Di's two girls. I most cordially hope it is true, that they may have bread to eat – if they are not eaten first, of which there is some danger, for as modern Conjurers are not greater adepts than the Pharaohs, and as that potent Sovereign's magicians had no power over lice, I doubt the visitation is inveterate.'[62]

The dreadful discrepancy between the earlier figure of the immaculate Macaroni and the present infested misanthrope must be attributed to his illness and laudanum dependency. Another witness to the decline was Lady Louisa Stuart, who referred to his personal hygiene as well as his moods:

This elegant and accomplished gentleman was what the French call 'cynique' in personal habits beyond what one could have thought possible in anyone but a beggar or a gypsy. He and Lady Di were part of a great Christmas party at Blenheim, when soon after the company was met, they found themselves strangely annoyed, as the court of Pharaoh were of old, by certain visitants *in all their quarters*. It was in the age of powder and when stiff frizzing and curling with hot irons and back pins made the entrance of combs extremely difficult. In short, the distress became unsupportable. The origins being clearly traced to Mr Beauclerk, one of the gentlemen undertook to remonstrate with him, and began delicately hinting how much the ladies were inconvenienced. Beauclerk replied 'What! Are they as nice as that? Why, I have enough to stock a parish'. I tell you the story as the Duchess of Marlborough told it herself. It happened at the same time Lady Di was taken ill and had a fever which lasted three or four weeks. During the course of it, she surprised her attendants by insisting on having clean sheets and linen every day. After this discovery they understood why. In the latter part of Beauclerk's life, the man of pleasure grew morose and savage, and Lady Di had much to suffer from his temper. So had his children, to whom he was a selfish tyrant without indulgence or affection. I used to hear much of him from Mrs Herbert, who learned it through Lady Pembroke.[63]

Boswell was another witness:

I told General Paoli that Topham Beauclerk found fault with Brompton's retouching the Pembroke family picture by Vandyke, and said he had spoiled it by painting over. 'Po, po' said Paoli, of whom Beauclerk had talked disrespectfully, 'He has not spoiled it. Beauclerk scratches at everything. He is accustomed to scratch' (scratching his head in allusion to Beauclerk's lousiness) 'and he'd scratch at the face of Venus.'

Like the Marlboroughs, Walpole had endured Topham as a guest and later told the tale to Farington:

Lord Orford [Walpole] mentioned many particulars relative to the late Mr Topham Beauclerk. He said he was the worst tempered man he ever knew. Lady Di passed a most miserable life with him. Lord O, out of regard to her, invited them occasionally to pass a few days at Strawberry Hill. They slept in separate beds. Beauclerk was remarkably filthy in his person, which generated vermin. He took laudanum regularly in vast quantities. He seldom rose before one or two o'clock. His principal delight was in disputing on subjects that occurred, this he did acutely.[64]

Despite, or because of, his extravagance on books and the new house, Beauclerk was also gambling very heavily during their current stay at Brighton. The high stakes shocked Mrs Thrale, who reported in November to Dr Johnson the rumour that Beauclerk had absconded rather than pay a debt to the Duke of Cumberland. Johnson sagely replied: 'If it be only report, I do not much credit it. Something perhaps he may have ventured, but I do not believe he had ten thousand pounds or the means of borrowing it. Of Beauclerk I suppose the fact is true that he has gone, but for his loss, can any body tell who has been the winner? And if he has lost a sum disproportionate to his fortune, why should he run away when payment cannot be compelled?' A few days later, he reproved Mrs Thrale for her spreading of gossip: 'Beauclerk ran no further than home, and is now, I hear, at his own house, perhaps Cumberland's distresses are in the same degree. When stories of this kind are told you, receive them with indifference, and do not by telling them seem to be pleased, but attend to them as traces of character, and hints for inquiry'. Writing to Boswell at exactly the same time, Johnson did not choose to pass on the tattle: 'Of our friends here, I can recollect nothing to tell you. I have neither seen nor heard of Langton. Beauclerk is just returned from Brighthelmstone, I am told, much better.'[65]

Major John Floyd, an old friend of the Marlboroughs and Pembrokes, and former companion of Lord Herbert on his Grand Tour, was shocked and saddened at the state of affairs between the Beauclerks that autumn: 'Lady Di Beauclerk was also at Brighthelmstone. She is quite broken in her looks, & leads the life of a dog with him. He lives to be a torment to himself & all about him.'[66]

A similar picture of these dreadful months was given to Fanny Burney by someone else who knew them well, Edmund Burke: 'He then, addressing himself to me as the person least likely to be acquainted with the character of Mr Beauclerk, drew it himself in strong marked impressions, describing the misery he gave his wife, his singular ill-treatment of her, and the necessary relief the death of such a man must give.'[67]

They returned to London at the end of November. Topham remained ill throughout the winter, although they continued to entertain, as if to show that nothing was wrong. He managed to attend the two January meetings of the Club, taking his turn as President at the first meeting, and felt sufficiently confident of the future to order several new sets of clothes from Le Duc, his Paris tailor. But the Club dinner on 17 January was the last appearance in company of this once most gregarious of men, and his friends recognized that the end was near – Johnson sadly said: 'I would walk the length of the earth's diameter to save Beauclerk'.

His condition deteriorated further during February; he died on 11 March 1780, at the age of forty-one. According to Walpole's conversation with Farington, Topham had sought a death-bed reconciliation with his wife: 'Before he died, he asked pardon of Lady Di for his ill usage of her.' The gentle but practical Lady Pembroke provided a frank epitaph to her son, which suggested the widow's real feelings, and prescribed the correct etiquette following the demise of an unloved relation:

Mr Beauclerk dyed last Friday night after ten days illness which was more than sufficient to put an end to the sufferings of his wretched constitution, it is certainly much happier for himself, & he did not act in a manner to be regretted by others. We put on our mourning next Sunday the 19th. It is a six weeks mourning for you, a month black buckles & sword, & a fortnight colour'd sword and buckles. You must mourn for him tho' abroad, as an Uncle is very near, & in France it will be well known. My Sister was shocked at first, but the way they lived together makes it quite unnatural that it should be a lasting sorrow. She went to Bob's for a few days, & today gets into the house she was in before they went to Russell St, in Hertford St which happens not yet to be let. [68]

Lord Herbert, still in Paris, recorded in his diary how he summoned his tailor and ordered a black coat to be made, but in the interim continued the social round wearing his brown.

Another Paris recipient of the news was Mme du Deffand, whose main reaction was a half-joking fear that her beloved Walpole might become a suitor of the liberated Lady Di unless another old admirer, Fish Craufurd, got in first: 'Regretterez-vous M. Beauclerk? Non, et vous consolerez aisément sa veuve. Que fait le petit Craufurd? [Will you miss Beauclerk? No, and you will easily comfort his widow. What is little Craufurd up to?]' Just a week later: 'Ne serez-vous point tenté de devenir le troisième mari de la nouvelle veuve? Votre goût pour elle est-il aussi vif qu'il a été? Cette question n'est point captieuse, elle ne doit ni vous scandaliser ni vous embarrasser: je mérite, à toutes sortes d'égards, votre parfait confiance – nous avons des mariages ici bien singuliers. [Aren't you tempted to become the third husband of the new widow? Do you still fancy her as much as you used to? This is not a frivolous question, it shouldn't shock or embarrass you; I'm entitled to your full confidence in everything – we have equally unusual marriages here.]' Four months later the joke is getting a little stale: 'Le jour n'est donc point pris pour votre noce? [Haven't you fixed the wedding day yet?]'[69]

Mrs Thrale, moved by his death and by the grave illness of Boling-broke, took the opportunity of writing some of her terrible verses:

I heard the death of Beauclerk last week, and made the following epigram improviso; 'tis a distant imitation of Ausonius' famous 'Infelix Dido'.

> Ah lovely luckless Lady Di
> So oddly linked to either spouse,
> What can thy Gordian knot untie
> Or what dissolve thy double vows?
> And where will still our amazement lead to
> When we review thy various life,

> Whose living lord made thee a widow
> Whose dead one leaves thee still a wife?[70]

Johnson was deeply grieved and described Topham's death as 'a loss that perhaps the whole nation could not repair' (just as he had felt that Garrick's death 'eclipsed the gaiety of nations'). He wrote to Boswell, then in Edinburgh, about their old friend:

Poor dear Beauclerk – nec, ut soles, dabis joca.* His wit and his folly, his acuteness and maliciousness, his merriment and reasoning are now over. Such another will not often be found among mankind. He directed himself to be buried by the side of his mother, an instance of tenderness which I hardly expected. He has left his children to the care of Lady Di, and if she dies, of Mr Langton, and of Mr Leicester, his relation and a man of good character. His library has been offered for sale to the Russian ambassador.

In the following year, Boswell described a touching conversation with Johnson after an evening in company when Topham had been remembered and mourned: 'Dr Johnson and I walked away together. Stopping by the rails of the Adelphi and looking on the Thames, I said with tenderness I thought of two friends we had lost who lived here: Garrick and Beauclerk. 'Ay', said he, 'and two such friends as cannot be supplied.'[71]

Boswell's attitude to Beauclerk was generally one of respect rather than close friendship. His own immediate reaction to the news of the death was slightly qualified: 'After a long silence, I received a letter today from Dr Johnson. He mentioned Topham Beauclerk's death, which some time ago affected me a good deal; for the death of one so fashionable and spirited and knowing and witty as he was dampened my spirits'. And in a letter to Reynolds, Boswell did not scruple to recall the sharp tongue: 'We have lost Beauclerk and Chamier since I was with you. These are sad losses. The first can never be repaired, though his acidity sometimes made me smart'.[72]

Topham had rewritten his will on 6 March 1780, a week before his death, realizing that there was not going to be another recovery. It left all his goods and chattels to Lady Di, specified arrangements for Langton's guardianship of the children in the event of her death, and made a generous bequest to his valet, Thomas Clarke, of all his clothes,

---

* 'No more with wonted humour gay', according to Byron's translation of a poem by the Emperor Hadrian.

his French gold watch and fifty guineas. (A year later, Walpole would be chasing up, on Lady Di's behalf, the fate of the suits Topham had ordered in Paris.) Although it was not specified in the will, Lady Di gave to Langton the portraits of Johnson and of Garrick which Topham had commissioned as duplicates from Reynolds in the previous year, to which he had attached inscriptions. For Garrick, it was a line from *Love's Labour's Lost*: 'a merrier man within the limit of becoming mirth, I never spent an hour's talk withal'. For Johnson, it was a quotation from Horace's *Satires*: 'ingenium ingens inculto latet hoc sub corpore',* which Langton removed. According to the *Life*, 'Johnson said complacently: "It was kind in you to take it off"; and then after a short pause, added, "and not unkind in him to put it on." '[73]

---

* 'A huge talent lurks beneath this uncultivated exterior'.

NINE

The Merry Widow

(1780–87)

'I think you must do like other widows –
buy yourself weeds and be cheerful'

JOHN GAY, *The Beggar's Opera*

Deciding to leave London was a mark of new and necessary independence. It was a chance for Lady Di to establish a completely different
way of life, a positive escape from the unhappy connections of the last
few years and even from the memories of the divorce which still
resonated in metropolitan circles. Her name, and that of Bully, had
recently figured in a cruel satirical serial, *The Picture Gallery*, which
cunningly imitated the format of an art exhibition review in order to
attack the characters of well-known men and women of the day by
providing commentaries on the imaginary but appropriate pictures
they might be thought to have painted. The fifteenth edition, published
in 1779, had a preface which mocked Reynolds' Discourses to the
Royal Academy: 'noble artists are actuated with no other view than to
rescue Great Britain from the imputation of inferiority to her neighbours in Italy'. One of the artists is Viscount B . . . ng . . . ke, who has
painted *The Spendthrift and the Swallow*, after the fable by Aesop, in
which 'the hero of the tale is depicted in a truly tattered condition . . .
having been born in the height of splendour, emblematical representation of cards, dice etc . . . is very characteristic and excellently
fancied'.[1]

The 1780 edition is devoted to 'the softer sex [who] have made a faint attempt to rival the glories of their husbands and brethren'. To Lady D . . . a B. . . . . .k are attributed two works. The first, *Scylla and Charybdis*, shows that the boat 'which leans so indiscreetly towards Charybdis has undoubtedly been shattered by Scylla . . . how it ever escaped out of the jaws of the latter is worthy the attention of the curious. . . . the captain's wife a pattern of evil-doing . . . after having escaped from the teeth of one lord and master, she was induced to try her success with another. The second gave rise to the English proverb "Out of the Frying Pan."' The other picture is *Jupiter and Leda*: 'to inveigh against Leda's breach of chastity would be acting the part of moralists rather than critics . . . Jupiter is hideously frightful, and must certainly have been indebted to Tyndarus (Leda's spouse) for a kindred ugliness in the success he meets with as a suitor. His married rival is presented in the bath scene gambling and so earnest in the amusement that there is little danger of interruption'.

This is very cruel stuff, with so many different barbs springing from the cleverly chosen subjects, attacking all three of them twelve years after the divorce and rubbing in her unhappiness with Beauclerk as well as Bolingbroke's continuing profligacy. She was not the only woman attacked, for the 1780 *Picture Gallery* described 'near two hundred paintings by the most distinguished ladies in Great Britain'. Her sister-in-law Lady Charles Spencer had produced a *Lucretia*, with 'not a hint of female delicacy . . . the texture of her petticoats [reveal her as] a finished courtesan'. To Bob Spencer's mistress Mrs Bouverie was attributed *Liberty*, revealing a 'becoming licentiousness . . . tipsy dance and revelry'. The Dowager Duchess of Bedford, known for her strong character and ruddy complexion, was associated with *Medusa's Head* and *Boudicca*. The Duchess of Devonshire got off quite lightly, with reference only to her failure to breed after six years of marriage, *Cymon and Iphigenia* depicting an apathetic lover, while *The Careless Husband* preserved the chastity of his wife.

Another recent, hurtful publication was *Trials for Adultery*, which came out in 1779 (and was so popular that a second volume was published in 1784). This provided the full texts of the depositions given in the more notorious divorce hearings at Doctors' Commons during the 1760s and '70s. So the full accounts of the Bolingbroke divorce, including the servants' descriptions of the rumpled couch and the secret visits of Dr Hunter, were now available to anyone who could read.

Moving out of London represented an attempt to distance herself from those who knew most about these old stories, and was also a necessary effort to live more cheaply outside the capital, since she was now solely responsible for three young children and a crew of servants. The sophisticated Thameside towns of Richmond, Kew and Twickenham were already familiar territory, the home of old and more recent friends, centres of social and intellectual life – the theatre in Richmond attracted the best actors of the day, and a new building had just been opened in 1776 – providing a rural ambience within fairly convenient coach ride of central London. The only disadvantage was fear of the highwaymen who preyed upon travellers to London: the German tourist and novelist Sophie von la Roche describes a dinner at Richmond in 1786 'interrupted by the fact that all these guests feared highwaymen . . . so they all decided to depart together, as the robbers would hardly hold up four coaches at once'. A further precaution was 'all the gentlemen hiding their watches and only keeping a third of their money in their purses'. Sophie's coach fell behind the convoy because her coachman was drunk but she got back to London safely, despite much anxiety.[2]

Lady Di was familiar with such problems, for she had often visited Walpole at Strawberry Hill and the Garricks further up the Thames at Hampton. Another acquaintance and occasional local resident was Sir Joshua Reynolds, who had a house built on Richmond Hill in 1771, where he often used to spend his Sundays entertaining friends. (However his niece later reported his description of it as 'a place I hate, for one has all the inconvenience of town and country put together, and not one of the comforts – a house stuck upon the top of a hill without a bit of garden or ground near'.) This was where his sister the artist Frances Reynolds was living in 1781. Some of Bully's old friends were also drawn there; the Duke of Queensberry purchased a villa in 1780, despite his opinion of the Thames: 'I am quite tired of it – there it goes, flow, flow, flow, always the same'. Selwyn moved there two years later, and Bob's friends the Sheridans lived at Douro House on Richmond Hill. Other distinguished neighbours included the Duke of Clarence, the King's third son, who owned Ivy House near the river, and of course the King and Queen, who still occasionally stayed at Kew.[3]

The best form of support for Lady Di, following Topham's death and the move, was the company of her sister, who quickly joined her in Richmond as the first step in a subtle separation from her husband. Lady Pembroke wrote to her son in April 1780:

I am just now delighted with having leave to take some Lodgings at a Keeper's Lodge in Richmond Park; it is a leave they do not in general like to give, but the K and Q have said a thousand civil things at the same time they have given me leave . . . it is but nine miles & in just the place I like. You know a Villa has always been my Hobby Horse. Sister Di has just taken a house at Richmond, & the Duke of Montagu's, where the Dss of Buccleugh (his Daughter, my cousin) & the Courtowns are forever, is in Richmond, so that is quite comfortable.

Betty later took a house on the north-west side of the Green (her name still commemorated in the current Pembroke Villas which now stand on the site), which was famous for its beautiful gardens and massive holly hedge; her final Richmond residence was another Pembroke Lodge, in Richmond Park, where she first rented part of a house previously called the Molecatcher's and was then granted the whole property by George III.[4]

Lady Di first lived in Petersham, an arcadian but elegant village set on a bend of the river, nestling between the foot-slopes of Richmond Hill and the peaceful watermeadows which ran down to the broad Thames. There were still stocks on the village green, and the medieval maypole had only been demolished some fifty years earlier. Here she rented a 'cottage' whose genteel neighbours included Petersham Lodge, occupied by the Earl of Harrington, and later by the Duke of Clarence, and Douglas House, owned by the Duchess of Queensberry. Lady Di's cottage itself contributed to the panoramic prospect from the far grander house of Sir Joshua high up on the Hill, a view which he sometimes painted. She also found inspiration in the scenery of Richmond, sketching views of Hill and river; one large watercolour shows two ladies enjoying a picnic and conversation in a setting which could well be the Park, rural but tamed Nature.[5]

It was here one Sunday in 1782 that the conversation of a group of Reynolds' guests, who included Edmund Burke and Edward Gibbon, turned to Lady Di, as recorded by the sharp pen of another guest, Fanny Burney:

From the window of the dining-parlour, Sir Joshua directed us to look at a pretty white house which belonged to Lady Di Beauclerk. 'I am extremely glad' said Mr Burke, 'to see her at last so well housed; poor woman! the bowl has long rolled in misery; I rejoice that it has now found its balance. I never, myself, so much enjoyed the sight of happiness in another as in that woman when I first saw her after the death of her husband. It was really enlivening to behold her placed in that sweet house, released from all her cares, a thousand pounds a year at her own disposal, and – her husband was dead! Oh it was pleasant, it was delightful, to see her enjoyment of her situation'. 'But, without considering the circumstances' said Mr Gibbon, 'this may appear very strange, though, when they are fairly stated, it is perfectly rational and unavoidable'. 'Very true', said Mr Burke, 'if the circumstances are not considered, Lady Di may seem highly reprehensible.'[6]

Lady Di soon established an active social life, with the freedom to be with the sort of people whom her late husband had antagonized. She saw a great deal of Walpole, and it is through his letters that we continue to see much of her. For example, there was an evening in June 1780, when the dangers of being in London during the anti-Catholic Gordon riots were realized: 'I have been with Lady Di at Richmond, where I found Lady Pembroke, Miss Herbert and Mr Brudenell. Lord Herbert is arrived. They told me the melancholy position of Lady Westmorland. She is sister of Lord George Gordon and wife of Colonel Woodford, who is forced to conceal himself, having been the first officer who gave orders to the soldiers to fire, in the attack on Lord Mansfield's house. How many more deplorable calamities from the tragedy of this week that one shall never hear of!'[7]

Liberated from having to attend to a bad-tempered invalid with whom she had thoroughly fallen out of love, her main concern was lack of money. Recalling the demand for her engraving of the Duchess of Devonshire, she now commissioned Bartolozzi to engrave and distribute another of her works, a recent pastel portrait of Mary and Elizabeth, the elder in profile, reading aloud from a book, and gesticulating with a finger, to her sister. This was on the large scale she preferred for portraiture, nearly four feet wide, which made her pastels resemble oils, revealing the considerable skill and confidence she was developing in this very different medium. She handles the pastels very effectively, managing to contrast the most precise details of her daughters' features – the slightly uneven line of Mary's nose, the bluish shadow under the eye, the highlights on their hair, the crisp details of the tiny ruffles on their sleeves – with a loosely blurred effect away from the centre extending out to a soft hazy background. Her palette is deliberately restricted to pink and greyish-blue tones. This work was much admired by Walpole, who described it as 'another specimen of her singular genius and taste. The gay and sportive innocence of the younger daughter, and the demure application of the elder are as characteristically contrasted as Milton's Allegro and Penseroso'.[8]

Bartolozzi's engraved version moved a long way from the original, by substituting a formal setting for the immediacy and informality of the pastel. He extended the subject, so that instead of just the three-quarter-length figures of the two girls they are now full-figure, seated on a day bed which has exotic, Egyptian-looking legs, and above which is suspended a massive Reynolds-style draped curtain; a column separates the interior view from a landscape at the extreme left. The question of payment has to remain speculative; Bartolozzi was responsible for selling the edition, which proved as popular as the engraving of the Duchess of Devonshire. Therefore it is possible that, at this time of need, Lady Di did accept a fee from him for the right to reproduce and distribute her original – this is certainly what she was doing some ten years later.

The engraving was agreed to be a great artistic success, and one print was sent as a thank-you present by her nephew Lord Herbert to William Hamilton, with whom Lord Herbert had spent much time on the Naples leg of his Grand Tour. Herbert courteously wrote to Hamilton, in August 1780: 'I have sent to town for some music for you that Lord P thought would be to your liking. My servant, who leaves me in a month for Rome, will be the bearer; I shall desire at the same time your acceptance of Lady Di Beauclerk's two girls, which Bartolozzi has lately published from the original which was by Lady Di herself'. Herbert had gone to some trouble to obtain the print, sending instructions from Wilton to John Morris, their London steward. Morris replied that he had managed to obtain a copy, but only through the personal influence of Lord Pembroke and the distinguished Italian violinist and director of the London Opera, Felice de Giardini: 'My Lord desired Giardini, he being very intimate with Bartolozzi, to apply for it, in order that a good impression might be obtainable'.[9]

The print was successfully delivered, for Hamilton replied in December 1780:

Your servant Nicolas Laurent sent me the packet of Musick and the charming print of Lady Di Beauclerk's, for which I really am most obliged to your Lordship. The Musick is just what I wanted and the Etching does one's heart good to look at it. I always thought Lady Di had more true taste than any creature living and I defy any artist in England to compose two figures with more grace and elegant simplicity than these two delightful little girls. Do kiss the hand that produced them (as my proxy) and tell her Ladyship that I can never cease being her admirer, as I was long before you were born, and when your graceless Papa used to laugh at my tender feelings, for with him you know – sh-cum-sh is the beginning of love and kiss my A – e is the end of it.[10]

Her nephew was well aware of Lady Di's commitment to her work; even from icy St Petersburg, which he visited on his extremely Grand Tour, he had sent her information about the local ores as constituents of coloured pigment. His graceless Papa, Pembroke, was happy to tease Hamilton about his old passion, when he wrote early the next year, describing her latest project: 'If you was to see six pieces of Lady Di's from a story in Ossian, you would fall down and worship her more than ever. She lives totally at Richmond with her children and paints all day long'.[11]

The poetry of the ancient Celtic Ossian was in fact an entire fabrication by the modern Scottish poet James Macpherson, although this was not appreciated at the time, and the public were flocking to read a wild neglected genius; that she was looking to illustrate such themes shows her engagement with a particular type of subject matter, that of the dramatic conflicts and powerful emotions already expressed in the *Mysterious Mother* drawings. Pembroke's reference to her painting all day long suggests that she had at last obtained the freedom to do what she really wanted.

It was at this time that Walpole attempted to commission reproductions of the *Mysterious Mother* set; he was perhaps aware of her financial situation, but also realized that the furthering of her career would enhance the status of her great commission for him. He was now seriously considering publishing the play, and so may have been contemplating an illustrated edition. In July 1780, he wrote to William Mason:

I expect Sandby every day, who is to attempt Lady Di's drawings for my play in his new aquatinta. It is a thousand pities they should exist only in one septinity, and that the world should have no idea of the powers of her genius if the originals should perish. Bartolozzi has executed very well the drawing of her two daughters, but they have not half the ingredients, passions, graces, horrors, scenes, expressions of my seven pictures. I am writing in their own closet, and it is having the continence of Scipio to say no more about them, though you know them so well; but how infinitely pleasanter if you was sitting here and talking them over.[12]

The artist Paul Sandby was respected not just for his watercolours of landscapes and figures but also for his interest in the techniques of print-making. In the mid-1770s he had pioneered a technique called aquatint, by which an etching could reproduce the subtle nuances of wash drawings, such as Lady Di's use of bistre for the *Mysterious Mother* sequence. But nothing seemed to come of this potential collaboration, and the play was published, unillustrated, in the following year.

Lady Di was also trying to raise funds by selling Topham's famous library. This was in order to pay off her brother's loan of £5,000, against which the library had been pledged as security. There was an optimistic attempt by the Earl of Pembroke, whose own finances were always precarious, to attract the attention of that enthusiastic collector of Western art, the Empress Catherine the Great of Russia. James Harris, British Ambassador at St Petersburg, wrote to Lord Herbert (who had met the Ambassador on his Grand Tour):

If Lord Pembroke ever wrote to me about Lady Di Beauclerk's Library, his letter never came to hand; if it had I should have told him that tho' I would endeavour to dispose of it in the manner desir'd as well from his recommendation and from its real value, yet I should think my success very doubtful, since the Empress does not give greatly into that particular branch of belles-lettres, and will scarcely be induced to purchase it at a moment when she has made already such expensive acquisitions in the picture way; I must say the same as to Lord Pembroke's medals. I spoke of those to her myself, but medals are not her Imperial Majesty's taste.

Pembroke was obviously trying to kill two birds with one stone, helping out his needy sister-in-law, and easing his own problems by selling off family treasures.[13]

The book collection was disposed of in the following year in a massive sale organized by the auctioneer Samuel Paterson, in the Society of Arts' old premises in the Strand. The sale lasted from 9 April to 6 June 1781. The catalogue lists over thirty thousand books 'in most languages and upon almost every branch of science and polite literature'. They show Topham's extraordinary breadth of interests (or undiscriminating acquisitions policy) – the arts and sciences, early and modern literature, travel, medicine, many with his own annotations such as an anecdote told to him by Garrick in the *Life of Colley Cibber*. The sale eventually realized just over £5,000, enough for the unsupported widow to clear the debt she had inherited to her extremely wealthy brother. The playwright Malone wrote to Charlemont (for whom he had been trying to purchase some books): 'the rage for all sorts of ancient English literature is so great at present that all books of that kind went extremely high, Mr Garrick having made a collection of old plays, every manager now thinks it necessary to do the same . . . Beauclerk's books are thought to have sold extremely well . . . the Duke of Marlborough had a mortgage on them for £5000, and the money every day paid to his banker. He has, you see, a tolerably good guess how far he may venture to go when he opens his purse.'[14]

The sale provoked a conversation between Johnson and John Wilkes, on only the second occasion of their meeting. Boswell reported how

Mr Beauclerk's fine library was this season sold in London by auction. Mr Wilkes said he wondered to find in it such a numerous collection of sermons, seeming to think it strange that Mr Beauclerk should have chosen to have many compositions of that kind. JOHNSON. 'Why, Sir, you are to consider that sermons make a considerable branch of English literature, so that a library must be very imperfect if it has not a numerous collection of sermons; and in all collections, Sir, the desire of augmenting grows stronger in proportion to the advance in acquisition, as motion is accelerated by the continuance of the impetus. Besides, Sir' (looking at Mr. Wilkes with a placid but significant smile), 'a man may collect sermons with intention of making himself better by them, I hope Mr Beauclerk intended that some time or other that should be the case with him.[15]

One of the many conveniences of Richmond was its proximity to London, so that visits could easily be made or received. Miss Lloyd, now companion to Lady Clermont, came to see Lady Di in 1781, and another familiar face was that of Boswell, who spent a few days in Richmond that spring: 'Day passed charmingly. Called Lady Di; in London. Card came evening to come at 11. Mrs White with us'. On the next day, he reports having breakfast with Lady Di, and her performance as a devoted mother: 'fine to see her with the children, hearing one French and t'other harpsichord'. He returned to her house later in the day, with expectations raised: 'Sorry for being so long absent. Quite tender friendship'. But he was perhaps becoming too assiduous a visitor, for on 28 April, he was informed 'Lady Di not up'.[16]

He went back to Richmond three weeks later, and called again, despite a bad hangover:

Rose with a severe headache, coldness and giddiness. Breakfast did me some good. Visited Lady Di Beauclerk. Her gay conversation did me good. I said gaiety, by making animal spirits well, would cure every complaint. 'Every nervous complaint', said she. I complained of Langton's worthy, dull, Lincolnshire-goose justice. 'O, Massenberg,' said she [the name of Langton's lawyer-neighbour in Lincolnshire]. 'I have seen them all. One is not to die of these worthy people'. 'No,' said I, 'and a sad death: the reverse of "Die of a rose in aromatic pain" [Pope, *Essay on Man*]. They overlay one'. I begged to see a particular painting by her Ladyship from Spenser's *Faerie Queene*, and read the passage: Book 4, Canto 7, SS 35–36, and looked at the picture and was charmed. I said the representation was such, one could not say whether the poetry was taken from the painting or the painting from the poetry; whether the poetry or the painting was first. Said she: 'That is the finest compliment I ever had paid me. I'll write that in a book, as you do'. She went in a carriage to the Park with her daughters. I crept down the hill, cold and not well. Was obliged to take peppermint drops and sit by the fire.[17]

Her *Faerie Queene* cycle survives as six large watercolours, which depict (as in the *Mysterious Mother* sequence) significant moments that demonstrate her total empathy with the text, as Boswell had remarked. From the three lengthy books of Spenser's uncompleted epic (he had originally intended twelve), an allegory presenting the moral virtues as chivalric knights, she chose incidents in which women played key roles. The depiction of strong female protagonists was a strategy also adopted by Angelica Kauffmann, many of whose history paintings show the actions and choices of women rather than men. The illustration which Boswell admired revealed the brave Belphebe's realization of her betrayal by the lovely Amoret, whom she had just rescued from the monster Lust, but who had charmed Belphebe's love, the Squire Timias. The painting shows the moment when Belphebe returns victorious from killing the monster, bearing her bow and arrow, but gazes in sudden horror at Timias' absorption in another woman, which drives her on a further quest.

> But drawing nigh, ere he her well beheld,
> Is this the faith? She said, and said no more
> But turned her face and fled away for evermore
> (BOOK IV, CANTO 7)

Another heroine is Britomart, who wore male armour but revealed herself to the knight Arthegal after fighting with him: Lady Di has shown the moment when Britomart removes her helmet:

> .... her yellow heare
> Having through stirring, loos'd their wonted band
> Like to a golden border did appeare
> (BOOK IV, CANTO 6)

The unloosed hair is the focal point of the picture, gleaming out of the muted surrounding glade: Britomart, with raised sword in one hand and shield in the other, her close-fitting armour resembling mermaids' scales, looks gravely at an awed group of knights, one of whom has knelt and laid his own sword and shield at her feet.

There is another image of Britomart, again in armour, this time rescuing the hapless Amoret from the Enchanter's Chamber (Book III, Canto 12), whose alien nature is symbolized by an exotic Moorish arch supported by glazed columns with stylized Arabic patterns in the spandrels, which frames the whole scene. These details must have been based on something that she had seen – wall panels in the gallery at Strawberry Hill, for example, used intricate oriental-looking patterning, and designers and architects drew cheerfully on an eclectic mix of styles. Another proactive heroine is Una, shown rescuing the Red Cross Knight from the Cave of Despair (Book I, Canto 9), whose terrible sense of desolation, 'dark, doleful, drearie, like a greedie grave' is captured by a gaunt tree, with branches like skeletal fingers, the cave mouth strewn with skulls and bones, the dark tones of the whole, redeemed only by Una's white robes and fair hair.

Lady Di's close analysis and sensitive, accurate interpretation of the meaning arose from an intimate study of the original; she copied the relevant portions of the text, and the verses describing the Belphebe–Amoret scene survive in her elegant handwriting. As Walpole's library at Strawberry Hill held a fine vellum-bound three-volume edition of Spenser, illustrated not particularly sensitively by Kent, she may have borrowed these particular volumes to work from. The accurate details of much of the armour also suggest that she had studied and sketched Walpole's extensive collection of helmets, gauntlets, swords and mail. The drawings have a unity of structure – the main characters are generally framed by a background of trees, they relate dramatically to one another by facial expression and by gesture, the effects of light and darkness are well expressed through highlights and shadows. The colour tones are soft and smoky, with the Rubens-like shades of browns, yellows and greens, with touches of blue or red (Britomart's scarf, the blood dripping from Amoret's bosom) to concentrate the eye.[18]

Although her illustrations to Spenser got no further than these watercolours, she was undoubtedly intending them for publication, either as a set of engravings for sale, or for a projected new edition of *The Faerie Queene*. Their dimensions and format (large and ambitious for watercolours, each measuring almost three feet by two) are almost identical to the watercolours which she later undertook specifically for engraving by Bartolozzi and his team as a commission to illustrate a new edition of Dryden's *Fables*. This is reinforced by Walpole's reference to the project, as typically recorded by Letitia Hawkins: 'Mr Walpole used to talk of Lady Di's engaging in making designs from Spenser – there were many employments that would have suited her better'.[19]

Scenes from *The Faerie Queene* were a popular source for illustration in the 1770s and '80s. Joshua Reynolds had painted Mary Beauclerk as Una with the Lion in 1778, a work which was exhibited at the Royal Academy in 1780, where Walpole had described it as 'very sweet'. Lady Di now wanted to buy this picture, and asked Langton to find out discreetly from Sir Joshua, in whose studio it still was, 'without telling him that I made this enquiry', how much it might cost. 'The case is that if I find it not beyond what I can afford, I should be very happy to buy it, but dare not mention it till I know, as it may be a great sum'. It was too expensive for her to acquire.[20]

It was during this burst of visits to Richmond that Boswell also took the opportunity of calling upon Walpole at Strawberry Hill. The two did not get on. Walpole disapprovingly told William Mason how 'Boswell, that quintessence of busybodies, called on me last week and was let in, which he should not have been, could I have foreseen it'. Boswell's view of Walpole was only slightly more charitable: 'genteel, fastidious, priggish'. The thought of a polite conversation between these discrepant characters, both perhaps boasting of their special relationship with Lady Di, the one thing they had in common, can only be imagined.[21]

Another admiring visitor at this time was 'Fish' Craufurd. Lady Louisa Stuart made a characteristically snide comment: 'The last I remember of James Craufurd was his loitering about Richmond as *cicisbeo* to Lady Di Beauclerk when she was quite old enough to have done with that sort of thing and he rather past the middle age'. Selwyn reports a dinner in 1781 attended by 'The Fish', and by Everard Fawkener, whose sister was involved with Bob Spencer; in the same letter, he describes how Bob has been very ill but that 'Lady Di has promised to send to me as soon as he is permitted to see anybody'.[22]

In the spring of 1782 she moved across the river and a little way downstream, to another delightful property which overlooked the Thames. It was in the grounds of Marble Hill House, a Palladian villa commissioned by Lady Suffolk, George II's former mistress, Queen Caroline's Mistress of the Robes, and an old crony of Horace Walpole, who often visited her; it was designed by Henry Herbert, ninth Earl of Pembroke (the father of Lady Di's brother-in-law) and the grounds were said to have been planned by another illustrious Twickenham resident, Alexander Pope. Lady Suffolk's brother then bought the adjacent land, including a pretty cottage to the east of the estate, which Lady Suffolk acquired from him in 1756. As described in 1760, in *A Short Account of the Principal Seats and Gardens in and about Twickenham*, although the building was small, this was offset by 'the extreme neatness of the outside, which is perfectly white, and makes it a striking and pleasing object from the River'. There was a 'large room with a bow-window to the water . . . the garden is laid out to as much advantage as so small a piece of ground is capable of'. It was then extended into 'a sweet little box', called Marble Hill Cottage, by Daniel Giles, a director of the Bank of England, who had rented it during the 1770s and early '80s. Lady Di was the next tenant, and she stayed there for seven years. The pretty villa consisted of two storeys and an attic; French windows opened onto the lawn which led down to the water; and there was a summerhouse.[23]

Here she was described by Pembroke to Hamilton to be working on another portrait of her daughters: 'She has done the girls again, & differently, & still better, but it is not engraved. She has given it to Fawkener'.[24]

Perhaps it was the terrible weather and influenza epidemic recorded by Walpole in the summer of 1782 (after two days of downpour when 'I found everybody at Twickenham as ill as they have been in town . . . both Lady Di's daughters were in bed') that inspired her to tackle a new genre, that of mural decoration, creating a permanent vista of summer blossoms entwined on trellis. She was also working for the first time in the subject thought most appropriate for women artists, that of flower painting, which was then ranked at the very bottom of the subject-matter hierarchy because it required mere imitative skills. Walpole did not share the common contempt, and expressed his adulation in verse:

> Here genius in a later hour
> Selected its secluded bower
> And threw around the verdant room
> The blushing lilac's chill perfume,
> So loose is flung each bold festoon –
> Each bough so breathes the touch of noon –
> The happy pencil so deceives
> That Flora, doubly jealous, cries
> 'The work's not mine – yet trust those eyes,
> 'Tis my own Zephyr waves the leaves.'

As he enthused to Mason:

Lady Di Beauclerk is painting a room at her charming villa that was Mr Gyles's, and that I have christened *Spencer Grove*. It is nothing but a row of lilacs in festoons on green paper, but executed in as great a style as Michael Angelo would have done for a pope's villa; and without even making a sketch. You would know the countenance of every single flower, and call them by their names, but alas! those glorious wreaths that you would wish to cut out and glaze, were any glasses large enough, are painted in water colours, and will not last two summers. In each panel of the surbase she has painted a sprig or chaplet of geranium, or ivy, or periwinkle, and every one is a capital picture. Every plant has its identical character, as her human figures have. You have never seen my picture of her gypsies telling a country girl's fortune, but I don't pity you; you might see it if you would, but I never wish any one to do what is not done but by solicitation.[25]

Finding just the right colours for her schemes was a constant challenge. She sought the advice of Lord Harcourt, one of a group of learned amateurs and connoisseurs who corresponded with one another about styles and techniques – these included Mason, John Gilpin, the watercolourist, and Walpole himself. In the previous year, for example, Walpole was informing Mason that Gilpin was anxious to master Sandby's aquatinta technique in order to provide colour illustrations for Mason's forthcoming book. A few days later, 'Lord Harcourt has just been here and tells me he believes he can procure the method of the acquatinta for Mr Gilpin' from 'Taylor at Bath'. Again Walpole was the intermediary for Lady Di's approach to Harcourt: 'I beg your Lordship's pardon for giving you this trouble, but Lady Di Beauclerk desired me to ask if you have not a receipt for a beautiful green for house painting, and if I thought you would be so good as to let her have a copy. I said, I did not doubt of your lordship's complaisance, if it is no secret, yet that I conceived you would still be more ready to oblige her with it if it were to paint anything rather than a house'.[26]

Her decorations inspired local interest. Another tenant on the Marble Hill estate was George Hardinge, a Welsh justice, who rented a house called Ragman's Castle (and who broke the terms of his lease through planting unauthorized fir trees and raising forbidden fowls). Hardinge was fascinated by his neighbour and begged Walpole to introduce him:

Did I see you in the act of sipping coffee at Lady Di's on Sunday evening? What a scene it is! N.B. – I have seen the lilac festoons. But will you forgive my ambition to know the artist? If that is more than I can hope to obtain, may I have the entree of her sweet gardens when she is from home? . . . apropos of the lilac. Suffer me to explain our trespass. Mrs Hardinge and I rambled and saw the birds were flown. We asked leave to peep; and the Major-Domo would have my name, whether I would or no. As a misconstruction is possible, pray guard me against it.

This demonstrates the practice of hopeful visitors simply turning up at interesting properties and, if the owner was not at home, asking to be shown around by the housekeeper or other senior servant. That was why people with more prestigious homes, such as Strawberry Hill or the Muswell Hill villa, had to restrict visitors to those who had booked in advance.[27]

Walpole made it clear that he thought Hardinge had overshot the mark, and provoked an anxious reply:

I am concerned that you should think me capable of intruding myself either upon Lady Di Beauclerk's acquaintance or upon her family in her absence. I have never entertained for a moment so indelicate a thought; but what I named upon was the idea that as I am your friend and her immediate neighbour, she would not be averse to me; and that when her *whole* family, except the servants, were from home, I could now and then, without offence, drop in upon her sweet place as a part of my walk. But as I find from your account that it cannot be with propriety,

I beg it as a particular favour that you will be so good as to leave me in my natural obscurity, drop no hint of my wishes to Lady Di Beauclerk, and trust to me that I shall commit no further trespass.

Walpole was expressing his instinct for the proprieties and the desire to protect Lady Di – for a single lady with a hint of a past, the presence of a married man turning up unannounced with free access to her house and garden, whether or not she was at home, would have done her fragile reputation no good at all.

Walpole was always anxious to encourage her progress and advance her fame. Just as he had tried to have her drawings reproduced in aquatint, still aware that her technical limitations restricted her to watercolour rather than the oils necessary for history painting, he approached William Mason, a more experienced practitioner, for guidance as to how her range might be extended and made more permanent:

I want to know how your pupil Mrs Harcourt advances by your marriage of oil and water colours. Next, if it answers, I should be glad to have the receipt, that is if you have no objection, and do not intend to keep your nostrum a secret till you can announce the discovery to your own honour – not that I will rob you of it – I have two purposes to serve, one to communicate the process to Lady Di, the other to employ a painter to oil some of her drawings, if your method will do that end, and will not hurt them; but I repeat that I do not desire you to acquaint me with the process if you have the least objection.

Mason did send his formula, which, it has been suggested, was a mixture of oil paint with minium, or red lead, the body-colour used in miniature painting.[28]

Having done one room, she started a new mural scheme, painting this time not directly on the walls but onto large panels, which could therefore be moved. Walpole boasted to Lady Ossory:

There will be a much prettier room soon at the other end of the village. Lady Di is painting another with small wreaths of flowers – 'flowers worthy of paradise'* – there is already a wreath of honeysuckles, surpassing her own lilacs, and such as she only could paint and Milton describe; and there is a baby Bacchus so drunk! and so pretty! borne in triumph by Bacchanalian Cupids. Twickenham does not vie with the pomps of Stowe, but, like the modest violet, *qui se cachoit sous l'herbe* [hiding itself beneath the grass], has its humble sweets.[29]

* Milton, *Paradise Lost*, iv, 241.

By the following spring it was complete.

Lady Di has painted a new room at her cottage, since you saw it, with small pictures of peasants and children, in rounds and squares, that are chained together by wreaths of natural flowers that exceed her lilies, and all flowers that ever were painted. What a pity that they are in water colours, and consequently almost as perishable as their originals. Van Huysum's finical and elaborate works will pass for standards because Lady Di's bold characteristic touches will not exist! They are like the excellence of a great actor or musician, whose perfections live only in tradition, and cannot be compared with the merit of prior or subsequent performers. If the Apollo Belvedere were not extant, who would believe that it has never been equalled?[30]

He described her Marble Hill murals in one of his addenda to the second edition of the *Description of Strawberry Hill*: 'she painted in the boldest style, though in water colours, a room hung with green paper, which she adorned with large festoons of lilacs, and the surbase with wreaths of different plants, in a style superior to the greatest flower painters. She afterwards painted another room there on brown paper with lunettes of peasants and children, chained together by garlands of different flowers, which were still more excellent and natural than even the lilacs'. He noted that when she moved from Twickenham these portable panels were given to Lady Pembroke, and that she also decorated a whole room in Bob Spencer's house in Berkeley Square with painted panels which were set on velvet.

As a further encouragement of these botanical skills, Walpole presented her with a copy of the French version of his essay on *Modern Gardening*, translated in 1785 by the Duc de Nivernois, with whom her name had been linked in the days when she was a court lady.

Another connoisseur who admired her work was William Gilpin, the artistic clergyman whose formulation of the Picturesque – an emphasis on the rugged qualities of landscape which were necessary to stimulate the imagination – was manifested as much by his thousands of sketches of wild countryside as by his theoretical writings. Generous in his advice to aspiring artists, Gilpin had an extensive circle of admirers, pupils and correspondents, with whom he exchanged drawings, theories and technical tips on a whole range of practical matters such as the preparation of paper, obtaining and mixing pigments, recipes for inks and so on. One of his most assiduous correspondents was that other artistic vicar, William Mason; for over twenty years they exchanged hundreds of letters, arguing in a scholarly way about styles and techniques.

In 1784 Gilpin expressed to Mason his admiration for Lady Di's work:

While my drawings have the honour to please Ladies, the drawings of a Lady have excited great admiration in me – those of Lady Di Beauclerk. I am never very solicitous about seeing *wonderful works* of art; I feel myself so often disappointed. But a Lady, visiting in this neighbourhood last autumn, Miss Crewe, sent for two of Lady Di's drawings from a friend, on purpose, I believe, to show them to me. I was indeed greatly surprised at their beauty; they were masterly in a high degree: and I took the liberty to desire Mr Walpole, if he could by any means, to put me in possession of a sketch of Lady Di's. He gave me a very obliging answer – promised to do his utmost; but told me of the extreme difficulty of getting hold of them – not from the value she sets on them; but from the extreme unwillingness, with which she takes up her pencil.[31]

This alleged unwillingness to draw does not ring true and is more likely to be Walpole's polite way of declining to share the work of his own favourite and protégée with another influential man, especially one who had more expertise and influence than himself in this area; he may never even have passed on the request. Four years later Lady Di was sufficiently impressed by Gilpin's work and reputation as teacher and critic to seek his advice on her own drawing style by sending him an example for comment. The artist Miss Emma Crewe was again the intermediary, who wrote to Gilpin:

I saw Lady De [sic] Beauclerk the day before I left Richmond, and mentioned to her your criticism on her drawing, she said she would be very happy to *endeavour* to do one which you would approve, upon conditions, that you would do her the favour to make an exchange, & give her a drawing of yours, she says Mr Walpole has one at Strawberry Hill which she covets and admires beyond expression – I promis'd her to deliver the Message & I shall write to her soon, if you wish to have a drawing of hers, & have a fancy for any particular size or sort (I mean Landscape or figures) if you will inform me I can give her a hint – I *did* venture to say, that you did not lay much stress upon finishing, which seem'd to please her.[32]

Gilpin did provide her with one of his drawings, and later in 1788 she visited his house at Vicar's Hill in the New Forest, and gave him four of hers. These were of figures, however, rather than the landscapes which he had encouraged so many other leisured practitioners to tackle. He had reservations about some aspects of figure drawing, feeling that images of people in modern dress jarred with wild nature (although banditti were permitted); but he approved of Lady Di's nonspecific depictions, which he preferred to Emma Crewe's 'ladies with caps, and stays, & gowns & petticoats & shoes & stockens. I always reprobated them. Another Lady, who sent me one of her drawings, Lady Di Beauclerk, drew in much better taste. She covers her figures with loose gowns – puts hats, or handkerchiefs upon their heads; & their feet into slippers'. The use of loose gowns and slippers shows that Lady Di had well absorbed the lessons of Sir Joshua Reynolds, as expressed in his Discourses and undoubtedly tested around the dinner table, on the unsuitability of a painter showing modern dress, 'the familiarity of which is enough to destroy all dignity' as opposed to figures 'with something like the general air of the antique'.[33]

Her reputation as a member of an influential family now outweighed for many people the memories of the divorce. One persistent petitioner at this time was a struggling young scholar, John Pinkerton, who over the next few years would seek Lady Di's influence to gain access to the library of John Moore, former tutor to Charles and Robert Spencer, and now Archbishop of Canterbury. In Walpole's letters to Pinkerton, there are references to Lady Di's mediation: 'I am acquainted with another person, who I believe has some interest with the present Archbishop'; 'as soon as I can see the lady, my friend, who is much acquainted with the Archbishop, I will try if she will ask his leave for you to see the books you mention in his library, of which I will give her the list' . . . 'Her Ladyship was so good as to write to his Grace directly and has sent me the enclosed answer favourable as far as it was in his Grace's power to comply'. Two years later, Walpole reports the Archbishop being less cooperative: 'I have had no more success for you than I expected, yet from no want of application in Lady Di or me, as you will see by the pontiff's letter'. And Pinkerton also came to irritate Walpole through the continuing attempts to exploit Lady Di. In 1790 he applied for a post in the Department of Printed Books in the British Museum, of which the Archbishop was a Trustee, again involving her, again against the Archbishop's inclination: 'I could have shown you a very Jesuitic letter from the prelate in answer to Lady Di's application at my request'. In 1795, the desperate Pinkerton, now applying for another post in the Museum, that of assistant librarian in the Department of Coins and Medals, again asked Walpole to use his friends: 'any recommendation from the Marlborough family will be of great weight with the Archbishop of Canterbury, in whose nomination the office chiefly is'. This provoked a furious reply from Walpole:

I have told you over and over, that knowing I have not a glimpse of interest with any one man in power, nor claim to be asking favours of any one, I am extremely averse to making use of that no-interest, I have also repeated to you that I have not the smallest connection with any of the house of Marlborough but with Lady Diana Beauclerk. To her I have applied for you once more, enclosing your own letter which states your pretensions and claims better than I can; nor indeed could I have written myself, not being able to move either arm with the gout, but trusting to her Ladyship's showing or sending it to the Archbishop.[34]

She seems to have been very hard up at this time, a problem likely to result from trying to maintain the lifestyle that she was used to, but which a woman without a husband or proper financial settlement could no longer expect. Her own family's support for her was perhaps tempered by the attitude that she had brought about the situation through her own actions. In the early 1780s, for example, her brother the Duke, who was then spending thousands of pounds on modernizing Blenheim, asked her for the £50 interest on a loan which he had made to her, at a time when she claimed she 'had not five guineas'. There was a distinct cooling off between brother and sister, and she ceased for the moment to be invited to Blenheim.

Walpole was always there to help; even his efforts (especially during a painful attack of gout) to help her find a particular wine show his tactful acknowledgement of her lack of money and space, as well not being experienced in dealing with wine suppliers:

Your ladyship said here t'other night that you wished to know where to get some good Frontignac wine. I have inquired and got some that I am assured is very good; but as I am no judge, I have taken only a dozen bottles for a trial, and those to be returned if they do not prove good; so pray do not say you like them if you do not, and I will get you some other, and a large quantity. Mr Selwyn brings this and will bring your answer. Tell me at what hour I shall send them. I suppose early in a morning. If you please I will send you a smaller quantity, and can do this as often as you want them, that they may not go in the cellar. I am not able to wait on you yet, as you see by my writing my hand is still bad, and the fog yesterday hurt me a good deal and brought back some pain to my foot.[35]

It was therefore a boost to her reputation when her designs began to be used by another significant patron, one who was affecting contemporary taste just as much as Walpole, but whose deliberate neoclassicism contrasted totally with Walpole's Gothick fantasies. The popularity of the works produced by the firm founded by Josiah Wedgwood was the result of his dazzling technical experiments, innovative design commissions and hard-headed marketing strategies. In 1765 he had managed to establish an important connection with the court by creating a green and gold tea service for Queen Charlotte; the Queen was already aware of his products, for he had targeted her via court lady Miss Deborah Chetwynd, and her father, the Master of the Mint, a former Member of Parliament for Staffordshire, and therefore concerned to further a local industry. As a result, Wedgwood was graciously permitted to name his new cream-coloured line Queen's Ware, and saw sales rocket as a result. Lady Di, then still a Bedchamber Lady, would have been familiar with the product. As he defined his business plan in 1771, royal patronage was crucial because one should 'begin with the Head first and then proceed to the inferior members'. Lady Di's family also supported Wedgwood. For example, the Duke of Marlborough and Charles Spencer visited him in Stafford-shire in July 1765: 'they have bought some things and seemed much entertained and pleased – the Gentlemen wonder I have not a ware-house in London where patterns of all the sorts I make may be seen'. Later that year, Wedgwood and his wife spent some weeks in London, when he went to St James's Palace to meet the Queen, as well as visiting members of the aristocracy, both to take orders and to study their works of art. On the way home, they spent half a day at Blen-heim.[36]

During the 1770s Wedgwood had extended the output of his pottery from domestic wares to a wide range of functional and ornamental items, even including three-dimensional statues, together with decora-tion applied to furniture and architectural features. He adapted the neoclassical style (as interpreted in architecture and interior design by the Adams) for pottery, thus bringing what had been perceived as a minor decorative art in line with the tastes of the day; his ornamental references to classical literature and mythology complimented the learning of his patrons. Indeed, he jumped on the bandwagon of the classical revival inspired by the renewed appreciation of the archaeology and architecture of ancient Greece and Rome during the 1760s. This included the first accounts of the excavations at Herculaneum and Pompeii, the writings of James Stuart on Athens and Robert Adam on Rome. What had been a general awareness of classical taste and literature turned into a more focused and deliberate revival of specific idioms.

Wedgwood managed to combine a sense of mission, in his genuine desire to improve standards of taste and design, with the ability to profit from it too. When debating with his partner Bentley the issues of security raised by the piracy of their designs, he pondered the advantages of a more open policy: 'Do you think when our principles were known, the Nobility would not still make it a point to patronize and encourage Men who acted upon such different principles from the rest of mankind . . . that we generously lay our works open to be imitated by other Artists and manufacturers for the good of the community at large . . . upon the whole, this scheme might bring us as much *profit* as *loss*?' Yet, in his concern for quality, and ability to strike the balance between beauty and function, he can be regarded as a worthy forerunner of the Arts & Crafts movement.[37]

In order to be more directly in contact with his powerful London patrons, as the Spencers had advised, he took premises in St Martin's Lane, an area which was the centre of artistic practice and trade in London. Joshua Reynolds' studio was in nearby Leicester Fields, and the neighbouring streets housed many specialist craftsmen. On the ground floor was a shop for seconds and bargains, on the first floor a display room for general wares, and a more exclusive room for the finest products, only accessible to the more valued patrons and customers, who included the Duke of Marlborough and also Miss Chetwynd, who continued to negotiate on behalf of the King and Queen. He recognized the purchasing power of women, although deploring the timidity of the lower orders: 'Few Ladies, you know, dare venture at anything out of the common stile till authorised by their betters – by the Ladies of superior spirit who set the ton', and therefore insisted that the showrooms should be designed to attract to such influential female as well as male clients. (This was almost too successful – 'Lady Littleton told me she visits our Rooms so often as to be almost afraid of becoming a trouble, but is always very good and quiet, till all who came before her are serv'd, and makes a point of bringing everybody she can along with her'.)[38]

Wedgwood and his family occupied the second floor when on their various visits to London, while Bentley, a man who moved more easily in influential circles, settled permanently in London in order to control the flourishing business. Wedgwood recognized the significance of attracting elite patrons, not just to purchase his wares, but to be flattered by having their opinions sought; this provided him with endless free publicity, which would 'cascade' down to the lower-status purchasers, whose money was equally sound. Bentley's friends in the 1770s included 'Athenian' Stuart, Solander and Banks, people who were also dining at that time with the Beauclerks. Wedgwood wrote to Bentley in 1770: 'Be so good to let us know what is going forward in the Great World. How many Lords and Dukes visit your rooms, praise your beauties, thin your shelves and fill your purses?' But he also recognized the purchasing power at the bottom end of the market 'for there are and ever will be a numerous class of People to purchase shewy and cheap things'.[39]

The original showrooms soon became too small for the expanding business, and Wedgwood tried to move to the newly built Adelphi; this was partly to be near the Adam brothers, in order to liaise more closely with them in the hope of encouraging their use of his terracotta inlays in their designs. However, this scheme fell through, and he opened a new showroom in Greek Street in 1774.

But London was not the only focus for peripatetic patrons, and the works in Etruria, Staffordshire, also proved a magnet and a cultural holiday activity. In August 1770 Wedgwood reported to Bentley, 'Whilst I have been at Etruria here, they have had Lady Gower, Lady Pembroke & Lord Robert Spencer to breakfast. This is the second time the Trentham family have been there whilst I have been abroad'. Lord Gower (another old flame of Lady Di's), whose family seat was nearby Trentham Hall, was now a member of the government, and therefore an influential connection for Wedgwood. In 1771 a showroom was also opened in Dublin, whose patrons included the Earl of Charlemont.[40]

It was jasper ware that became Wedgwood's best-known product; the perfecting of a new clay composition which could take strong colour tints, retain precise details, and be capable of being fired with reliefs in another colour was the result of some thousands of experimental firings. The shapes of the wares produced, and the cameo-like plaques with which they were decorated, struck the right balance for the decorative arts of the last quarter of the century, when the more austere features of neoclassicism began to be tempered by a romantic sensibility. Wedgwood already employed a range of freelance artists – both painters and sculptors – to produce designs and models. Despite the technically successful development of jasper in the years after 1775, there were problems with marketing a new product, and it has been suggested that in order to attract the attention of the women customers who were the main purchasers of domestic tablewares, he needed new women designers. Not only would their work be more in tune with the customers' needs, but there could be useful publicity in using such women. One of these new designers was Lady Di, another was Lady Elizabeth Templeton, and there was also Lady Di's acquaintance, and fellow-artist, Miss Emma Crewe. Wedgwood already employed women as skilled painters of his more delicate tablewares, but his recruitment of them as designers for relief plaques was something new. Among the professional male artists already designing for Wedgwood were George Stubbs, the Gosset family (who also sculpted in wax), Thomas Stothard, John Flaxman and a group of Italian sculptors who worked from Rome, under Flaxman's supervision. While promoting the modern, tasteful neoclassical style, it was perhaps to contrast with the purer classicism of Flaxman and his Roman pupils that Wedgwood chose to employ ladies who worked in a more charming and even sentimental manner.

The contact was made in 1783 through Charles James Fox, with whom Wedgwood was currently in negotiation; Wedgwood had petitioned Fox, now Foreign Secretary, in April on behalf of the Staffordshire pottery makers in the hope that he would bring pressure to bear to reduce French import tariffs, as a part of the commercial agreements being negotiated under the Versailles Peace treaty. (Fox had already opposed Pitt's attempts to lift duties on Irish products.) With his private hat on, Fox then approached Wedgwood on behalf of Lady Di, the sister of Fox's close friend Bob Spencer, and submitted some of her designs. Wedgwood responded, in July 1783, offering 'A thousand thanks for the beautiful drawings he has received, and will be much obliged to Mr Fox, if he will be so good as to signify to Lady Diana Beauclerk how much he esteems himself indebted for this flattering mark of her Ladyship's notice. He has sent a few bas-reliefs, which were modelled from some beautiful cut Indian paper which Lady Templeton favoured him with – just to shew the manner in which he will attempt to copy the drawings he is now honoured with – Mr Fox is desired to dispose of the bas-reliefs as he thinks proper.' The connection with Lady Templeton had been established earlier that year, and Wedgwood had written to her in June, in similar language, expressing pleasure that his 'attempts to copy in bas relief the charming groups of little figures her ladyship was so obliging as to lend him' had met with her approbation, and hoping that he might be 'indulged in copying a few more such groups'.[41]

Despite the flowery language, this was a commercial transaction of great benefit to Wedgwood. He had recruited one genteel, marketable name, and was now using that to attract another – this time not simply an aristocratic designer, whose work was admired by such influential patrons as Walpole and Hamilton, who were already well known to Wedgwood, but one whose reputation also carried a tinge of scandal.

Her particular speciality for Wedgwood was the motif of the chubby cherub or cupid figure which she frequently drew and painted, often called the 'Bacchanalian Boy'. The revelries and processions of Bacchus were a recurrent theme on jasper ware and such figures were already well established in Wedgwood's vocabulary of motifs. As early as 1774, he was describing various 'bas-reliefs of Boys . . . they will be in pairs and represent hunting in two medallions, Music & the Arts in two more, & War – if you please to have so horrid a subject represented by innocent Babes'. And throughout the 1770s he refers to the production of various Bacchanalian figures, Cupids, Pans and Boys with Drapery. So a revamp by a respected specialist in such popular themes would undoubtedly sell well, although these saccharine forms were far removed from the priapic and frenzied figures of the original, and worship of the cult of Dionysus seems particularly inappropriate to the refined interpretations of Wedgwood's designers.

Four of her designs were listed in the sixth edition of Wedgwood's *Catalogue*, issued in 1787:

241. Group of three boys, from designs by Lady Diana Beauclerk 5½ x 4½
242. Group of two boys, from the same. 5½ x 4½
    The same, different sizes, to 3½ x 2¾
243. Four boys, single, from the same. 4½ x 3¾

The same, different sizes, to 3 x 2¼
244. Bacchanalian tablet of the six preceding articles under arbours, with pan-
    thers' skins in festoons etc. 16 x 5½⁴²

The first design, of two boys swinging a third between them, has
been described as her reworking of the group, 'Bacchanalian sacrifice',
by C. M. Clodion, a French sculptor whose terracottas and bas-reliefs
of nymphs and satyrs provided inspiration for several of Wedgwood's
designers. Another related influence was the work of Duquesnoy, who
had been designing for Wedgwood up to 1780. His products included
two boys standing, one of whom holds a spear, and two boys dancing.
Lady Di's 'group of two boys' shows a pair of figures seated at the
base of a tree, one, a faun, holding a spear. Of her four single figures,
one is a boy with a bunch of grapes, and one, seated, plays a pan-
pipe, while the other two are fauns, one eating grapes, and one
holding an ivy stem. But the most popular was the set of three boys,
No. 241, which was chosen to ornament foot bowls, lidded boxes,
cups, bowls, and urns and tubs for flowers, even clocks, a piano and a
fireplace.

The subject matter of the cameos, intaglios and bas-reliefs listed in
Wedgwood's catalogues shows the eclectic range of late eighteenth-
century taste. There were ancient Egyptians, classical gods and goddesses, characters from the Trojan War, poets, philosophers and
orators, and portraits of illustrious men and women of the present as
well as the past. It is a mark of David Garrick's popularity and fame
that he is almost the only non-royal contemporary figure to be
included in the 1779 catalogue; the 1787 supplement had a wider
selection, among whom were the Duchess of Devonshire, Mrs Siddons,
Mrs Montague and Lady Charlotte Finch (another amateur artist as
well as former court lady and divorcee). The cameos and intaglios in
hard and highly polished ware imitated closely the antique gems prized
by connoisseurs such as Lady Di's brother, the Duke of Marlborough,
already a friend of Wedgwood, and through whom Wedgwood may
also have become aware of Lady Di's design skills. The catalogue lists
among its cameos 'No. 1674, "The Marriage of Cupid and Psyche";
in the cabinet of the Duke of Marlborough'. The first version of this
was originally copied from a cast modelled by James Tassie, a man
who had started his career as a gem modeller in sulphur wax and
paste and who was later allowed to model directly from the gems,

supplying Wedgwood with many impressions of cameos and intaglios. The later version of the Duke's favourite cameo was taken from the original, a mark of the respect and support which Wedgwood engendered in his wealthy patrons, and its sturdy little cherubs are very much of the type drawn by Lady Di. The Duke's collection, engraved by Bartolozzi, had been published in 1781. Other collections copied by Wedgwood included those of Sir William Hamilton, 'Athenian' Stuart, and Sir Watkin Williams Wynn. Such patrons actively assisted Wedgwood not only by providing originals to be copied, but also through the loan of books and prints, as well as casts of antique sculptures. His interpretation of 'classical' incorporated an exotic mix of Greek, Hellenistic, Roman and Renaissance.

The support and friendship of Hamilton was crucial to Wedgwood; as British representative to the court at Naples, Hamilton had amassed a vast collection of Greek and Etruscan vases, and his publication of them brought them to the attention of a wider audience as well as providing a further source of inspiration for Wedgwood. Hamilton's motivation was more than that of mere acquisition; through his excavations, purchases and publications, he sought to make the educated public more aware of the excellence of antique art. He commissioned Italian and French draughtsmen to illustrate his collection for a series of catalogues, beginning in 1766; Wedgwood was allowed to draw on this source material from the very beginning. Hamilton gave him vases, and casts of bas-reliefs, as well as lending gems and cameos to copy, and commissioning many items. As usual, Wedgwood was alert to the uses that could be made of this significant mark of interest from such an influential man, who could be unobtrusively recruited in his advertising campaign. He wrote to Bentley in 1776: 'Sir Wm Hambleton [sic], our very good Friend is in Town – suppose you show him some of the Vases, & a few other Connoisieurs, not only to have their advice, but to have the advantage of their puffing them off against the next spring, as they will, by being consulted & flatter'd agreeably, as you know how, consider themselves as a sort of Parties in the affair, & act accordingly'.[43]

Wedgwood's intention, as stated in his Catalogue, was to produce fine copies because 'nothing can contribute more effectually to diffuse a good Taste through the Arts than the Power of multiplying Copies of fine Things, in Materials fit to be applied for Ornaments, by which Means the public eye is instructed and all the Arts receive Improvement

. . . the more Copies there are of any Works, the more celebrated the Original will be, and the more Honour derived to the Possessor'.

Jasper products were not confined to table and other ornamental wares, but could also be used more widely as part of a whole scheme of interior decoration, appearing on the integral features of a room such as fireplaces or mirror surrounds. The Adam style already incorporated medallions with classical subjects in low relief but Wedgwood had found it difficult to persuade such designers to work with him ('we were really unfortunate in the introduction of our jasper into public notice, that we could not prevail upon the architects to be godfathers to our child . . . they have cursed the poor infant bell book and candle'). Less of such furnishings have survived, owing to loss and destruction as a result of the extreme changes of taste in the nineteenth century, but there is the record of a fireplace commissioned by a Mr Uppleby of Barrow on Humber, which was to be decorated by Lady Di's Bacchanalian boys; he received the plaques on approval in 1789.[44]

Another supporter of Wedgwood was Joseph Banks, who had brought back samples of clay from New South Wales for Wedgwood's experimental firings. Banks ordered an ornamental chimney piece for his house in Soho Square; this had figures representing scenes of a Sacrifice to Flora, including two cupids of Lady Di's type. The Empress Catherine the Great was an even more prestigious patron. Not only had she commissioned the famous 'Frog' dinner service, but her architect Charles Cameron incorporated Wedgwood plaques as an integral part of his work for her at Tsarskoe Selo, in a florid version of the Adam style. The chimney breast in her bedroom included Bacchanalian figures, a mark of the appeal of Lady Di's subject matter.

One of Wedgwood's greatest challenges in jasper was attempting to copy the Portland vase, a celebrated example of Roman glass. Walpole mentioned this in a letter concerning his own acquisition from the sale of the Duchess of Portland's collections, a basalt head of Jupiter Serapis (which Hamilton had earlier bought from the Barberini Collection in Rome before selling it to the Duchess): 'I told Sir William Hamilton and the late Duchess, when I never thought that it would be mine, that I had rather have the head than the vase. I shall long for Mrs Damer to make a bust to it and then it will be still more valuable. I have deposited both the illumination and the Jupiter in Lady Di's cabinet, which is worthy of them. And here my collection winds up. I will not purchase trumpery after such jewels.'[45]

The recipient of this letter was Walpole's cousin, General Conway (with whom Hamilton had served as aide-de-camp nearly thirty years earlier), a friend of Joshua Reynolds and of Angelica Kauffmann, whom Conway had helped introduce to London circles. Mrs Damer was his daughter Anne, who had often stayed with Walpole as a little girl when her parents were abroad. She married in 1767, but was widowed at the age of twenty-seven when her husband committed suicide after his father refused to pay his gambling debts. It was the freedom from the demands of children, yet with the acceptable social status of widowhood, that made possible her career as a sculptor, which included travelling on the Continent, and studying sculpture in Italy. She was recorded as sometimes wearing man's clothing, a not infrequent strategy among professional women artists, and an exceptionally practical course of action given the wide and trailing garments of the 1760s and '70s. As his third 'female genius', her work was frequently linked by Walpole to that of Lady Di, and in the same extravagant terms: 'I am in possession of her sleeping dogs in terra cotta . . . Mr Wyatt the architect saw them here lately and said he was sure that if the idea was given to the best statuary in Europe, he would not produce so perfect a group. Indeed with these dogs and the riches I possess by Lady Di, poor Strawberry may vie with much prouder collections'. William Hamilton also admired Anne Damer's work, stating on one occasion to Walpole: 'I can believe anything you say of Mrs Damer, whom I always thought was the cleverest creature in the world next to Lady Di.'[46]

Walpole continued to collect and display Lady Di's work throughout the 1780s. An especial favourite of his was her watercolour drawing of 'gypsies telling a country-maiden her fortune at the entrance of a beech-wood' (of around 1781) which hung in the Red Bedchamber. Another was 'A masquerade at Vauxhall, in bistre . . . there is a wonderful expression in the faces and attitudes, though some of the figures are quite masked, and others have half masks'; this dates from around 1784. His enthusiasm for this piece provoked Lord Harcourt to write in exasperation to Mason:

he showed me a beautiful drawing by that injurious friend and corruptress of her own sex, Lady D--- B-----. It was a masquerade scene at Vauxhall, with two very lovely young women in half masques, sitting on a bench, and an old woman sitting on the ground, reading a ballad. This was the whole, and all I am persuaded the artist designed to represent, yet a long story was made out, or not made out, of one of the young men being much more in love than the other, of one of the females being a woman of strict virtue, the other an errant coquette, and infinite praise bestowed on the idea of making the old woman reading, as a *vulgar* artist would have represented her *watching*. The countenance and character of the bunches of lilac came into my head and I was ready to laugh.

As well as mocking Walpole's snobbery and earlier rapturous accounts of her mural decorations, Harcourt is also implying that Lady Di was still being judged on her morals rather than her artistic talent. He was also harsh on Walpole, whom he summed up as having 'the talent of giving an air of importance to the most trifling and least uncommon occurrences, of persuading others (and himself I really believe also) of events the most improbable'.[47]

Her other great admirer, Hamilton, motivated perhaps by old love as much as connoisseurship, touchingly hung one of her drawings in his private apartments in the Palazzo Sessa, his official residence in Naples, whose state rooms ostentatiously displayed his fine art collection. The difference between public and private display was perceptively noted by Wilhelm Tischbein, a German painter who accompanied Goethe on his Italian journey (and who would stay on to become the Director of the Neapolitan Academy in 1787). He wrote:

I have never seen a more pleasant room than the one where [Hamilton] lived and slept. The paintings on the walls were of little importance, but they all had a meaning and content that he enjoyed, and recalled things to his mind in the most pleasant way. Thus there was among them a pen-drawing scribbled by a lady friend, who had shown her children in a nice group as they tumbled about together on the ground. Many people would not have kept this sort of drawing but Hamilton respected it for the naive way the figures were caught, and which a painter concerned with the rules of art would never have been lucky enough to capture . . . the whole arrangement [of the room] seemed chaotic but, looked at in the right way, it revealed the sensibility of the man who was at home in this cabinet and who had assembled these various objects with discrimination and taste.

Tischbein's grudging and rather patronizing recognition of spontaneity in a work by one so unlucky as to be a woman and a poorly trained amateur shows a more typical response than the partialities of Walpole and Hamilton.[48]

Walpole remained the most supportive of friends, constantly in touch, always ready to protect and defend her. He served as embassy for her persistent neighbour George Hardinge, who had so admired her 'lilac festoons' the previous year and was still desperate to improve his acquaintance with her. Hardinge wrote unhappily to Walpole about the correct etiquette required to make the acquaintance of the woman who clearly fascinated him but who was resisting his advances:

I thought no more of your generous offer to me than Lady Di thinks of my passion for her. . . . I have more business to do with your friendship. It is a message to the dear Lady Di. Be so good as to abuse her in my name (whatever you may tell her in your own) for not liking me or Mrs Hardinge. We have seen her for a quarter of an hour (which flew like half a quarter of a minute) in our castle. A little after this tantalising peep at her, we left the neighbourhood, but a long week is past since we left our card at her door, and that was the first moment after my return that we could wait on her. Etiquette says, that we must now (to borrow a metaphor from our constant object the Thames) lye upon our oars; that we must go to her next, and for that purpose, wait for a summons from her; else I would ask her to us, or invite ourselves to her, for Mrs Hardinge and I are enchanted with her. [49]

Lady Di realized that she could not put off the invitation any longer, and submitted – although inviting Walpole along to share the strain: 'She told me she would ask you and Mrs Hardinge to-morrow evening; and she desired I would meet you. She told me how much she admired Mrs Hardinge, and, as I agree with her Ladyship, I shall not tell you what she said of you.' This is an example of Walpole's cunning ambiguity, since what she had said was unlikely to have been at all flattering.

But she made the most of Hardinge's devotion, and used him for informal legal and financial advice, though still delicately employing Walpole as an intermediary, as the following note from Walpole to Hardinge implies: 'I think you go this morning to Lady Di's. Be so good as to carry the enclosed, and deliver it when Mr B is not present, which I suppose he will not be. I will trouble you too to leave her answer here as you return'. 'Mr B' sounds a rather formal term for her son Charles, then aged ten. [50]

Walpole's crammed, annotated and updated editions of the inventories of Strawberry Hill show how his wide circle of friends and acquaintances contributed to this treasure house and were recorded for posterity as donors. Referring ironically to her knowledge of his 'shyness about receiving presents', he asked on one occasion for Lady Di's help in trying to obtain from the Trevor cousin who owned it a rare edition of Latin poetry for the library. Her own artistic presence was evident in all the public rooms of his house and therefore on open display to the many polite visitors admitted to view the house. His preface to the 1784 edition of his *Description of Strawberry Hill* singles her out in the very second paragraph: boasting of the master-pieces in the collection (whose miniatures and enamels, he claimed, exceeded those of the King and that other great collector the Duke of Portland), he carries on: 'the drawings and bas-reliefs in wax, by Lady Diana Beauclerk, are as invaluable as rare'. And the following pages list an extensive range of her works. In the Breakfast Room, there were three elaborately presented pieces: the wax sculpture framed to her own design, the Duchess of Devonshire print, in a matching frame 'with Wedgwood's cameos, and two flies engraved and painted by Hill', and the print of Mary and Elizabeth 'in a blue and gold frame painted in mosaic with lions and flower-de-luces, in allusion to the arms of Beauclerc'. Here was also the Masquerade at Vauxhall drawing. In the Green Closet, there was 'a washed drawing of the walnut-tree covered with ivy on the terrace at Strawberry Hill, in winter' (sharing space with Anne Damer's 'two kittens in marble'). In the Red Bedchamber, the Gypsies watercolour hung beside the chim-ney, and the Great North Bedchamber housed the wax sculpture with Walpole's poem rating her above Praxiteles and Phidias, adjacent to the Wedgwood flower containers painted to her designs.

Also in this state bedchamber was an exotic item of furniture called the Beauclerc Cabinet especially designed in 1784 to Walpole's com-mission by Edward Edwards (one of the copyists whom he employed, who also painted two watercolour paintings of Little Marble Hill). This 'ebony cabinet, ornamented with ormolu, lapis-lazuli, agates, pieces of ancient enamel, bas-reliefs of Wedgwood and nine capital drawings by Lady Diana Beauclerk ... with strawberries and Mr Walpole's arms and crest' was intended as a further shrine both to her genius and to his patronage. A Gothic–neoclassical hybrid with a hint of the Chinese, the cabinet stands on spiky legs which are separated by a row of gilded arches with spandrels inlaid with painted glass and lapis panels at the corners, the whole effect being that of a medieval reliquary. The interior drawers are concealed by a door, set into the surface of which are nine gilt-framed rectangular panels, each of which contains one of her drawings 'of a gypsy girl, and beautiful children'. The central and largest drawing, the gypsy, who carries a bundle on her back and leans on a stick, is surmounted by a classical swag of embossed gilt, and it is surrounded by eight smaller panels which contain various chubby children – almost certainly some of the bistre drawings that Walpole was enthusing about in 1775. When the door is opened, the inner panel reveals the vivid colours of Walpole's collection of semi-precious stones, presented in highly polished section in oval and circular settings, juxtaposed with brightly patterned roundels of 'ancient enamel' and ornamental metalwork inlaid into the drawer fronts and contrasting with the almost black mahogany background. More of these textured inlays are set into the sides and top of the cabinet. Another type of ornament commemorates her association with Wedgwood: in the middle of the stone settings is an oval of blue and white jasper showing cherubs frolicking by a tree. On the two sides of the cabinet are more ceramic relief plaques with cherubs, each surmounting another inlaid wash drawing under a mask, of figures holding musical instruments. The top is equally ornate, embedded with a large plate-like roundel whose centrepiece is a boy on a dolphin, surrounded by a laurel wreath, and borders of swags and more classical figures; in the outer corners are more jasper roundels. The top could easily be seen and admired, for the whole cabinet is on an exquisitely miniature scale, being just over four feet high. Lest we forget, on the inside of the cabinet's door is a brass plaque bearing the inscription: 'This cabinet was ordered by and made at the expense of Mr Horace Walpole in 1784 to receive the Drawings which were all design'd and executed by the Right Honourable Lady Diana Beauclerk.' A smaller inscription below acknowledges Mr E. Edwards as the designer.

Other acquisitions for Strawberry Hill were 'a two-leafed screen, painted on Manchester velvet with the heads of a Satyr and Bacchante', which she did in 1788, and 'A Copy of Virgil, printed by Baskerville, with drawings on the covers by Lady Diana Beauclerk. On the edges, which are highly gilt, is a view of Blenheim, which disappears altogether when the volume is closed'.

The culminating experience at Strawberry Hill was the Beauclerk Closet itself. As well as the 'sublime drawings' for *The Mysterious Mother*, he had hung her drawing of 'two young women and a boy' in a black and gold frame, and the copy which he had commissioned from Powell of the Reynolds portrait of Viscountess Bolingbroke, the artist and Muse of Art.

Her growing artistic reputation at this time seemed to have effected some rehabilitation of her personal one. Fanny Burney reports a tribute from the King himself, surprisingly generous towards someone who had so let him down. During Fanny's very first meeting with the King and Queen at the house of their adored mutual friend Mrs Delany, the conversation touched on those who lacked an ear for music and shifted to those who were colour-blind. The King cited the Duke of Marlborough, and then courteously added, 'I do not find, though, that this defect runs in his family, for Lady Di Beauclerk draws very finely'. This was a generous tribute, and one which showed George's appreciation of current artistic taste (and perhaps his memories of her as a Bedchamber Lady before her fall from grace). His experience of Bully as a Lord of the Bedchamber may also have helped modify his judgement.[51]

As further evidence of reinstatement, a portrait of her in chalk, drawn by her collaborator Bartolozzi (also the Royal Engraver) was acquired by the royal family for the collection at Windsor (as was the version of her portrait of the Duchess of Devonshire). The drawing belonged to Queen Charlotte, and was later obtained by the Prince of Wales following the dispersal of much of his mother's collection after her death. Royal friendship with the Marlborough family is also suggested by the presence of three drawings in Charlotte's collection by the Spencer daughters, Lady Di's nieces.[52]

In 1787 Walpole noted her working on a new project, while he also took the opportunity for a jibe at Reynolds, whose work he had never particularly admired: 'I called at Sir Joshua's while he was at Ampthill, and saw his Hercules for Russia [commissioned by Catherine the Great]. I did not at all admire it . . . if Sir Joshua is satisfied with his own departed picture, it is more than the possessors of posterity will be . . . Lady Di has done two pictures for *Macbeth* and *Lear*: the latter with the madman is very fine'.[53]

Illustrating the Bard may have represented her hope of earning some money through contributing to the famous Shakespeare Gallery which had been established by John Boydell, a professional printmaker and seller, also an alderman, and then Lord Mayor of London. Described by the assiduous visitor Sophie von la Roche in 1786 as 'London's most famous print-dealer', his shop exemplified for her 'the excellent arrangement and system which the love of gain and the national good taste have combined in producing, particularly in the elegant dressing of large shop windows, not merely in order to ornament the streets and lure purchasers, but to make known the thousands of inventions and ideas, and spread good taste about'. Boydell's great project was the concept of a permanent exhibition of pictures illustrating scenes from Shakespeare. This was both altruistic and patriotic, a further attempt to reinstate the moral and dramatic nature of history painting, but also self-interested – by commissioning drawings and paintings of these noble topics, he also acquired the rights to have them engraved by his team of forty-six printmakers and then to sell these copies of the original exhibits, not just to the viewing public but to a far wider market. He shrewdly realized that this created a double profit: people paid to see the exhibition then bought their favourite images from it as uplifting souvenirs. This was clearly where the future lay. Betsy Sheridan visited the gallery soon after its opening in May 1789: 'I liked some of the pictures very well, in particular two from *The Winter's Tale* . . . yesterday we went to the Shakespeare Gallery again. There was less company and I saw the pictures better . . . this kind of painting has long been wanted to show the real genius of painters'.[54]

Boydell was officially acknowledged as a public benefactor and popularizer when he was toasted by the Prince of Wales at the Royal Academy banquet of 1789, in words composed by Burke, as someone who had done 'more for art than the grand Monarque of France'.

This would have been an excellent bandwagon for Lady Di to join, and her choice of these passionate tragedies indicates her continuing attempts to extend her range, to move on from feminine subjects in response to the sensibilities of the day. Boydell's artists included Angelica Kauffman and Anne Damer, but Lady Di's name does not appear in any of the catalogues to the exhibitions, which ran for several years. However, Boydell did later publish Bartolozzi's engraving of her portrait of the Duchess of Devonshire.

TEN

The Grandmother

(1787–1808)

EDMUND: Incest! Good Heavens!
COUNTESS: Yes, thou devoted victim! Let thy blood curdle to
   stone! Perdition circumvent thee!

HORACE WALPOLE, *The Mysterious Mother*

Although Lady Di had preferred to distance herself from the hothouse circles of London, she ensured that her children did not suffer from her self-imposed exile. Mary Beauclerk was observed, for example, by Lady Mary Coke at a prestigious ball at Bedford House held by an old ally, the Duchess of Bedford, in 1783: rehabilitation is demonstrated by the presence of Princess Amelia, the Prince of Wales and his younger brother at the party. This represents the introduction of Mary, then aged sixteen, into the marriage market in the company of other more desirable debutantes such as the daughters of fellow Bedchamber Ladies the Duchess of Ancaster and Lady Weymouth.

But it was Mary's younger sister, Elizabeth, who was the first to find a husband. In March 1787 she became engaged to her first cousin Lord Herbert, the only son of Betty Pembroke. Lady Louisa Stuart informed her sister:

I think Lord Herbert's match with Elizabeth Beauclerk, his pretty little cousin, broke out the day after I wrote to you last; we have all suspected it for some time. Lady Pembroke is the happiest creature I ever saw in my life, and there must be some wonderful revolution in the mind of her lord, for he has consented without making one objection, and written the kindest letters imaginable to them. It is a prodigious match for her and the poor little girl seems heartily in love but I think Lord H has rather grown attached to her by degrees, from the habit of living with her, for I do not take him to be a passionate character. Our friend [Mrs Herbert, a Pembroke cousin] was not trusted with the secret, and therefore I think not so well used as she might have been. She whispers to me it is a bad breed and Lady Diana will govern them all, but she puts the best face on it and says she likes it as well as they do.[1]

Lady Louisa was well aware of Lady Di's reputation: when the former became the subject of mild gossip, being thought to be courted by an elderly uncle by marriage, she wrote to a friend:

I tell you this nonsensical story chiefly for the sake of an admirable *bon mot* (tant soit peu libertin) which it drew from Lady Dye Beauclerk. Soh! said she to Mrs Herbert, your friend Lady Louisa Stuart is to marry her grand-father, is she? If she can hold her nose and swallow the dose, it may do very well. But most people would be apt to take a little sweetmeat in their mouths afterwards.[2]

The match had initially come as a grave shock and severe disappointment to the Earl of Pembroke – not because of the Beauclerks being seen as a 'bad breed' (although it was obvious that this still remained the view of some parts of society), or because of fears of Lady Di as a domineering mother-in-law, or even because of Elizabeth's lack of a title. His reservations were entirely based upon her not being an heiress. Lady Louisa was also unfair in her interpretation of Lord Herbert's feelings: they may have originated in familiarity rather than passion, but he was wholly committed. He dutifully and formally requested the approval of his father – absentee and spendthrift, even now interfering in Lord Herbert's careful management of the estates: 'You have repeatedly urged me to marry and I would have complied with your request long ago had I found a person with whom I thought I could live. About two years ago, I really thought I had made such a discovery; I was mistaken however . . . I have at last found one with whom I am confident I shall be happy, and who is of the same opinion on her side and has accepted my offer. The person of whom I so thoroughly approve and who so thoroughly approves of me is Lady Di's second daughter, Elizabeth Beauclerk'. (His earlier unsuccessful passion had been for another first cousin, the much richer Lady Caroline Spencer, daughter of the Duke and Duchess of Marlborough; but Caroline did not feel 'that kind of liking for you without which she is determined not to marry any man . . . she likes you well enough but not as a lover'. This was according to her uncle Charles Spencer, writing at the time to his heart-broken nephew.)[3]

Lord Pembroke had been urging his son to marry, as long as the bride was an heiress; this was the only means of recouping the family fortunes which he himself had wasted. Even on the boy's Grand Tour, amongst his father's frequent instructions about good health (including thorough tooth-cleaning) and cultivated behaviour, there were constant reminders: 'Miss M. is not rich enough and nothing can save us but your taking to an opulent one'; 'Pray keep a journal & give it to me when your travels end in repose & a rich wife at home, sans quoi you & I & Co shall end in Newgate'; 'I have enlarged a bed big enough to hold you & a rich wife too' ; 'You will be a Parliament man by the time ye return and soon after married, I hope, to some Miss, as beautiful as ye please & as rich as Croesus'; 'Pour l'amour de nous, get yourself a good matrimonial bedfellowess & de plus riches as soon as ye can after your return, ou nous sommes tous, tutti quanti, f----s'; 'I am afraid I should be Villain enough to marry the Devil's Grandmother with one quarter of Miss Child's fortune. Apropos have you ever seen her? and do you think you could bring yourself to lay your chaste Leg over her for the dirty consideration of two, or three hundred thousand pounds?' Sarah Child, 'the richest heiress on the British Dominions', was the daughter of a wealthy banker, to whom Lord Herbert dutifully but unsuccessfully paid court in 1780. By 1786, Pembroke was still reminding him that 'our family circumstances want a good fortune'; and 'though you missed aim at Lady S. I hope ye will try again for I have a passion for grandchildren & a handsome sensible and opulent young daughter-in-law, rien que ca and the sooner the better'.[4]

Although Pembroke had ensured that his son's Grand Tour lasted four and a half years, and covered most of Europe, the constant need for economy had sometimes caused the young man's tutors to protest. And Lady Pembroke also had to make sacrifices, complaining bitterly at being forced to stay at Wilton during the London season; on one occasion she had to postpone a long-desired journey to London until after one of the royal birthdays because she could not afford the new gown in which court etiquette compelled her to appear. Yet Pembroke had never stinted on his own requirements (Walpole referred to his 'profligacy counteracting his avarice').

It was therefore a mark of Pembroke's love for his son and affection for his sister-in-law and her family (he and Betty were also fond of her second son by her first marriage, Frederick St John, who often visited them at Wilton) that he was able to give a warm although qualified approval to the engagement. But he was not prepared to accede to Herbert's request for an increase in the figure of £1,000 per annum which was on the table as a marriage settlement (an ungenerous increase on his bachelor allowance of £800 a year). He wrote from Paris, where he spent most of his time, and even more money, when not in the south of France or Italy (it was this selfish extravagance, as well as the discovery of the existence of another illegitimate child, which eventually drove Betty to leave him in the following year and settle permanently in her Richmond bolt-hole):

I own your letter of the 27 ult. surprised me very much. The greatest pleasure I can feel is to know that you are happy, and I need not then say that I most ardently wish you may be so. Everything I have will always be more yours than mine, and the thousand pounds ye mentioned before and now repeat, seems to me at present, as it did then, very reasonable. Pray have matters settled accordingly. With every thing I hear to the advantage of Elizabeth B. and my own good opinion of her, I will however fairly own to you, that though I should have been sorry to see you a fortune hunter, I could have wished ye had chosen somebody with some fortune. Ye know how very much our affairs stand in need of at least thirty thousand pounds. I now fear them irretrievable for our time, at least; it would have been lucky for us had ye found a thirty-thousand-pounder as agreeable to ye as Elizabeth. Had I been given to guess, I should have guessed the other sister. I once suspected ye of a liking there.

Although Lord Herbert had begged him not to mention the engagement to anyone else, Pembroke added 'as Lady Di tells me she has told it to her brothers, it must be known'.[5]

Herbert fervently thanked his father for 'the generous and friendly treatment . . . nothing will ever efface it from my memory . . . I wish with all my soul Elizabeth had £30,000 but ladys who have that sum are exceedingly apt and not perhaps unreasonably in the extreme to expect a free permission of great extravagance'. He denied that he had ever had any thoughts of Mary. His father's approval obtained, he now informed the King and Queen, and Charlotte wrote to Betty to congratulate her. There was a fulsome account of the engagement in the gossip column of *The Times* on 31 March 1787, which implies that, for *Times* readers at least, Lady Di's reputation was no longer in question:

The Grandmother

The approaching nuptials of Lord Herbert and Miss Beauclerk promise well, and Hymen, who has been rather in the dumps during the winter, appears to be in high spirits on this occasion. There are those qualitites and graces on both sides which form the constituent part of connubial happiness, and we hope and trust that no envious daemon will possess the power of troubling the pure fountain of their felicity.

Just before their wedding the young couple attended a ball at Lady Hopetoun's, where Lady Louisa Stuart proved to be a rather more critical observer than the *Times* columnist: 'Eliza Beauclerk and Lord Herbert were there; neither of them danced, and they take no notice of one another in public – a proof, in my humble opinion, that he is not in love. People may say what they will about being stared at now, but when a man's mind is taken up with one object, he forgets that there is anybody else in the room . . . true lovers are scarce things'.[6]

The wedding took place on 8 April 1787, a deliberately select and quiet occasion planned by Lord Herbert, who refused to invite an unwanted guest suggested by his father (who had not chosen to leave Paris for the event):

You certainly were joking when you proposed I should ask him to my marriage, for tho' his family are well known to you, you must recollect he is a very slight foreign acquaintance of mine, and that no one likes to faire Spectacle de son Marriage, and I have absolutely refused to let any of my nearest connections and greatest friends to be at it. Lady Di, Lady P, Lord Charles, Bob and Frederick St John will be the only people present (the Archbishop excepted, who is to marry us).[7]

However, the *Times* correspondent must have been lurking behind a pillar, for the paper reported on 17 April that

the matrimonial scene on Sunday evening was a most charming picture of domestic felicity – Lord and Lady Herbert and the two mothers appeared to be equally, because supremely, happy. Indeed nothing can occasion any interruption of their well established harmony, unless this time twelvemonth the two grandmothers should quarrel about who should nurse the bantling.

The presence of Frederick St John, Elizabeth's half-brother, who was then aged twenty-three, shows that Lady Di was fully reconciled with at least one of the sons she had abandoned. This was easier to do following Topham's death; one of the factors contributing to her unhappiness in the later years of that marriage could have been the realization that she had sacrificed her two sons for this bad-tempered man. Links were further reinforced just four weeks after the wedding, when Bully himself died, on 5 May 1787, and the young men no longer had to take sides. The death of the second Viscount Boling-broke was regarded as a merciful release. He had been mad for six years, and in some circles Lady Di was still held responsible for his mental decline. The obituary which was published in the following month's edition of the *Gentleman's Magazine* had no reservations about blaming her, and the divorce was yet again dragged into the public eye – though it was tastefully conceded that 'to investigate the facts that produced this would be an office painful and improper'. However, after mentioning Bully's 'generosity and goodness of heart . . . affability . . . his wit, his mirth, his conversation', it was stressed that all these excellent qualities were negated by the state of apathy that he fell into as a direct result of the divorce, which gave rise to 'the miseries under which he laboured for the latter part of his life'. The tragic conclusion 'that such a mind should shiver, that so able a fabric should decay' left no doubt as to the cause.

The newly-weds went to Brighton for a six-week honeymoon. Elizabeth immediately became pregnant, miscarried, and conceived again. *The Times* coyly reported on 9 September that 'nothing is said of Lord and Lady Herbert; we scarcely know whether they are in the town or the country and we augur well of the circumstances'. The columnist then went on to give a warm account of Lady Di, great mother and artist, who 'is at her beautiful little cottage on the banks of the Thames, employing herself in the most elegant duties of maternal care and adorning the peaceful interval with all the graces of her pencil'. By 19 September, the young couple had been tracked down: 'Lord and Lady Herbert are now on a friendly visit for a fortnight at Lady Diana Beauclerk's elegant villa on the banks of the Thames, opposite Richmond Hill. It would be superfluous to declare that the Graces are partial to a mansion where so bewitching and refined a hostess presides'. The reality was that Elizabeth had been in very poor health during the summer, and Lady Di had also been ill. Lord Herbert had written to his father, requesting suitable remedies (the sort of thing that Duchess Sarah would have had at her finger-tips):

I should be obliged to you if you would send to Gibbs and desire he would write down and send to me by the return of the post, what quantity of what ingredients (and how taken) cured his son of the jaundice a year or two ago; Lady Di is confined with it, and I told the Apothecary here I would write for the cure of which I had heard.[8]

Pembroke's remedy was hardly encouraging:

A vomit is the first thing for the jaundice; after that, every morning a Seville orange roasted with saffron; cut a plug out of the orange, fill the hole with saffron, put the plug in again, roast and eat the orange, the whole of it, rind and all. This must be done fasting, and do not eat for an hour or two after. In the course of the day, a raw egg every three hours; three or four in the course of a day. You know I had the jaundice at Lisbon. The Portuguese have it very much and always cure it so, keeping the body always open, and eating ripe fruit. Tell Lady Di that Le Mousquetaire a Genoux, Monsieur Vise au trou (the hinder one, I mean) Clysters, in short, are very useful also, and tres raffraichissant toujours.

The recommendation of clysters (enemas) shows that colonic irrigation was already popular in smart circles.[9]

Although not a thirty-thousand-pounder, Elizabeth soon proved herself to be an effective breeder; despite the first mishap, she gave birth to a son eleventh months after the wedding. This was not Lady Di's first grandchild; her eldest son George, now the third Viscount Bolingbroke, had already produced three legitimate children. But these were not the only ones.

George was a young man who had inherited most of his father's extravagant habits but whose income was so low that marriage to an heiress could be his only salvation. As Selwyn had pointed out in 1781: 'he will have £600 a year, but he wants a wife and how he will be diverted from that extravagance, I know not'. But George made the most unsuitable choice, by marrying Charlotte Collins, the daughter of the Reverend Thomas Collins, rector and second master at Winchester College. This had to be a love match, for Charlotte had neither the necessary rank or fortune appropriate to the heir to an impoverished viscountcy. He fell for her in 1780, when he was an impressionable nineteen-year-old (then living in Winchester because Lydiard was rented out, receiving private tuition from her father) and she rather older. This was a far worse entanglement than Lord Herbert's match with Elizabeth, who was at least of the same kin and rank, and younger than her husband, but a very desirable one for the Collins family. Bully, then gravely ill and in the first throes of mental illness, was even less capable of making his son marry an heiress than

Pembroke had been. However, George's sudden departure for Germany in 1781 may have represented his family's attempt to put an end to things by sending him on a belated Grand Tour. According to her sister, Charlotte 'though exceedingly hurt, bears up better than I could have expected, I hope, and firmly believe that nothing on his part will ever give her uneasiness'; such optimism was rewarded, for George remained faithful, returned to England to stand successfully for election as Member of Parliament for Cricklade, and married Charlotte in February 1783. However, it took him nearly two years to make any form of marriage settlement on her. He had by then borrowed over £16,000 from the money-lender and proprietor of White's Club, Robert Mackreth, which would be payable after Bully's death.[10]

George and Charlotte had three children in rapid succession and were staying in Paris at the time of Bully's death, which must have been eagerly awaited. Despite these strains, Charlotte had sufficient looks and character to make an impression on Lord Pembroke, who visited them in France and wrote to his son: 'Tell Lady Di I am in love with her daughter in law, and shall go and see her again if I have time. Lady Bolingbroke hits my eye, or rather my head vastly.'[11]

Pembroke would have been even more impressed had he known that Lady Bolingbroke was at this time colluding with her husband and his mistress to conceal a criminal relationship – for George's mistress was his own half-sister Mary Beauclerk, who had already borne him one child and was now expecting another. Elizabeth Beauclerk's marriage showed how romance could blossom between first cousins. Mary had taken a close family relationship a degree too far.

Early in 1787, soon before her sister's marriage, Mary had gone on an extended visit to her half-brother, his wife and the little niece and nephews. Something happened there for sibling intimacy to turn into illicit passion. George, perhaps tiring of his permanently pregnant wife (three babies in under four years) and the Christian virtues of his schoolmaster father-in-law, even liberated at the prospect of the imminent death of his father, seduced his half-sister. Mary represented transgressive desire – herself the little bastard produced by his own mother's lust for a man who was not his father, the cause of his parents' divorce, his own unsettled childhood and his need for security through marriage to the clinging Charlotte. There were too many forbidden fruits. Their sin was punished by Mary almost immediately falling pregnant, which put her into a situation infinitely worse than that of her mother twenty years earlier. The guilty couple took the bold and manipulative option of telling Charlotte; with astonishing charity or the determination to hang on to her husband and title, she went abroad with Mary, looked after her during the birth, and returned to England with a new baby to add to the three little St Johns at home, which she may even have claimed as her own.

But Mary and George had learned no lessons and carried on with their affair. There was a second pregnancy resulting in another trip across the Channel with Charlotte, who brought the next baby, again a boy, back to England. This was late in 1788. That winter Mary went through the motions of doing the London season, attending parties, balls and masquerades, the routine of an impeccable young lady of minimal fortune in search of a husband. She was chaperoned by her uncle Bob's mistress, Mrs Bouverie. A fellow party-goer that winter was Betsy Sheridan, the sister of Bob's great friend Richard Brinsley Sheridan. Betsy described Mary as 'about one-and-twenty but does not appear more than eighteen and I thought had a look of innocence and simplicity'. Mary was a fine actress, for it was during this period of empty pleasures that she and George were starting to consider running away to the Continent with their two babies and leaving their families for ever. They knew that when the relationship became public their reputations would be destroyed, quite apart from the effect that the revelations would have on their closest relations: George may even have obtained some strange convoluted satisfaction by taking a terrible revenge on Lady Di for her earlier abandonment of him. Not only was he echoing her own pattern of behaviour by walking out of his own marriage and commitments, but he was destroying her daughter, and therefore her own peace of mind.

Incest was a sin; the Church followed Old Testament law as defined in the prohibitions against sexual relationships between 'any that is near of kin' in the Book of Common Prayer's Table of Affinity, with its ultimate Old Testament source in Leviticus xx 17: 'If a Man shall take his Sister, his Father's Daughter or his Mother's Daughter, and see her nakedness and she see his nakedness, it is a wicked thing: and they shall be cut off in the sight of their People. He hath uncovered his Sister's nakedness. He shall bear his Iniquity.' Incestuous relationships and proscribed degrees of consanguinity were being keenly debated in the latter part of the century. The legality of marriage between first cousins had already undermined some perceived barriers. Current discussion mainly concerned a man's entitlement to marry the sister of his deceased wife, a not infrequent need given the hazards of child-birth. In the controversial tract *The Case of Marriage between Near Kindred* (1756), relationships between brother and sister were defended, on the grounds that Eve was made out of Adam's flesh and bone, and that their own sons and daughters had necessarily coupled in furthering God's command to multiply. The patriarch Abraham was also cited, as were various other brothers and sisters from biblical to early historical times. But this was a highly contentious contribution to an ongoing theological and legal argument. The reality was that a sexual relationship between half-siblings was deeply shocking, and the reactions to Walpole's play and Lady Di's illustrations of it showed society's real response to incest.[12]

It was Mary's third pregnancy that finalized their decision to escape: adopting the names of Mr and Mrs Barton, they went with the toddler and the baby to Paris in June 1789, a city in turmoil and the month in which the fast-growing constitutional crisis was coming to a head. Mary now wrote to Lady Di, who learned for the first time the whole dreadful story, the committing of a grave sin, the destruction of a marriage, the ruin of a daughter's and of a son's reputation, the existence of two grandsons whose birth was a crime. The letter's final hurt was the instruction never to try to find them because they had changed their names and intended to spend the rest of their lives abroad.

The shattered families – the present and the former Lady Boling-broke – got together and sought advice. Lady Di was supported, as ever, by Walpole, and by the lawyer George Hardinge, whose company she at last genuinely sought. Walpole was again the intermediary:

I am now with Lady Di, who is ill from great distress by a misfortune relative to her family. If you could come hither for ten minutes, you would do a great act of charity, as you can perhaps give her some advice, which I cannot do. It is not a point of law, but compassion; and yet I do not know how to put her in a way of doing any good. I send you my own chaise, because it is ready; and it shall carry you back directly. You will oblige Lady Di extremely, as well as yours ever.[13]

Somehow the guilty couple were tracked down and an express mes-senger was sent with a letter begging them to return, with the promise of forgiveness and discretion, but there was a flat refusal. Betsy Sheridan, cheerfully recounting these events to her sister in Dublin (and therefore to a wider Irish circle), described how 'poor Lady Di was near dying and is now very ill ... she has never gone into Public since her divorce'. Regarding Lady Bolingbroke, 'you may judge what the poor woman must have suffered, who doats on her husband, tho' cruelly treated by him, and three children she has by him entirely neglected. Yet the hope of saving from disgrace the family she was connected with made her submit to her unfortunate lot'. Betsy would have got the story, via her brother, from Bob Spencer, uncle to Mary and to George. And it also leaked quickly to other London circles: Viscount Wentworth discussed the affair with his sister despite not being in possession of the full facts: 'I suppose you have heard of the shocking piece of scandal which lately has been much talked of, Lord Bolingbroke going off with his sister Miss Beauclerk, who is in a way to make him at once an Uncle and a Father'. The recipient quickly spread the news to her family in County Durham: 'Lord Bolingbroke, I suppose you have heard, is gone off with his sister Miss Beauclerk who, it is said, is with child – a merry world my Masters!'[14]

And the story inevitably reached the national press. On 7 July 1789 *The Times* hinted at the facts, describing how Lord Bolingbroke 'had often quoted a Shakespearean passage on love for sisters' (presumably dinned into him by his father-in-law tutor). It might also have pointed out that his own father had owned a horse named Incest in 1765.

In touch with the real thing, the author of *The Mysterious Mother* must have felt a vicarious thrill of excitement. He did rush to sympathize with the devastated Lady Di, but at the same time relished the telling of the tale to Lady Ossory:

I have certainly seen the most unfortunate of all mothers upon earth, as soon as I could; it was not a moment to neglect one for whom I have so much regard. The blow was very nearly killing her ... she looks as deplorably as you may imagine, madam. Where the wretched pair are, I know not. The wife, whose patience and conduct has proved her a prodigy of discretion, is gone to her father, and has her jointure of £800 a year. Dreadful as her case is, still she is the least to be pitied, for time may assuage her grief and the esteem of the world will reward her innocence; but there being no resource for the guilty pair, their miseries can only increase; and consequently the mother must always suffer for what they have brought on themselves and to which she can never be insensible.[15]

It was a terrible irony that Lady Di's reputation as an artist had been established by her sympathetic interpretation of incest in her drawings for *The Mysterious Mother*. Some of the lines of the play must have come back to haunt her. The Countess tells her daughter Adeliza, the product of the Countess's incest with her own son, 'Thou must fly, must wed, must never view the towers of Narbonne more, fly ere it be too late'. Adeliza does wed, but it is to her own brother-father. And the play culminates in the grand climax where the Countess stabs herself, Adeliza is banished to a convent and Edmund goes off to seek death on the battlefield. Real life was mundane and painful, the days had to be got through, people stared and gossiped about yet another Spencer scandal.

Another concerned family member was Lady Pembroke. As well as having to cope with her niece's disgrace and sister's devastation, she was suffering from a grave public embarrassment of her own. As a Lady of the Bedchamber, and a loved and trusted friend of the Queen, she had just been revealed as the subject of George III's secret sexual fantasies. Her appointment as Bedchamber Lady in November 1782 was the result of Lord Pembroke's successful application on her behalf for the vacancy created by the death of Lady Hertford, as a useful supplement to the family income. The King succumbed to his first major bout of mental illness in 1788; his ramblings included the revelation of his lust for Lady Pembroke: 'he called himself Ahasuerus and the Queen Vashti and Lady Pembroke Esther – he told the Queen he could not lie with her until the year 1793 and said he would make Lady Pembroke Marchioness of Kingston'. On bad days, his thoughts and conversations were fixated upon her and frequently unrepeatable. This all got out – horrified accounts of the King's symptoms and treatment were public news, but were also recorded in the case accounts of his doctors. He wrote notes to her: 'Oh dear Eliza, ever love thy Prince, who had rather suffer death than leave thee'. Betsy Sheridan reported in February 1789 how the King 'has been quiet now for some time but not one bit more rational . . . he carries the Queen of Hearts in his pocket, and calls it Lady Pembroke's picture, for she is the object of his affections ever since his mind has been disordered'. And this analogy was confirmed during the therapeutic card-playing sessions with his doctors. Holding the King of Hearts, he said: 'Oh, if the Queen of Hearts would fall to the King'. An outing had to be aborted when it was realized that the King's innocent-sounding desire to visit Richmond Park masked a cunning scheme to call at Betty's house there, for which he intended to put on his best white breeches. He was so upset by the cancellation of the excursion that he had to be put back into his straitjacket that evening. He fantasized about marrying her and his recovery was actually measured by the reduction in his references to her, Dr Willis noting in late February 1789 that the King was 'quite right except for a hint or two of Lady Pembroke'.[16]

His condition continued to improve and the threat of a regency was removed, to the dismay of the Prince of Wales, Fox and the Whig circle. There was a service of thanksgiving in St Paul's Cathedral, and in the early summer the royal family went to the resort of Weymouth to complete his convalescence. Betty was due on duty as a Bedchamber Lady – this was very sensitive, considering that the last time she had seen the King was at an early stage in his recovery, when he had slipped away from the Queen 'and got to the other end of the room where Lady Pembroke was, and there was extremely gallant, and that Lady Pembroke seemed distressed and behaved with a becoming and maidenish modesty'. And now news of the family scandal had just broken. Mrs Harcourt, wife to the King's Equerry, kept a beady eye on her, but Betty, as ever, behaved with dignity:

she has been very ill in London, probably from agitation about the King's conduct towards her, and also on account of her niece, Lady Diana Beauclerk's daughter, going off with her Brother . . . at Weymouth she acted with such propriety that her visit, which was much dreaded, proved most serviceable, for in a short time they met her with perfect ease . . . previous to her coming she had some explanations with the King which entirely destroyed his hopes of succeeding with her. The Archbishop of Canterbury spoke to her seriously on the subject.

The Archbishop was of course the former family tutor. Later that year, the King's hostile younger brother, the Duke of Gloucester, claimed that the Prince of Wales and the Duke of York had seriously plotted to win over Lady Pembroke and so control the King through his infatuation for her.[17]

The passion of Mary Beauclerk and George, Viscount Bolingbroke, did not survive. She produced another two sons (four in all), but by May 1794 he had abandoned her too – being free to live together rather than conducting a secret relationship meant that the forbidden fruit lost its flavour. Having moved his family from France to Germany, as Paris became too dangerous to live in, George formed a new relationship with a seventeen-year-old girl, Isabella, daughter of Baron Hompesch. He did have the grace to arrange financial support for Mary and his son-nephews, Charles, George, Robert and Edward Barton, by a deed which provided annuities for them and their mother. He then eloped with Isabella, whom he married bigamously in Austria.

Another victim, his real wife, Charlotte Bolingbroke, also left Britain, depriving Lady Di of the presence of her legitimate grandchildren. Accompanied by her father and sister, Charlotte spent four years in Italy, living in Pisa, Vicenza and then Venice. But of course her story was known to the expatriates and Grand Tourists, and she became another item on the itinerary. Despite her trying to live 'very retired', one visitor wrote: 'Poor thing, how interesting she is in her present unfortunate situation. I feel quite grieved for her'. They eventually returned to live at Lydiard, where her eldest son died in 1803, and the younger, Henry, became the heir to the title. Charlotte developed consumption, and died, in great poverty and an atmosphere of sanctity, in Bristol in January 1804.[18]

Following the scandal of Mary's flight, Lady Di distanced herself from the prying eyes of Twickenham by giving up the lease on Little Marble Hill and moving back across the river to Petersham, where she rented a cottage tucked in between the foot of Richmond Hill and the river, overlooking the meadows. Here she again sought to escape from the painful realities of life by immersing herself in her art. She began a major mural project for the new house, designing a scheme which was again intended to be portable because it was painted on paper mounted on to large wooden panels; although still in watercolour, her mastery of the medium has ensured that the colours are still vibrant today. She was working on a very large scale, which would have required weeks of work: six rectangular panels, each over twelve feet high by three feet wide, and three smaller ones, to go over doorways, totalling several hundred square feet of painted surfaces. Each panel is different in detail but follows the same formal structure. There is a strong cornflower-blue background, against which are vertical bamboo trellis supports, wreathed with different types of leaves, flowers and tendrils – jasmine, pinks, roses, passion flowers, honeysuckle – which carry on across the top and bottom. At the base of each there is a bouquet of three or four contrasted flowers, in a different permutation for each of the six panels – carnation blends with honeysuckle and narcissus, briar rose with dahlia and lily, all entwined together and depicted with exquisite detail and botanical accuracy. These provide an exotic frame for the centre zone of each panel, which has a creamy ground linked to the cornflower-blue frame by rows of tiny stitch-like leaves all around. In the middle of each is painted a motif – a basket, hanging by ribbons from a medallion and containing more variegated bouquets (in one, fuchsias, daffodils and sweet peas) or a group of figures involving the familiar cherubs. On one is a roundel showing a group of eight naked chubby babes, carefully composed into two sets of four placed against a delicate background of trees. On another, four cherubs are arranged around a basket of flowers, the roundel itself wreathed with a complex garland of blue and white convolvulus, while the two smaller panels, of cupids sacrificing at an altar, imitate the effects of a jasper or wax bas-relief. The overall effect is fantastic and decorative because of the combination of surreal precision with a vivid use of colour.[19]

Walpole described the whole scheme as 'natural and masterly'. The resources of Strawberry Hill may have provided a source of inspiration, for he owned an example of Mrs Delany's flower collages, as well as companion pieces by her pupil, a 'Miss Jennings of Shiplake'. Mrs Delany's use of a plain, strong-toned ground provided a superb and striking background for her own delicate flowers of tissue paper. Lady Di would undoubtedly have been familiar with these works and their visual effect. Combinations of different flowers were also available for copying from the pages of the many art training manuals which were being produced in the 1780s and '90s. Carington Bowles published and sold works about painting in watercolour, and *Bowles's Florist* listed various colours, including the fourteen main tones which could be obtained from his shop, plus sixty plates of flowers to colour. Brown's *A New Treatise on Flower Painting, or Every Lady her own Drawing Master* ran to three editions by 1799, and sought to improve the status of the genre by teaching ladies to master the exact replication of the beauties of nature for the sake of 'the honour and credit of ladies and the nation' through 'containing the most familiar and easy instructions . . . to obtain a complete knowledge of drawing flowers with taste and by practice alone'. Brown recognized the flaws in women's training unless they were 'first taught the proper rudiments' by following his tasteful instructions for drawing and colouring. This series was an early example of a part work, issuing sets of progressively challenging flowers, grouped three or four to a page. Such combinations as hyacinth/fuchsia/campanula/Michaelmas daisy, and sweet pea/pink/ *Linum tenuifolium* (shown in three stages, first in outline, then lightly tinted, and finally more vividly coloured) suggest that Lady Di was copying directly from such a model rather than observing her blooms from nature; she has also followed the precision and perfection of these drawing aids, achieving effects quite unlike the looser, sketchier style of so many of her other drawings.

Another source may even have been the Sèvres china collected by her first husband, some items of which, bought on their Paris honeymoon, could have remained in her possession. The vivid blue backgrounds in 'bleu-celeste' or 'turquoise', the panels of cherubic children, the garlands of wild and cultivated flowers, painted naturalistically and entwined in varying combinations, all typical features of the china, are echoed in her murals.

Walpole continued to visit and admire, not quite so frequently, however, because she had moved a little further away and because he had found a new passion in life, his friendship with the sisters Mary and Agnes Berry, who had recently come to live in Twickenham. He regarded these girls as 'the best informed and the most perfect creatures I ever saw at their age', and his close relationship with them, particularly the elder, Mary, would enliven his remaining years. He reported to Lady Ossory his attempts to improve their artistic education through loaning one of his favourite pictures to Agnes Berry: 'The younger draws charmingly and has copied admirably Lady Di's gypsies, which I lent, though for the first time of her attempting colours'.[20]

His letters to them (when they were away travelling) as well as to his other correspondents continue to provide glimpses of Lady Di. 'Coming out of Lady Di's in the dark, I missed my way and pitched headlong down a perpendicular bank into a brick pavement laced with orange tubs and flower-pots, broke two of the latter to powder, and yet only bruised my hand and slightly hurt my hip. Had I weighed more than gossamer I must have been dashed to pieces'. A few months later:

I met the Marlboroughs at Lady Di's. The Duchess desired to come and see Strawberry again, as it had rained the whole time she was here last. I proposed the next morning: no, she could not; she expected company to dinner; she believed their brother Lord Robert would dine with them: I thought that a little odd as they have just turned him out for Oxfordshire; and I thought a dinner no cause at a distance of four miles. In her Grace's dawdling way, she could fix no time; and so on Friday, at half an hour after seven, they arrived; and the sun being setting, and the moon not risen, you may judge how much they could see through all the painted glass by twilight.

The Marlboroughs owned a house in nearby Isleworth, and now appeared to be on tolerable terms with Lady Di. As a result, Walpole was able to scotch rumours which had intrigued Miss Berry concerning the allegedly imminent marriage of the Marquess of Blandford; although she claimed he was due to be married in four days' time, Walpole insisted that 'his aunt, at the foot of yonder hill, has heard nothing of it four days ago nor believes a word of it'.[21]

As the revolution in France progressed, Richmond became an attractive refuge for many émigrés, as it was cheaper than London. 'I am still here: the weather, though very rainy is quite warm; and I shall have much more agreeable society in Richmond, with small companies and better hours than in town, and shall have till after Christmas, unless great cold drives me hither. Lady Di, Selwyn, the Penns, the Onslows, Douglases, Mackinseys, Keenes, Lady Mount-Edgcumbe all stay, and some of them meet every evening. The Boufflers too are constantly invited and the Comtesse Emilie sometimes carries her harp'. In 1793, Joseph Farington, describing his visit to Strawberry Hill, reported how Walpole 'mentioned that at Richmond and in the neighbourhood there are a great number of French emigrants, many of them being high fashion; that party spirit rages among them, some being Royalists, others, as they call themselves, Constitutionalists, which makes it necessary to be cautious not to assemble them together, though they labour under the common grievance of being expelled from their native country'.[22]

There was also a royal neighbour, the King's third son, William, Duke of Clarence, who sometimes joined their circle. 'We have had several beautiful days, a vast deal of rain and high winds. Richmond is still full and will be so till after Christmas. The Duke of Clarence is there, and every night at Mrs Bouverie's, Lady Di's, at home, or at the Duke of Queensberry's, with suppers that finish at twelve. I have been at three but do not think seventy-three just suited to twenty-five'. The Duke, then aged twenty-five, was committed to the active naval service which his father had made him follow, but was also the Ranger of

Bushey Park. Here he passed his leisure time subsidized by the earnings of the actress Dora Jordan, with whom he lived in domestic stability for a number of years – although she seldom accompanied him in public. He also preferred the laid-back riverside life to the pomposity of the court in London or Windsor, such as the sailing match in the summer of 1791 in honour of the Duke's birthday, at which Bob Spencer presented a cup to the winner: 'On Monday was the boat-race. I was in the great room at the Castle with the Duke of Clarence, Lady Di, Lord Robert and the house of Bouverie, to see the boats start from the bridge to Thistleworth [Isleworth], and back to a tent erected in Lord Dysart's meadow, just before Lady Di's windows whither we went to see them arrive and where we had breakfast . . . the scene, both up river and down, was what only Richmond upon earth can exhibit'. This event was also described in the *Oracle* for 24 August, which reported how the grand folk, including Lady Di, had been cheered by 'the mob with three huzzas'.[23]

That same summer, for the first time in over thirty years, Lady Di encountered William Hamilton, who had come to England to marry his long-time mistress Emma Hart. The couple visited Richmond and were seen by Walpole at the Duke of Queensberry's house two days before the birthday boat-race. The new Lady Hamilton, whose upwardly mobile career had included semi-nude posing as a goddess at the famously naughty Temple of Health in the Adelphi, with its Viagra-like Celestial Bed (£50 a night), and being mistress to three men in succession, had so entranced the third, Sir William, that he married her. As a connoisseur of classical art, he saw in her the epitome of ideal beauty, which he now encouraged her to display to the world through the public performances known as Lady Hamilton's Attitudes, based on dramatic gesture and poses taken from classical art. Wearing a Greek costume which Hamilton had especially designed for her, 'she lets down her hair, and with a few shawls, gives so much variety to her poses, gestures, expressions etc. that the spectator can hardly believe his eyes . . . In her he has found all the antiquities, all the profiles of Sicilian coins, even the Apollo Belvedere'. This was the reaction of Goethe. Walpole missed the local performance but Lady Di managed to attend: '[Hamilton has] actually married his gallery of statues and they are set out on their return to Naples. I am sorry I did not see her Attitudes, which Lady Di (a tolerable judge) prefers to anything she ever saw'.[24]

Lady Di continued to provide innocuous copy for the *Times* social column, which reported on 13 September 1790 that 'Lady Diana Beauclerk continues to employ herself with her pencil in giving those beauties to the canvas which Sir Joshua himself might be proud to acknowledge'. Her abilities as a literary illustrator were beginning to receive wider recognition. Although her illustrations for Ossian, *The Faerie Queene* and Shakespeare had not been published, either as prints or as book illustrations, her designs continued to sell Wedgwood's products, and Walpole remained a voluble admirer and collector of her work. In 1791 she received a commission to illustrate a prestigious new edition of Dryden's *Fables* to be published by the book- and print-sellers J. Edwards and E. Harding of Pall Mall; her drawings would be engraved by the distinguished team of Bartolozzi and his pupils Vandenberg, Cheesman and Gardiner. Bartolozzi's reputation was now such that his Fulham studio was on the sightseeing itinerary of visitors to London, such as Sophie von la Roche in 1786: 'we came upon the eminent artist with his worthy pupils at a nice house situated in the midst of a large flower garden, busts of his friends in the alleyways, and Apollo on a hill, overgrown with laurel, in front of his window . . . I was fascinated to note what grade of art his pupils had attained, at the same time observing that his mind had not only influenced their hand and vision but their character'. Sophie was also delighted that Bartolozzi engraved and praised the work of Angelica Kauffmann, 'the honour of her sex and of our century'.[25]

In the preface to the first edition of his *Fables Ancient and Modern* (1700), Dryden, the former Poet Laureate, stated his intention of paying tribute to Chaucer, the father of English poetry, through producing a modern English version of some of the *Canterbury Tales*, together with selections from Homer, Ovid and Boccaccio, as well as a Chaucerian-inspired piece written by Dryden himself, 'The Flower and the Leaf'. The tales were allegedly selected because of their morally improving conclusions, but they variously involved love and lust, battles, murder, revenge and the supernatural as necessary aids to catharsis. It was a controversial volume when first published, not least because of Dryden's updating of a sacrosanct national monument. So this was a prestigious commission for her, the very first illustrated edition, requiring an artist who could highlight crucial moments in dense and complex narratives, and one who was not afraid to be associated with the bawdiness and violence that was embedded in the text – Chaucer and Boccaccio were hardly celebrated for their gentility.

Twenty-four engravings were made from her original drawings and watercolours. The illustrations consisted of one full-page scene for each of the seven tales selected, with the exception of the longest, the Knight's Tale, 'Palamon and Arcite', which had three. There were also little scenes which were used as a headpiece and a tailpiece to each story. Lady Di's output therefore consisted of nine large watercolours for the full-page plates and fourteen pencil and red chalk vignettes. The title page boasted that the *Fables* were 'ornamented with drawings from the pencil of the Right Honourable Lady Diana Beauclerc', using the more medieval version of her name favoured by Walpole; but in the captions to the plates it is spelled Beauclerk, which is how she always wrote her own name.

One of the engravers, William Gardiner, would later complain that 'some of the plates to Lady Diana Beauclerk's edition of Dryden's *Fables* were entirely my own and many of those with the name Bartolozzi affixed were mine'. The collaborative process of engraving depended upon a subtle and sympathetic interpretation by the engraver; many amateur ladies did have their designs reproduced by professionals who frequently had to improve radically the far from perfect originals. However, Gardiner's comments seen unreasonable in relation to the one original watercolour which has survived. This illustrates the dreadful tale of 'Theodore and Honoria' and has infinitely more life and delicacy than its engraved version (attributed to Cheesman). It also gives some idea of the impressive scale on which she was able to work, being around two feet wide. Reduced to a quarter of the original, the engraved version inevitably loses the subtlety of her colour tones, although her palette is deliberately restricted to yellowish and brown washes, with a very few touches of blue and pink. In some places Cheesman has completely altered the original intention, for example by darkening a light patch. Nor are her sketchy pen strokes and light washes really captured by the far more detailed and concentrated engraver's line, which turn her simplicity into over-elaboration. Apart from the tonal imbalance, the facial expressions are not truly interpreted, particularly the mad eyes of the phantom Knight.[26]

She has chosen to depict the climax of a particularly horrible story, in which Dryden/Boccaccio gives a graphic account of the hunting down and disembowelling by two Hell-hounds of a haughty maiden who has rejected her suitor, 'a knight of swarthy face . . . with flashing flames his eyes were filled'. This is not even a single event, but is endlessly repeated in a time-loop: she is fated to be eternally punished for her arrogance – once slain and ripped apart, she leaps up again intact and the chase resumes. The awful pageant is demonstrated by another spurned lover, Theodore, as a warning to Honoria, who has rejected his suit. Theodore invites Honoria and her family to picnic at the spot where he knows the phantoms will appear; the hunt and the kill are re-enacted, and Honoria is so terrified by this prospect of retribution that she begins to relent. This is the moment depicted, although Lady Di delicately manages to omit the grisly physical details described earlier – 'her heart and bowels through her back he drew And fed the hounds that helped him to pursue', and now repeated: 'piercing through her inmost heart Drew backwards, as before, th'offending part, The reeking entrails next he tore away, And to his meagre mastiffs made a prey'. The Hell-hounds are shown leaping towards the head and shoulders of a recumbent lady, who is however cleverly placed at the far right of the design so that the rest of her body, with its cascading entrails, is fortunately not visible. But the emotions of the characters are finely captured, the passionate Knight with swarthy face gesturing threateningly with his sword (his other hand grasps the reeking dagger), the swooning Honoria, supported by horrified companions. Theodore, who has seen the ghost-hunt before, leans against a tree, his folded arms and casually crossed legs suggesting a degree of detachment, while he studies Honoria's expression. Extra emotional effects are provided by the Knight's sinister horse, with rolling eye and pawing leg; and by the large central tree, which separates the spectres from the living, its branches tossing uneasily. As in *The Mysterious Mother* drawings, we can read the whole story from the expressions in the characters' eyes and faces.[27]

The other tales contain equally lively material, calculated to shock the sensitive, and thrill the broader-minded. Boccaccio's 'Sigismonda and Guiscardo' deals with the improper lust of the recently widowed Sigismonda for the handsome young Guiscardo. Her possessive father, King Tancred, has Guiscardo murdered; Sigismonda discovers his heart, and drinks poison, her final request to her father being that she be buried with the man she loved. Lady Di shows the last moments of

Sigismonda recumbent on her deathbed (a scene also tackled by Hogarth), declaiming: 'Tancred, restrain thy tears, unsought by me, And sorrow unavailing now to thee.'

Chaucer's 'Wife of Bath's Tale' concerns one of King Arthur's knights, who has committed rape but is offered a reprieve from punishment if he can answer the question 'what it is that women most desire?' His researches require him to marry and bed an old crone 'fouler far Than grandam apes in Indian forests are', who, satisfied by his sexual performance, turns into a beautiful young woman, and they live happily ever after. The illustration shows the moment when the knight first meets the old hag, who has a skull-like face and twisted body, and is propped against a tree in a moonlit grove, just as described in the text.

Boccaccio's 'Cymon and Iphigenia' involves the loutish Cymon committing visual rape by gazing at the nude sleeping Iphigenia, titillatingly described as 'a sleeping maid . . . Her bosom to the view was bare Where two beginning paps were scarcely spy'd . . . The fool of nature stood with stupid eyes And gaping mouth, that testified surprise, Fix'd on her face, nor could remove his sight'. This is the inspirational moment in which love begins to transform the young man, and the one that Lady Di has selected; her illustration makes Cymon rustic rather 'brutish', but her Iphigenia is certainly exposing a naked breast.

For 'The Nun's Priest's Tale',* her drawing again shows thorough familiarity with the text; the illustration contains all the details lovingly described by Chaucer at the start of the story: Chanticleer stands on top of the hen-house and dreams of the fox, which lurks in shadow in the foreground. Against the background of humble cottage, and cows in a meadow, the old woman feeds her pig, while her two daughters (remarkably clean and ladylike) scatter corn to the chickens. The tale contained one passage which must have hurt. Although it only referred to the cockerel-hero, Chanticleer, and his wives, it raised the issue of incest:

> Scandal, that spares no King, though ne'er so good,
> Says they were all of his own flesh and blood;
> His sisters both by sire and mother's side;

---

* This was thought too bawdy to be studied, except in a bowdlerized version, by 'A' level English Literature candidates in the 1960s!

And sure their likeness showed them near allied.
But, mark the worst, the monarch did no more
Than all the Ptolemies had done before.
When incest is for int'rest of a nation
'Tis made no sin by holy dispensation.

This was Dryden's insertion, and not Chaucer's text at all, as an intervention in the debate over degrees of prohibited marriages between near kin; it followed the line of a tract of 1673 which accused the Pope of granting dispensations 'for Lucre's sake' from such prohibitions, especially if they were members of the Spanish royal family.[28]

The vignettes which begin and end all the stories are composed of naked cherubs or little children, who are enacting or suggesting the events in the texts they frame, aided by appropriate props. This represents a delightful and clever way of making strong material more palatable to the readers; her familiar light-hearted classical style, employing the resoundingly successful Wedgwood bacchanalian figures, deliberately subverts the Gothick spirit of the violent passions being expressed. It also suggests her knowledge of contemporary book illustrators and adaptation of a popular formula; for example, Thomas Stothard had depicted a group of antique-style cherubs playing at geometry as the frontispiece to a mathematical textbook published in the 1780s, which had inspired the book's engraver, William Blake, to explore further the potential dichotomies between image and text in his own works, such as *America* (1793).[29]

The scheme of course found favour with Walpole, who described her working on the originals to Mary Berry: 'I am just come from Richmond, first having called on Lady Di, who is designing and painting pictures for prints to Dryden's *Fables*. Oh, she has done two most beautiful: one of Emily walking in the garden, and Palamon seeing her from the tower, the other, a noble free composition of Theseus parting the rivals, when fighting in the wood. They are not, as you will imagine, at all like the pictures in the Shakespeare Gallery; no, they are worthy of Dryden'. The letter continues with a further enthusiastic mention of 'Lady Di's gypsies and Mrs Damer's dogs. I defy your favourite Italy to produce . . . such monuments of female genius'.[30]

Her skills were acknowledged at this time in the *Oracle*, which also provided a little puff for Walpole: 'Lady Di Beauclerk, in this age of refined taste, is busy in the improvement of the pallet. Her Ladyship is distinguishable by a rapid masterly style, which is visible in her charming suite of drawings for Horace Walpole's play . . . *The Mysterious Mother* was composed for Mrs Pritchard's benefit. Mature consideration, however, convinced the elegant author that the horror would be much too powerful for an audience to bear.'[31]

Although she started work on the Dryden in 1791, the large scale of the project and the time required for the engraving process meant that it would not to be published until 1797. The considerable work required, the commercial nature of the project and the employment of Bartolozzi's team would suggest that she received a fee in return for her skills and name, which is prominently mentioned on the title page.

In the meantime, art continued inevitably to be intersected with private life. She lost a daughter-in-law and a grandson when Mary, the wife of her second son, Frederick St John, died following childbirth in February 1791. Frederick was now an army major, and his marriage had been celebrated at Little Marble Hill in 1788. There was even greater loss two years later when Lady Di's own daughter Elizabeth Herbert died in March 1793 after the birth of a fourth baby. Three months later, Elizabeth's eldest child, George, also died, shortly followed by the new baby. Grandmothers had an important role in these sadly frequent circumstances. Lord Herbert turned to his own mother, Lady Pembroke, for help with the two surviving children, Robert and Diana, with whom they spent much time until his remarriage in 1808. And Lady Di often looked after Frederick St John's surviving son, 'little Bob', after Frederick's remarriage and rapid production of seven more children. The Earl of Pembroke died in January 1794 and Lord Herbert succeeded to the title.

During the sad year of 1793, with one daughter already lost through scandal and the other in childbirth, as well as the continuing absence of her disgraced eldest son, Lady Di was additionally worried about the health of her youngest son, Charles Beauclerk. He was now aged nineteen, and had been educated at Eton, and Oxford, like his father. She decided to combine Grand Tour with health cure and sent him straight to Naples, where she knew she could call upon William Hamilton to keep an eye on Charles. Her letter of introduction sums up her depressed state and sense of everything going wrong:

The bearer of this letter is by far the dearest thing to me upon earth and I do flatter myself that you have enough friendship for me to be kind to my son Charles Beauclerk. Nothing would make me so happy as a certainty that during his residence in Naples you would grant him your protection and I think you will find him worthy of it. Overwhelmed as I am by repeated misfortunes, parting from him is very painful indeed but it must be. A thousand compliments to Lady Hamilton, and pray tell her if it is possible she should feel such a spark of gratitude for the admiration of such a poor animal as I am, she can fully repay me by joining you in the protection of my son. If I was something younger, not quite so poor, nor quite so unhealthy, there are few things I should like better than going myself to Naples, and assuring you both how much I am yours etc.[32]

Sir William and Lady Hamilton did more than their duty, as Lady Di gratefully acknowledged when she wrote again (from Marlborough House, while staying with the Duke and family) in January 1794:

I cannot resist the desire I have to thank you and Lady Hamilton for your great goodness to Charles, though boring you with a letter you will perhaps think rather troublesome. Charles writes me word that nothing was ever equal to both your goodness and Lady Hamilton's to him, and my gratitude is in proportion to my affection for him, which I do assure you is unbounded . . . pray order Charles when he writes to say how his health is, for that is a matter he never thinks of mentioning, and I am a little fearful of the heat of the climate. I hope you and Lady Hamilton will like him half as much as he likes you both.

There is a flirtatious postscript: 'This letter is intended for Lady Hamilton as well as you, only I prefer being troublesome to you, as an old friend.'[33]

Charles was travelling with a group which including his 'bosom friend' the current Lord Holland (Charles James Fox's nephew). According to Lady Webster, another member of their circle, Charles was 'silent and sulky and when he speaks it is to tease his friend'; but she conceded that for those who got to know him he was 'remarkably sensible, good humoured and pleasing'. When he moved on to Rome, he joined one of the many parties of English visitors, which included his mother's friend and cousin Lady Bessborough (younger sister of the Duchess of Devonshire), whose friendly intimacies with Charles provoked, according to Lady Webster, 'a fit of jealousy' by Lord Bessborough so severe that it brought to an abrupt end an expedition to Tivoli. But Harriet Bessborough already had a younger lover, Granville Leveson-Gower, with whom she had been involved for many years but for whom she would not disrupt her own marriage (he eventually married her own niece, Georgiana's daughter). Harriet's fondness for Charles was sufficiently marked to provoke teasing by Granville, to whom she later wrote: 'As to Beauclerc, I like him better and mind him more than ever I did; but tho' it is possible he may have been upon the whole more hours (not many, many, however if any) in my Company than you, yet I am certain no creature that ever saw us together could for a moment imagine he thought of me one bit more than he does . . . I am not angry with you for preaching but I find the warning on this head so little wanted that you must not wonder if it does not make much impression'.[34]

Having visited Venice and Switzerland, Charles returned home with his health restored in the summer of 1794. His mother and Lady Bessborough remained in touch, and Lady Bessborough later described a visit to this artistic if not moral exemplar: 'in the evening we drove to Lady Di's, who always delights me and does me good in every way. I came home in full drawing humour and set to work with industry'. Lady Di's more optimistic mood following his return was perhaps reflected, as recorded in Farington's diary, in her sitting for a portrait drawing by Nathaniel Dance, a former professional artist and founding member of the Royal Academy, but now of vastly improved status, as Member of Parliament and baronet, following the inheritance of a fortune.[35]

Walpole, now in his late seventies, maintained his active social life: 'I have been with Lady Di, and *voici* what I heard. Nel of Clarence plays Ophelia tonight at Richmond. Miss Hotham has issued cards for a tea on Friday. I have not received one, though last year she *swore* by me; but this year has not noticed me. I shall not break my heart'. Nel of Clarence, better known as Dora Jordan, had already performed in *The Tempest* at Richmond on 17 August and would repeat Ophelia on 26 August. In the following month, 'I went to the Palace at Fulham this morning and have been at Lady Di's and Lady Betty's this evening, and could not bring away a scrap of novelty except that the Parliament is to meet on the 29th of next month. What care you or I? . . . Last night I was near tumbling headlong down Lady Di's steps but her footman caught me in his arms'. He had already fallen down her 'perpendicular bank' in 1789.[36]

By the later 1790s, some of Bartolozzi's engravings from her drawings were available as individual coloured prints, published by the print-seller Dickinson. The subjects included two of the Bacchanalian boy groups, as originally done for Wedgwood, one of cherubs in a roundel, and two of 'Children at play'. Bartolozzi, who admired her 'exquisite taste', also drew her portrait in red chalk at this time. Another craftsman interpreting her work was Mariano Bovi, one of Bartolozzi's pupils, who had come to London from Naples to train as an engraver, with the support of King Ferdinand IV and possibly at the instigation of William Hamilton. Bovi later took premises at 207 Piccadilly, where he engraved, published and sold prints; the catalogue he issued in 1802 included various prints of Lady Di's drawings, such as 'Amorini in a woodland setting', together with those from other popular artists of the day, including Kauffman, Sandby and Cipriani; the works were displayed in his exhibition room as well as being available for purchase. These professional artists received fees for the engraving rights; Lady Di was also paid, for she would later refer bitterly to the rascally practices of such print-sellers who exploited their artists, and she was well aware that this was an unpredictable source of income – Bovi, for example, went bankrupt in 1805, and his entire stock was sold off in a sale which lasted for three days.[37]

As well as producing drawings for engraving as single prints, Lady Di began work in 1796 on another set of illustrations for a book. *Leonora* was the English version of the tragic ballad *Lenore* written by the German poet Gottfried Burgher, the tale of a woman fatally punished for selfish passion, and so Romantic that it would later be translated by Walter Scott and by Dante Gabriel Rossetti. Set in the time of the Crusades, the ballad begins with Leonora waiting impatiently for her soldier lover to return; she fails to realize that the mysterious horseman with whom she recklessly elopes is not her betrothed but Death. They gallop through the night, past a symbolic funeral procession and sundry wraiths and spectres, achieving a climactic moment when the lover turns into a grinning skeleton and Leonora dies. This project was an example of quite underhand practice by the Spencer family. The young amateur poet and artist Mr (later Baron) Stanley had already translated the poem but modified it with a happy ending. As described by Maria Holroyd, his future wife: 'Mr Stanley was very ill used . . . he lent his translation to Lady Diana Beauclerk, who took advantage of it to make beautiful drawings from it, and Mr Spencer, her nephew, undertook to improve the translation and publish it with engravings from Lady Diana's drawings. Mr

Stanley did not intend to publish but hearing of this he was affronted and had his translation printed in hot haste'.[38]

The nephew, William Robert Spencer, another society poet, was the son of Lady Di's middle brother Charles. With the publicity bonus of illustrations by his celebrated aunt, again engraved by a team which included Bartolozzi, this was a potentially lucrative project for the equally hard-up aunt and nephew. William had been educated at Harrow and Oxford, where he started to write poetry. His Grand Tour covered France (where he spent the evening of 5 October 1789 at Versailles with Marie Antoinette and Louis XVIII, awaiting the arrival of the mob from Paris), Italy, Switzerland and Germany. Here he met and married the widowed Countess Spreti, the former Susan Jenison-Walworth. She had been born in England, but her father had thrown up his position as a Justice of the Peace in County Durham, and sold off the ancient family estate in order to become an officer of dragoons, and then chamberlain, in the service of the Elector Palatine, Charles Theodore. Her brother, Francis Jenison-Walworth, served in the court of the Margrave of Hesse-Darmstadt, where he was rumoured to be the Margravine's lover (his mother was conveniently employed as the Margravine's maid of honour). The suicide of Susan's husband, Count Spreti, was rumoured to have been caused by his wife's relationship with the young English poet; whatever the truth, in 1791 William married Susan 'as a gross take-in concerted by the brother and the Margravine' in order to acquire the grandson of a Duke of Marlborough and the name of Spencer.[39]

William and Susan lived in Curzon Street, Mayfair, and maintained a hectic social life. William was a popular member of the Devonshire House set, his wit and humour eliciting from Fox the compliment that 'Mr William Spencer exceeded every man he had ever met with in the happy talent of conversation'; although another member of that circle, Harriet, or Harryo, daughter of Georgiana, Duchess of Devonshire, thought that 'Mr William Spencer looks like a starved cat, tries every one's spirits by his perpetual rattle . . . people say he is brilliant, but I think they must mean noisy'. The scale of his gambling meant of course that he was constantly deeply in debt. Susan would find her own ways of increasing her pin money, at one time from the Duke of Devonshire, filling the vacant post created when he married his mistress, Lady Elizabeth Foster, after Georgiana's death. From a later lover she obtained a handsome annuity, and ended her days back in Germany, to be near her daughter Harriet Spencer. The latter had become an unmarried mother at the age of nineteen, following seduction by one of her relations, either the Duke of Marlborough (Lady Di's nephew) or his son the Marquess of Blandford. This scandal obviously ruined her marriage prospects in England but she was successfully married off into the German family of the von Westerholts.[40]

Publication of the Spencer–Beauclerk *Leonora* was delayed, according to Spencer's introduction, because 'much time was required by the artists to do justice to these exquisite designs, which are its brightest ornament'. The illustrations consisted of five full-page plates, plus vignettes at the beginning and end, two each for the German and English versions of the text, which were published on facing pages. Spencer pays homage to Walpole in his introduction, which, while acknowledging the 'terrible and majestic' qualities of German writing, awards 'the palm of excellence' to 'our nation' because of 'the impregnable towers of *Otranto*', Walpole's seminal Gothic novel of 1765. The vignettes and the full-page frontispiece were engraved by Bartolozzi, the rest by Birrell and by Harding. Lady Di's interpretation again shows her absorption in the text and her ability to visualize and set down the smallest intricate details. Her artistic style is closer to Fuseli than Flaxman, bringing out the atmospheric and sinister nature of the piece.

The drawings are slightly repetitive, in that three of them show Death and Leonora riding on a horse, although at different stages of the dramatic narrative. In the first scene, when the horseman invites Leonora to mount behind him 'to reach our nuptial bed', and urges 'my fierce steed maddens to be gone', the drawing shows the blowing mane of the sturdy war-horse tossing its head and rolling its eyes. There are wonderful contrasts of light and shade: the dramatic ride takes place at night, but the moon casts highlights on the protagonists. For the final scene 'thin sheeted phantoms gibbering glide . . . charnels and tombs on every side Gleam dimly to the blood red moon', while light focuses on the swooning form of Leonora; we see that she is about to be pierced by the arrow gripped in the skeletal hand of the rider whose face turns to the front to reveal that it is just a skull.

Susan Spencer posed for the figure of Leonora and was quoted as saying that sitting for Lady Di had been the hardest work she had ever done. The tale, and Lady Di's illustrations, came to epitomize the romantic spirit cited sarcastically by the rational Mr Percival in Maria Edgworth's *Belinda* (1801) as an example of the adventures that might befall a lover and his mistress when they are out riding: the sudden appearance of bandits or footpads means that 'the lady must be carried off, robes flying! Hair streaming! like Buergers Leonora'. The work was so popular that two editions of the Stanley version were published in 1796, as well as another translation by H. J. Pye in the same year, a parody, *Miss Kitty*, in 1797, and a combined Stanley–Pye–Spencer edition in 1799. But it was only the 1796 Spencer edition which had full-page illustrations. *Leonora* was William's first major success, its fame undoubtedly enhanced by the reputation of his illustrator. His best-known and most enduring work was the ballad *Bethgelert* (1800), a convincingly medieval-sounding version of the ancient Welsh legend of the faithful hound.

The publication of *Leonora* was quickly followed by that of the long-delayed *Fables* in 1797. The revived boost to Lady Di's career from the publicity resulting from these projects meant that she obtained another significant commission from a new patron, which would result in a monumental three-dimensional sculpture in the excitingly modern medium of lithodipyra, or 'artificial stone'. This product, clay-based but weatherproof and therefore suitable for exterior use, was made from a secret formula first patented in the 1720s, then rediscovered and improved in 1769 by the enterprising Mrs Eleanor Coade; her highly successful manufactory in Westminster Bridge Road produced quantities of architectural ornament and free-standing items in a broadly neo-classical style. Taking Wedgwood as a marketing role model, and even viewed by him as a commercial rival, Mrs Coade employed a range of distinguished freelance designers and sculptors to work for her (including Flaxman) and a chief in-house sculptor, the Royal Academician John Bacon. In 1784, she issued a catalogue of some 800 items and, as a way of further improving sales on the model of Wedgwood's London showroom, opened an exhibition gallery in Lambeth. A second, expanded edition of the catalogue was issued in 1799, which also served as a guide to the gallery where the public could inspect samples of these 'statues, vases, . . . panels in bas relief, models from the antique . . .'; it stressed how the highly fired stone was as durable as jasper or porphyry. Items in the catalogue, which could be ordered as well as viewed, covered the whole spectrum of contemporary style, from classical to Gothic. The frontispiece to this catalogue was Lady Di's 1797 design for a pediment over the entrance to the Pelican Life Insurance Office in the City of London, a design which was also adopted as the heading on the policy documents issued by the Company as the development of an effective corporate image. The pediment was a free-standing three-dimensional sculpture, with over-lifesize figures, made out of Coade stone by John De Vaere, a former pupil of Flaxman in Rome and then one of Wedgwood's chief modellers. This massive piece was placed over the main door of the Company's new offices at 70 Lombard Street.

The work was most enthusiastically described in an article in the *European Magazine* for 1801, which stated that 'the ideas upon which this group was founded, we are informed, were taken from some of the elegant vignettes from the pencil of Lady Diana Beauclerk which decorate the late edition of Dryden's *Fables*'. This article was written four years after the commission, and drew on information in Mrs Coade's Catalogue, which however does not specifically mention Lady Di's name, despite using the image as a frontispiece. Nor do later versions of the engravings (as the policy documents were changed and updated) bear her name, although the figures are typical of her style, especially the cherub holding a torch, and a graceful seated figure with wide eyes and a sweet smile; some sort of collaboration must have been necessary to account for the invention of the particular symbols which were appropriate to the new policy.

What was being advertised was an innovative scheme which had been devised to fill a gap in the market by the recently founded Pelican Life Insurance Company. The new concept was emphasized by the inscription at the base of the design – 'Children Endowed' – since the company was providing policies for orphaned children which matured when they reached the age of twenty-one, a time when they stood in most need of 'such assistance and for want of which too many are precluded from settling advantageously in the world'. Through 'a most laborious investigation', the company claimed it was able to offer rates below that of any competitor; the purpose of the scheme was 'to liberate the widows or guardians from any burden of payment, yet preserving the title of the endowed orphan as if the whole of those latter instalments should have been fully paid up'.

Like her more literary illustrations, Lady Di's drawing seeks to explain the facts and show the emotions of the protagonists. The group of figures, constrained into the flattened triangle of a pediment, are all in classical dress or undress; the focal point is a Roman, wearing only a helmet and a tactically draped cloak. In one hand he holds up what looks like a standard, which is however surmounted not by the Roman eagle but by the company's logo of the pelican stabbing its own breast to feed its young; the usual Roman inscription SPQR is wittily replaced by the company's acronym, PLIC. In his other hand the soldier holds out the laurel wreath of victory to the ladies running towards him, the one in the lead apparently pushing the other back: does this imply that insured orphan girls will have greater success in the race of life than those unendowed with a policy? Behind the Roman is a sacrificial altar, its legs ornamented with entwined snakes, and a cuirass, and to the left is a draped male figure; the triangular design is maintained by a thumb-sucking, torch-bearing cherub (perhaps an invitation to start endowing one so young), and by a graceful seated male on the far right. Beside him is a real emblem of mortality, a skull surmounted by an hourglass.[41]

Lady Di's reputation at the very end of the century was sufficient to merit her inclusion in a verse polemic, *The Unsex'd Females*, published in 1798 and written by a reactionary vicar, Richard Polwhele, as an attack upon Mary Wollstonecraft. Polwhele blamed her advocacy of women's liberation and self-expression for causing revolution and a decline in religious faith. His long poem listed other dangerously free women, among whom were artists – the over-sensual Angelica Kauffmann and Emma Crewe – and the actress Mary Robinson (ex-mistress of the Prince of Wales and also of Fox). However, he also mentions women of whose activities he approved: the Blue-stockings, the writers Anna Seward, Mrs Radcliffe and Fanny Burney and an acceptable artist, Lady Di. His couplet might have helped to boost sales of *Leonora*: '. . . if Beauclerk paint Leonora's spectre horse, The uplifted lance of death, the grisly corse . . .'[42]

This late flowering of commercial success and artistic recognition coincided with a period of revived private happiness. In 1796, Mary Beauclerk re-entered her mother's life. There was no mention of the four incestuous grandsons – two had perhaps already died, the other two (known to be in America by the early nineteenth century) may have been sent or even taken there by George Bolingbroke, who moved to the States with his bigamous child-bride and newest illegitimate child in the same year. Mary remained in Germany but, freed of encumbrances, had evidently renewed contact with her family and had thus met and married Francis, or Franz, the second Count Jenison-Walworth, whose sister Susan was already married to Mary's poet cousin, William Robert Spencer. Franz clearly charmed Lady Di, as he had captivated Mary; but he was always short of money, always trying to pull strings to find an appropriate appointment. He may have been as mistaken as his sister Susan in the assumption that marrying a Spencer would mean influential contacts and automatic prosperity. In 1796, Mary and Franz were married in Heidelberg, then came to England on their wedding tour. They stayed in Richmond with Lady Di: she had forgiven Mary, received them warmly and made them part of her life again.

After their return to Heidelberg, Lady Di began a regular correspondence with her daughter and son-in-law. More than forty of her letters to them survive (although none of their replies), dating from 1797 to 1808, in which she paints a picture of the last decade of her life, set against the distant background of the turbulent years of Britain's war with France, and, at times, most of Europe. There were invasion threats, victories and defeats, temporary peace, the apparently unstoppable rise of Napoleon, inflationary price increases and increasing taxation. Despite her own growing poverty and declining health, these years were lit up for her by the company of her granddaughter, the eldest child of Mary and Franz, whom they left in England after their second visit in 1798, when the baby was just a few months old. Their departure was hard to bear – 'I have not yet left off expecting you to walk into the room, and I still look into the meadow often expecting to see the Count and the dogs coming home' (July 1798). But they never came back, and the baby, Caroline Mary, became Lady Di's sole responsibility, providing a new lease of life although also a considerable responsibility for a single ageing woman. Mary Beauclerk never attempted to visit or to reclaim this child, although she went on to have other children with Franz. Perhaps, given her earlier traumatic experiences of motherhood, there was some dreadful failure to bond with this first legally permitted baby; and she may even have been relieved by the loss of her incestuous sons. From the way Lady Di writes about her adored charge, there is no suggestion that she is ever going to be handed back – the arrangement was clearly a permanent one.[43]

Lady Di acknowledged her daughter's problem: 'I wish to God you knew her: you will one time or other love her, when you have her and study her'. But Mary never reached this stage; she and her husband never returned to England, although visits were sometimes suggested, perhaps just to keep Lady Di happy. The ultimate fate of the little girl was of constant concern to Lady Di, and at one stage she beseeched the Count for 'a promise from you. . . . if I do not see you and Mary before my death, you will give me your honour to come yourselves to fetch my little Mary whenever you may wish to have her – not send a servant for her' (memories surfacing of George Selwyn's anguish when he had to make arrangements to return Mie-Mie to her parents in France). Whatever the Count may have promised, they had no intention of reclaiming their daughter. They assuaged their consciences by sending little gifts and drawings of the next child, although apparently no money; they wrote occasionally but months often passed without any word, and Lady Di did not always know where they were.

Mary Beauclerk had an income of her own – one of the reasons why the Count was prepared to marry a woman with such a terrible past – as a result of George Bolingbroke's settlement on her when he left her for Isabella. Lady Di reminded her in December 1802 that '£400 a year is settled upon you entirely in your own power and that you have £3000 of your own in ready money, so that your annual income will be between £500 and 600 a year – besides the 3000, you are therefore perfectly independent'. With this amount of capital and income, Mary could easily have afforded to contribute to her child's upbringing or come to her own mother's assistance. But she was also subsidizing the Count's search for lucrative employment, in which Lady Di was sometimes involved. If there had been something in England, he might taken it up: at one stage, she urged them to come and live with her, mentally reorganizing the rooms in her house so as to make space for them. Increasing fragility, however, produced a shift in attitude, and when it seemed that Mary was intending a visit, she was flung into a panic – she needed a whole floor for herself, the only spare room was damp, another bedroom was reserved for her grand-nephew, there would be no space for Mary's new baby. But 'if when the Count is placed and richer, you and he would come and take a few lodging rooms near me, I should be delighted' (October 1801). Given this tepid response, it was no wonder that Mary did not make the visit. One reason for the long exile was the fact that Franz himself, although English-born, can have felt little sense of belonging since most of his life had been spent in Germany. And the wars and shifting European alliances were hardly conducive to normal travel, financial stability or employment prospects.

But Lady Di did try to use what little influence she had to help, for example writing in August 1800: 'It is impossible for me to find out how far the great person dislikes you ... I have employed different people but there is no getting at the truth'. She even tried to call upon William Hamilton to bring his influence to bear, but 'not having received any answer, I could not begin another request; however Mr Trevor will speak to Lord Nelson, I believe' (December 1800). By December 1801, Franz had found what seemed like a suitable appointment, as Chamberlain and Privy Councillor at the Court of Wurtemberg, but continued to press for something better, with an unrealistic determination that things might be easier in England. In 1806, she was forced to tell to Mary: 'they say if you understood the thing you would see the impossibility of what the Count and you ask, the nature of our Government makes the difficulty and always has'. Their situation was then so bad that Mary had even been suggesting that the Count's brother-in-law William Spencer be approached to help them out, another completely wild request: 'As for the Spencers sending anything to their sister, that is also out of the question as they have not one single shilling except what I believe is lent him' (August 1806). In the autumn of 1806, Mary and Franz were in Lisbon.

But the main factor in Mary's long exile was her personal history. The letters imply that although the Spencer family was prepared to accept the company of little Mary, who did see her aunt, uncles and cousins, the presence of her mother in England remained problematic. In 1802 Lady Di sounded hopeful that her son's and her daughter's crimes were being forgiven, if not forgotten: 'I think people are a little softening, my sister and Lord P. quite adore Mary'. But George, Viscount Bolingbroke also chose to stay away from Britain for many years, apart from a secluded year in Wales in 1795, when his Isabella gave birth to the first of many children. They then moved to America, living not entirely successfully incognito until they were able lawfully to marry following Charlotte's death. Lady Bess Foster's son Augustus, then serving in Washington, wrote to his mother from New Jersey in

1805 of 'Lord Bolingbroke, who lives a mile off under the name of Mr Bellasyse and the German lady his wife, now declared so and married over again to him . . . she is anything but handsome, a little square German with broken teeth, but they say very amiable . . . he flatters himself that he is not known here . . . he is disgusted with the manners of the people of this country, ragamuffins and adventurers that flock here from all parts of Europe, and particularly the Irish'. George, Isabella and their nine children returned to England in 1806. His long absence had pained Lady Di, who had also managed to find forgiveness in her heart for him. She refers to him in a letter to the Count, who clearly knew the whole story of his wife's former disastrous liaison: 'What you say about my poor G. is exactly truth. His is the noblest mind spoilt by an entire giving way to passions, but the fond remains. I had a letter from him last summer that made me cry for a week, it was so full of real affection for me – poor soul! The lady has not such a mind, with all her virtues' (January 1801). And she tried to remain in contact with George, writing after Charlotte's death how 'receiving a few lines from you has been a great comfort to me, and now I hope to have a much greater, that of seeing you, as I understand you *must* come to England now . . . how dreadfully you must have suffered in the horrible climate you mention, come away as fast as you can' (January 1804).[44]

When they did return, George went to see his mother, who reported to Mary: 'I have seen G. and Lady B.; she is not a beauty but seems pleasing' (August 1806). By the end of that year 'G. and Lady B are living at Lydiard, the people round them are very civil and visit them – in this part of the world it is very different'. If this remained the attitude to George, no wonder that Mary could never return.

Despite domestic stability, George remained haunted by his past, as reported two years later by Harriet, Lady Bessborough, during a visit to Perthshire in 1808:

My second adventure . . . might really figure very tolerably in a novel. We went to the Falls of Moness. While Lord B was drawing, W and I scrambled up the rock; I sat to rest on a stone while he went on to explore. After a little while I was startled by hearing my name. I look'd up and saw a man I did not know standing by me (the noise of the water had hinder'd my hearing him come). He again repeated my name and said 'have time and misfortune so compleatly altered me that you can find no trace to recollect me by?' . . . I stared at him and growing quite frightened got up, thinking he was mad; but he took hold of my hand, and said 'look at me again'. I did so, and his *Spencer* face and Moving (more than any thing else) made me recollect him: it was Lord Bolingbroke. I never saw any creature so agitated, but yet neither his long banishment, his crimes and sufferings, seem to have subdued the violence of his Character'.

As Harriet (no stranger to romantic drama in her own life) defined it, this was not merely from a novel but from the most Gothic of tales, with wild mountainous scenery and rushing waters, all perfectly complemented by a remorseful madman of genteel birth.[45]

Although often cheerfully emphasizing that she does not want to write dull or depressing letters ('I have not written for some time having been so very unwell and to write dismal letters is very bad', November 1803; 'my letters must be very insipid for I live so entirely out of the world that it is by mere chance if I hear of any event till a month after it happens', June 1802), Lady Di makes many references to her health over the years. One previous ailment, defined as 'gallstone colic', had been relieved by a practitioner at Bath; according to Walpole, writing to another sufferer in 1795, 'she was so thoroughly cured that . . . she has not felt the smallest return of her disorder since'. Now she described a range of ailments – general disorders such as headaches and bilious fits, which she recognized as being caused by her nerves. But there were also attacks of depression triggered by her sense of isolation during the winters in Richmond, when rural charm was replaced by damp, cold and the sight of the flooded river awash over Petersham meadows: 'Here I am as if in the main Ocean – a flood as far as one can see – boats coming over the railing at their ease' (January 1799). She always felt better in the summer, and consequently increasingly came to dread the winter months. The only alleviation was a few weeks in London, following the pattern of the old Season, but paying the extra rent was always a problem. Yet she contradictorily dreaded company and longed to be alone, writing for example in one letter, which urges Mary and Franz to come and stay with her, but to keep a separate house in which to entertain their friends and family: 'my health and spirits would not bear people coming . . . I rather dread a lonely winter here'. If wanting to live alone was a natural result of having had to live with two incompatible husbands, it was worse to feel abandoned. And there was a general sense of failure; when Mary named her second daughter Diana, this provoked the comment: 'I should like to see my little namesake, but it is not a lucky name' (June 1799).

The particular physical complaints were a general weakness, affecting her eyes and hands, and something more specific, described as a 'spasm' – 'My sister has sent a note to ask to come. I have put her off, having (in reality) a sad spasm, and indeed seeing her would increase it' (1798); 'my spasms, as they call them, are worse than ever before perhaps; if we ever have summer, they may be better' (July 1802). The only effective remedy was a too familiar and high-risk solution: 'my health has been so bad, such frequent Spasms, and then I can do nothing but groan and take Laudanum' (March 1802). But unlike Topham, and perhaps because of her intimate knowledge of how he was affected by his addiction, she was well aware, in a perfectly detached way, of the side effects upon her: 'Having a little Laudanum in my writing makes it swim, so adieu my dear Mary' (January 1800); 'You must not expect me to write often or much, my dear Mary, my health is very bad and I am old and my hands shake from taking Laudanum perhaps, but this cannot be helped' (August 1802); 'I have again thrown the ink all about, my hands are so trembly and the ink so thin' (April 1805); 'I have been so long silent because my health has been so very bad that I am bound to take Laudanum every other day almost and this confuses one's head too much to write or do anything' (November 1805). A swimming mind and a shaking hand were a small price to pay for the relief of pain, and sometimes depression too – Anne Damer, for example, recorded the drug's efficacy: 'my spirits were depressed and my head grew confused. I took a few drops of laudanum, possibly without necessity, and slept quietly'.[46]

Teeth were another source of self-mockery: 'You would laugh were you to see what a horrid old Mumper I am – lost every tooth in my upper jaw that it had, the last pull'd out because they were loose' (June 1799). Two years later, 'old as I am, I look a good deal older, thin, yellow and one solitary tooth left . . . indeed you never saw such a monster as I am'. This was a slight exaggeration, for in the spring of 1802, 'there will soon be an end to my eating, for I have only four teeth left and these I must have pulled out to-morrow, they ache so. I am exactly the figure of Old Mother Shipton'.

For an artist, weak eyes, the wearing of spectacles, and shaking hands were a cause for despair – although she claimed that writing letters was more fatiguing to the eyes than drawing. But, even incapacitated, other areas of design were possible, and she was stimulated by the Count's request for her to plan a garden for him, although it was 'a commission that drives me almost mad, because I am incapable of performing it at present. I suppose the part shad'd in the plan means higher ground, is the house in the middle to be an ornamented one or a useful one? I never saw a vineyard. All these things I must know before I myself can attempt anything. What are those cross-lines through the whole? and what is the little thing in the fence so? If I can get at any good garden designer I will – my part even when these questions are answer'd must wait till I am well enough to see or hold a pencil' (March 1797). She also responded to Mary's request for ideas about room decoration: 'I wonder whether Mary received some sketches for painting a room? They are very bad and coarse, only an idea and indeed so are these pictures. I have been too ill to draw tolerably. I am rather better at present' (February 1799). And she sent them drawings of their daughter: 'this is the most like her common face, tho' not half so handsome' (February 1799); 'I cannot draw my dear little Mary because nobody can draw ten thousand countenances in one face, and this is her beauty' (December 1800).

Another project was a piece of three-dimensional design in the form of a fountain for her nephew the Marquess of Blandford, at White-knights Park, Reading. Relations between the profligate heir and the Duke of Marlborough were not good, but his father had bought the estate for him in 1798. Blandford was as obsessed with collecting exotic plants (on which he would spend up to £500 each) as his father had been for antique gems, and it has been estimated that the garden cost him £40–50,000. The Duke of Wellington, visiting one January, was struck by the fact that the profusion of evergreens made it look like summer. The whole property was described and illustrated in a detailed account made in 1820, which praised the botanical collections and formal garden, Gothick chapel, rustic bridge and various bowers and groves, including a secluded lawn enclosed by a hexagonal trellis fence, whose centrepiece was Lady Di's fountain. This might have been inspired by her memories of an exotic shell seat in the gardens at Strawberry Hill, for the fountain's summit was a shell supported by dolphins, from which water poured into the basin below. A lower tier was supported by more dolphins and lizards drinking from shells, while tall conches and pillars of naturally coloured rocks jutted up out of the water in the bowl; the overall effect is Gaudi rather than the Piazza Navona, and the feeling baroque rather than classical.[47]

This was all unpaid art for the family. But in June 1800, feeling more vigorous, as usual, in the summer months, she announced: 'I have taken to drawing again, and am happy to find that everybody thinks I draw better, and this proceeds from growing old and being more patient of course'. Her motivation however was not just genteel pleasure; maturity and patience could also be harnessed to help her keep out of debt. Six months later, her efforts had paid off: 'I have drawn a good deal – and had I not, I should be in the King's Bench'. She echoes this in the New Year of 1801: 'As yet I have fed myself by my drawings, but when my eyes fail I must put on rags and beg at Blenheim'. And when the pain returned, her first reaction was fear of the loss of earnings: 'my drawing is and has been for some time at an end, it hurts me to apply, and this is a bad thing for my pocket' (October 1801). She also spoke bitterly of the middlemen she had to deal with, when her drawings were sold to be engraved – 'truly the print sellers are such greedy rogues'. By March 1802, 'there is an end of my drawing, my hands shake', and she recognizes the loss of it as an activity to ward off loneliness as well as to make money: 'I have lost all power of drawing, which will be a sad thing for me through a long winter' (June 1802). But she had still not given up hope, and, four years later, in the kinder summer months of 1806, announced 'I have begun again to try my eyes and my shaking hands in drawing'.

Her daughter also practised art, and now sent drawings of the namesake Diana – 'I am delighted with your drawings . . . little Di is beautiful . . . I ought perhaps not to add that she is exactly like a picture of myself done about a century ago, only handsomer as my eyes were grey' (January 1803). Mary also sent 'the most beautiful landscape I ever saw in water-colours' as a present for uncle Robert Spencer and asked her mother's help to organize having some of her own drawings engraved in order to try and earn some money by selling them.[48]

The sarcastic reference to begging at Blenheim showed how Lady Di resented the difference in attitude between her mean rich brother George and her generous poor brother Robert. She regarded the Duchess of Marlborough as worse than the Duke: 'they really are become callous to all (but themselves), when I say they, I mean particularly the female' (July 1802). When referring to the dire economic situation following the likely resumption of war in 1803, 'I am poverty myself and so is everybody I believe, except a few great people and they keep all snug to themselves' (January 1803). But there is no other mention of any contact with them, a couple who could have shared a little of their great wealth and luxury. The gulf between them is stressed by her exclamation marks when Betty Pembroke and little Mary were staying in London in 1806: 'My sister carried her one day to Marlbro' House on a visit! Only think of that!!'

More evidence of the Marlboroughs' cold behaviour emerged with regard to the marriage of their daughter Lady Charlotte Spencer. Charlotte had been very grudgingly permitted to marry beneath her perceived station, to the Revd Edward Nares, who had been at Oxford with Lord Henry Spencer, the Duke's younger son. Nares visited Blenheim a number of times, originally to take part in the theatrical performances that the younger members of the family engaged in. Unkind reports commented on the poor audibility and static nature of some of the performers, but putting on plays was a popular activity in the country house, cunningly subverting the rules of rank and conduct (so well described by Jane Austen in *Mansfield Park*). Disguised in their costumes and make-up, Charlotte and Nares had fallen in love. The Duke and Duchess at first refused their consent to such an unsuitable match but eventually gave in; however they took revenge by cutting Charlotte off with a mere £400 a year and banning Nares for ever from Blenheim. Other members of the family were more sympathetic, including Lady Di, who had more experience than most of breaking out of a tight little circle. Nares' memoirs record how, in the spring of 1797, 'accident had thrown us, without previous knowledge, into the neighbourhood, not only of many of the nobility, but of some very nearly related to the Marlborough family . . . Lady Diana Beauclerk, the Duke of Marlborough's eldest sister, invited us to her house at Richmond'. This would not have pleased her brother. She was aware of Charlotte's distress at her parents' behaviour: 'Poor thing, I feel her parents' hardheartedness helped to break her heart' (July 1802). When Charlotte died following childbirth in January 1802, there was a belated reconciliation between Nares and the Marlboroughs, and Charlotte was buried in the family vault. Nares recalled that 'Lady Blandford wrote to me and expressed an earnest solicitude about my children. I had similar letters from Lady Diana Beauclerk and the Countess Dowager of Pembroke'.[49]

Lady Di told Mary of her cousin's death and the Marlboroughs' insensitivity: 'poor thing, the story is too horrid to write. Her husband behaved with the utmost affection during her illness (others not so!);

there are sad cold hearts about the world!' and mentioned to the Count 'the horrid behaviour of those who ought to have loved her'. Nares' subsequent distinguished career, from curate and theologian to Regius Professor of Modern History at Oxford, was interspersed by a curious interlude in which he wrote anonymously a humorous novella *Thinks I to Myself*, which became a bestseller and was read by the royal family, among many other fans. It earned him over £1,000, a vast sum for an author by the standards of the time, and it was still being reprinted as late as 1836.

Robert Spencer was Diana's favourite brother. Nicknamed 'Comical' Spencer, he remained an intimate friend and close political ally of Charles James Fox – Robert's epitaph read 'He lived the friend of Fox' – and he was at the centre of the Whig circle in the 1790s. Another close friend was Richard Brinsley Sheridan (whose sister Betsy recorded in August 1788 how, when Sheridan's coach was unable to pick up Betsy and their gravely ill father, he used Lord Robert Spencer's instead). Bob was an addicted gambler, like the rest, so committed that his former tutor, now turned Archbishop of Canterbury, had tried to persuade him to give up, without success. A series of financial disasters had culminated in bankruptcy in 1781, from which he had recovered by setting up as banker running his own private game within Brooks's Club; with the massive profits, he had been able to buy a country house, Woolbeding, near Midhurst in Sussex.

Harriott Bouverie still remained officially with her husband, but had given birth to a daughter who was the 'tell-tale Bouverie . . . there never was such a perfect indisputable Spencer, Lord Robert's walking picture', according to Lady Louisa Stuart. The child was named Diana. Lady Di described Bob as 'the real guardian of all the family' and the one she saw most often; he helped her out with money, when he could afford it. ('Were it not for my brother Bob I should be in a very disagreeable situation', January 1801). She maintained a friendly relationship with Mrs Bouverie too, and was pleased with 'Mrs B's' comparison between her own daughter Di and little Mary. Robert and Harriott came to her rescue in 1804, after she 'had passed 7 or 8 months in misery from bad health and spirits . . . when I dread another winter here alone' by insisting that she and Mary spend the autumn and winter with them at Woolbeding. This was a great success; her first letter reported: 'they are all so good to us that I have not been so happy for some years . . . I am much better and Mary is . . . mad with spirits and with happiness'. For the lonely child, brought up by servants and her 'poor dear old Granny' in a damp house overlooking only river meadows, it must have been a revelation to be with company: 'Di Bouverie has taken Mary quite under her protection and they do scamper about all over the place incessantly'. And there were lots of new cousins to meet: 'The Spencers are here, William at present in a gracious humour . . . is enchanted with her', as well as Robert's political friends – 'many men very superior in their understanding have been here, and each has declared they never saw a child with so clear a head and with such fine animal spirits joined to it'. Her next letter continued the theme: 'being with all the people I love has made me much better, and perhaps finding they are all so pleased with Mary may have done my health good as it has made me happier . . . I feel so happy and contented here that I dread going back to my own solitary house' (November 1804).

It was through Robert that she retained some sense of participating in the outside world: 'Thank God we now have a little glimmering hope of peace. Mr Pitt being gone, Charles Fox and all my friends are coming in, I believe. When I say all my friends, I only mean Charles Fox and my brother Robert, for I know few of the others by sight – but they are reckoned to possess all the abilities of the kingdom' (February 1806). The 'Ministry of all the Talents', headed by Fox, even included Robert Spencer as Surveyor-General of Woods and Forests, at last earning a regular salary. This new influential role for the Spencers, combined with the current peace negotiations, meant that Count Franz again sought his frail mother-in-law's assistance in finding him a place in England: he sent her a plea to forward to Fox's secretary, but she replied: 'I cannot give any hopes at present for never anything equalled the numerous requests and the hurry people seem to be in to get places' (February 1806). She mentioned the start of Fox's fatal illness in August 1806: 'I fear his complaint will be a lasting one in some degree, at least if he continues working so hard day and night'. Two months later he was dead. She took this hard – a man of such charm and gregariousness, her brother's friend, and her friend for so long, fifteen years younger than herself – and was for a time so devastated that little Mary, aged eight, had to become the correspondent to the mother she did not know: 'Dear Mama, Grandmama has been so unwell since the death of Mr Fox that she has been unable to write but she is better now. We wish there was any chance of peace that we might see you, Papa and my sister. Grandmama says she has not heard from you this long time. Dear Mama, I am your dutyfull daughter, C. M. Jenison'. Lady Di added a PS to this: 'The funeral is over. The whole Park of St James crowded as well as the streets and from high and low not a dry eye! They say there never was so moving a sight and if anything can be call'd a consolation for such loss, it was the exultation his friends felt to see the real grief of millions. I was sadly afraid it would have overset my brother Robert but I saw him since and he looks well in health' (October 1806).

She now saw very little of her brother Charles, long separated from his wife. He had been a Member of Parliament for some years, obtaining office in the beginning of the century when he served as Postmaster-General, then Master of the Mint, retiring in 1804 with a pension of £1,000 per annum. She was more frequently in touch with his son William Robert, reporting rather sarcastically 'I had the honour of a visit from W.S.' and telling his brother- and sister-in-law of his social successes – his 'employment now is to govern the P[rince] of W[ales]; Lady J[ersey] all in love with him . . . I never saw Mrs Spencer half so well or stout' (February 1799). By 1801, Susan Spencer had managed to enter the Duke of Devonshire's orbit – 'Your sister is still at Chatsworth, and William also'.

Her sister Betty Pembroke was looking after the little Herberts, the surviving children of Elizabeth Beauclerk. Lady Di did not see so much of these grandchildren and described in an almost detached way how Betty had spent nearly a year at Plymouth, providing sea air for 'the two poor remaining children. It is too dreadful to have them die off so' (January 1800). However, as Lady Di's pain decreased her mobility, Betty came to the rescue of the isolated little Mary and brought her into the company of her older cousin: 'my sister doats upon her and this will be of the greatest advantage to her when she is a few years older, and her cousin Lady Di Herbert loves her beyond description – you must see that these are the two happiest things that can happen to her there' (November 1805). By 1806, when 'I am just able to crawl down to my garden and sit there . . . I never go to London . . . my sister takes Mary for a day or two there, I cannot spare her any longer' (June 1806). Granddaughter Di was spotted by Farington in 1804: 'At one-o-clock went in the chaise to a public Breakfast . . . several young people and children danced – the first dance was led off by a beautiful girl, Lady Diana Herbert, daughter of Lord Pembroke, who, with her brother Lord Herbert was there with their grand-mother the Dowager Countess of Pembroke'. This was the sort of social life that Lady Di knew her sister could provide so much better than she could.[50]

Her son Charles Beauclerk remained a close friend of the third Lord Holland, although he had not made such a good impression on the Dowager Lady Holland: 'I am told that he is remarkably sensible, good humoured and pleasing for those that know him, but this must be taken on trust . . . I understand that I am odious to him; je me venge [I get my revenge] in feeling as much against him as he possibly can towards me'. However, Lady Holland claimed responsibility for making the match between Charles and Lord Holland's first cousin Emily (known as Mimi) Ogilvie. Mimi was the daughter of Emily Lennox, now Dowager Duchess of Leinster, and her second husband William Ogilvie, former tutor to some of Emily's twenty children by her first husband the Duke, and the Duchess's twenty-second and last child. The marriage between the dowager and the tutor had upset the Richmond and Fox families; this match between two young people with the slightly tainted names of Beauclerk and Ogilvie was therefore appropriate – given their backgrounds, they would not do much better. Lady Di did not attend the wedding, but wrote to Mary that 'Charles is at this moment marrying, I believe, at the Dss of Leinsters . . . I have seen her [Mimi] twice and her manner is really delightful and interest-ing, I don't think her so very handsome, tall and of a good figure, and in short a very fine-looking woman. Charles is wild with spirits, and I hear Ld Holland jumps about the room for joy – she is his cousin, you know, and he looks upon her like a sister' (April 1799).[51]

Lady Bessborough, who always admired Charles more than Lady Holland did, inspected the young couple and confirmed Charles' re-served nature:

Beau looked very handsome today and was so amiable I am half in love with him. She pale but very pretty; but she begins to complain a little of the excessive retirement and solitude they live in (these are all secrets, pray observe), and she wanted Lady Holland and me to persuade Beau to stay. This I declined. Lady H said she would try, but I am sure any attempt of this sort will completely fail and only make him imagine there is a plot against him. Poor fellow, with the most generous, best heart in the world, he is not formed to make himself or those that he loves happy![52]

After a visit to them in 1800, Lady Holland confirmed his wife's sense of isolation (especially considering her crowded and cosmopolitan childhood).

Beauclerk did not articulate ten words; he seems happy but it is the bliss of torpor . . . one should think his precept was that conversation spoilt society, he rarely incurs that risk. It is to be regretted, as he has a most acute perception, and an uncommon degree of subtlety in his argument. No person is clearer on the obscure subject of abstract metaphysics; his definitions are ingenious and brilliant. Finance is also a branch of the political economy he is profound in, and had he entered Parliament, he would have distinguished himself. At present he is lost; shyness, indolence and a sort of content, deprive society of his exertions and his friends of his company.

Ten years later, in 1811, she had seen no change: 'Mr B more silent and Mrs B more blooming than ever.'[53]

Like the rest of his family, Charles was spending beyond his income and eating into his capital. In December 1802, he bought a country estate in Sussex, where he intended to have a new house built. After less than three years of marriage, his family was expanding rapidly: 'a fourth child is arriving – sad work! – her mother had 21 – tremble at that!' (December 1802). And the new property was 'not yet begun, not even the foundation, so he has taken a small house near to overlook his workmen. He is half-ruined by this purchase, as this detestable war will make him lose 6 or 7000 pounds in drawing out his money from the funds' (January 1803). Things got worse; by the time a sixth child was due ('she is constantly in that state'), because of the costs of farming his new land, he found he could not afford to build a new house after all and had to continue living in the small rented property for another year or two. He did feel a sense of responsibility for his mother, as she became increasingly frail: 'Charles says he will make me come to him when his new house is ready, alas! he must then take some years off my age!' (December 1806). A year later she referred to his occasional visits, when he can afford it, but 'he has just built a house and has eight children'. At this rate, having given birth to eight living children in eight and a half years of marriage, Mimi Ogilvie was on track to beat her own mother's record. The prospect of living in the remote countryside with a silent son, a fecund daughter-in-law and eight very young children was not attractive to someone who suffered from nerves and needed her own space.

The grandchild who far exceeded the rest was little Mary Jenison-Walworth. Over the ten years of the letters, it is touching to see Lady Di's adoration of her granddaughter develop from the earliest almost dutiful comments ('Your little girl is quite well', July 1798). From 'the little girl', there is a shift to the possessive 'my little girl'. By April 1799, 'I am actually in love with this child'. There are endless accounts of little Mary's intelligence, humour, sweet nature, pretty looks and ways; she becomes the chief topic of the letters and the focus of Lady Di's life: 'I am more afraid of dying since I had her' . . . 'the only thing that keeps me alive'. The pleasures were immeasurable, but so was the anxiety: 'little Mary has been innoculated and is now intensely well again . . . I tried to write to you and the Count without mentioning a word but I thought too much about it to be able to write upon anything else so I would not write at all' (February 1799). Inoculation against the dreaded disease of smallpox had been practised for the last fifty years, but could itself prove equally fatal: the far safer use of cow-pox rather than infected human material was being pioneered by Edward Jenner in 1796.

Despite 'the bad moments when I consider what will become of my little angel when I die. I have nothing to leave her' (August 1799), she revels in the child's activities, and provides a wonderful record of her development from babyhood – the delay in teething, the changes in her appearance: 'she has but one slight fault in her face, her nose is rather too small in proportion, but this will certainly alter . . . she has a good right to Nose on both sides of her family' (December 1800). As the child grew older, there were new needs and worries: 'I wish I was rich enough to give her Masters or healthy enough to teach her the little I know' (December 1801). By the next April, some money had been found: 'I have just got a master to teach her to write, as I am incapable, and she has got a dancing master, a cheap one but good enough at present just to put her in good posture'. Mary was then aged barely four but already 'reads as well as I do and has a rage for it; she reads and understands everything correctly'. The prodigious child was soon writing fluent notes to her parents and little sister Di. At five, 'she grows like her grand-father . . . she bewitches everybody' (January 1803). Despite her mother's independent income, little Mary's education remained the charge of Lady Di: 'You must not expect what is called an accomplish'd Miss. I cannot afford the fine Masters. She is learning of a very good Musician here the grounds of

music, and a little dancing from a middling sort of dancing master . . .
I cannot give 2 guineas a lesson for dancing, or 3 guineas for music
. . . I have a Frenchwoman with her whom I like but she costs me 20
guineas a year' (September 1805). As a result of this expenditure, she
was 'too poor to go to Woolbeding this year'. The sacrifices were
worth it; there is not a letter which does not include a rapturous
account of little Mary's charm, intelligence and wonderful behaviour
– attributes which contrast with all that is known of her mother – and
she is the yardstick by which the responses of friends and family are
measured. Her presence made more bearable the last painful years of
Lady Di's life – 'she is the most pleasing creature possible and
everybody likes her – to me she is everything, my life depends upon
her' (November 1805); 'the comfort of my life – she has fine animal
spirits, thank God, and more sense and good feelings than anybody'
(August 1806).

Writing about Mary brought out Lady Di's sense of humour too,
despite the pain and money worries. One letter enthuses about 'the
most intelligent little thing you ever saw and the most beautiful – I
wish you could see her running about stark naked'; then there is a
hasty postscript: 'I don't mean that she is always naked'. This evident
intelligence meant that Lady Di was not too worried at her delay in
beginning to talk: 'she speaks but a few words' however 'her Gibberish
is very fluent' (June 1800). In the next year, she laughs at herself
endlessly praising Mary – 'all this you will place to the account of my
dotage'.

As well as being the guardian of her granddaughter, Lady Di was
also for a time responsible for her grandson Robert, called 'Little Bob',
the son of Frederick St John. As he was not really welcome at home
during the school holidays by his frequently breeding stepmother,
Lady Di warmly added him to the Richmond household, as if trying
to compensate her second son for her own abandonment of him when
a schoolboy: 'I have been in distress about Little Bob who I hear has
the whooping cough at school . . . the next holidays I must contrive
something' (June 1799, when it was so cold that she noted 'a fire in
my room'). Two months later he has joined her and Mary, although
at some cost and inconvenience: 'Poor little Bob is just arrived here:
you cannot think how they neglect him. I fear I shall not be able to go
to Woolbeding or Money Hill [Charles' house] as I cannot take two
children about, the journeys would be too expensive and I cannot

leave them certainly'. She felt unable to have him over the next Christmas holidays because of 'having no man to keep him in order. I was too unwell myself to undertake it as he is now a great riotous schoolboy but with the best heart possible' (January 1800). In April 1800, Frederick, his wife and younger children set off for his new posting at Madras, with the intention of staying four or five years and making his fortune as a nabob; en route they had a terrible experience when their ship caught fire and they lost all their possessions. 'Little Bob is left to my care and his Uncle Robert's . . . I am very incapable of the charge, as I grow old and infirm and cannot bear the least exertion, and a schoolboy is a violent undertaking in so small a house and family as mine'. This action by Frederick again suggests the rather selfish confidence her children placed in her, disregarding her fragility and lack of funds – unless, by comparison, they felt that their own situations were even worse. However, the boy was like a brother for little Mary: 'Little Bob is now here and she is so fond of him! and he of her, you have no idea of it.' By 1802, she had heard that 'his father is making a great deal of money' but Frederick's wife was clearly determined that it should not be shared with her mother-in-law or stepson – 'in her letters she says the contrary, the first is the fact I believe' (April 1802). Bob was now being educated privately: 'I see him only six weeks in the year as he is educating near Northampton, a clergyman who takes in only two or three boys, and his improvement is great' (August 1802). He then went on to Harrow: 'Little Bob is just come for his holidays looking very well and really an amiable boy . . . Mary tags about him all day' (June 1803). Frederick and family returned in 1805. He had not made his fortune but remained 'the same open-hearted good soul as ever . . . one of the best-hearted creatures breathing'. His son was now made welcome at his own home for the holidays: 'Fred is delighted with little Bob – poor Mary is very sorry to lose him' (September 1805).

Lady Di's frailty and sense of isolation (as well as shortage of money) contributed to her withdrawal from the Richmond social round. A void was created by the death of the oldest and most loyal friend, Horace Walpole, in March 1797: 'poor Lord Orford is dead and I have lost a real friend in him'. More recent local residents with whom she was on visiting terms included the Austrian Ambassador and his wife, M. and Mme Starhemberg, 'the best natured people I ever met'. Count Starhemberg, delicately appreciating her poverty, assisted with her postal expenses through receiving and sending letters for her, and also did his bit in passing on information about possible positions for Franz. There was also Lady Buckinghamshire (sometimes nicknamed Mme Blubber), one of the Devonshire House circle of ladies, who lived at Marble Hill, which she had inherited through her husband's aunt, Lady Suffolk. Her reputation was somewhat tainted by the bad publicity generated by the notorious private gambling club she had run at her London home (where Harriet Bessborough had recently been arrested, a scapegoat for all ladies who gambled). Sher received a more qualified welcome: 'I am reduced to Lady B. who is a good natured creature – but—'. It was this lady whose advice Lady Di sought when Mary had asked her impractical mother how to run a dairy: 'Lady B. says when you make butter it must be with two broad wooden things (something like the Cymbals) . . . she says she has lately discovered that it should not have salt put in it or be washed – only squeezed over and over again to get the Buttermilk – there – I am sure I am very good to write all this – I am astonished at my own patience!' (December 1798). She had clearly never played at being a dairymaid. Lady Buckinghamshire was occasionally entrusted with the care of little Mary, as when Bob was suddenly sent home from school with scarlet fever.[54]

Another local friend was a second cousin, Mrs Trevor, with whom she visited to Brighton in the summer of 1798 for therapeutic 'warm sea-bathing', ungratefully commenting that she would prefer to have been alone: 'Here I am in a dark, dismal, stinking House. Mrs T. likes it, but I shall try for a small lodging for myself. This will be better in every respect, for I find its impossible to live with anybody (except you) . . . it is impossible to say how tired I am of being married!' Otherwise the holiday was a success: 'The Steyne . . . is really a beautiful sight, millions of *Beauties* walking around and the Regimental Band playing in the middle of it every evening. I have just been in the Tepid Bath. This moment' (August 1798).

But a very few years later she was deliberately avoiding the company even of these familiars: 'the Starhembergs are acting plays here, very well too they say. I go nowhere or I would have gone there. I like her extremely' (1803). Poverty, as much as attacks of nerves and depression, was a very real factor; visiting other households was an expensive activity, since all the servants lined up in the hall, each expecting a compulsory tip from the guest. But she was still prepared to receive people in her own house: 'I see my old friends, when they are in Town they come here' ... 'I had the real pleasure of a visit from Charles Fox the other day, who looks well and comfortable. He admired Mary very much, thought her like you' (October 1801). There was also a meeting with a very old acquaintance and local resident, Mrs Garrick, in 1804. Nor had William Hamilton entirely forgotten her; he wrote her in February 1802 'a very civil and indeed friendly letter ... still abroad but means soon to come here'. A useful new friend in Richmond was 'Mr Clark, an old man with the most benevolent heart and clear head possible', whom she managed to charm into letting little Mary be taught French by his family's governess (June 1802). A year later, he was 'a remarkable sensible man, grave, old, and has nieces of his own that he don't seem to love half so well as Mary'.

The occasional fees for her work made little impression on the overall problem of what she described as 'that nasty thing, money'. In March 1797, 'we are so poor here! I have not means to pay for a letter even', and there was constant difficulty in paying rates and bills: 'the Assess taxes are even more than last year and however to pay them, God only knows ... two years bills to Mr Dundas just paid, £50!!' (February 1799). The war with the French had a disastrous impact on inflation. By 1800: 'so you think living is cheap in England! Alas! Everybody except the enormous estates like my brother Marlborough, Duke of Bedford etc are ruined. My income will not pay half the establishment of my small family ... every article is raised to three times what it was when you were last in England, and our great men (as you call them) don't care a straw about it! ... my brother Bob has sold his house in town and very ill, and his pictures, very ill! we are all in a bad way as to money, as well as you' (August 1800). When the preliminaries to peace were announced, there was a joyous comment at the head of her letter: 'Peace is agreed! Peace! Peace! Fireworks, illuminations, guns without end day and night' (October 1801). But this was too late to help her own dire situation, especially when the extra income from drawing had dried up: when she heard that the Count might be about to get a place, she joked that she needed one herself: 'I should not be sorry myself to have one for I am forced now to live like a poor beggar (as I am) to get back into a tolerable situation. I cannot bear the idea of begging again or leaving debts behind me' (October 1801). She had been helped out on one particularly bad occasion by Charles Beau-clerk – 'I am obliged to be eternally thinking about money, afraid of every shilling, for were I to get into the same scrape that Charles relieved me of, I should really abhor myself' (April 1802). But Charles' expanding family and domestic expenses meant that she could no longer rely on him to bail her out. She also enjoyed another job fantasy: 'I think now I am so poor it would be a good thing for me to keep a day school' (October 1802).

The dream of escaping to London for the winter months was always hindered by the reality of her poverty: 'it would be better for me to go for the next two months to London, I know, but I cannot by any means afford it' (December 1801). Yet there was the same ambivalence about facing company – 'I almost dread going to Town, though I want to be among my few friends for a short time'. She did manage to find some money that winter, by selling off family treasures, the dwindling remains of the fine furniture and possessions which had attracted crowds to Muswell Hill, and so impressed Boswell at the Adelphi, and managed to afford six weeks in London. Her self-diagnosis was correct for 'I have been better since I came to Town than in the country this nasty weather – but I must go back as I am at the fag end of my money' (February 1802). She planned the same the following year: 'If I can sell some more old candlesticks (as I did last year) I will go to town for two months, as it is too cold for me here all winter' (October 1802). But not enough could be raised: 'I am too poor to go to town, though perished and blown away here'. 'I wish I could afford a lodging in Town for the months of February and March, for I fear this place will half kill me at that time, but this is out of the question unless I can borrow a house, for never will I borrow any more money' (December 1802). This must refer to the scrape with the money-lenders from which Charles had rescued her. The following summer, she was again hoping 'to go to Town this winter, which perhaps I may, for I am sometimes too low-spirited here and quite alone'. There was a visit in the New Year of 1805, but in the next year she was again 'dreading the damp of this place during the winter' but now feeling incapable, through pain, of moving anywhere else, despite an invitation from her brother to Woolbeding. As well as its damp and remoteness, she now felt that Richmond lacked the facilities of London in every way, especially in the crucial topic of little Mary's education as a lady: 'next Spring, if I am alive, I will carry her to London to have her get a good dancing master' (August 1806).

She would have travelled further too, in the false peace in 1802, when 'people will all be running to Paris instead of passing their summers here or in watering places'. Later that year, 'all the world have been at Paris, if I was twenty years younger and somewhat richer, I should have gone also'. But the resumption of hostilities with France put an end to such jaunts, and imposed further financial strains: 'this odious War will prevent our meeting, I fear, and utterly ruin me among many others' (June 1803).

One miraculous solution to her poverty would have been a win on the state lottery, in which Lady Di and her opportunist son-in-law placed their hopes. Run by the government at least once a year in order to fund particular projects (such as the building of Westminster Bridge or the setting up of the British Museum) or simply to provide revenue, there had been a change in the type of prizes during the century, sensible annuities being replaced by more desirable lump sums. Participants in the lottery raffle received one portion of a ticket, some numbered, some blank; if numbered, the other portion (rolled up and tied with string) was drawn from a rotating drum, secured by seven locks, transported by a massive, horse-drawn vehicle. The cost of a ticket was high – in 1797, £13 – but £500,000 was distributed in prize money, with three top prizes of £20,000, and the lowest £17. The government made over £250,000 and twenty thousand people received prizes. Lady Di bought a ticket on behalf of herself and the Count – 'I hope he got my letter with the No. of the Lottery – 7:50,671, and that I am to have one third' (March 1797). Their number did not come up. They tried again the next year, when the tickets cost £11 15s. and there were rather fewer prizes, but with even less luck: 'Oh dear! I am sorry to tell you the Lottery ticket is – a Blank! there are nothing but Blanks (or worse) in the world I believe' (August 1798).

The servant problem was both created by and caused further lack of money. She had a small household of five or six staff but seemed not to be in control. There was a turnover of the women looking after little Mary, a Mrs Wright, then a Mrs Murray, who was soon 'gone from me, thank heavens – she grew too ill natured and too bad in many respects'. To make things worse, 'I find I have kept not only Mr Por: but his two brothers – sad work! No wonder I am so poor' (June

1799). This upheaval produced a new nurse and a new maid, with little Mary 'quite adored by all the servants, it is a continual romp'. In June 1801, she was content: 'her nurse is a treasure, the best servant I ever saw and must never be parted from Mary I think – indeed she does half the work of the house'. But by 1805, the often-mentioned dampness of the house was causing disruption: 'the servants' rooms were so damp nobody can live in them and I am forc'd to give up my rooms below to them . . . some are driven into the Garetts, the rest into the best spare bedchamber'. This was not all: 'in two days I am to go through the worry of having all my servants changed, except my own old H. Mary is having a French maid'. She was evidently being forced to sack the whole household, and mentions 'the sad work of turning away people I am quite afraid of' (April 1805).

In the final year of her life, she described herself as 'not able to stir out at all', although still loyally visited by Bob Spencer and Charles Beauclerk, and she managed to write only two letters. The very last includes a bitter epitaph on herself. Commenting on Charles' situation, she adds: 'alas! I feel I was but an ignorant Guardian – nothing more painful. I know nothing (nor ever did) about Money!' (December 1807). This was being unfair to herself. She had been a wonderful guardian to little Mary (and, when needed, to Little Bob), providing these grandchildren with the emotional support which had been less freely given to her own children. As to money, the Spencers were always reckless, but she had managed to turn her own skills and reputation into a marketable activity which at least helped to pay some of the bills.

Unlike Sarah Churchill, she had little to leave in her will, and this was one reason for her despair, particularly in respect of little Mary's future. Like Sarah's, Lady Di's will was modified by codicils, expressing afterthoughts and anxieties about the future. But the spirit of the two documents could not be more different, for hers showed all the love she felt for her family and friends without the desire to control them. The will was written in 1806, with Robert and Charles appointed as executors. She left 'whatever effects I happen to have in my possession' to Charles, apart from a number of bequests, including mementoes to Mrs Bouverie – 'the small alabaster Venus under a glass' – and to Mrs William Spencer – 'the large blue china vase' – and more china to Betty Pembroke. To Charles James Fox, she had left the Reynolds portrait of Robert Spencer, but a subsequent codicil after Fox's own death gave it to Charles Beauclerk. Little Mary was obviously not going to be reclaimed by her parents, since 'my son Charles and Mrs Beauclerk have been kind enough to promise to take care of my Dear little Girl (and by this promise have made my last moments less terrible)'. Another codicil provided that if she had any money left, this should be used on Mary's behalf by 'whoever is kind enough to take charge of her'. To her daughter she left her books, apart from those already belonging to little Mary – 'she has many books now in her own property'. To Frederick St John, 'the portrait of my father in regimentals'. There was no bequest to George, Viscount Bolingbroke or his wife. Bob Spencer would receive 'all the green-house plants' and 'two marble statues and pedestals'. Little Mary was left the piano and the music books, as well as 'the two new Globes that I bought for her', an important part of her education in geography. The final codicil, dated May 1808, left all her clothing to Nurse Egerton (just as Topham's will had left his clothes to the servant who had cared for him at the end), and to little Mary 'the silver tumbler I generally drink out of' together with two beds and 'all my painting apparatus and drawing paper' in case they might be 'of use to those who keep her'. This crucial part of her life was the very last thing she recorded.

She died three months later, on 1 August 1808. Robert and Charles arranged for her to be buried in Richmond parish church, where the parish register simply records her death at the age of seventy-three. No inscribed monument survives in the church itself, and in the graveyard, now truncated to a tranquil, overgrown oasis surrounded by suburban traffic jams, the lettering on those gravestones still remaining has completely weathered away.

Epilogue

The Gentleman's Magazine for 1808 decided that Lady Di was worth a brief obituary. This described her only in relation to her family and husbands; she was the 'relict of Topham Beauclerk, sister of the Duke of Marlborough and the Dowager Countess of Pembroke ... first married to Frederick St John, Viscount Bolingbroke, from whom she was divorced in 1768'. The writer then expanded on Topham, 'well known for his intimacy with Dr Johnson, Edmund Burke and other men of learning and genius'. But there was no recognition of Lady Di as an artist or individual – court lady, witty hostess to those men of learning and genius, the admired friend of Walpole, Wedgwood's popular designer, talented book illustrator, painter of botanical murals and family portraits.

Just as the facts of her existence have been eroded from any gravestone, so her artistic reputation rapidly dissolved in the nineteenth century: the contents of Strawberry Hill were sold at auction in 1842 and Walpole's treasured collection was dispersed in a sale that lasted for thirty-two days. From Lady Di's works, the Gypsies watercolour sold for £6 10s, one of the wax sculptures for £1 0s 6d and the other for £2, and the *Mysterious Mother* drawings for thirteen guineas. Others vanished without trace, as the products of the eighteenth century, let alone works by a non-professional woman working mainly within the decorative media, became deeply unfashionable. Some restitution began when she was included in Elizabeth Ellet's pioneering study *Women Artists in All Ages and Countries* (1859), a book which made a significant contribution towards the wider debates of the 1850s and '60s about the status of women generally; it recognized

Lady Di's 'elegant and fertile imagination, with a truly classic taste' in her drawings for the *Mysterious Mother*, *Leonora* and Dryden's *Fables*. This was followed by a mention in Ellen Clayton's *English Female Artists* (1876), and she then became the subject of Beatrice Stuart Erskine's major study, *Lady Diana Beauclerk, her Life and Work*, published in 1903. This was a richly illustrated work in the anecdotal style of contemporary writings about the eighteenth century, which presents her as a 'brilliant and accomplished woman' whose work was now entirely neglected. The book included a list of works known to Mrs Erskine in 1903; some of these have now disappeared from their cited locations. Mrs Erskine also published an article in *The Connoisseur* (1903), describing in more detail the contents of an album of Lady Di's drawings and watercolours then kept at Woolbeding, the former home of Bob Spencer, where a number of her drawings and paintings were also displayed.

It was perhaps as a result of this study that subsequent references to her art continue to be moderated by rank, by gender and by the nineteenth-century perceptions of 'amateur'. Richard Sée, *English Pastels 1750–1830* (1911), regarded her style as 'a trifle loose.... drawing grievously at fault.... a little mannered'. For Hugh Stokes, in *The Devonshire House Circle* (1917), she was 'a woman of gifts, but her work was always strongly derivative', dependent upon Fragonard, Cosway, and Reynolds, yet he also cited her as a forerunner of Morland, Stothard and their followers. Iolo Williams' judgement was harsh; his *Early English Water-colours* (1952) describes her Gypsies, so loved by Walpole, as 'pretentious and vapid', and he sourly comments on 'how small a part women have played in the development of watercolour in England ... their total contribution seems curiously unimpressive'. Adrian Bury, in an article in *The Antique Collector* (1958), stressed her aristocratic background, resulting in an untrained style that was 'adequate to her gentle, refined and felicitous muse'. Martin Hardie, in *Water-colour Painting in Britain* (1966), defined her as 'an English amateur of birth and distinction', and said: 'her facile and expressive draughtsmanship, obviously based on Italian models and encouraged by her friendship with Reynolds, brought force and charm into her drawings ... her pictures rely on drawing and decorative design and she rarely fails as a designer'. Germaine Greer's *The Obstacle Race* (1979) grouped her with other lady amateurs whose works represent the emergence of the leisured class in the eighteenth century, and stressed the variety of her work, citing the combination of pastel portraiture, book illustration and mural decoration.

By the end of the twentieth century, Lady Di had become subject to two different sorts of interpretation. On the one hand, she still figured in the brief biographical format, originating in the old *Dictionary of National Biography* entry, which emphasized the fact that she remarried two days after her divorce; this is still being repeated, as in the article about her in *The Dictionary of Women Artists* (1997). But she had also been set in the wider context of later eighteenth-century art practice, as defined by Kim Sloan's '*A Noble Art*': *Amateur Artists and Drawing Masters* (2000); as one of a galaxy of neglected talents, she could be seen helping to play a part in the undermining of the stereotyped views of 'amateur' and 'professional', and even between the work of 'ladies' and 'gentlemen'.

And her works do well at auction; she has become collectable again. The revival was inaugurated by Wilmarth Sheldon Lewis in the 1920s, as just one element in his life work, the collection and study of the works of Horace Walpole and his circle. Through a combination of dedicated research, dogged perseverance, luck, and a generous chequebook, Lewis' acquisitions included the 'lost' Beauclerk Cabinet and six of the *Mysterious Mother* drawings. In *Rescuing Horace Walpole* (1978), he included both these items in a 'Desert Island Discs' selection of his very favourite things. A number of her works came on the market in the early 1970s following the sale of the contents of Woolbeding, which included an album of her drawings, her portrait of Fox, the pastel of her son George with Selwyn's pug Raton, and several other framed works. The album was acquired by the Gerald Norman Gallery, its contents were separated and sold as a total of sixty-three separate lots in 1971. These continue to change hands through the auction houses, as do other drawings and paintings and the Bartolozzi and Bovi engravings of her works. At the time of writing, her work is on public display only at Blenheim and at Lydiard House, in these family contexts of childhood and first marriage, which so defined the course of her life, and which still apparently determine the reception of her art.

Viewing her works now, from the perspective of the twenty-first century, we have learned that the question, 'Why have there been no great women artists?' is an ironical and irrelevant one. What women artists produced was entirely affected by society's perceptions and needs, in which the role of wife and mother was supreme. For Lady Di, art training and practice were initially the standard accomplishments expected of one of her class, both before and after marriage, and her own talents were not necessarily greater than those of many of her dedicated and industrious contemporaries. However, she retained a very serious commitment throughout her life, and her style had its distinctive features as well as being impressive in its versatility. Her subject matter – the wide-eyed nymphs and children, the exuberant, playful fauns and cherubs, the bold choice of literary illustrations and empathetic interpretation of the texts – contains both drama and humour. In her application of techniques, with her confident line, delicate application of colour and wash, and bold handling of pastels, as well as wax modelling and provision of motifs for Wedgwood's jasper ware, she shows great confidence and understanding of the varied media involved; the flower murals are still full of impact for their formal properties of colour and design as well as for their botanical accuracy. She was able to change and develop, mirroring the shifts in taste from the 1760s to the end of the century, moving from light-hearted neo-classicism to Gothick Romanticism as her own life veered between happiness and sorrow, love and loss.

But it was her private life and family background which contributed to her reputation as an artist in her own day, as they still do now. These were factors from which she could never fully escape. Trying to assert her own will and live how she wanted, by finding the passionate courage to leave Bully for Topham, and later by turning her absorption in art into a means of paying the bills, resulted in the continuing attention of society. Her second unhappy marriage was seen by some to be a just retribution for her abandonment of the first one, reinforced by the later scandal of her children's incestuous relationship. Yet it was the public knowledge of these personal affairs, the result of her having chosen to flout convention, that positively enhanced the demand for her art, ensuring the popularity of her Wedgwood products, the book illustration commissions and the constant sales of her prints. Disentangling her private life from her work is ultimately impossible.

After Lady Di's death, little Mary remained unclaimed and unwanted by her parents. It was Betty Pembroke, not Charles and Mimi Beauclerk, who became responsible for her, despite Lady Di's intentions. Betty enlarged and continued to live in The Molecatcher's in Richmond Park, with Mary. After Betty's death in 1831, Mary moved to Germany where she finally resumed contact with her mother on the latter's deathbed. The descendants of her Jenison-Walworth half-siblings appreciated the family connection enough to have Lady Di's letters to her daughter and son-in-law privately printed, and the family owned some of her works. One of Lady Di's Jenison-Walworth great-great-granddaughters, Ellen Sommer, became a distinguished medieval theologian, and was a Research Fellow at Newnham College, Cambridge, from 1929 to 1932; the College's obituary refers to her sense of fun, her striking red hair, and the warmth and openness of her personality. Another descendant was the fin-de-siècle artist Charlotta Jenison-Walworth.

Charles and Mimi Beauclerk went to live in Italy, where the 'blooming' Mrs Beauclerk was a noted hostess in Pisa and Florence during the 1820s. She was a friend of Caroline, Princess of Wales, and knew Shelley and Byron. Mimi died in 1832, and Charles in 1846. One of their seven surviving daughters became a close friend of Mary Shelley (who was also a friend of the widow of one of George Bolingbroke's sons) and various cosmopolitan Beauclerks are mentioned in Mary Shelley's letters.

Elizabeth Beauclerk's daughter Diana Herbert married the Earl of Normanton in 1816; Lawrence's portrait of her was exhibited in the Royal Academy in 1827.

Bob Spencer and Harriott eventually married after the death of Mr Bouverie, in 1811. Their daughter, Diana Bouverie, inherited Woolbeding on Bob's death in 1831.

Betty's son, the Earl of Pembroke, married, as his second wife, Catherine Woronzow in 1808. They had four children, and he died in 1827.

George Bolingbroke did not manage Lydiard effectively, and after his death in 1824 neither his son nor his grandson could halt the decline; many parts of the estate had to be rented out and in the early twentieth century it was broken up and sold. Swindon Corporation bought the virtually derelict house in 1943, together with 147 acres of the parkland, for £4,500, and a loving programme of repair, restoration and refurnishing was begun, as a result of which many of the original contents and fittings have been reinstated. In 1955 the house and park were first opened to the public. The refurbishment continues, including what is now named the 'Lady Diana Spencer' room, Lady Di's former dressing room with the stained-glass window; here can be seen some of her botanical murals, the pastel of George learning to write, a watercolour of children with baskets of grapes, and some prints of her work, together with a copy of the Reynolds portrait of her as artist.

Notes

ONE *The Dowager and the Duke*

1 Wharncliffe I 107.
2 Toynbee 1924 87.
3 King 1930 xi; Toynbee 1924 75;
   Halsband 1967 134.
4 For these and the following citations of
   Sarah's correspondence, see Harris,
   1991.
5 Thomson 1943 51–2.
6 Ibid. 52.
7 See Rowse chapter 1, for a fuller account
   of Charles' upbringing and time abroad.
8 Holland 1822 I 483; Rowse 20.
9 King 1930 296.
10 Toynbee 1924 75.
11 Ilchester 1950 59: 9 September 1730.
12 Ibid. 87: 12 September 1731; 92: 25
   September 1731.
13 Ibid. 80: 26 August 1731; 98: 1
   October 1731.
14 Ibid. 120: 7 December 1731.
15 Ibid. 294: 1 March 1733.
16 BL Add. MSS 61446 f.2: May 1732.
17 Ilchester 1950 135: 9 May 1732.
18 Toynbee 1924 89.
19 Sarah's letters to Diana are published in
   Thomson 1943 from which this and
   subsequent extracts are taken.
20 Ilchester 1950 288: 14 July 1732.
21 Ibid. 289: 23 November 1732.

22 BL Add. MSS 61447 f. 145.
23 Ilchester 1950 180: 19 November 1733.
24 Lippincott 1983 113.
25 Ilchester 1950 212: 2 November 1734.

TWO *The Duke's Daughter*

1 Lady Di's date of birth has been
   conventionally given as 24 March 1734.
   According to the old style Julian
   calendar, in which the New Year began
   on 25 March, 24 March was the last
   day of the Old Year. However, by the
   1730s, 1 January was being increasingly
   regarded as the defining date and the
   period 1 January to 24 March can
   therefore be described, during this
   period of overlapping usage, as
   belonging to both years, expressed as
   1734/35. However, as her mother was
   pregnant in the autumn of 1734, it is
   more logical to ascribe the birth to the
   spring of 1735; for the Duchess of
   Bedford's correspondence, see Massey
   1999 213, 215.
2 Thomson 1943 168: 16 August 1735.
3 Delany 1861–2 I 545. A map of
   Windsor Castle and Park, engraved by
   J. Roque in 1738, is dedicated to the
   Duke and mentions 'une des maisons et
   jardins du Duc de Marlborough'.

4 Hertford 1805 49.

5 Delany 1861–2 II 107.

6 The 38th Foot is now part of The Staffordshire Regiment (The Prince of Wales's).Toynbee 1924 143; BL Add. MSS 61451 f. 149: 31 March 1738.

7 Toynbee 1924 89.

8 Delany 1861–2 II 228; Hertford 1805 7: 9–1738; Rathbone 1899 90: 26 July 1751.

9 The painting hangs at Ickworth, Suffolk. See Laing 1995 62 for full discussion.

10 See BL Add. MSS 61666, 61667 for Charles' letters to Elizabeth.

11 Delany 1861–2 II 228; BL Althorp D49: 26 November 1743.

12 See Burford 1986, citing Goadby's *Nocturnal Revels*. Johnny is loosely disguised as the Hon. Jack Spindle.

13 Halsband 1967 254.

14 Sarah's will was published as *A True Copy of the Last Will and Testament of Her Grace Sarah, Late Duchess Dowager of Marlborough* (1744).

15 *An Inventory of the Pictures at Blenheim and Marlborough House*, signed by Sarah on 20 December 1740, BL Add. MSS 61473.

16 Halsband 1967 211; Greig 1926 4: 18 September 1752; Aspinall-Oglander 1940 114: 26 September 1748; HW 9 289: 19 July 1760.

17 Ilchester 1928 81.

18 Fitzgerald 1949 273.

19 Walpole 1822 I 483.

20 BL Add. MSS 61678 for the Blenheim accounts.

21 Rouquet 1755 119.

22 For the boys' letters, see Herbert 1939.

23 Delany 1861–2 IV 268: 9 June 1770; Delany 1861–2 II I 412 refers to a school in London in the 1750s run by Mrs Holt, a 'gentlewoman', which took twenty pupils, including titled ones.

24 See Thomson 1940 for the Bedford accounts.

25 Halsband 1967 22; 40; 83.

26 Halsband 1973 262.

27 Halsband 1967 24.

28 Greig 1922 311: 13 August 1801.

29 Harcourt III 280; see Roberts 1987 for royal practice.

30 Delany 1861–2 II I 246; 293; 473; 621.

31 Ibid. 209; 545.

32 Ibid. 356; 544; 469.

33 Ibid. 207.

34 See Whitley 1938 II for George III's training, Sloan 1997 for men's training generally; and Sloan 2000 for drawing masters; Turnbull cited in Solkin 1993 220; Delany 1861–2 III 179.

35 Vlieghe 1987 no. 141. The painting was sold in 1885 and is now in the Metropolitan Museum, New York. See Logan 1986 for Lens and the Marlboroughs, and Ribeiro 1984 for the significance of Rubens/Van Dyck fancy dress.

36 Coke 1889–96 II 306.

37 Foreman 1998 4 on John Spencer's fortune; Halsband 1967 51; Delany 1861–2 II 28.

38 HMC *Hastings* 86: 18 May 1754; 89: 13 December 1754. The 3rd Guards are now the Scots Guards.

39 Ibid. 105: 10 October 1755; 110: 21 October 1755.

40 Harcourt III 67; Fitzgerald 1949 14: 12 May 1755; HMC *Hastings* 96: 26 May 1755; Harcourt III 72.

41 HMC *Hastings* 117: 25 May 1756.

THREE *The Viscountess*

1 Delany 1861–2 II I 465: 5 September 1757 for the proposal. Hollingsworth 1965 suggests that peers' daughters of Lady Di's generation might delay marriage because of the shortage of suitors of equivalent rank. His claim that twenty-five was the median age for marriage has been challenged by Cannon 1984 on the basis of inadequate sampling methods.

2 HW 37 499: 1757 (n.d.); 30 137: 6 September 1757.

3 BL Add. MSS 34196.

4 *Gentleman's Magazine* 1787 407.

5 Chesterfield quoted by Carne 1988 19–20, who provides the most thorough

account of Frederick, plus a detailed list of his porcelain and silver purchases. I am most grateful to Peter Collier for calculating the value of the *louis d'or* at this period.

6 Lewis 1928 12; Home 1899 81, 85.

7 *Town and Country Magazine* IV, March 1772, 121–5; Burford 1986 175 for Charlotte Hayes' career.

8 Ilchester 1915 44: May 1750; 53: December 1750.

9 HMC *Hastings* 117: 25 May 1756.

10 Fitzgerald 1949 49: 17 June 1757.

11 The bills are included in BL Add. MSS 61678; Rathbone 1899 158: 14 April 1755.

12 Ibid. 134: 31 January 1754.

13 Sieveking 1930 1912 78. Mrs Giberne's son was an unreliable secretary to Horace Mann in Florence, and she would later seek Horace Walpole's advice about his future career.

14 Stirling 1956 50, 52.

15 See Dasent 1895 for a history of the Square.

16 Ilchester 1915 112.

17 See BL Add. MSS 61667 for the Duke's 1758 campaign letters.

18 Cokayne 1912 499; Halsband 1967 192; HW 9 259: 27 November 1758.

19 Fitzgerald 1949 273: 12 February 1760.

20 Ibid. 277: 6 March 1760; 281: 8 April 1760.

21 Ibid. 272: 31 January 1760; 299: 29 October 1760.

22 HW 20 338: 20 October 1751; Jesse 1883–4 I 173: HW 9 307: 14 October 1760.

23 Jesse 1883–4 II 84; Thomson 1940 282.

24 See Jacob 1988 for full account.

25 Cited by Egerton 1984 84.

26 Ibid.

27 Home 1899 90; see Black 1891 for the history of the club.

28 See Cannon 1984 72 on Northumberland's status; Greig 1926 160: 27 September 1771; Rouquet 1755 58. For discussion of Stubbs' achievement, see Deuchar 1988, Egerton 1984, Parker 1984.

29 Kerr 1909 78; Jesse 1883–4 I 305.

30 BL Add. MSS 61666 f. 131, 135 for the two letters.

31 Sedgwick 1939 120.

32 Porter 1985 9 has pointed out the disadvantages which William Hunter overcame – the younger son of a humble man, the wrong country, the wrong religion, the wrong university, initially the wrong subject; McLaren 1984 13 on John Hunter; John's collection of 3,500 specimens can be seen in the Hunterian Museum in the Royal College of Surgeons of England in Lincoln's Inn Fields.

33 See McLaren 1984 for the conflicting eighteenth-century approaches; Boswell 1936: 16 May 1763.

34 Brock 1983; Porter 1985 8; see Stark 1908 for the detailed record of Hunter's obstetrical approach.

35 HW 38 45: 1 November 1764. Miss Lloyd's career is a fascinating example of the opportunities open to those with no fortune; after Kensington she worked for the Fitzroys, with whom she travelled to Paris and spent a year from 1766 to 1767. During this time, she obtained entrée to Mme du Deffand's salon, and joined the household of Lady Di's sister, Lady Pembroke, during her stay in Paris.

FOUR *The Lady in Waiting*

1 Ilchester 1915 100: 7 April 1761.

2 Greig 1926 27; HW 9 377: 10 July 1761; HW 38 96: 14 July 1761.

3 Hedley 1975 136.

4 This letter is in the Earl of Bute's papers at the Mount Stuart Trust Archive, Isle of Bute.

5 Barrett 1904–5 IV 47: 26 July 1788; II 421: 3 August 1786.

6 Howard 1824 291.

7 Greig 1926 97.

8 HMC *Various* VIII 178: 8 August 1761; McKendrick et al. 1982 81.

9 HW 38 116: 9 September 1761; Greig 1926 29.

10 Broughton 1887 I 9; Stokes 1917 60.
11 Greig 1926 31.
12 Thomson 1943 104.
13 Stokes 1917 60.
14 Greig 1926 33, 34.
15 HW 38 121: 25 September 1761; 127: 27 September 1761; 143: 28 November 1761.
16 Fitzgerald 1949 102: 15 August 1761.
17 HW 9 387: 24 September 1761; Greig 1926 36; Buck 1979, citing Bocage; Rouquet 1755 48; see HW 10 237 on Lady Fortrose 'at the point of death, killed, like Lady Coventry and others, by white lead, of which nothing could break her'; see Williams 1957 on history of cosmetics.
18 *Gentleman's Magazine* 78 (1808) 1068 for an account of the visit to the Barclays.
19 Broughton 1887 I 2. Mrs Papendiek was the daughter of Charlotte's page, Frederick Albert.
20 Ibid. 17; Fitzgerald 1949 58; Barrett 1904–5 II–IV for Fanny Burney's court diaries.
21 Farrer 1903–6 II 33: 8 July 1771.
22 Harcourt 1871–2 44.
23 Barrett 1904–5 II 314.
24 Blunt 1923 181.
25 Sedgwick 1939 125: 26 July 1762.
26 Home 1899 24.
27 Barrett 1904–5 II 473; 363.
28 Ibid. 351; 469.
29 HW 20 28 August 1764; Home 1899 114; Broughton 1887 I 33; Ilchester 1901 178.
30 HW 38 143: 28 November 1761; Sedgwick 1939 71: 28 November 1761.
31 Fitzgerald 1949 17: 15 May 1757; Hyde 1972 37: 4 August 1770.
32 Greig 1926 43: 23 May 1762; 111: 16 May 1770.
33 Ibid. 47; Stark 1908 for Hunter's diary.
34 Greig 1926 50: 8 September 1762.
35 HW 22 104: 30 November 1762; Ilchester 1901 129: 24 December 1762; Fitzgerald 1949 359: 22 January 1763.
36 HW 10 14: 22 February 1762; 22 16: 25 February 1762.

37 HW 10 16: 25 February 1762.
38 Fitzgerald 1949 318: 27 February 1762.
39 Ibid. 321: 9 March 1762.
40 Blunt 1923 16.
41 HW 22 16: 22 March 62; 24: 13 April 1762
42 HW 22 24: 16 April 1762.
43 Herbert 1939 34: 18 September 1762.
44 HW 10 52: 25 March 1763.
45 Fitzgerald 1949 112: 5 September 1761; 318: 27 February 1762.
46 Ibid. 319: 27 February 1762.
47 Ibid. 337: 18 August 1762; Blunt 1923 30.
48 See Fowler 1989 for the Duke's refurbishment of Blenheim; Sedgwick 1939 168: 27 November 62.
49 See Carne 1988 for details of Bully's financial problems and attempts at solution.
50 HW 22 148: 5 June 1763.

FIVE *The Amateur*

1 See Bennett 1992.
2 See Cormack 1968–70, and Leslie & Taylor 1865, for Reynolds' practice; Mannings 2000 80.
3 HW 10 52: 25 March 1763. Nelly's portrait is in the Wallace Collection.
4 Rouquet 1755 40; Lady Burlington, cited by Mannings 1977 285.
5 HW 22 105: 30 November 1762; Meteyard 1865 II 78: March 1768. The vase in the portrait was inspired by the ewer designed by Jaques Stella and illustrated in his 1667 *Livre de Vases* – see Clifford 1978. It would be recreated by Wedgwood out of Staffordshire clay in 1770.
6 Broadley and Melville 1913 54.
7 Greig 1926 94.
8 This portrait was sold at auction by Dreweatt Neate, of Donnington, Berkshire, on 5 April 2000.
9 See Roberts 1987 for a full account of the industrious royals.
10 See Ellet 1859 for a pioneering account of women artists, Whitley 1938 and Greer 1979, chapter 14, on the privileged amateurs. Alexander 1983 19

suggests that Lady Di had also learned to etch.

11 Krill 1987 64.

12 See Clarke 1981 for a general history of watercolours.

13 Greig 1922: 1 August 1800.

14 Whitley 1938 249.

15 Herbert 1939 60, 74.

16 See Whitley 1938 for these and other success stories.

SIX *The Adulteress*

1 Ilchester 1915 160.

2 Jesse 1883–4 I 225.

3 Ibid. 316, 345.

4 Ilchester 1901 114: 16 December 1764.

5 Jesse 1883–4 I 401.

6 Ilchester 1915 245: 21 July 1765.

7 Ibid. 241: 19 July 1765.

8 Ibid. 240: 7 August 1765.

9 Society of Antiquaries of London MS 444/18/22, 23: 31 August 1765, 11 September 1765.

10 Jesse 1883–4 I 413–15: 28 October 1765.

11 HW 14 141: 12 November 1765.

12 Ilchester 1901 182–83: 9 January 1766.

13 King 1930 328; see Adamson and Dewar 1974 for the Beauclerk family history.

14 These various anecdotes are recorded in Boswell's *Life of Samuel Johnson*.

15 Ingrams 1984 14.

16 Hardy 1812 209.

17 Chapman 1952 I 142: 20 July 1762; 146: 21 December 1762; see Ingamells 1997 for English visitors to Italy; Jesse 1883–4 II 126.

18 See Hawkins 1822 and Welby 1940 for accounts of the Club.

19 The visit was originally described by Dr John Sharp in the *Gentleman's Magazine* for 1785; see also Basker 1996 on Johnson in Cambridge.

20 Jesse 1883–4 I 251: 1 July 1763; Kerr 1909 189.

21 Jesse 1883–4 I 358.

22 Earl of Townshend, cited by Draper 1963 5; HW 10 14: 22 February 1762.

23 Coke 1889–96 III xviii.

24 Erskine 1903a 55.

25 Jesse 1883–4 I 350; HW 31 68: 4 November 1765.

26 The evidence from which the following account of the events of 1765 to 1768 is drawn was first published in 1779 in *Trials for Adultery, or the History of Divorce*, reprinted Trumbach 1985 (B).

27 See Hecht 1956 on servants, and Murray 1998 chapter 4 for calculations of the cost of keeping horses.

28 See Johnson 1952 for the history of Berkeley Square.

29 See Cruickshank & Burton 1990 on the practicalities of living in eighteenth-century London.

30 HMC *Carlisle* 270: 1774; Lefanu 1960 53–5: 12 June 1785.

31 Coke 1889–96 I 57: 22 September 1766.

32 Ilchester 1915 261: 24 July 1766; Jesse 1883–4 II 57: October 1766.

33 Ibid. 84.

34 Ibid. 86: 21 November 1766; 68: 4 November 1766.

35 Fitzgerald 1949 467: 29 September 1766.

36 Jesse 1883–4 II 113: December 1766.

37 Coke 1889–96 II 95: 9 November 1766; Rousseau 162: 9 December 1766.

38 Brooke 1956 259.

39 Jesse 1883–4 II 109: 1766; Ibid.33: 1766.

40 Ibid. 110: 16 December 1766.

41 Ibid. 118: December 1766.

42 Ibid. 170: 1767; 309: 21 June 1768.

43 Ilchester 1901 195: 8 May 1766; Jesse 1883–4 II 42. This may have been William Pitt's sister Anne, a former Maid of Honour to Queen Caroline, celebrated for her witty tongue; but Lady Louisa Stuart, in her comments on Jesse's edition of Selwyn's letters, suggests that it was more likely to be Anne's sister Betty, 'in her day a much more famous person and more likely to have Macaroni friends'.

44 Coke 1889–96 II: 2 January 1767.

45 Cited by Stone 1993 507.
46 McLaren 1984 74; for the use of condoms in the eighteenth century, see Burford 1986 144.
47 McLaren 1984 127; 95.
48 See Matossian 1989.
49 Cunnington 1951 111.
50 See Gloag 1990 325; the bed's covered-wagon type of canopy was designed to hinge or be removed (Lady Coventry managed to take her tent-bed on honeymoon). Chippendale provided six different designs in his 1762 *Directory*.
51 Ilchester 1915 280: 28 August 1767; 281: 5 September 1767.
52 Coke 1889–96 II 126.
53 HW 18 185: 3 March 1743. For separation and divorce procedure at this time, see Stone 1990 and 1993.
54 Stone 1993 12 has calculated that, in the middle of the eighteenth century, only 0.1% of marriages ended in court-approved separation or divorce; see Wagner 1982 127 on the Grosvenor divorce.
55 HW 30 250: 16 October 1767.
56 Coke 1889–96 II 148: 27 October 1767.
57 BL Add. MSS 61674 f. 56.
58 Coke 1889–96 II 158; 160: 27 November 1767.
59 Greig 1932 II 173: 20 November 1767.
60 HW 22 567: 2 December 1767.
61 Jesse 1883–4 II 208: 10 December 1767; ibid. 211: 23 December 1767; HMC *Carlisle* 225: 29 December 1767.
62 Cited Stone 1993 54.
63 Blunt 1923 291: 31 October 1775.
64 Coke 1889–96 II 164: 11 December 1767.
65 HMC *Carlisle* 222: 11 December 1767.
66 Ibid. 228: 12 January 1768.
67 Greig 1926 97.
68 HMC *Carlisle* 226: 5 January 1768; HW 35 344: 25 August 1771; see Burford 1986 126 for the *List of Covent Garden Ladies*, and Bleackley 1909 152 on the confusion between Jones and Kennedy.
69 HMC *Carlisle* 230: 17 January 1768;

Jesse 1883–4 II 246: 27 January 1768; Coke 1889–96 II 186: 8 February 1768.
70 HMC *Carlisle* 236: 2 February 1768; ibid. 239: 17 February 1768.
71 The proceedings were reported in the *Journal of the House of Lords* for 1768.
72 Coke 1889–96 II 201: 27 February 1768; Stone 1990 285. Such a Bill was introduced in 1779 by the Bishop of Landaff, and passed by the Lords but rejected by the Commons, swayed by the advocacy of Charles James Fox; see Jesse 1883–4 IV 145: 18 May 1779. Attitudes to divorce in the 1770s and '80s continued to put the main blame on the woman: for example, Fanny Burney records in 1786 a discussion about the wife of Warren Hastings, who had been divorced from her first husband in Germany in 1777. This was thought by the company to be shocking, until Fanny pointed out that in Germany the remarriage of a divorced person did not imply a scandalous history since divorce was only permitted as a result of irreconcilable differences and not from adultery; but in England, every divorced woman could be assumed an adulteress, since divorce could only result from her misconduct, Barrett 1904–5 II 442.
73 Jesse 1883–4 II 321: 26 August 1768.
74 Coke 1889–96 II 211: 13 March 1768.
75 Jesse 1883–4 II 275: 3–1768; Bleackley 1909 152.
76 Coke 1889–96 II 214: 15 March 1768; Jesse 1883–4 II 275, 280: 3–1768; Bleackley 1909 106.
77 HW 39 104: 9 August 1768.
78 Balderston 1951 332: July 1778.
79 Coke 1889–96 II 204: 1 March 1768; ibid. 430: 20 December 1768.
80 Greig 1922 44; Jesse 1883–4 II 358; Coke 1889–96 III 18 February 1769.

SEVEN *The 'Femme du Monde'*

1 Collison-Morley 1909 148; see also Robinson 1992 on Reynolds' image of Baretti.

2 Hardy 1812 327: 5 July 1773; see also HMC *Charlemont* I 316–19.

3 See Evans 1956 for a history of the Society of Antiquaries.

4 See Harris 1998 for the British Museum Library, and Lamb 1951 for the Royal Academy.

5 See Miller 1948 for the Club.

6 Ellis I 1889 113; Hawkins 1822 24; the poem is cited in the Gerald M. Norman Gallery Catalogue of the 1971 exhibition of Lady Di's work.

7 HW 32 108: 27 March 1773.

8 HW 5 372: 8 August 1773.

9 HW 6 79: 3 July 1774; ibid. 6 460: 13 July 1777.

10 According to Draper 1963, the house was demolished in the 1860s to make way for the railway line running to Alexandra Palace, but the name survives in an area of park named the Grove, in the Palace grounds.

11 HW 32 122: 11 June 1773; Barrett 1904–5 III 481: March 1788.

12 HW 32 170: 14 December 1773; Royal College of Surgeons, Hunter-Baillie papers I, f. 12, n.d. Reproduced by kind permission of the President and Council of the Royal College of Surgeons of England.

13 Delany 1861–2 V 265.

14 Pottle & Ryskamp 1963 158: 17 May 1775.

15 Adamson and Dewar 1974 73.

16 Pottle & Wimsatt 1960 172: 7 April 1773. In 1773 Selwyn had to lend Topham £300, which was repaid with some difficulty. Society of Antiquaries MS 444/6 f. 25: 18 September 1773.

17 Ibid. 180: 27 April 1773.

18 Ibid. 192: 30 April 1773.

19 Boswell 1936 II: 246; Pottle & Wimsatt 1960 194; *Life* III 349: 12 May 1778.

20 Erskine 1903 93.

21 Ellis II 1889 154; Broughton 1887 I 1887 113.

22 Pottle & Ryskamp 1963: 27 March 1775; 1 April 1775. Pottle's suggestion is that Johnson used the powdered peel as an aid to digestion.

23 Hardy 1812 345: 20 November 1773.

24 Ibid. 348; Erskine 1903 131: 12 February 1774.

25 Farrer 1903–6 II 207: 30 November 1774.

26 Burford 1986 225; *The Lady's Magazine* 94–96, cited Ribeiro 1994.

27 HW 32 77: 6 January 1772.

28 Pottle & Ryskamp 1963: 23 March 1775.

29 Ibid. 27 March 1775.

30 Ibid. 118: 3 April 1775.

EIGHT *The Artist*

1 See Riely 1975 on Walpole and Bunbury.

2 See Hill 1997 for an account of the dispersal of Walpole's art collection.

3 HW 35 425: 23 October 1775. According to Harley 1970 144, bistre was not popular until the second half of the eighteenth century, and its limited use in England was because the best quality bistre was made from French beechwood. Its slightly resinous character made it difficult to use, and it was generally superseded in the nineteenth century by the transparent brown wash provided by sepia, or cuttle fish. Hardie 1966 25 claims that wood soot or coal soot dissolves well, and that there is enough grease in the soot, or plus the addition of a small amount of gum, to make it as adhesive to paper as any watercolour; bistre produces a brownish ink, hardly distinguishable from sepia. Paul Sandby even experimented with pigments made from burnt brioche crust and burnt split peas!

4 Six of the seven drawings survive, in the Lewis Walpole Library, Farmington, Connecticut. For their almost miraculous rediscovery after the 1842 dispersal of the contents of Strawberry Hill, see Lewis 1978.

5 HW 41 321: 16 December 1775; 28 9: 27 December 1775.

6 Ibid. 244: 18 February 1776.

7 Ibid. 259: 8 April 1776.

8 HW 32 292: 20 June 1776

9 HW 28 275: 17 September 1776; 318: 6 July 1777; Toynbee 1927 166.

10 HW 24 524: 31 October 1779.

11 HW 29 142: 15 May 1781.

12 HW 31 216: 1782; Coke 1889–96 III: 29 August 1782.

13 Barrett 1904–5 III 119.

14 Greig 1922 3: 21 July 1793.

15 Hawkins 1822 103.

16 See Mowl 1996, who places a heavy emphasis on Walpole's homosexuality.

17 HW 35 425: 23 October 1775.

18 The Wilton wax sculpture and the Amorini have proved untraceable; the other two are in the Department of Coins & Medals, Fitzwilliam Museum, Cambridge, acquired from the Pyke collection.

19 Farrer 1903–6 II 207 30 November 1771; 357 4 May 1777.

20 The pastel of her daughters hangs at Blenheim; the Fox portrait is in the Lewis Walpole Library (there was also a preliminary version, showing his head only, which was at Holland House in 1903).

21 HW 6 340: 14 July 1776.

22 HW 32 406: 17 December 1777; 39 275: 30 June 1776; 32 293: 23 July 1776.

23 HMC *Charlemont* I 317.

24 See Berridge & Edwards 1981 Part II on the early nineteenth-century recognition of the distinction between narcotic and recreational use. I am indebted to Louise Foxcroft for facts and figures about opium consumption.

25 HMC *Charlemont* I 318.

26 Chapman 1952 II 4, 307.

27 HW 6 286: 27 March 1776.

28 Herbert 1939 75; Hilles 1952 16: 1 April 1776.

29 HW 32 292: 20 June 1776.

30 Stokes 1917 106; HW 32 319: 22 August 1776; 39 172: 30 August 1773. Walpole inherited the title on his nephew's death in 1791.

31 Jesse 1883–4 III 125: 6 April 1776.

32 Ibid. 125: 8 April 1776; 142: 1775 (n.d.).

33 Ibid. 153: December 1776.

34 Ibid. 162: 21 November 1776.

35 Ilchester 1901 179:9 January 1766; Balderston 1951 221: December 1777. In 1755, Johnson's Dictionary simply defined 'to bore' as 'to pierce with a hole'.

36 Bleackley 1909 152 ff. on the Kennedys; Angelo 1904 I 37.

37 HW 10 232: 22 October 1766. In another note to Selwyn, she refers to the 'raffish' and 'dismal' nature of Bath out of season. Society of Antiquaries MS 444/6 f. 25: n.d.

38 Erskine 1903 166.

39 Jesse 1883–4 III 132: n.d. 1777.

40 Ibid. 179; Chapman 1952 II 162: 18 February 1777; HW 32 365: 6 July 1777.

41 HW 33 292; Broughton 1887 I 68, when Charlotte Albert was sent to Brighton to recover from the measles.

42 Balderston 1951 45: 28 May 1777; 149: 8 September 1777.

43 Ingrams 1984 250; Herbert 1939 244.

44 Chapman 1952 II 224: 16 October 1777; 225: 18 October 1777.

45 HW 6 483: 12 October 1777.

46 HW 7 73: 27 January 1778.

47 HW 28 386: 18 April 1778. One version of the watercolour is in the Royal Collection, where it was described by Oppé 1950 60 as 'after Diana Beauclerk', and is currently defined as 'possibly by another hand'. According to Lewis (in HW 28) the original was in the possession of Mrs D. V. Garstin of New Haven in 1950.

48 Ibid. 419: 19 July 1778; 421: 24 July 1778.

49 Pottle & Reed 1977 83: 15 April 1779.

50 Boswell 1936 III 384: 16 April 1779.

51 Pottle & Reed 1977 92.

52 Herbert 1939 164: 8 April 1779; 334: 28 November 1779. A plaque still commemorates the Beauclerks' occupation of 100 Great Russell Street. I am grateful to Paul Petzold for drawing this to my attention.

53 HW 30 267: 5 July 1779; HMC *Carlisle* 301: 7 November 1775.

54 Jesse 1883–4 III 200: 5 July 1777; 247: 9 December 1777; Orchard 1954 103.

55 Coke 1889–96 citing HW **33** 107: 27 June 1779.

56 Ibid.; HW 30 269: 7 July 1779.

57 Herbert 1939 202; Jesse 1883–4 IV 316: 13 July 1779; Herbert 1939 203.

58 Herbert 1939 202: 2 July 1779; 259: 20 September 1779.

59 HW 30 272: 21 September 1779; Herbert 1939 301: 28 October 1779

60 Balderston 1951 I 18 December 1777.

61 Barrett 1904–5 II 282–3, 287.

62 HW 30 272: 4 October 1779.

63 Home 1879 II 36. Confirmation of such hazards comes from a contemporary Italian hairdresser criticising the English adoption of French fashions: 'three rows of pins thrust into the skull will not fail to cause a constant itching sensation that much distorts the features of the face and disables it so that a lady by degrees may lose the use of her face; besides the immense quantity of pomatum and powder laid on for a genteel dressing that after a week or two breeds mites' cited by Williams 1957 89

64 Greig 1922 66: 31 July 1794.

65 Chapman 1952 II 322, 325, 326.

66 Herbert 1939 351: 15 December 1779.

67 Barrett 1904–5 II 91.

68 Herbert 1939 429: 14 March 1780.

69 HW 7 213: 14 March 1780; 215: 22 March 1780; 239: 23 March 1780.

70 Balderston 1951 434: 26 March 1780.

71 Chapman 1952 II 336: 8 April 1780; Pottle & Reed 1977 329: 20 April 1781.

72 Ibid. 199: 12 April 1780; Hilles 1952 16.

73 HW 36 192: 13 April 1781; according to Reynolds' ledgers, Topham made an advance payment in February of £26 15s, and paid the remaining half in November 1779, see Cormack 1968–70.

NINE *The Merry Widow*

1 Printed for G. Kearsly, 46 Fleet Street.

2 Williams 1933 235.

3 Whitley 1938 197; Jesse 1883–4 I 225.

4 Herbert 1939 464.

5 According to Cundall 1925 96, the house was later named Devonshire Cottage, after a subsequent tenant, Duchess Georgiana; other tenants would include Walpole's adored Berry sisters, who would rent it from Georgiana's granddaughter Caroline Lamb. The watercolour is in the Lewis Walpole Library.

6 Barrett 1904–5 II 91.

7 HW **33** 195: 10 June 1780.

8 The original was acquired by the Lewis Walpole Library in 1999.

9 Herbert 1950 31ff: 12 August 1780, 17 August 1780.

10 Ibid. 76: 26 December 1780.

11 Ibid. 86: 6 February 1781.

12 HW **29** 71: 15 July 1780.

13 Herbert 1950 122: 30 June 1780.

14 HMC *Charlemont* I: 18 June 1781.

15 Pottle & Reed 1977 350: 8 May 1781.

16 Ibid. 331: 26, 27, 28 April 1781.

17 Ibid. 359: 17 May 1781.

18 Five of these works are in the Lewis Walpole Library, acquired by W. S. Lewis in 1948, together with the text Lady Di copied from Book IV, Canto 7, describing the sixth scene. The watercolour showing this scene, however, is in the Dept. of Prints & Drawings, Victoria & Albert Museum, whose catalogue describes it as 'Two lovers, reclining in a forest glade, surprised by Diana'. There is also a preliminary version of this scene; Society of Antiquaries MS 444/6 f. 24.

19 Hawkins 1822 103.

20 Hilles 1952 178.

21 HW **29** 144: 22 May 1781; Hilles 1952 102.

22 HMC *Carlisle* 461: 15 February 1781.

23 Draper 1970, citing Ironside's *History and Antiquities of Twickenham* (1797).

After 1820, the property was known as Little Marble Hill.

24 Herbert 1950 201: 7 June 1782.

25 HW **29** 272: 4 August 1782.

26 Ibid. 101: 2–1781; 35 530: 1 March 1783. See Sloan 2000 for Harcourt's artistic activities and influence.

27 HW **25** 624: 30 July 1783.

28 HW **29** 311: 22 September 1783 and FN 3, 4.

29 HW **33** 473: 30 June 1785.

30 HW **36** 238: 8 April 1786.

31 Barbier 1963 154: 22 April 1784.

32 Ibid. 155: 29 September 1788.

33 Ibid. 145: 20 December 1791; Discourse VII, delivered in 1776.

34 HW **16** 280 and ff.

35 HW **42** 450.

36 Farrer 1903–6 II 38: 7 September 1771; Meteyard 1865 I 383.

37 Meteyard 1865 II 215.

38 Farrer 1903–6 II 363: 21 June 1777; 169: 6 December 1773.

39 Meteyard 1865 II 175; Farrer 1903–6 II 177: 7 March 1774.

40 Meteyard 1865 II 176.

41 Ibid. 542; Farrer 1903–6 III 12: 27 June 1783.

42 There seem to have been more than the four designs, as shown on the 'Bacchanalian tablet' in the Nottingham Castle Museum; there is a second tablet with a different permutation of figures in five scenes, in the Dwight Collection, Birmingham Museum, Alabama. See Reilly 1989 on jasper ware.

43 Farrer 1903–6 II 308: 12 September 1776.

44 Ibid. 494: 19 June 1779; Kelly 1965.

45 HW **39** 443: 18 June 1786.

46 HW **35** 385: 7 September 1784; 438: 19 February 1788.

47 HW **29** 353: 1 January 1785. The Gypsies painting is in the Dept. of Prints & Drawings, Victoria & Albert Museum; there is a photograph of the Masquerade in the Witt Library of the Courtauld Institute.

48 Gage 1993 765. I am grateful to John

Gage for permission to quote from his translation of Tischbein's letter.

49 HW **35** 650: 16 September 1784.

50 Ibid. 632: 1784 (n.d.).

51 Barrett 1904–5 II 328: 16 December 1785.

52 See Oppé 1950 55.

53 HW **33** 573: 6 September 1787.

54 Williams 1933 237; Lefanu 1960 159, 161.

TEN *The Grandmother*

1 Clark 1895–8 II 60: 23 March 1787.

2 Coke 1889–96 I xlix.

3 Herbert 1950 340: 27 February 1787; 316: 10 October 1786.

4 Ibid., various letters from 1779 to 1786.

5 Ibid.: 8 March 187.

6 Clark 1895–8 II 74: 6 April 1787.

7 Herbert 1950 347: 3 April 1787.

8 Ibid. 357: 20 August 1787.

9 Ibid. 358: 21 August 1787.

10 HMC *Carlisle* 462: 17 February 1781; Cannon 1984 198 has calculated that only 3.76% of peers born between 1690 and 1779 married the daughters of clergy; Carne 1973 94.

11 Herbert 1950 38: 2 April 1788.

12 Reprinted in Trumbach 1985 (A).

13 HW **35** 636.

14 Lefanu 1960 176: 25 June 1789; Elwin 1967 340, 341: 27 June 1789, 3 July 1789.

15 HW **34** 56: 22 July 1789.

16 Trench 1964 136, 151, 152; Lefanu 1960 147.

17 Harcourt 1871–2 28, 41.

18 Ingamells 1997 102; Carne 1973.

19 Some of the panels are displayed in Lydiard House.

20 HW **34** 25: 11 October 1788.

21 HW **11** 18: 12 September 1789; 81: 3 July 1790; 120: 16 October 1790.

22 Ibid. 148: 27 November 1790; Greig 1922: 21 July 1793.

23 HW **11** 163: 17 December 1790; 341: 23 August 1791.

24 Goethe's *Travels in Italy*, cited Jenkins

& Sloan 1996 252; HW 11 349: 11
September 1991.

25 Williams 1933 231.

26 Erskine 1903 222, citing Tuer's
Bartolozzi.

27 The original watercolour is in the Lewis
Walpole Library.

28 *The Marriages of Cousin Germans
Vindicated*, reprinted Trumbach 1985
(A).

29 See Essick 1992 for full discussion.

30 HW 11 248: 15 April 1791.

31 Ibid. 248.

32 Thibaudeau 1893 179: 20 July 1793.

33 Ibid. 187: 20 January 1794.

34 Granville 1917: 20 January 1796.

35 Ibid. 164: July 1797; Greig 1922 171:
14 March 1794.

36 HW 12 172: 18 August 1795; 189: 18
September 1795.

37 Examples in the Dept. of Prints &
Drawings, Victoria & Albert Museum.
See Vesmé & Calabi 1928.

38 Adeane 1896 368: 22 February 1795.

39 See Howell-Thomas 1978 for further
discussion of these families.

40 Ibid. 20, chapter 5.

41 The Pelican merged with the Phoenix
Assurance Company in 1907; the
Phoenix became part of the Sun
Alliance in 1984, which has
subsequently expanded to become the
Royal & Sun Alliance. In 1915 the
sculpture was moved to the Sherborne
Lane entrance to the building following
demolition of the Lombard Street
entrance. Here it remained until it was
removed in 1930 and, in 1933,
presented by the Phoenix to the London
County Council, where it became the
property of the Education Committee of
the LCC (subsequently ILEA). It was
erected outside the Geffrye Museum,
Kingsland Road, in 1934, and Listed in
1951. In the mid-1950s, now the
responsibility of the London Residuary
Body, it was moved to the Horniman
Museum, Forest Hill. It was restored
and conserved in 1991. I am most
grateful to Martin Cruys, Archivist of
the Royal & Sun Alliance, and to Karen
Scadeng of the Horniman Museum
2001 project for their assistance.

42 Polwhele 1798.

43 The letters, from which the subsequent
quotations are taken, were privately
published by the Jenison-Walworth
family in Heidelberg (n.d.), and are
also printed as an appendix to Erskine
1903.

44 Foster 1898 240: 22 September 1805;
the letter to George is an unpublished
MS at Lydiard, Lyd 1994/137.1.

45 Granville 1917: 4 September 1808.

46 Melville 1913 25: 10 October 1790.

47 Described and illustrated in Hofland
1820.

48 Amongst the drawings pasted into
Walpole's extra-illustrated volume of
the Strawberry Hill catalogue was a
little work by Mary Beauclerk, a
playing card whose pips are
transformed into an animated figure.
This became a popular genre, adopted,
for example, by a descendant, Charlotta
von Jenison-Walworth, in the sequence
Jeanne d'Arc – see Rothenstein &
Gooding 1999.

49 White 1903 133, 151.

50 Greig 1922: 22 August 1804.

51 Sermoneta 1940 162.

52 Granville 1917 273: November 1799.

53 Sermoneta 1940 214; Granville 1917
395.

54 See Ashton 1898, chapter 5, on the
ladies who gambled.

Bibliography

Manuscript Sources

British Library: Blenheim Papers, Add. MSS 61473, 61666–9, 61672, 61678
Royal College of Surgeons of England Library, Hunter Baillie Papers H-B i 12
Society of Antiquaries of London MS 444/18
Isle of Bute: The Mount Stuart Trust Archive
Lydiard House: Lyd 1994/137.1

Published Sources

Adamson, D. & Dewar, P., *The House of Nell Gwynn: the fortunes of the Beauclerk family 1670–1970* (London, 1974)

Adeane, J. H. (ed.), *The Girlhood of Maria Joseph Holroyd* (London, 1896)

Alexander, D., *Amateurs and Print-making in England 1750–1830* (Oxford, 1983)

Angelo, H., *The Reminiscences of H. Angelo*, 2 vols. (London, 1904)

Arch, N. & Marschner, J., *Splendour at Court: dressing for royal occasions since 1700* (London, 1987)

Aspinall-Oglander, C. (ed.), *Admiral's Wife: being the life and letters of the Hon. Mrs Edward Boscawen from 1719 to 1761* (London, 1940)

Ashton, J., *The History of Gambling in England* (London, 1898)

Attfield, J. & Kirkman, P. (eds), *A View from the Interior: feminism, women and design* (London, 1989)

Bailey, M., *Boswell's Column: being his contributions to the London Magazine from 1777–1783* (London, 1951)

Bailly's Racing Register. Vol. I, 1709–1800 (London, 1845)

Balderston, K. (ed.), *Thraliana: the Diary of Mrs Hester Lynch Thrale (later Mrs Piozzi) 1776–1809* (Oxford, 1951)

Bibliography

Barbier, C. P., *William Gilpin, his drawings, teachings and theory of the picturesque* (Oxford, 1963)

Barrell, J. (ed.), *Painting and the Politics of Culture* (Oxford, 1992)

Barrett, C. (ed.), *The Diary and Letters of Madame D'Arblay 1778–1840, as edited by her niece, with preface and notes by Austin Dobson*, 6 vols (London, 1904–5)

Basker, J., 'Dictionary Johnson amidst the Dons of Sidney: a Chapter in Eighteenth-Century Cambridge History', in *Sidney Sussex College, Cambridge: Historical Essays*, ed. D. E. D. Beales & H. E. Nisbet (Woodbridge, 1996)

Beauclerk, D., *Letters, from 1797 to 1807* (Printed by J. Hoerning, Heidelberg, n.d.)

Bennett, B. T. (ed.), *The Letters of Mary Wollstonecraft Shelley* vols II, III (Baltimore & London, 1983, 1988)

Bennett, S., 'A Muse of Art in the Huntingdon Collection', in *British Art 1740–1859*, ed. G. Sutherland (San Marino, 1992), 57–80

Bermingham, A., 'The Origin of Painting and the Ends of Art: Wright of Derby's *Corinthian Maid*' in *Painting and the Politics of Culture*, ed. J. Barrell (Oxford, 1992), 135–64

– 'The Aesthetics of Ignorance: the accomplished woman in the culture of connoisseurship', *The Oxford Art Journal* 16:2 (1993), 3–19

– A., *Learning to Draw: Studies in the Cultural History of a Polite and Useful Art* (New Haven, 2000)

Berridge, V. & Edwards, G., *Opium and the People: opiate use in nineteenth-century England* (London, 1981)

Bicknell, P. & Munro, J., *Gilpin to Ruskin* (Cambridge, 1988)

Black, J., *The Jockey Club and its Founders* (London, 1891)

Bleackley, H., *Ladies Fair and Frail: sketches of the demi-monde during the eighteenth century* (London, 1909)

Blunt, R. (ed.), *Mrs Montague, 'Queen of the Blues': her letters and friendships from 1762 to 1800* (Edinburgh, 1923)

Bocage, A.-M. Du, *Letters concerning England, Holland and Italy. Translated from the French* (London, 1770)

Borzello, F., 'Leisured Ladies', *Women's Art Magazine* 55 (November/December 1993), 10–13

Boswell, J., *The Life of Samuel Johnson*, ed. G. B. Hill (Oxford, 1936)

Boucé, P. & Porter, R., *Sexual Underworlds of the Enlightenment* (Manchester, 1987)

Brewer, J., *The Pleasures of the Imagination: English Culture in the Eighteenth Century* (London, 1997)

Broadley, A. M & Melville, L. (eds), *The Beautiful Lady Craven* (London, 1913)

Brock, C. H. (ed.), *William Hunter 1718–83: A Memoir by Samuel Foart Simmons and John Hunter* (Glasgow, 1983)

Bibliography

Brooke, J., *The Chatham Administration 1766–68* (London, 1956)

Brooks's Club, *Memorials of Brooks's* (London, 1907)

Broughton, Mrs V. D., *Court and Private Life in the time of Queen Charlotte: being the Journals of Mrs Papendiek, Assistant-Keeper of the Wardrobe and Reader to Her Majesty*, 2 vols (London, 1887)

Brown, G., *A New Treatise on Flower Painting, or Every Lady her own Drawing Master* (3rd edn. London, 1799)

Brownell, M. R., *Samuel Johnson's Attitude to the Arts* (Oxford, 1989)

Bryant, J., *Marble Hill: the design and use of a Palladian estate* (Borough of Twickenham Local History Society Paper 57, 1986)

Buck, A., *Dress in Eighteenth-century England* (London, 1979)

Burford, E. J., *Wits, Wenchers and Wantons: London's low life – Covent Garden in the eighteenth century* (London, 1986)

Burgher, G. A., *Leonora: translated from the German by W. R. Spencer with designs by the Right Honourable Lady Diana Beauclerk* (printed by T. Bensley for J. Edwards and E. and S. Harding, Pall Mall, 1796)

Bury, A., 'Lady Diana Beauclerk and her Art', *The Antique Collector* (August 1958), 153–7

Buten, D., *Eighteenth-century Wedgwood* (London, 1980)

Cannon, J., *Aristocratic Century: the peerage of eighteenth-century England* (Cambridge, 1984)

Carne, B., 'George Richard, Third Viscount Bolingbroke', *Friends of Lydiard Tregoz Annual Report* 6 (1973), 91–114

– 'Frederick, Second Viscount Bolingbroke', *Friends of Lydiard Tregoz Annual Report* 21 (1988), 15–39

Chancellor, E. B., *The History of the Squares of London* (London, 1907)

Chapman, R. W. (ed.), *The Letters of Samuel Johnson*, 3 vols (Oxford, 1952, reprt 1984)

Clark, Mrs G. (ed.), *Gleanings from an Old Portfolio*, 3 vols (Edinburgh, 1895–8)

Clarke, M., *The Tempting Prospect: a social history of English watercolours* (London, 1981)

Clay, H., 'Coade's Artificial Stoneware', *The Connoisseur* 82 (1928), 79–87

Clayton, E., *English Female Artists* (London, 1876)

Clifford, J. L., *Hester Lynch Piozzi (Mrs Thrale)* (Oxford, 1952, reprt 1968)

Clifford, T., 'Some Ceramic Vases and their Sources', *English Ceramic Circle Transactions* 10 part 3 (1978), 163–80

Cokayne, G. E., *Complete Peerage* (London, 1912)

Coke, Lady Mary, *Letters and Journals*, 4 vols (Edinburgh, 1889–96)

Colley, L., *Britons: Forging the Nation 1707–1837* (London, 1992)

Collison-Morley, L., *Giuseppe Baretti and his Friends* (London, 1909)

Bibliography

Cormack, M., 'The Ledgers of Sir Joshua Reynolds', *Walpole Society* 42 (1968–70), 105–69

Cotton, W., *A Catalogue of the Portraits Painted by Sir Joshua Reynolds* (London, 1857)

Cruickshank, D. & Burton, N., *Life in the Georgian City* (London, 1990)

Cundall, A. M., *Bygone Richmond* (London, 1925)

Cunnington, C. W. & P., *The History of Underclothes* (London, 1951)

– *Handbook of English Costume in the Eighteenth Century* (London, 1964)

Dasent A., *The History of St James' Square* (London, 1895)

Delany, M., *The Autobiography and Correspondence of Mary Granville, Mrs Delany*, ed. Lady Llanover, 6 vols (London, 1861–2)

Deuchar, S., *Sporting Art in Eighteenth-century England* (Yale, 1988)

Donald, D., *The Golden Age of Caricature: Satirical Prints in the Age of George III* (London, 1996)

Draper, F. W. M., 'Topham Beauclerk at The Grove, Muswell Hill', *The New Rambler* June 1963, 5–8

Draper, M., *Marble Hill House and its Owners* (London, 1970)

Eeles, H. S. & Earl Spencer, *Brooks's 1764–1964* (London, 1964)

Egerton, J., *George Stubbs 1724–1806* (London, 1984)

Ellet, E. F., *Women Artists in All Ages and Countries* (London, 1859)

Ellis, A. R. (ed.), *The Early Diary of Fanny Burney* I (London, 1889)

Elwin, M. (ed.), *The Noels and the Milbankes: their letters for twenty-five years, 1767–1792* (London, 1967)

Erskine, B., *Lady Diana Beauclerk, her Life and Work* (London, 1903)

– 'Lady Di's Scrap-Book', *Connoisseur* 7 (1903), 33–7, 92–8

Essick, R. N., 'Visual/Verbal Relations in Book Illustration', in *British Art 1740–1820*, ed. G. Sutherland (San Marino, 1992)

Evans, J., *A History of the Society of Antiquaries* (Oxford, 1956)

Ewen, C. L., *Lotteries and Sweepstakes* (London, 1932)

Farrer, K. E. (ed.), *The Letters of Josiah Wedgwood. Vol. II, 1771–1780. Vol. III, 1781–1794* (Manchester, 1903–6, reprt 1973)

Fitzgerald, B. (ed.), *Correspondence of Emily, Duchess of Leinster* vol. I (Dublin, 1949)

Foreman, A., *Georgiana, Duchess of Devonshire* (London, 1998)

Foster, V. (ed.), *The Two Duchesses* (London, 1898)

Fothergill, B., *The Strawberry Hill Set: Horace Walpole and his Circle* (London, 1983)

Fowler, M., *Blenheim: Biography of a Palace* (London, 1989)

Gage, J., 'Lusieri, Hamilton and the Palazzo Sessa', *Burlington Magazine* 135 (November, 1993), 765–6

Bibliography

Glaze, D. (ed.), *Dictionary of Women Artists* (London, 1997)

Gloag, J., *Dictionary of Furniture*, rev. by C. D. Edwards (London, 1990)

Goadby, M., *Nocturnal Revels, or the History of King's Place* (London, 1779)

Granville, C. (ed.), *Lord Granville Leveson Gower: Private Correspondence 1781–1821. Vol. 1* (London, 1917)

Greer, G., *The Obstacle Race* (London, 1979)

Greig, J. (ed.), *The Farington Diary. Vol. I, 1793–1802* (London, 1922)

– *The Diaries of a Duchess: extracts from the diaries of the First Duchess of Northumberland* (London, 1926)

– *The Letters of David Hume* (Oxford, 1932)

Halsband, R. (ed.), *The Complete Letters of Lady Mary Wortley Montagu. Vol. III, 1752–1762* (Oxford, 1967)

– *Lord Hervey, Eighteenth-century Courtier* (Oxford, 1973)

Harcourt, E. W. (ed.), 'Mrs Harcourt's Diary of the Court of King George III', *Miscellanies of the Philobiblion Society* 13 (1871–2)

– (ed.), *The Harcourt Papers, Vol. III* (Oxford, 1880–1905)

Hardie, M., *Water-colour Painting in Britain. Vol. I, The Eighteenth Century* (London, 1966)

Hardy, F., *Memoirs of the Political and Private Life of James Caulfield, the Earl of Charlemont* (London, 1812)

Harley, M. D., *Artists' Pigments c. 1600–1835* (London, 1970)

Harvey, A. D., *Sex in Georgian England* (London, 1996)

Harris, F., *A Passion for Government: the life of Sarah, Duchess of Marlborough* (Oxford, 1991)

Harris, P. R., *A History of the British Museum Library 1753–1973* (London, 1998)

Hawkins, L. M., *Anecdotes, Biographical Sketches and Memoirs* (London, 1822)

Hecht, J. J., *The Domestic Servant Class in Eighteenth-century England* (London, 1956)

Hedley, O., *Queen Charlotte* (London, 1975)

Herbert, Lord (ed.), *Elizabeth, Henry and George (1734–80)*

– *The Pembroke Papers (1780–1794)* (London, 1939)

Hertford, Countess of, *Correspondence between Frances, Countess of Hartford (afterwards Duchess of Somerset), and Henrietta Louisa,Countess of Pomfret, between the years 1738 and 1741* (London, 1805)

Hibbert, C., *George III: a Personal History* (London, 1998)

Hill, B. (ed.), *Eighteenth-century Women: an Anthology* (London, 1978)

Hill, P., *Walpole's Art Collection: Horace Walpole's Oil Paintings, Water Colours and Drawings at Strawberry Hill* (Twickenham, 1997)

Hilles, F. W. (ed.), *Portraits by Sir Joshua Reynolds* (New York, 1952)

Historical Manuscripts Commission:

Carlisle 1897

Bibliography

Charlemont I 1891

Hastings III 1934

Various VIII 1913

Hofland, B., *A Descriptive Account of the Mansion and Gardens of 'White-Knights'*, (privately printed for the Duke of Marlborough, London, 1820)

Hollingsworth, T. H., 'The Demography of the British Peerage', *Supplement* to *Population Studies* 18 (1965), 1–108

Home, J. A. (ed.), *Lady Louisa Stuart: Selections from her Manuscripts* (Edinburgh, 1899)

Howard, H., *Letters to and from Henrietta, Countess of Suffolk, from 1712–1767* (London, 1824)

Howell-Thomas, D., *Lord Melbourne's Susan* (Old Woking, 1978)

HW, see Lewis 1937–83

Hyde, M., *The Thrales of Streatham Park* (Cambridge MA, 1972)

Ilchester, Countess of, & Stavordale, Lord (eds), *The Life and Letters of Lady Sarah Lennox, 1745–1826* (London, 1901)

Ilchester, Earl of (ed.), *Letters of Henry Fox, Lord Holland* (London, 1915)

– *Lord Hervey and his Friends, 1726–1738* (London, 1950)

– & Mrs Langford-Brooke, *The Life of Sir Charles Hanbury-Williams* (London, 1928)

Illingworth, C., *The Story of William Hunter* (Edinburgh, 1967)

Ingamells, J., *Dictionary of Travellers to Italy* (New Haven, 1997)

Ingrams, R. (ed.), *Dr Johnson by Mrs Thrale: the anecdotes of Mrs Piozzi in their original form* (London, 1984)

Jacob, W. L., 'Frederick, Second Viscount Bolingbroke – "Lord of the Turf"', *Friends of Lydiard Tregoz Annual Report* 21 (1988), 40–46

Jenkins, I. & Sloan, K., *Vases and Volcanoes: Sir William Hamilton and his Collection* (London, 1996)

Jesse, J. H., *George Selwyn and his Contemporaries*, 4 vols (London, 1883–4)

Johnson, B. H., *Berkeley Square to Bond Street: the early history of the neighbourhood* (London, 1952)

Jones, V. (ed.), *Women in the Eighteenth Century* (London, 1990)

Kelly, A., *Decorative Wedgwood in Architecture and Furniture* (London, 1965)

– *Mrs Coade's Stone* (Upton-on-Severn, 1990)

Kerr, S. P., *George Selwyn and the Wits* (London, 1909)

King, W. (ed.), *Memoirs of Sarah, Duchess of Marlborough, together with her Characters of her Contemporaries and her Opinions* (London, 1930)

Krill, J., *English Artists' Paper, Renaissance to Regency* (London, 1987)

Laing, A., *In Trust for the Nation: Paintings from National Trust Houses* (London, 1995)

Bibliography

Lamb, W., *The Royal Academy* (London, 1951)

Lefanu, W. (ed.), *Betsy Sheridan's Journal: letters from Sheridan's sister, 1784–1786 and 1788–1790* (London, 1960)

Leslie, C. R. & Taylor, T., *The Life and Times of Sir Joshua Reynolds, with Notices of some of his Contemporaries*, 2 vols (London, 1865)

Lewis, J. S., *In the Family Way: Child-bearing in the British Aristocracy 1760–1860* (New Brunswick NJ, 1986)

Lewis, W. S. (ed.), *Notes by Lady Louisa Stuart on 'George Selwyn and his Contemporaries' by John Heneage Jesse* (New Haven, 1928)

Lewis, W. S., *Collector's Progress* (London, 1952)

– *Rescuing Horace Walpole* (New Haven, 1978)

– (ed.), *The Yale Edition of Horace Walpole's Correspondence*, 48 vols (New Haven & London, 1937–83)

Lippincott, L., *Selling Art in Georgian London: the rise of Arthur Pond* (New Haven & London, 1983)

Logan, A.-M., 'Bernard Lens the Younger and the Marlborough Collection', *In Honour of Paul Mellon*, ed. J. Wilmerding (Washington, 1986), 203–16

Macht, C., *Classical Wedgwood Designs* (New York, 1957)

McKendrick, N., Brewer, J., & Plumb, J. H., *The Birth of a Consumer Society: the commercialisation of eighteenth-century England* (Bloomington, 1982)

McLaren, A., *Reproductive Rituals: the perception of fertility in England from the sixteenth century to the nineteenth century* (London, 1984)

Mankowitz, W., *Wedgwood* (London 1953)

Mannings, D., 'At the Portrait Painter's', *History Today* 27 (1977), 279–87

– *Sir Joshua Reynolds: a Complete Catalogue of his Paintings* (New Haven and London, 2000)

Manwaring, E. W., *Italian Landscape in Eighteenth-century England* (New York, 1925)

Marlborough, Sarah, Duchess of, *A True Copy of the Last Will and Testament of Her Grace Sarah, Late Duchess Dowager of Marlborough* (London, 1744)

Massey, V., *The First Lady Diana: the life of Lady Diana Spencer 1710–1735* (London, 1999)

Matossian, M., *Poisons of the Past* (New Haven, 1989)

Melville, L., *Society at Royal Tunbridge Wells in the Eighteenth Century and After* (London, 1912)

– *The Berry Papers* (London, 1913)

Meteyard, E., *The Life of Josiah Wedgwood*, 2 vols (London, 1865, reprt 1970)

Millar, O., *The Later Georgian Pictures in the Collection of Her Majesty the Queen*, 2 vols (London, 1969)

Miller, C. A., *Anecdotes of the Literary Club* (New York, 1948)

Bibliography

Montagu, Lady Mary, *Lady Mary Wortley Montagu, the Letters and Works*, ed. Lord Wharncliffe, 2 vols (London, 1893)

Mowl, T., *Horace Walpole, the Great Outsider* (London, 1996)

Murray, V., *High Society: a social history of the Regency period 1788–1830* (London, 1998)

Oman, C., *David Garrick* (London, 1958)

Oppé, A. P., *English Drawings, Stuart and Georgian Periods, at Windsor Castle* (London, 1950)

Orchard, V., *Tattersalls: Two Hundred Years of Sporting History* (London, 1954)

Oswald, A., 'Woolbeding, Sussex II', *Country Life* (15 August 1947), 329–31

Parker, C. A., *George Stubbs: Art, Animals and Anatomy* (London, 1984)

Penny, N. (ed.), *Reynolds* (London, 1986)

Percy, T., *The Life of Oliver Goldsmith* (Introduction to *The Miscellanous Works of Oliver Goldsmith*) (London, 1801)

Perry, G. & Rossington, M. (eds), *Femininity and Masculinity in Eighteenth-century Art and Culture* (Manchester, 1994)

Piozzi, H. L. (Mrs Thrale), *Observations and Reflections made in the Course of a Journey through France, Italy and Germany* (London, 1789, reprt Ann Arbor 1967)

Pointon, M., *Strategies for Showing: Women, Possession and Representation in English Visual Culture 1665–1800* (Oxford, 1997)

Polwhele, R., *The Unsex'd Females. A Poem* (London, 1798, reprt New York, 1974)

Porter, R., 'William Hunter, a surgeon and a gentleman', in *William Hunter and the Eighteenth-century Medical World*, eds W. F. Bynum & R. Porter (Cambridge, 1985), 7–34

– 'A touch of danger: the man-midwife as sexual predator', in *Sexual Underworlds of the Enlightenment*, eds G. S. Rousseau & R. Porter (Manchester, 1987), 206–33

– & Hall, L., *The Facts of Life: the Creation of Sexual Knowledge in Britain 1650–1950* (New Haven 1995)

Pottle, F. A. (ed.), *The Yale Editions of the Private Papers of James Boswell* (New Haven, 1950–86)

with W. K. Wimsatt, *Boswell for the Defence: 1769–1774* (1960)

with C. Ryskamp, *Boswell – the Ominous Years: 1774–1776* (1963)

with J. W. Reed, *Boswell, Laird of Auchinleck: 1778–1782* (1977)

Rathbone, A. (ed.), *Letters from Lady Jane Coke to her friend Mrs Eyre at Derby 1747–1758* (London, 1899)

Reilly, R., *Wedgwood*, 2 vols (London, 1989)

Bibliography

– & Savage, G., *The Dictionary of Wedgwood* (London, 1980)

Ribeiro, A., *A Visual History of Costume: the Eighteenth Century* (London, 1983)

– *The Dress Worn at Masquerades in England 1730 to 1790* (New York, 1984)

Riely, J., 'Horace Walpole and the Second Hogarth', *Eighteenth-century Studies* 9.1 (1975), 36–47

Roberts, J., *Royal Artists, from Mary Queen of Scots to the present day* (London, 1987)

Robinson, D., 'Giuseppe Baretti as "a Man of Great Humility"', in *British Art 1740–1820* ed. G. Sutherland (San Marino, 1992), 81–94

Rogers, K., *Feminism in Eighteenth-century England* (Brighton, 1982)

Rothenstein, J. & Gooding, M., *The Playful Eye* (London, 1999)

Rouquet, J., *The Present State of the Arts in England* (London, 1755, reprt 1970)

Rousseau, J.-J., *Correspondence Générale, vol. 16* (Paris, 1931)

Rowse, A. L., *The Later Churchills* (London, 1958)

Sayer & Bennett's Catalogue of Prints for 1775 (London, 1775, reprt 1970)

Sedgwick, R., *Letters from George III to Lord Bute 1756–1766* (London, 1939)

– (ed.), *Lord Hervey's Memoirs* (London, 1952)

Sée, R., *English Pastels 1750–1830* (London, 1911)

Sermoneta, V., *The Lockes of Norbury* (London, 1940)

Shevelow, K., *Women and Print Culture: the construction of femininity in the early periodical* (London, 1989)

Sieveking, I. G., *The Memoirs of Sir Horace Mann* (London, 1912)

Skrine, F. H. (ed.), *Gossip about Dr Johnson and others. Being chapters from the memoirs of Miss Laetitia Matilda Hawkins* (London, 1926)

Sloan, K., 'Drawing – a "Polite Recreation" in eighteenth-century England', *Studies in Eighteenth-century Culture* 2 (1982), 217–40

– '"Industry from Idleness". The rise of the amateur in the eighteenth century' in *Prospects for the Nation: Recent Essays in British Landscape 1750–1880*, eds M. Rosenthal, C. Payne & S. Wilcox (New Haven, 1997), 285–304

– '*A Noble Art': Amateur Artists and Drawing Masters c. 1600–1800* (London, 2000)

Solkin, D., *Painting for Money* (New Haven, 1993)

Stark, J. N., 'An obstetric diary of William Hunter 1762–1765', *Glasgow Medical Journal* 70 (1908), 167–77, 241–56, 338–56

Steegman, J., *The Rule of Taste from George I to George IV* (London, 1968)

Stephan-Maasen, R., *Mythos und Lebenswelt: Studien zum 'Trunkenen Silen' von Peter Paul Rubens* (Hamburg, 1992)

Bibliography

Stirling, A. M. W., *The Merry Wives of Battersea and Gossip of Three Centuries* (London, 1956)

Stokes, H., *The Devonshire House Circle* (London, 1917)

Stone, G. W. & Kahrl, G. M., *David Garrick, a Critical Biography* (Carbondale, Ill., 1979)

Stone, L., *The Road to Divorce: England 1530–1987* (Oxford, 1990)

– *Broken Lives: Separation and Divorce in England 1660–1857* (Oxford, 1993)

Taylor, J. G., *Our Lady of Batersey* (London 1925)

Thibaudeau, A. W. (ed), *The Hamilton and Nelson Papers Vol. I, 1756–1797. (The Collection of Historical Documents formed by Alfred Morrison, 2nd series, 1882–1893)* (London, 1893)

Thoms, W. J., *The Book of the Court* (London, 1838)

Thomson, G. S., *The Russells in Bloomsbury 1669–1771* (London, 1940)

– *Letters of a Grandmother 1732–1735. Being the correspondence of Sarah, Duchess of Marlborough with her grand-daughter Diana, Duchess of Bedford* (London, 1943)

Tillyard, S., *Aristocrats* (London, 1994)

Toynbee, P. (ed.), *The Reminiscences of Horace Walpole* (Oxford, 1924)

– *The Strawberry Hill Accounts* (Oxford, 1927)

Trench, C. T., *The Royal Malady* (London, 1964)

Trumbach, R., *The Rise of the Egalitarian Family: Aristocratic Kinship and Domestic Relations in Eighteenth-century England* (New York, 1978)

– (ed.), *The Marriage Prohibition Controversy: Five Tracts. Vol. 4 in Marriage, Sex and the Family in England 1660–1800* (reprt New York, 1985) (A)

– (ed.), *Trials for Adultery: or the History of Divorces. Vol. 9 in Marriage, Sex and the Family in England 1660–1800* (reprt New York, 1985) (B)

Vesme, A. de & Calabi, A., *Francesco Bartolozzi* (Milan, 1928)

Vickery, A., *The Gentleman's Daughter: Women's Lives in Georgian England* (New Haven & London, 1998)

Vlieghe, H., *Rubens' Portraits of Identified Sitters Painted in Antwerp (Corpus Rubensianum L. Burchard XIX, Portraits II* (London, 1987)

Wagner, P., 'The Pornographer in the Courtroom', in *Sexuality in Eighteenth-century England*, ed. P. G. Boucé (Manchester, 1982), 120–40

Walpole, H., *Memoirs of the last ten years of the reign of George II*, ed. Lord Holland (London, 1822)

Watkins, J., *Memoirs of her most excellent Majesty Sophia Charlotte, Queen of Great Britain* (London, 1819)

Welby, Earl of, et al., *Annals of the Club 1764–1914* (London, 1940)

White, G. C. (ed.), *A Versatile Professor: Reminiscences of the Reverend Edward Nares* (London, 1903)

Bibliography

Whitley, W. T., *Artists and their Friends in England 1700–1799* (London, 1938)
Williams, C. (trans. & ed.), *Sophie in London 1786* (London, 1933)
Williams, I., *Early English Water-colours* (London, 1952)
Williams, N., *Powder and Paint: a history of the Englishwoman's toilet, Elizabeth I to Elizabeth II* (London, 1957)
Wood, H. T., *A History of the Royal Society of Arts* (London, 1913)

Young, H., *The Genius of Wedgwood* (London, 1995)

Acknowledgements

There can be no such thing as a definitive biography – the more you study a person, the more avenues open up for future exploration. But writing a book has to be a finite process, and this book would have been far less complete without the assistance of those mentioned here. With so much support, all omissions and errors remain my own.

I would like to thank the helpful staff of the following institutions, libraries and archives: Birmingham Museums & Art Gallery; British Library; Department of Prints and Drawings, British Museum; Witt Library, Courtauld Institute; Fitzwilliam Museum, Cambridge; Archives, Keele University Library; Kenwood; Leicestershire Record Office; Liverpool Museum; Mount Stuart Trust, Isle of Bute; Castle Museum, Nottingham; Paul Mellon Centre for Studies in British Art; Royal College of Surgeons of England; Departments of Prints and Drawings, and of Sculpture, Victoria & Albert Museum; Royal Archives, Windsor Castle; Society of Antiquaries of London; Spode Museum, Stoke on Trent; St Mary's College, Strawberry Hill; Wedgwood Museum, Barlaston.

In particular, Sarah Finch-Crisp, Keeper of Lydiard House, John Forster, Education Officer at Blenheim Palace, and Karen Scadeng, of the Horniman Museum's 2001 Project, all gave most generously of their time.

Kind permission has been given to quote from unpublished manuscripts in their collections by the following: Department of Manuscripts, British Library; the Library of the Society of Antiquaries of London; the Mount Stuart Trust Archive; the Royal College of Surgeons of England.

Visiting the Lewis Walpole Library in Farmington, Connecticut (now a part of Yale University) and the Yale Center for British Art was essential, both for the chance to study many of Lady Di's works at first hand, including the *Mysterious Mother* drawings, and also for the opportunity to use a superb, open access collection of books and journals devoted to the eighteenth century. The trip was made possible by a travel award from the Library and accommodation at Farmington, where Anna Malicka and Joan Sussler provided invaluable assistance, as did Hugh Glover of the Williamstown Art Conservation Center, Massachusetts. I was also most grateful to Jean Wilson and Norman Hammond for hospitality in Boston en route, as well as many helpful discusssions.

I am indebted to Brian Allen of the Paul Mellon Centre for providing encouragement and advice, and to Kim Sloan of the British Museum for finding the time to read and comment on sections of my text when she was finalizing her own *A Noble Art*. Canon Brian Carne shared with me his extensive knowledge of the Bolingbroke family. Among Cambridge and other friends and colleagues, Sarah Baylis, Mark Blackburn, Peter Collier, Louise Foxcroft, John Gage, Yasmin Haskell, Freya Johnson, Brian Outhwaite, Liz Pitman and Paul Petzold have all helped with references, translations and comments on the text, while conversations with Germaine Greer, one of the few people who had actually written about (or even heard of) Lady Di, were an early source of inspiration. I am grateful to the Board of Continuing Education, University of Cambridge, for a term's sabbatical leave; and to Newnham College, where quite a lot of the writing took place, with a special award to Delia Pluckrose, Head of the Tutorial Office, for rescuing me from potential disasters with disks and printouts. A very important Newnham link is Elsie Duncan-Jones, who was there in the 1930s with Lady Di's great-great-grand-daughter, and who has provided invaluable references and unflagging enthusiasm, as well as reading and commenting on the whole text. This book is dedicated to her.

Above all, I owe thanks to my agent, Clare Alexander, for realizing what I was trying to do, and for her continuing support and involvement. For Macmillan, Tanya Stobbs provided gentle but firm editing, while Becky Lindsay, Anya Serota and eagle-eyed Nicholas Blake have all worked wonders.

I once heard a distinguished author being asked how he had managed to produce his latest book while also holding down a demanding day job. The answer was: 'By neglecting my family'. That was certainly true for me, and mine deserve an honourable mention here.

Index

Index

Index

Index

Index

Index

Index

Index

Index

Index

Index

Index

Index